D0298191

050755

Tourism policy and performance

An understanding of the tourism industry and the economic factors which drive it is essential to any professional involved in tourism, as well as to students on tourism-related courses. *Tourism Policy and Performance* is the only book in the field of tourism research to open up the debate on connections between tourism performance and government policies on an international level. The authors focus on the real-life example of the Irish Government's tourism policy and bring to light a range of issues of central importance to tourism planners and governments world-wide. The book explores:

- the Irish Government's economic imperatives and the targets they aimed to achieve
- tourism and regional development
- the implications of a single market in Europe
- the promotion of the tourism industry.

Tourism Policy and Performance is the only book of its kind. It will prove invaluable to lecturers and students of tourism, management and public policy as well as to practitioners working within the tourism industry.

James Deegan is a lecturer in economics and Director of the National Centre for Tourism Policy Studies at the University of Limerick. He has presented papers at national and international business conferences and has made scholarly contributions to books and journals on many tourism issues. He has also undertaken tourism consultancy work for the European Commission and governmental agencies.

Professor Donal Dineen is Associate Dean of the College of Business and Head of the Department of Economics at the University of Limerick. His research interests, apart from tourism policy analysis, include labour market issues and local economic development of small firms, on which topics he has published widely. He has undertaken several consulting assignments for international, national and regional bodies on aspects of economic policy.

To
Dorothy
(J.D.)
and
Margaret
(D.A.D.)

Tourism policy and performance
the Irish experience

James Deegan
Donal A. Dineen
University of Limerick

INTERNATIONAL THOMSON BUSINESS PRESS
I ⓉP An International Thomson Publishing Company

London • Bonn • Boston • Johannesburg • Madrid • Melbourne • Mexico City • New York • Paris
Singapore • Tokyo • Toronto • Albany, NY • Belmont, CA • Cincinnati, OH • Detroit, MI

NTA 338.4791415

Tourism policy and performance: the Irish experience

Copyright © James Deegan and Donal A. Dineen

First published 1997 by International Thomson Business Press

I(T)P A division of International Thomson Publishing Inc.
The ITP logo is a trademark under licence

All rights reserved. No part of this work which is copyright may be reproduced or used in any form or by any means – graphic, electronic, or mechanical, including photocopying, recording, taping or information storage and retrieval systems – without the written permission of the Publisher, except in accordance with the provisions of the Copyright Designs and Patents Act 1988.

Whilst the Publisher has taken all reasonable care in the preparation of this book the Publisher makes no representation, express or implied, with regard to the accuracy of the information contained in this book and cannot accept any legal responsibility or liability for any errors or omissions from the book or the consequences thereof.

Products and services that are referred to in this book may be either trademarks and/or registered trademarks of their respective owners. The Publisher and Authors make no claim to these trademarks.

British Library Cataloguing-in-Publication Data
A catalogue record for this book is available from the British Library

First edition 1997

Produced by Gray Publishing, Tunbridge Wells, Kent
Printed in the UK by Cambridge University Press, Cambridge

ISBN 0 415 09315 5

International Thomson Business Press
Berkshire House
168–173 High Holborn
London WC1V 7AA
UK

International Thomson Business Press
20 Park Plaza
14th Floor
Boston, MA 02116
USA

http://www.thomson.com./itbp.html

£53·00

GALWAY - MAYO
INSTITUTE OF TECHNOLOGY
1 2 SEP 2000
WESTPORT ROAD
CASTLEBAR
CO. MAYO

Contents

Preface

Tourism is predicted by many international agencies to be the biggest industry in the world by the year 2000. The technological development of the jet aircraft in the 1950s, increased affluence in the industrialized economies, demonstration effects of the mass media and an increasing desire by millions of people to experience different cultures, climates and environments have been the major catalysts behind this development. While tourism growth has been particularly pronounced since the 1950s it is only recently that governments across the world have fully recognized the importance of the sector and the contribution it can make to economic development.

This book traces the evolution of tourism policy and performance in a small European economy from the emergence of the new state in the 1920s to the fully participating Member State of the EU as the century draws to a close. Ireland presents an interesting case analysis for many of the issues which confront governments today in their efforts to develop a tourism sector. Issues such as the environment, sustainable tourism, tourism and regional development, product development in tourism, problems of seasonality and access transport, the human resource dimension, the role of the private sector and innovation in tourism and the efficiency in the application of public sector funds are common to tourism development across the globe. All of these issues are addressed in this book, set in the context of changing visitor numbers, composition and expenditures since the 1960s, changing policy approaches and institutional arrangements, and significant tranches of external funding made available through the EU Commission's Structural Fund transfers since 1989.

This book provides a comprehensive analysis of the development of tourism in Ireland and is unique in that it brings together a focus on tourism on both parts of the island. While more emphasis is placed on the recent policy milieu and attendant developments, the recurrence of issues and the failure to learn from past policy failures is a constant theme throughout the book. In a small open economy with significant unemployment problems the tourism sector can play an important role in sustainable economic development. It is our hope that this book can contribute to a clearer understanding of the issues that have and will continue to determine tourism growth in Ireland and as a result help to avoid policy mistakes that would be deleterious to a sector of the economy that is so important for Irish economic development.

James Deegan
Donal A. Dineen
Department of Economics
College of Business
University of Limerick

List of tables and figures

FIGURES

Acknowledgements

This book would not have been possible without the enormous support and encouragement of numerous colleagues both at the University of Limerick and elsewhere; at an early stage, and throughout the writing, Brian Deane (then at Bord Failte) was most helpful and encouraging; his colleagues at Bord Failte, Brian Maher and Richard O'Keeffe, were extremely forthcoming with the numerous and frequent data and reference requests we presented as was George Burke (Central Statistics Office); likewise Rab McConaghy of the Northern Ireland Tourist Board could not have been more helpful; others to contribute in a variety of ways which helped to make the book more comprehensive and enriching include Professor Eamonn Henry (Economic and Social Research Institute), Paul Tansey (Tansey Webster and Associates), Brendan Leahy (Irish Tourist Industry Confederation), Jim Fitzpatrick and John McEniff (Jim Fitzpatrick and Associates), Tony Brazil (Limerick Travel), Brendan Russell (Shannon Development), Dr Bernadette Whelen, Mary Walsh, Leonie Allen, Paul Murphy, Adrian Harte, Mary Dundon, Marie Dineen, Rita Gallaher and Majella O'Halloran (University of Limerick), Professor Peter Johnson (University of Durham), Sean Gorman, Agnes Aylward and Paul Appleby (Department of Tourism and Trade), Brendan O'Regan and the staff of the National Archives, Dublin.

We would like to acknowledge the help and support of our colleagues at the Department of Economics, University of Limerick, and the encouragement of the Dean, College of Business, Dr Noel Whelan. We are indebted also to the generous support of an anonymous donor to the National Centre for Tourism Policy Studies.

We owe an especially enormous debt of gratitude to Grainne O'Connell, Secretary in the Department of Economics, University of Limerick, for the thoroughly professional and patient manner in which she handled the word-processing and production of the manuscript, the interaction with the publisher and for generally ensuring that the volumes of disks and hard copies were efficiently and smoothly handled right through the process. Any remaining errors are entirely our responsibility.

1 Introduction

BACKGROUND

While Ireland has several natural, cultural and ethnic advantages which could be exploited in numerous ways to develop its tourism sector, the historical experience (with some recent exceptions) has been such that Ireland's relative share both of European and world tourist arrivals and revenues has been declining. There are numerous reasons for this ranging from the difficulties of promoting a destination so closely located to and aligned with a world 'trouble-spot' (Northern Ireland) to lack of attention to the changing world tourism market trends and failure to reflect these in appropriate product development measures. The tendency to lay the blame for much of Ireland's economic ills, including those in the tourism sector, on external factors is a residue of a dependency culture, once political, later economic and more recently both political and economic. The substitution of an internal dependency relationship (for example, on the national Government) for an external one perpetuates the feeling of helplessness which the main players in the industry experience. At the same time it can create opportunities, as under the EU, which may be exploited to considerable advantage (as witnessed in Ireland's ability to extract considerable fund transfers from the EU to invest in Irish tourism since 1989).

In common with several other countries the composition of the tourism industry in Ireland[1] is heterogenous, fragmented and disjointed. The principal Government agency charged with responsibility for promoting and developing the sector – Bord Failte Eireann (BFE) – has played a pivotal role in the evolution of Irish tourism. This role has become more muted in recent years but continues to be influential in directing the industry towards a more sophisticated and mature approach to its future development. However, tourism has generally been treated by Government as less central to delivering employment policy objectives than the manufacturing sector though this situation has been altered also in the past decade. Indeed, tourism is now perceived as very central to delivering the employment objectives of Government not only because of linkages to the goods producing sectors of the economy but also because of the forecasted growth projections for international tourism spending in real terms of over 5 per cent per annum over the next decade (Edwards, 1992).[2]

This book primarily examines the development and performance of a tourism industry in a small open economy and links this to the strategic and other policy initiatives taken over a number of decades. While the context and institutional characteristics in which the industry developed are unique, many of the variables, policy issues and strategic options are probably echoed in several other countries seeking to develop an industry which is taking an increasing proportion of the world's disposable income. While Ireland has often been described as a 'latecomer' in industrial development terms, the emphasis in tourism has been much more on promotion than development. Not unrelated to this is the fact that a 'commodity'-based rather than 'mature product'-based approach to tourism expansion had evolved (Tansey Webster and Associates, 1991). Ironically the failure to develop Irish tourism or at least to maintain its international market share has led to the present situation where the problems of over-rapid expansion and decline experienced elsewhere can be avoided.

Furthermore, the increasing emphasis on environmental protection and sustainable tourism development in the 1980s and 1990s can inform the debate on the future development of the industry on the island and thus optimize the welfare gains for the residents and tourists alike. It is an opportune time to take stock of an industry with enormous potential particularly since there have been significant sums of public monies invested in the sector under the EU's Structural Fund transfers since1989 and set to continue to 1999. These funds have been targeted at infrastructural and product developments primarily (in addition to market development measures) and provide the basis for the upgrading and modernization of Irish tourism into the next century. It has also represented a unique injection of funds into an industry which has traditionally given rather too poor a return on investment to be able to generate sufficient funds for re-investment and renewal of the primary assets.[3] Many of these issues are revisited throughout the book.

TOURISM INDUSTRY – COMPOSITION AND ROLE

Tourism embraces two principal actions – travel plus activity. Both actions involve expenditures on a variety of goods and services in the country from which the tourists travel (the 'origin' country) and in the country where the holidays are spent (the 'destination' country). These are one and the same country in the case of domestic tourism. Travel may be short or long, domestic or overseas/international and may involve extended overnight stays or day trips. Those engaging in the latter are referred to as excursionists. The activity in tourism will typically involve spending on meals and overnight accommodation, on visits to tourist attractions, e.g. museums, theme parks, heritage centres and on retail goods such as souvenirs, local products and craft goods.

The industry may be defined in terms of what tourists do as the following 1973 definition from the National Tourism Resources Review Commission specifies:

A tourist is one who travels away from home for a distance of at least fifty miles (one way) for business, pleasure, personal affairs, or any other purpose except to commute for work, whether he/she stops overnight or returns the same day. Quoted in Lavery and van Doren (1990: 1)

The 50-mile factor may seem incongruous as shorter trips frequently involve crossing international frontiers but otherwise this is a useful working definition and helps to classify the various sub-sectors which make up the industry. Through the exclusion of travel for working purposes a key dimension of international tourism is noted which is that the tourist brings purchasing power generated in one economy to be spent to the benefit of the destination economy and this underpins much of the economic rationale for the development of tourism.

Tourism is not a neatly defined sector within the economy. Though the principal sub-sectors are the carriers, accommodation and tourist attractions, several other sub-sectors are affected by the fortunes of the industry either through indirect purchases of goods and services (food, drink, craft goods, financial services) or through the incomes generated in shops, bars and restaurants frequented by tourists. Indeed, many of the principal sub-sectors derive only a part (though often quite a substantial part) of their earnings from tourism which arises particularly from the seasonal nature of the industry. Furthermore, employment in tourism organizations whether industry based or Government funded are part of the economic fabric of the industry. The principal sub-sectors providing direct employment in the sector are summarized in Table 1.1.

Table 1.1 Principal tourism sub-sectors and associated industries

1. Travel: airlines, sea-carriers, car-hire firms, bus companies and coach-tour operators, railways, airports, tourist guides, travel agents, tour operators
2. Accommodation (including meal service): hotels, guest-houses, bed-and-breakfasts, self-catering, tourist hostels, caravan and camping sites, restaurants, fast-food outlets
3. Recreation and leisure facilities: historic houses and sites, interpretative centres, folk villages, museums, theatres, heritage centres, cabin cruising, angling/fishing, golf, equestrian centres, summer schools, camping sites
4. Tourism organizations: national tourism agency, regional tourism organizations, rural tourism bodies, hotel industry association, tourism industry confederation

This list is not exhaustive but does cover the main players in the tourism industry.

Economic role

The tourism industry in Ireland has developed erratically over the last 30 years against a background of a more rapidly rising world tourism industry and increasing pressures in Ireland to solve her endemically high unemployment problem.

The generalized inability of macroeconomic, industrial and other sectoral policies to generate sufficient jobs to reduce unemployment has meant that more
attention and resources (particularly from the EU's Structural Fund transfers)
have been diverted to the tourism sector in an attempt to realize some of the
Government's employment objectives. Overseas visitors to the Republic of
Ireland reached 3.7 million in 1994 and generated over IR£1.1 billion in revenue
while employment dependent on all tourism domestic and out-of-state reached
88,600 or 7.5 per cent of the total employed. The industry also generates net
inflows in the balance of payments current account, contributes positively to gross
national product (GNP) through the expenditures generated and accounts for
an important proportion of the tax revenue of the Government. While these
economic effects are not additive benefits, since they are different expressions
of the gross expenditures derived principally from overseas tourists, they reflect
the variety of impacts which the tourism industry can bring to an economy. The
industry is an important export earner and because it tends to have stronger
linkages to other sectors in the economy than, for example, some of the foreign-
owned manufacturing firms the import content of much of its output is low.
Figure 1.1 summarizes the principal tourism flows and the economic variables
affected.

   The primary source of the economic benefits from tourism is based on the
number of overseas visitors and their propensity to spend while on holiday in
Ireland. The latter is a function of the composition of overseas visitors both in
terms of countries of origin (and particularly their socio-economic status) and
reasons for visiting the country together with the length of stay.

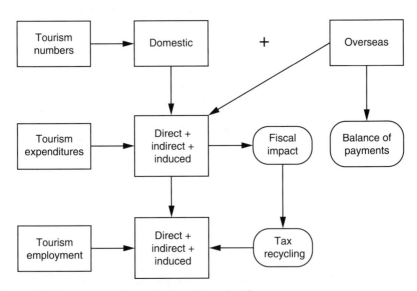

Figure 1.1 Schematic outline of principal tourism flows

Domestic tourism is important also though it is more difficult to be accurate about the extent of it from year to year.[4] The extent to which domestic holidays substitute for foreign holidays is unknown but such an import-substitution effect could justify the use of public funds to a greater extent in product development for the domestic market. Indeed, it is one of the problems of evaluating public expenditure in tourism to be able to separate the impact on foreign compared with domestic visitor numbers. Because of seasonality problems any upgrading of facilities must generate benefits for both domestic and overseas visitors to justify the expenditures incurred.[5] It has been observed internationally that origin countries generally have higher incomes and living standards than destination countries so that tourism assists the distribution of incomes between countries, e.g. northern EU to southern EU countries.

Within Ireland the same is true on a smaller scale where both domestic and overseas tourism generate some regional income re-distribution effects to the less-developed western parts of the island. Offsetting this is the fact that the relatively high-income Dublin region is the most popular destination sub-region for overseas visitors, followed by the South-west (Cork–Kerry) region. However, though tourism is growing more rapidly in revenue terms in the eastern regions of Ireland it contributes proportionately less to regional GDP and employment there than in the less developed western regions, e.g. in the West region, almost 12 per cent of regional GDP was derived from tourism in 1992.

KEY ISSUES IN IRISH TOURISM

Successful tourism destinations are characterized by three principal assets, namely, good and competitively priced transport networks, price competitiveness and quality of product. The existence of these three assets can make the promotion of a tourism destination a relatively easy task. In the absence of any one or more of these attributes the task of a national tourism promotional agency can be very difficult. In this regard the role of Government in establishing an appropriate macroeconomic and infrastructural support framework is particularly important. Ireland, like many other destinations has suffered over the years due to a lack of emphasis on these three important characteristics. As an island destination the lack of appropriate air and sea international linkages has and continues to hamper the development of the tourism sector. In tandem with poor and expensive access transport networks Irish tourism has also underperformed for many years due the perception that the country was a high cost destination. When the relative neglect of product development and quality is added to these two factors the poor performance of Irish tourism for many years is readily understood.

In recent years progress has certainly been made on all three elements deemed vital for a dynamic and successful tourism industry, yet much remains to be undertaken if the impressive growth is to be maintained. Access transport still constrains the development of the sector and will remain a priority issue for many years to come. Competitiveness has been dramatically improved since the late

1980s due to the pursuance of more prudent fiscal and monetary policy by the Irish authorities. It is imperative that the policies implemented in these years be continued if the competitive position is to be maintained. The Operational Programmes for Tourism have certainly contributed to an increased investment in the sector but it is still somewhat unclear as to what effect the investment has had on overall quality of product. The dearth of appropriate qualitative instruments to measure the human resource improvements is also deemed an important issue for the future.

While recent improvements in performance have obviously been welcomed by Governmental and private sector agencies it is appropriate to question the extent to which this performance can be attributed to the policies pursued. Is it possible to detect a strong line of causation? What can we say about the role of Governmental policy? Can we detect a very focused approach to the development of the sector? Is there an appropriate mechanism in place to monitor the return on investment in the tourism sector? These and other important issues of policy permeate the main chapters of this book.

PLAN OF THE BOOK

While retaining a strong policy focus throughout, this book is structured in such a way that the historical evolution of policy is first considered, followed by the regional dimension and, later, a European perspective. The performance of the industry is assessed in these diverse though complementary contexts. The parallel, if less dynamic, recent development of Northern Ireland's tourism industry is examined, including the policy issues arising there and the North–South dimensions of the industry. The importance of the environment as a prime tourism asset and the policy issues relevant to this are considered while organizational factors and the policy instruments applied to develop the sector are analysed against the background of changing international demand trends, EU and Government support for investment in the industry. This leads to a consideration of the critical influences likely to shape the future of the tourism industry in Ireland.

Historical evolution of tourism policy

To set the scene for the more recent developments in Irish tourism the historical context since independence is set out in Chapter 2. The chapter charts the development of the tourism sector from the early days of independence in 1922 through to the 1960s. The general lack of attention to the sector in the early years of the state, the relative tourism boom of the late 1940s and an analysis of the contribution of tourism to the economy are among issues that are considered in depth. Many of the policy issues that emerged in the period from 1922 to 1960 are still central to the development of Irish tourism in the 1990s.

The dramatic adjustments which occurred in the two decades, 1960–1980 are presented in Chapter 3 which saw the steady if not exceptional expansion of the 1960s broadly reversed in the 1970s as the image problems associated with the 'troubles' in Northern Ireland affected the tourism industry in both parts of the island.

Ireland as a whole lost market share of international tourism though not all of this can be blamed on the 'troubles'. The limited investment in product development and relatively unsophisticated nature of the industry (poor infrastructure, limited training expenditures) meant there was an over-reliance on the twin attributes of 'beautiful scenery' and 'friendly people' to sustain the growth of Irish tourism. By the end of the 1970s, the Republic of Ireland had regained its level of 'pre-troubles' (1969) visitor numbers while it took Northern Ireland more than another 10 years to do likewise.

The performance of Irish tourism since 1981 is analysed in Chapter 4. This captures the dramatic upsurge in visitor numbers and revenues from 1987 onwards. The liberalization of air fares, particularly on the Dublin–London route, through the break-up of cartel arrangements of the existing carriers, played no small part in encouraging a larger flow of tourists across the Irish sea. The shift towards 'green' tourism also benefited Ireland. The considerable increase in investment in product development, levered by substantial EU structural fund transfers of c. IR£190 million from 1989 to 1993,[6] also helped though had more of an impact in the 1990s. The growing importance of the industry to the economy is noted. The most dramatic recent impact on the industry was the announcement of the IRA ceasefire on 31 August 1994 which generated significant increases in tourist flows to both parts of Ireland from overseas and north–south/south–north on the island.[7]

Regional, European and Northern Ireland aspects

The regional dimensions of tourism in Ireland are examined in Chapter 5. Regional expenditure levels are used to determine the distribution of the economic benefits of tourism within Ireland since 1981. The relative advantage of the poorer (western) regions has been eroded in recent years as the eastern regions have gained a disproportionate share of the growth which has occurred, with Dublin and the south-east benefiting most. The regional distribution of the second round of EU Structural Funds (1994–1999) will further exacerbate this bias towards the capital city. Rural tourism is a small but significant component of tourism development and emphasizes a strong community contribution in successful ventures. The chapter concludes with an analysis of the changing organizational structures at the regional level.

Chapter 6 explores the complicated interaction that exists between tourism and the environment and provides an explanation why the allocation of resources dictated by private markets may lead to sub-optimal outcomes for the environment. New approaches to environmental protection are discussed and Irish policy for the environment is evaluated in this context. The overall lack of attention to the role of the environment in Irish tourism is explored and serious policy failures are outlined.

Chapter 7 gives an in-depth overview of the role that the EU Commission plays in policy for tourism. It details the slow emergence of a focus on tourism within the Union and evaluates significant changes that have taken place in recent years to Structural Fund arrangements and how these changes have impacted on funding for the development of tourism in Ireland and other EU countries. The contribution of tourism to the economies of the EU is evaluated and the future role of a European tourism policy is considered.

The weak performance of the Northern Ireland (NI) tourism sector and its development since the 1960s are analysed in Chapter 8. There was an excessive dependence on tourists who visited friends and relatives rather than on 'pure' tourists, partly a result of the 'troubles'. The limited investment in the sector for over two decades generated an industry ill-attuned to the changing needs of the international market place. A 'dependency culture' is seen by the policy-makers in NI as both a dominant feature of the industry and a constraint on its future development. A greater role is envisaged for the private sector with the Government's function being one of creating the right macroeconomic conditions and incentive structure for greater self-reliance by those in the industry, which continues to enjoy considerable funding subventions from public bodies. The start of the 'peace process' in 1994 represents the most significant recent event impacting on the sector and, if sustained, will presage a much brighter future for the industry in a broader all-Ireland context.

Chapter 9 focuses on the design and delivery of Irish tourism policy, taking particular note of the organizational adjustments made to facilitate this process. The changing roles of the national tourism organization (BFE) and the Government department(s) to which it reported provide an interesting backdrop to the strong growth in the industry from 1987 onwards and the allocation of significantly increased funding stimulated under the EU's Operational Programmes from 1989. Apart from the direct subsidies provided, fiscal measures were introduced which benefited the sector also with the BES[8] being one of the most prominent. As in Northern Ireland, the underlying view of Government was to open up competition in the industry, to develop a more self-reliant tourism sector and to lessen the role of the state in the extent of its 'hand-holding' of tourism providers. In short, the development of a mature tourism industry would henceforth be left more to the industry itself.

The final chapter takes a reflective look at the main issues in Irish tourism, in the light of the current state of the industry, and considers, in a prospective sense, the policy measures required to shape the future of the industry as it prepares for the competitive environment of the 21st century.

NOTES

1. This book is primarily concerned with tourism policy and performance in the context of the Republic of Ireland (ROI), which is an independent political entity which gained independence through cessation from Britain and the then British Empire in

1921; Northern Ireland (NI) comprises the remaining six counties (there are 32 in all) of the island of Ireland and is politically ruled from Westminster as part of the United Kingdom of Great Britain and Northern Ireland. The development of tourism in NI is examined in Chapter 8. Unless explicitly stated otherwise, references throughout the book to Irish tourism and tourism in Ireland refer to the Republic of Ireland.

2. Edwards forecast international trips growth of 5.1 per cent per annum from 1995 to 2000 and 4 per cent per annum from 2000 to 2005; the corresponding expenditure growth rates were 5.6 and 4.7 per cent, respectively. He refers to both time and expenditure ceilings which are likely to affect the longer term expansion of the industry particularly in the developed economies and change the nature of trip and spending patterns.

3. While direct empirical evidence on this is not readily available, one can infer, from the limited private investment in Irish tourism which occurred down the years, in the absence of subsidies or tax breaks, that these subventions were necessary to give a return on the investments required; furthermore, in the first Operational Programme for Tourism, 1989–1993 (see Department of Transport and Tourism, 1989) the private sector investment fell far short of what was anticipated, clearly demonstrating the returns elsewhere were more favourable.

4. O'Hagan and Waldron (1987) provided some estimates of the importance of domestic tourism in different EU countries and examined alternative methodologies of data collection. Surveys are used in a number of countries which can be refined by reference to two concurrent checks – the ratio of domestic to international tourism expenditures and the share of total tourism expenditures in private final consumption. Ireland was grouped with small non-Mediterranean countries in this context (with Belgium/Luxembourg, The Netherlands and Denmark) and remarkably consistent ratios of domestic to international tourism expenditures of 0.5 were estimated. The shares of total tourism expenditures in private final consumption were broadly similar also at approximately 8 per cent.

5. The extent of displacement, which arises when one tourism facility is developed only to divert visitors and employment away from other facilities leaving no or very little net employment gain, is crucial to the investment appraisal process involving public funds; the related concept of additionality, where net gains arise through the expansion in the numbers of overseas visitors to the country as a whole, features perhaps all too infrequently in the project appraisal process. For a discussion on these concepts and their application to tourism evaluation methodologies, see Industry Department for Scotland (c. 1989) and Deegan and Dineen (1992).

6. Under the first *Operational Programme for Tourism, 1989–93*, see Department of Tourism and Transport (1989).

7. The ending of this ceasefire in February 1996 may have equally dramatic negative consequences should it be sustained and violence resumed on the pre-1994 ceasefire scale.

8. Business Expansion Scheme (see Chapter 9).

2 The development of tourism 1922–1960

INTRODUCTION

The growth of international tourism is essentially a modern phenomenon resulting from improved transportation networks, the growth in disposable incomes, increased leisure time, better education and increased promotion of tourism by international agencies. This growth has been particularly pronounced since the beginnings of the jet age of the 1950s. It would, however, be a mistake to ignore the developments that occurred before the 1950s in any evaluation of Irish tourism policy and performance. This chapter analyses the developments to the early 1960s and, *inter alia*, establishes a number of important links to the present. The final section of the chapter discusses the economic performance of tourism in the emerging Irish economy.

TOURISM DEVELOPMENT 1922–1945

Irish political independence in 1922 brought little fundamental change to the economic environment. The economy was tightly linked to her former colonial master, Great Britain, and the early years of economic development conform very well to the predictions of dependency theory.[1] The economy was heavily dependent on agriculture and virtually all agricultural exports went to the UK. The most industrialized part of the country in the north-east had remained part of the UK at independence. Agriculture accounted for one-half of employment, one-third of income and nine-tenths of exports (Gillmor, 1985).

Despite the generally poor economic climate the development of a tourist movement began very soon after the establishment of the state. The Irish Tourist Association (ITA) was established in January 1925, as a result of a conference held in Government buildings under the presidency of the Minister for Industry and Commerce. The conference succeeded in amalgamating regional tourist associations into a national tourist body, Fitzpatrick (1961) notes, the founders of the organization were regarded with some scepticism 'The country in 1925 was at a low ebb economically ... holiday traffic was negligible, services and facilities were disorganised'.

From the outset the ITA was hampered by a lack of funds which limited promotional and publicity activities. Although tourism came within the ambit of the Department of Industry and Commerce, the economic conditions of the time dictated that tourism was not a priority of Government. Nonetheless, section 67 of the Local Government Act (1925), empowered local authorities to contribute to the funds of an approved association (the ITA) for the purpose of developing tourist traffic. In the absence of central fund allocations the ITA, was dependent on funding from the local authorities and income from subscriptions of 250 members. In 1925 only one local authority County Council in Ireland (Kerry) contributed to the ITA but by 1928 24 councils made contributions. The ITA saw this as evidence of the importance of the tourism industry and continued to lobby the Government for an allocation from central funds. The association argued that similar support was given by practically all European Governments. In addition, the ITA argued for special credit facilities for hotel development similar to that which had been introduced to aid agriculture. It was some time before this facility was extended to the industry. Although hampered in their activities by a lack of funds the association did publish a handbook of tariffs of 80 per cent of Irish hotels as early as 1926. A party of 30 hoteliers undertook an extensive tour of French resorts in 1927 in order to familiarize themselves with best practice on the continent.

Despite favourable speeches and nuances from Government circles the development of tourism in the early years of the state was effectively left in the hands of the voluntary ITA. The association co-operated in many initiatives with the transport companies, in particular the Great Western Railway Company of England. It was, however, only in 1931 that the next important initiative in tourism development occurred. Measures to encourage the development of tourist traffic were included in the Tourist Traffic (Development) Act of 1931. The Act ensured that the ITA was the official beneficiary of local government finance. With the extra finance available in the 1930s the association published guides, folders and maps, set up its own photographic and film units, and intensified its drive to promote Ireland's attractions abroad (Fitzpatrick, 1961).

The role of aviation

The 1930s evidenced a period of protectionism across the world which was not conducive to the growth of international tourism. Nonetheless, the period was extremely important in the development of aviation. During the 1930s the new Fianna Fail Government became very aware of Ireland's strategic position in the developments of North Atlantic aviation routes (O'Riain, 1986). In anticipation of a North Atlantic service an agreement between the Governments of Britain, Canada, Ireland and the provincial government of Newfoundland was reached at the Ottawa conference in December 1935. The conference dealt with the establishment of mail and passenger services. The Irish Government approved this agreement in early 1936 after the then Taoiseach, DeValera, included a vital clause, which in later years, assumed huge significance: 'Subject to force majeure, all eastbound aircraft on the transatlantic air service on the direct route shall stop at the Irish Free State Airport as the first European port of call and all westbound aircraft on the direct route shall stop at the Irish Free State Airport'. (Quinlan, 1988: 43).

At that time Ireland did not have any facility for the landing of transatlantic planes. During 1936 the Government commissioned surveys to find a suitable location for such a base. A site was chosen at Rineanna, County Clare, and work began on the now internationally renowned Shannon Airport. The Government realized that work at Rineanna would not be completed in time for the North Atlantic sea plane flights of 1937 and a decision was taken to use Foynes on an interim basis. On 9 July 1939, Pan-Am's luxury flying boat *Yankee Clipper* landed at Foynes. It was the first commercial passenger flight on the direct route between the United States and Europe. These new exciting developments in commercial aviation were halted abruptly with the outbreak of war in September of 1939. The last commercial flight left Foynes in October of that year. Throughout the war years Foynes played an important part in international aviation. Although Ireland was a neutral country, most passengers travelling through Foynes were top-level military and diplomatic personnel. At first, the airlines were careful to hide the true identity of these passengers on their way through neutral Ireland but as the war dragged on, Foynes, with the quiet blessing of the Irish authorities, had clearly become an important transport link in the allied war effort.

Legislative change

The major developments in aviation in the 1930s led to a greater recognition of the value of the tourism industry. A Government White Paper published in the 1940s summarized the background to the Tourist Traffic Act, 1939, as follows: 'In subsequent years there was more general recognition of the value of the tourist industry as a factor in the national economy and also of the inadequacy of existing measures for its development. These measures were confined to local authorities.' (Stationery Office, 1946: 1). The document went on the discuss the benefits which other countries had gained from tourism and suggested that few countries had as many natural advantages as Ireland.

The 1939 Act provided for the establishment of the Irish Tourist Board, with wide powers to extend and develop accommodation and other amenities for holidaymakers. It stated:

> The Board is empowered to engage in these activities directly or to provide financial assistance to others for the same purpose, and it may require land compulsorily, including fishing rights and sporting rights over the land, to enable it to exercise fully its functions under the act. It is also empowered to register as such, hotels, guest-houses, holiday hostels, youth hostels and holiday camps. (Tourist Traffic Act, 1939: 1)

A National Economic and Social Council (NESC) report (1980b) noted that the legislation set out in the Tourism and Traffic Act, and subsequent amendments to it, provided 'very little direction on basic issues of tourism policy'. The preamble to the Act indicated that the reason for establishing the Board was 'to make further and better provision for the development of tourism traffic', Heneghan (1976) remarked:

> If this was to be regarded as a statement of the Board's objectives, it was too vague to be of assistance in solving difficult policy decisions. For instance it would be of little help in resolving the problem of what types of tourists should be persuaded to visit Ireland. Moreover, the statement was also ambiguous. One interpretation could have been that the Tourist Board's objective was primarily the provision of tourist amenities and facilities, no mention having been made concerning the promotion of tourist traffic. In addition it was not indicated whether the Bord should have been concerned with either export or domestic tourism or both. (p. 395)

In addition to the absence of a clear focus on policy it is interesting to note the long list of functions that were assigned to the Board while it was stated that the grant for all these purposes was not to exceed IR£45,000 per annum. While there was provision for repayable advances up to an aggregate of IR£600,000, these were earmarked for works of a profit-sharing character. It was inevitable (as proved to be the case) that this proviso would prove very cumbersome and that it would curtail much needed capital investment.

The outbreak of war in 1939 interrupted the work of the newly appointed board and planned developments were deferred. The Board did operate in a limited way during the war. It proceeded with the preparation of preliminary plans for the development of certain existing holiday resorts. In addition, the grading of accommodation was undertaken throughout the country. In anticipation of an increase in the numbers employed in the hotel and catering trades the board formulated a scheme for the training of additional personnel.

EARLY POST-WAR DEVELOPMENTS

The end of the war in 1945 signalled the starting point for a major stimulus to commercial transatlantic travel. Aviation developments such as the development of the jet engine, pioneered in the USA during the war years had made the flying boats obsolete in the new environment. The Irish Government, with admirable foresight, had signed a bilateral agreement with the USA in 1944 which ensured that all US aircraft, in transit over Irish territory stop at Shannon. Provision was also made for an Irish airline to operate on the Atlantic in due course. The agreement opened up the Atlantic and Europe to US airlines and was vigorously opposed by Churchill, the British Prime Minister. So committed were the Americans to the agreement that the protestations of the British were simply ignored. The result of the agreement was that Shannon enjoyed international status as a transit airport for the early post-war years.

Pan American (Pan Am) was the first airline to resume transatlantic services and the first plane landed at Rineanna on 16 September 1945. Services through Rineanna increased during 1945 and by the end of the year 'Rineanna was the hub of transatlantic aviation with about 50 per cent of total North Atlantic traffic routing through the airport' (Quinlan, 1988). In 1945, there were 315 arrivals and 4323 passengers; in 1947 there were almost 6000 arrivals and over 170,000 passengers. The extent of Government support for Shannon was evident by the passing of the Customs Free Airport Act in 1947 which made Shannon the world's first duty-free airport. In 1947, Aer Lingus received delivery of five new aircraft and operation on the North Atlantic route began that year. A change of Government in 1948 led to the abandonment of the service and Irish transatlantic services did not resume until 1958. Throughout the 1950s Shannon was the hub of international air traffic with all flights between North America and Europe required to touch down in Shannon. The arrival of the jet aircraft brought the first overfly threat to Shannon. Some innovative tourism developments were developed to counteract the threat (see Chapter 3).

Post-war tourism boom causes conflict

Irish tourism encountered a short-term boom in the immediate post-war years. Two factors contributed to the upsurge in activity. First, in the immediate aftermath of the war strict food rationing remained in Britain. Ireland proved a major attraction to British visitors because of the plentiful and superior quality of food. Second, international currency restrictions and the poor state of transport infrastructure discouraged travel to Europe. The influx of British tourists placed considerable demands on the limited accommodation infrastructure and was not universally welcomed. Numerous articles appeared in national newspapers bemoaning the influx of tourists. An article in a national newspaper concluded:

> There is not enough hotel accommodation for our own people. Yet, the Government intends to permit visitors from other countries to encroach on that accommodation. The *Irish* people should have first claim on the food and board in this country. (*Irish Independent*, 1 May 1946)

A laissez-faire approach to tourism development

The problem of appropriate tourist accommodation was to preoccupy the Government and the Irish Tourist Board in the late 1940s and 1950s: 'The provision of additional accommodation is, therefore, considered the most urgent requirement' (Tourist Development Programme, 1946). The programme proposed a temporary measure to acquire and refurbish properties to alleviate the problem. It was proposed that the 1939 Act be amended to increase the limit on advances from IR£600,000 to IR£1,250,000. Again it was stipulated that advances would only be made for schemes certified by the board to be of a profit-earning character. This approach to tourist development was consistently criticized by the industry and it was suggested that it curtailed tourism development. This inadequacy was stressed by the chairman of the Killarney Tourist Association in December 1947:

> In fairness to the Board I think I should stress that they are greatly hampered by their own Act which makes it a condition that any money expended should show a decent profit. This I consider is quite a ridiculous way to approach tourist traffic development. Surely, it is the indirect benefit to be obtained by attracting large numbers of tourists by the development and improvement of the amenities of our tourist resorts that really counts. (Chairman's Address, 1947)[2]

The conservative attitude to tourist development is evidenced by internal government memoranda of the time. In reply to a re-organization scheme submitted by the Irish Tourist Board in 1952 the Minister of Finance replied as follows:

> The scheme submitted by the Irish Tourist Board is primarily one for increases in pay and personnel ... In no sense can the Board's memorandum be regarded as a coherent, practical plan for the development of the industry and the Minister for Finance shares the disappointment of the Minister for Industry and Commerce. The remedying of existing defects in the industry is primarily a matter for those engaged in the industry ... The Minister for Finance does not consider that large-scale expenditure by the state is necessary for the development of the tourist industry ... The Minister for Finance is satisfied that, if efficiency is to be encouraged and extravagance avoided, upper limits should be set on the annual grants to the Board. He has in mind limits of IR£30,000 and IR£70,000 respectively for administrative and other expenses and for publicity. (D/T File S13087B, February 1950)[3]

The influence of the United States in Irish tourism development in the 1950s

Ireland like many other European countries was in receipt of Marshall aid from the United States in the post-war years. Internal government communications in this period suggest that the US aid agencies were unhappy with the priority being afforded to tourism by the Irish Government. A memorandum from the Department of External Affairs (dated 27 July 1950) to the Government outlined some serious problems with respect to Ireland's allocation of Marshall aid. The memorandum details a private conversation between the Minister of External Affairs and Colonel Pozzi, Chief of the Travel Development Office of the Economic Cooperation Administration (ECA):

He [Pozzi] stated that the ECA in Washington were altogether friendly to us but that in this particular question of tourism their patience was exhausted and he could state, following his recent visit to Washington, that effective Government action in this field by way of reconstitution of the Tourist Board and otherwise was essential to avoid a complete deterioration of our position in Washington ... If Ireland did not show some real interest in increasing her dollar earnings in the line which seemed most feasible, the ECA could hardly be expected to continue their aid at the forecast level particularly when the overall demand for aid had now got so much keener. (D/T S13087c)[4]

It is unclear whether the views of Colonel Pozzi were exaggerated but subsequent developments would suggest that the pressure from the USA did have a role to play in changing policy for tourism in the early 1950s. This may have been due to the change of Government in 1951 but other factors were also at work. Prior to the change of Government a number of reports on tourism had been initiated. In order to obtain specialized advice on tourism development the Government had utilized facilities provided under the technical assistance scheme operated by the Economic Cooperation Administration. Ireland participated with other member countries in a joint tourism mission to the USA which was sponsored by the Organization for European Economic Cooperation (OEEC). The Minister for Industry and Commerce received several reports on tourism which were published as the *Synthesis of Reports on Tourism 1950–1951* (Stationery Office, 1951).

The reports were extremely thorough and very important in a number of respects. First, the issues outlined are still central to the development of Irish tourism in the 1990s. Secondly, the reports emphasized a number of serious deficiencies in the organization of Irish tourism. Thirdly, the reports emphasized the importance of tourism to the economy and the long run potential of tourism to contribute to foreign exchange earnings and employment creation. Fourthly, and most importantly the reports emphasized that the Irish Government would need to give a good deal more emphasis to the development of tourism.

The Synthesis of Reports on Tourism was the culmination of six separate reports conducted during 1950, both in Ireland and the USA. For purposes of the Synthesis the report prepared by the American expert, Christenberry, and his colleagues was taken as the basic document and became known as 'The Christenberry report'. The report concentrated on the following six areas:

1. Official organization.
2. Ireland's tourist areas.
3. Accommodation.
4. Hotel operation.
5. Publicity and advertising.
6. Transport facilities.

The reports did not deal exclusively with any one area and there were several overlapping recommendations. The following is a summary of the main findings and recommendations with respect to tourism policy.

The Christenberry report

The Christenberry report was extremely critical of the organization of tourism and the report began with the following missive. 'As presently constituted and financed, the Irish Tourist Board and the Irish Tourist Association are completely inadequate to handle the important mission to which they are assigned, that of actively promoting tourism to Ireland from abroad' (p. 1). This general view was echoed in the other reports. The main recommendations on official organization were as follows:

1. the Irish Tourist Board and the Irish Tourist Association should be merged into one body as it was believed that this would avoid needless duplication on publicity activities;
2. it was suggested that the previous record and criticism of the Board would make it imperative that a new name should be given to the organization;
3. the new Board should have members with proven skills in the tourism industry; the previous legislation which prohibited such membership was deemed flawed;
4. it was recommended that a new Board should expand and increase the scope of activities. It was envisaged that this would 'naturally mean a far larger budget' (Stationery Office, 1951).

The analysis in the Christenberry report on tourist areas split the country into seven geographic destinations as outlined in Figure 2.1.

The report focused on the potential for development in each area. Areas 1 and 2 roughly covered the entire east coast, with Dublin as the centre. It was suggested that this area offered few attractions for American tourists apart from Dublin. Area 3 which comprised sections of Counties Waterford, Cork, Tipperary and Kilkenny was deemed attractive because of the 'lovely rural countryside'. Area 4 consisting of County Kerry and most of Cork was deemed to justify its reputation 'because of the magnificent scenery'. There were some words of caution with respect to the development of Killarney. 'For example, in Killarney we found several hotels and restaurants which attempted to attract Americans by being "American" in their architecture and signs. Nothing can more easily destroy the Irish charm and individuality as an attraction for Americans' (p. 5). Area 5 consisted of Counties Limerick and Clare and was considered important primarily because of Shannon Airport. The Cliffs of Moher and other attractions in the area were deemed to make it 'a top flight' destination for one- and two-day tours. Sections of Mayo, Galway and Sligo comprised Area 6 and was considered of great interest to American tourists because of the 'magnificent wild scenery, the fishing and shooting opportunities' (p. 5). Donegal was designated Area 7 and although deemed to 'possess breathtaking countryside'

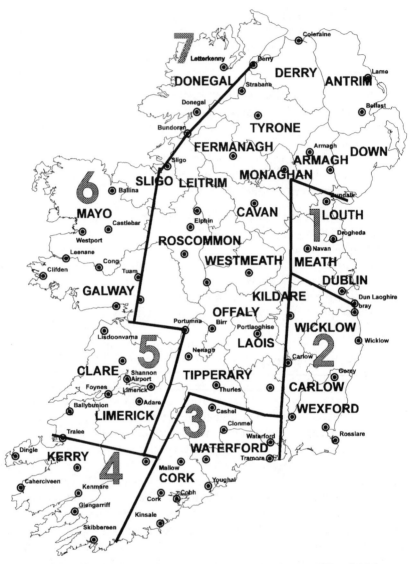

Figure 2.1 Map of tourism regions in Ireland. *Source*: Stationery Office (1951)

was considered very underdeveloped for tourism because of a dearth of public utilities, such as electricity and water. It was felt that these problems would take some time to overcome and consequently the area was not suitable for immediate promotion.

The reports dealing with accommodation considered 'the sound expansion and improvement of hotel and guest house accommodations in the strategic areas as of major importance in the building of a constructive tourist programme'. Bottlenecks in Dublin and Cork were identified as immediate concerns. The reports concurred on the necessity to provide incentives to 'stimulate the needed expansion and improvements' (p. 8). The section of the Synthesis report dealing with 'Hotel operation' highlighted poor standards of hygiene and sanitation. The report also stressed the need for improvement in the standard of management and service in many small hotels and guest houses throughout the country. It was suggested that the re-organized Tourist Board could actively participate 'in on the job training schemes' (p. 20). It was also recommended that 'in large cities, such as Dublin, there is room for the establishment of training schools which could attract suitable young men and women to enter the hotel industry as their career'. It was to be 13 years later before such a formalized structure was established, under the auspices of the Council for Education Recruitment and Training (CERT).

The section of the Christenberry report dealing with 'Publicity and advertising' was extremely critical of the Government's approach to tourism development. It described the expenditure for all forms of promotion as 'fantastically low' (p. 24). The report suggested a budget for the US alone of $200,000 which 'should be scaled upwards in subsequent years'. The Irish Hotels Federation[5] report was similarly critical and recommended 'Adequate funds (not less than IR£150,000) should be made available to the Tourist Board, a substantial proportion thereof to be expended on promotion in the USA and on a par with amounts expended by other European Countries' (p. 25). The Christenberry report outlined the attractions of Ireland that should be highlighted in the subsequent promotions. It was stressed that 'Few countries were as inexpensive for Americans as Ireland' (p. 26). The scenery, daylight hours in summer, fishing and shooting, good golf facilities and the friendliness of the people were seen as assets which were under-developed in promotional campaigns. In addition, several of the reports empha-sized the importance of extending the season. Transport facilities were only a minor element in the brief of the reports. The main considerations related to the curtailment of delays at border posts and it was stressed that the general reception conditions were in need of improvement. The Christenberry report detailed a number of suggestions as to how the 100,000 in-transit passengers who passed through Shannon Airport could be influenced to visit Ireland. The pro-vision of self-drive cars was considered an important aid to tourist development that required attention. Surprisingly, the reports expressed a general satisfaction with the condition of Irish roads, although a serious concern was expressed on the inadequacy of sign-posting, a deficiency that remains to the present day.

The publication of the reports on tourism were an important boost to an industry that considered itself relatively neglected by Governmental policy. The actual effectiveness of the reports in influencing Government policy is a little more difficult to determine. While the 1950s did evidence a more pronounced focus on tourism it was some time before the necessary resources were devoted to the sector. Nonetheless, the publication of the reports does appear to have given an immediate impetus to the Department of Industry and Commerce that was responsible for tourism development. The following is an extract from internal Government memoranda of January 1952. It suggests that the Department was now more serious in its attempt to foster tourism though this view was not readily accepted by the Minister of Finance:

> The Minister for Finance submits to the Government the following observations on the proposals of the Minister for Industry and Commerce regarding the tourist industry.
>
> The Minister for Finance fully recognises the importance of tourism in the national economy and in particular the significance of tourist income in the balance of payments. Despite the large and growing deficit of the exchequer which must be met from taxation, he is prepared to increase within reason the amount of public funds committed to the promotion of tourism. It is imperative, however, that state aid should not be given without the strictest regard to economy and to the probable effectiveness of the expenditure in producing early and substantial results. The Minister considers that there is no adequate justification for the extraordinary increase in the annual grant for administration, publicity, etc., from a maximum of IR£45,000 to IR£500,000 for which the Minister of Industry and Commerce proposes to provide in the forthcoming legislation. To justify annual assistance for tourism on such a lavish scale at the expense of the taxpayer it would need to be clearly established, particularly at a time like the present of unprecedented financial difficulty, either that there was a grave risk of a precipitative fall in tourist income which state assistance could effectively avert or that state assistance of the magnitude proposed could be relied upon to bring about the doubling of tourist income which The Department of Industry and Commerce regards as possible. The Minister is not satisfied that the proposals are justified on either score. (Department of An Taoiseach files, 1952)[6]

The general attitude displayed above is prevalent throughout the correspondence. The attitude to promotion is summarized neatly in the following extract:

> The inflow of visitors to this country is dependent on factors such as living conditions in the United Kingdom, the allowances for continental holidays given to UK residents, travel facilities and fares, and the international situation, which are largely outside our control. State aid has not had any significant influence on the recent prosperity and the good prospects of the tourist industry. It should, however, be borne in mind that the State has in fact contributed over IR£650,000 to the Irish Tourist Board since 1939 by way of grant in-aid and repayable advances almost all of which has had to be written off. ... The proposal to provide for an annual grant of up to IR£250,000 for publicity is altogether excessive in relation to present needs and the scale of expenditure in the recent past (IR£16,000 in 1950/51). If expenditure on anything approaching this scale were in fact incurred, it would be liable to cause considerable embarrassment to the tourist industry, for if it were effective in attracting greatly increased numbers of visitors before our ability to receive them had been improved and extended, irreparable harm might be done. (Department of An Taoiseach Files, 1952)[7]

LEGISLATIVE DEVELOPMENTS FOR TOURISM IN THE 1950s

Despite the aforementioned misgivings, the 1950s evidenced an increased focus on the development of tourism and the establishment of Bord Failte.

Establishment of Bord Failte

The Tourist Traffic Act of 1952 was introduced with the stated objective(s) to:

> make further and better provision for the encouragement and development of the tourist traffic and, in particular, to establish a body to engage in publicity in connection with such traffic, to amend and extend the Tourist Traffic Acts, 1939 and 1946, to amend the law relating to the licensing of hotels and holiday camps for the sale of intoxicating liquor, and to provide for other matters connected with the matters aforesaid. Part 2 Section 4, stated The Board heretofore known as The Irish Tourist Board shall be known as an Bord Failte. (Tourist Traffic Act, 1952)

The 1952 Act was important in a number of respects. First, it established Bord Failte, the organization that has been at the forefront of Irish Tourism for the last 44 years. Second, it established a new organization, Fogra Failte. It was anticipated that Bord Failte would concern itself with tourist development whilst this new body would concentrate on publicity. Third, the Act provided for an additional IR£250,000 to be expended by this new body. Fourth, it provided for Government guaranteed loans for improvements of hotels and guesthouses, with Bord Failte grants to cover the interest charges for the first three years (later extended to five years). A limit of IR£3 million was placed on the total of loans to be guaranteed.

The 1952 Act was welcomed by virtually all parties in Dail Eireann. Even though the amounts to be expended were still small relative to the income from tourism it did suggest that the malign attitude to tourist development had mellowed somewhat. Deputy Cafferky made the following contribution to the debate in the Dail which accurately summarizes the point:

> I would like to welcome this Bill and to say that I remember a time when it was anathema to this House to recommend the development of tourism and the invitation of tourists to this country. A big change in outlook has taken place during the past five or six years. When I was a member of this house during the years 1945, 1946 and 1947, quite a number of Deputies who have contributed to the debate and who have welcomed the Bill were very much opposed to the number of tourists coming to this country. (Dail debates, 28 February 1952)[8]

Fogra Failte

The most controversial element of the 1952 Act was the establishment of Fogra Failte. Many deputies saw this as a duplication of effort and as being administratively inefficient. It ran counter to the thrust of the Christenberry report which recommended one uniform body to coordinate the tourist effort. Concern

GALWAY - MAYO
INSTITUTE OF TECHNOLOGY

1 2 SEP 2000

WESTPORT ROAD

was also expressed that the creation of the new body was a snub to the ITA 'which has rendered excellent service to the nation' (Cowan–Dail debate, 28 February 1952).[9] Under the Act the ITA was to operate tourist bureaux and publicity functions within Ireland. In fact, the organization continued to do so until 1964, when this function and its local authority contributions were transferred to the regional tourism organizations. The elements of the Act that dealt with the licensing of hotels and holiday camps for the sale of intoxicating liquor were severely criticized by the more puritanical members of Dail Eireann. Some Deputies suggested that this would lead to excessive drinking by Irish citizens. The contribution of Deputy Desmond articulates this viewpoint rather well:

> It was before 12, Deputy, but even so, between 10 and 12 we had the misery of seeing young girls drinking in a bar attached to the hotel. My opinion is that if you are going to cater for tourists – including those from our own country – and if we are prepared to stoop to such a low level it will be a bad day for our country. (Dail debate, 25 February 1952)[10]

Although, only officially brought into existence by the 1952 Act the nucleus of Fogra Failte had been established in September of 1951. The annual report and accounts for the period 21 September 1951 to 31 March 1953 reveal that the following priorities had been established by the Board.

> In broad outline, the Board's policy is to plan and develop a continuous and integrated publicity effort, using every feasible technique of modern publicity to encourage increased traffic in and to this country. The primary objectives are (a) to develop the home traffic, through publicity designed to encourage the holiday habit among our own people, (b) to maintain and expand the volume of tourist traffic from Britain, which provides the bulk of our external tourist revenue, and (c) to encourage increased traffic from the dollar area by means of a carefully planned advertising and publicity campaign in North America. Prior to the establishment of Fogra Failte, and the provision of increased publicity funds, it had not been possible to undertake tourist publicity on any worthwhile scale in the United States of America. (D/T files 5647a)

The report recorded that publicity to attract traffic from the continent of Europe was at an experimental stage.

An Tostal

An important initiative of the new publicity board was a campaign to extend the tourist season. The 1953 report states 'The extension of the tourist season is one of the most urgent requirements of the tourist industry and the Board believed that the most effective way to extend the season would be by effecting an earlier commencement'. An Tostal, the first concerted effort to promote off-season traffic to Ireland, was held during the three weeks which commenced on Easter Sunday, 5 April 1953. From the outset it was recognized that the extension of the tourist season would require a long-term strategy and it would be unreasonable to expect an immediate return from An Tostal. While An Tostal was to be based in Dublin, it was expected to be of national interest. To that end 172 local An Tostal Councils were established throughout the country. It was 'intended that the whole country will, for the period of three weeks be AT HOME to Irish exiles and friends from everywhere' (*Irish Tourist Bulletin*, 1952[11]). While the national programme for An Tostal was well received, the shortage of events of national and international standard was deemed a deficiency that required attention. The development of An Tostal was overtaken by the change of Government in 1954 and the introduction of the Tourist Traffic Act, 1955.

Dissolution of Fogra Failte

The creation of Fogra Failte by the Fianna Fail administration (1951–1954) had been severely criticized by opposition parties in Dail Eireann. When the new coalition Government came to power in 1954 they quickly moved to dissolve Fogra Failte. The Tourist Traffic Act, 1955, was introduced as 'An act to dissolve Fogra Failte and transfer its functions to an Bord Failte and to provide for other matters connected therewith' (21 March 1955). The debate on this act illustrated the general divisions on tourist development and also on tourism policy.

The Minister for Industry and Commerce outlined that on coming to office he reviewed the workings of Bord Failte and Fogra Failte. He reported that the relationship of one board with the other was distinctly unsatisfactory, if not openly hostile. He also reported that although Fogra Failte was obliged by statute to act in accord with the policy of An Bord Failte, 'the body responsible for framing tourist policy', Fogra Failte 'did not regard it as their duty to consult An Bord Failte' (Dail debate, 9 February 1955).[12] Elsewhere he reported the existence of the two boards was wasteful of funds in that there were separate staffs, premises and transport arrangements.

Lemass, the former Minister for Industry and Commerce (who had introduced the 1952 Act) made a comprehensive speech dealing with many issues of importance to tourism policy. He suggested that the 'attitude of the Government to the development of our tourist business is somewhat ambiguous'. He went on to suggest that the support for An Tostal was not at the level required. In addition the process whereby decisions taken by Bord Failte and Fogra Failte had first to be approved by the Minister were also seen as a constraint to development. Lemass was dubious about the merit of having hoteliers on the Board of An Bord Failte:

> The extent to which it is desirable to have hotel proprietors directing the operations of An Bord Failte is a matter that we debated here in the past. It is clearly undesirable that An Bord Failte should be overloaded with representatives of hotel owners because its duties are very largely concerned with acting as policemen on

hotel-keepers and to seeing that they maintain proper standards of accommodation for visitors. If the representatives of the Tourist Association on An Bord Failte should be mainly concerned with the interests of hotel proprietors, then the whole work of An Bord Failte may get a wrong direction. (Dail debate, 9 February 1955).[13]

The issue of the advisability of having hoteliers on the board of An Bord Failte was also raised by NESC (1980b), yet the hotel senior management maintained a strong presence at board level until very recently.

In addition to the above concerns, Deputy Lemass (and other deputies) expressed dissatisfaction with the contribution of Bord Failte to tourist development. 'I refer to them merely to indicate the general impression I have got, both as a Minister and an ordinary Deputy, that an Bord Failte is not putting into this work of tourist trade development the effort that was expected of them. I think the Prime Minister will have to keep up pressure on them to get on with the job they were appointed to do and not to interfere with them in the doing of that job, if, by interfering, he is going to slow down the getting of results' (Dail debate, 9 February 1955). Not surprisingly, Lemass did not believe it appropriate that Fogra Failte be dissolved. He articulated an argument that has some relevance to recent developments in Bord Failte.[14] Lemass believed that the extra burden of publicity along with other duties would cause Bord Failte problems. It was suggested that it would be better to leave the publicity functions to a separate organization. In 1994 the Minister for Tourism and Trade commissioned a consultancy report on the functions undertaken by Bord Failte. The Minister apparently believed that Bord Failte should jettison all activities with the **exception** of the core publicity function. This report is discussed in Chapter 9.

An important facet of the 1955 Act was the transfer of the Fogra Failte grant to Bord Failte which in theory meant that the new organization would be entitled to an annual grant up to a maximum of IR£500,000 per annum. It is important to note that the maximum allocation had not been reached in any year up to that point in time. In December of 1957 a new Act was introduced. This Act, *inter alia,* was intended to introduce measures that would tackle the accommodation bottlenecks that still existed. The Act extended for five years the Guaranteed Loan Scheme for hotels and resorts and also grants towards the payment of interest on loans other than under the scheme. The Act also initiated the publication of a list of unregistered but approved premises. The 1957 Act did little to encourage an improvement in accommodation and a renewed attempt was made in the Tourist Traffic Act of 1959. From 1952 to 1957 the number of bedrooms in hotels and guest houses declined from just over 17,000 to 16,000. The major drawback to the expansion of accommodation was the heavy capital cost involved in relation to the comparatively short duration of the tourist season. In addition, although schemes of guarantees and grants had been in existence since October 1953 for the provision of amenities and services at tourist resorts, there had been relatively little improvement. The major barrier to development was the proviso that funds could only be used in cases where revenue would be earned to repay the loan. The nature of many 'merit' goods in tourism is that they have a public good component and as a result will inevitably be underprovided unless the state gets actively involved. It is imperative that capital investment of a non-remunerative type be engaged in order that profit earning activities may later be established. The legislation had not tackled this problem and as a result a lack of activity ensued.

The 1959 Act provided additional monies to Bord Failte to tackle the problems outlined above. The Act confirmed a commitment made in the First Programme for Economic Expansion (Stationery Office, 1958b) to set aside a sum of IR£1 million to assist by way of grants the financing of a 10-year programme for the development of major resorts. The Act also provided for a maximum of IR£0.5 million to grant aid the development of holiday accommodation. These additional funds for the development of tourist resorts and the expansion of hotel accommodation were additional to the existing annual maximum grant of IR£0.5 million available to Bord Failte for the general development and publicity for the tourist industry.

The passing of the four tourism acts in the 1950s suggested that the attitude to tourist development had become more benign. Subsequent developments were to prove that tourism was still very much the poor relation of Irish economic policy.

THE FIRST PROGRAMME FOR ECONOMIC EXPANSION

Throughout the 1950s Ireland had been engulfed by a severe economic recession resulting in widespread unemployment and emigration. In 1958, Whitaker presented a milestone report entitled 'Economic Development' to the Government (Stationery Office, 1958a). The ideas contained in the report were widely accepted and were incorporated in 'The First Programme for Economic Expansion' which the Government presented to the Irish Parliament in November of 1958 (Stationary office, 1958b). An eminent historian described the First Programme as follows:

> It was essentially a five year plan for expansion which was to involve many sectors of the country's economy, but principally agriculture and industry. In industry, the primary aim was seen to be the stimulation of private industrial investment. The abandonment of protectionism and the adoption of outward looking policies were at the core of the new programme. (Lyons 1985: 629)

The First Programme ran from 1959 to 1964. The programme of public capital investment outlined in the White Paper of 1958 covered the period from the beginning of the financial year, 1959–1960 to the end of the financial year 1963–1964. It contemplated capital expenditure of IR£220.5 million. Of this amount IR£2.5 million (a relatively minuscule amount) was projected for tourism development. The programme went far beyond its anticipated expenditure. This was most apparent in the case of transport, where expenditure was five times greater than the estimate. It was also true in the cases of agriculture, fuel and power, and telephones. On the other hand, fisheries and tourism fell below the projected amounts. The actual amount expended on the total programme was a little over IR£297 million (IR£76.5 million above target) yet the expenditure on tourism at IR£1.21 million was less than 50 per cent of the target. While the programme was undoubtedly a success as the performance of economic growth was beyond target it does appear that the new found emphasis on industrial development led to a relative neglect of the services sector in general and tourism in particular. This relative neglect was to continue for many years and the emphasis on tourism in the late 1980s only emerged when the relative failure of manufacturing industry became manifest.

THE ECONOMIC ENVIRONMENT

An evaluation of the contribution of tourism to the Irish economy in the years under review is made extremely difficult by the unavailability of comparable data. A reasonably comparable set of data for the major tourism components is available only from 1953. In this context the estimates of tourism revenue before 1953 are conjectural. Before reviewing this performance it is worthwhile to briefly chart the general performance of the macroeconomy from 1922 to the late 1950s. This can allow the reader to understand more fully the broader environment in which the tourism industry was operating.

Factors constraining economic development

There were many factors which inhibited Ireland's potential for economic development when the fledgling new state came into being. The fact that at independence 90 per cent of its exports went to the UK, and that 90 per cent were agricultural, was a doubly unfortunate combination for Ireland. The UK was to prove to be the 'sick man' of Europe for much of the period since independence, while agricultural prices and markets were for long unfavourable due to widespread agricultural protectionism. It has also been suggested that Ireland inherited a legacy of attitudes and institutions unfavourable to economic regeneration. A review of the economic performance conducted by Kennedy suggested that 'Ireland does not appear to have been as effective as other European countries in overcoming constraints, so that its economic performance, as well as its economic record, emerges as poor' (Kennedy, 1988) A significant result of the poor performance of the Irish economy was the long-term decline of population to 1961. The population fell to 2.8 million in 1961 from 4.2 million in 1926.

Ireland approached the end of the 1950s with few signs of any real improvement in the economic welfare of the populace. The initial laissez-faire policies of the First Free State Government were abandoned in the early 1930s by the incoming Fianna Fail administration. Fianna Fail embarked on a programme of generalized protectionism in 1932. As a result the level of effective protection of Irish industry was extremely high throughout the following three decades. Industrial employment grew from 109,000 in 1929 to 227,000 in 1951. Throughout the period agricultural employment continued to decline. Nonetheless the percentage of the population engaged in industry (at 18%) was far below our European counterparts. Northern Ireland at this time had 40 per cent of the population engaged in industry (O'Malley, 1987).

Balance of payments difficulties

Economic difficulties of the 1950s were mainly due to the emergence of a chronic balance of payments crisis. O'Malley (1987) suggests that this arose partly from the near exhaustion of the 'easy' stage of import-substituting industrialization,which meant that there was relatively little further replacement of imports by domestic production. This, coupled with the need to import capital goods and a continued failure to achieve significant growth in exports meant that it was inevitable that serious balance of trade deficits would emerge, leading to a balance of payments crisis. The balance of payments problems first became chronic in 1951, subsided a little in 1952 but emerged again in 1955 as a serious constraint. As the recession in industry occurred while the large agricultural labour force continued to decline, the total labour force fell dramatically. Emigration to the UK rose to 40,000 per annum. It was in this context that the 'First Programme for Economic Expansion' was launched (Stationery Office, 1958b). Economic Development (Stationery Office, 1958a) aptly described the sense of national crisis:

> The policies hereto followed, though given a fair trial, have not resulted in a viable economy. We have power, transport facilities, public services, houses, hospitals and a general infrastructure on a scale reasonable by Western European standards, yet large-scale emigration and unemployment still persist. The population is falling, the national income rising more slowly than the rest of Europe ... The common talk amongst parents in the towns, as in rural Ireland, is of their children having to emigrate as soon as their education is completed in order to be sure of a reasonable livelihood.

TOURISM PERFORMANCE

In the absence of a comparable dataset the best available option is to review the estimates of tourism revenues contained in the Irish Statistical Bulletins. In this context the most reliable data are available from the early 1940s. Ireland in this respect is no different to most countries in that tourism revenues and movements were afforded little priority until the early 1950s.

We have already mentioned that tourism assumed increased prominence in Ireland in the early post-war years. The 'official' estimates provided in the statistical bulletins suggest that the growth of net tourism receipts had in fact been on the increase since the early 1940s. The net receipts from tourism had increased from IR£2 million in 1942 to a peak of IR£33 million in 1948, thereafter a decline set in until 1953, stabilized until 1957 and increased from then until 1968 in every year except 1966.[15] The extent of the decline in receipts can be gauged from the fact that the net nominal value of receipts only reached the 1949 level in 1957 while the real value surpassed the 1949 level only in 1963 (Kennedy and Dowling, 1975: 128). The foregoing suggests quite a dramatic decline in fortunes that requires explanation.

There appears to have been a prevalent belief that the influx of British tourists in the post-war years would inevitably decline and that little action could be taken to avoid this. In addition, we have already mentioned that some elements in Irish society had not welcomed the influx of British visitors and thus were not unduly concerned to see a decline. While it does appear true that some decline was inevitable the lack of a proactive policy in tourism development also appears to have been a major element in the subsequent performance. The lack of attention to tourism development is even more startling when one evaluates the relative contribution of the sector to the balance of payments in the early post-war years.

The contribution of tourism to the balance of payments

Total net receipts from tourism were IR£18 million for 1946, IR£28 million for 1947 and IR£33 million for 1948. The total income from the exports of merchandise and invisible exports for these years were IR£103 million, IR£113 million, and IR£129 million respectively. The value of agricultural exports in the same years were IR£30 million, IR£30 million, and IR£35 million, respectively.[16] An internal Government memorandum in 1950 highlighted the importance of the tourism industry as follows:

> The importance of the industry transcends that of the agriculture industry so far as dollar earnings are concerned. Receipts from tourism are the largest single item in our dollar earnings as distinct from dollar income. The total dollar income in 1948 was equivalent to IR£7m, of which IR£3m represented emigrants' remittances and legacies (not regarded as earnings), IR£2m and IR£3/4m represented net earnings from tourism and IR£0.4m the earnings from exports of merchandise. It is clear, therefore, that neither in the field of agriculture nor in the field of industrial development is there any prospect of dollar earnings comparable with that provided by tourism. The Minister considers that the national interest requires that there should be a vigorous and determined effort to maintain and develop the industry. (D/T files S13087B)[17]

The overview presented in the previous sections has shown that the necessary commitment to develop the industry was far from enthusiastic and that while some decline may have been expected in the late 1940s it need not have been so disastrous if proactive policies were pursued earlier. The decline in the fortunes of tourism in the 1950s was particularly detrimental to Ireland as invisibles were an extremely important element in the Irish balance of payments. In 1949 invisibles accounted for 57 per cent of the exports of goods and services but fell considerably in the 1950s due to the slow growth of invisibles to visible exports. The growth rate of net invisibles was only 0.9 per cent per annum between 1949 and 1957. This to some extent reflects the increased emphasis in Ireland on industrial exports but it also reflects the relative neglect of the tourism sector and the poor performance of the macroeconomy in the 1950s.

Figure 2.2 presents total foreign exchange earnings from tourism. It shows that real foreign exchange earnings peaked in 1948 and declined more or less consistently until 1957 when earnings began to increase again. What is noticeable is that Ireland ended the decade of the 1950s with less real earnings from tourism than in 1948.

While estimates of tourism numbers have been available since the early 1950s it is only since 1955 that a reasonably reliable dataset of numbers and revenue can be used with any degree of confidence. A breakdown of tourism numbers and revenue is illustrated in Tables 2.1 and 2.2.

While the data presented in Tables 2.1 and 2.2 should be treated with some caution it does provide us with a reasonably good picture of developments. What is patently clear from the data is the heavy reliance on Britain as the principal source of revenue. This outcome was somewhat inevitable given the advantages Ireland enjoyed as a holiday venue for British visitors, such as geographical proximity, low travel costs and the same language. In the context of these advantages the rate of increase in visitor numbers and revenue from Britain in the 1950s was disappointing. Visitor numbers declined considerably in the early 1950s, due mainly to the improvement in the food situation in Britain and the cessation of most of the 'food conscious' traffic. The Irish Statistical Bulletin records a drop of 63,000 in 1953 alone (CSO, 1960). While some improvement was registered in 1955 and 1956 a decline again occurred in 1957. This was probably due to the very poor performance of the British economy, particularly in the earlier part of the year which affected bookings combined with the beginning of the border campaign by the IRA which began in December 1956. After 1957 both numbers of tourists and revenues began a steady increase.

While the performance in terms of visitor numbers showed improvement toward the end of the decade it did mask a worrying trend. The expenditure per capita was very sluggish. Commenting on the 1950s Quinn (1961) made the following observation 'The rate of revenue increase from tourism has been disappointing compared with most European countries. In the period 1955–1958 the increase in Ireland was 12 per cent, compared with figures of 25 per cent for Britain, 30 per cent for France, 48 per cent for Italy and 64 per cent for Germany' (p 155). This poor performance of Irish tourism requires some explanation and the answer is found in the constituents of Irish tourism demand at the time.

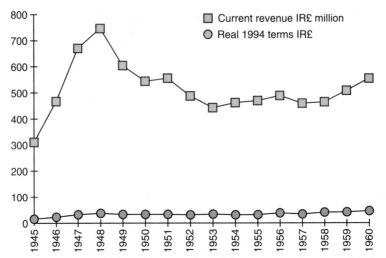

Figure 2.2 Total receipts from tourism, 1945–1960 in current and constant 1994 prices.
Source: Irish Statistical Bulletin, various years, published by the Stationery Office, Dublin

Table 2.1 Visitor numbers to Ireland 1955–1960 in thousands

Visitors from	1955	1956	1957	1958	1959	1960
Six Counties*	3288	3196	2724	2602	3092	3778
Britain	611	677	657	694	748	784
United States†	43	51	55	61	70	80

Notes
*The figures for the Six Counties (Northern Ireland) include day-trippers staying less than 24 hours. The number of day trippers did not fluctuate much in the six years and was estimated at 2.4 million.
†There is a slight element of duplication in the figures for US visitors since they include those who came directly from the US and those who came via Britain – the latter are also included in the British visitors.
Source: *Irish Trade Journal* and Irish Statistical Bulletin, various years, Stationery Office, Dublin.

Constituents of tourism demand

A more comprehensive picture of tourism developments can be ascertained if an analysis of the individual constituents is made according to purpose of visit. Of the total visitors from Britain in 1960 (784,000) about 45 per cent (356,000) were in the category 'visit to relatives'; 40 per cent (315,000) were in the 'tourist' category, i.e. comprising mainly British holiday-makers without family ties in Ireland; the remaining 15 per cent (113,000) fell into the category 'business and other'. While the number of 'visiting relatives' was substantially greater than the number of British holiday-makers the estimates of expenditure of the latter

Table 2.2 Tourist revenue* from visitors to Ireland by area of residence, 1955–1960 (IR£million)

Year	1955	1956	1957	1958	1959	1960
Britain	13.0	15.2	14.2	16.5	19.1	21.8
Six Counties						
Day	1.9	1.8	1.9	2.2	2.2	2.2
Other	10.0	10.0	9.9	8.2	8.0	8.9
Overseas†	4.0	4.3	4.3	5.4	6.1	6.8
Transport	2.0	2.1	2.1	2.3	2.4	2.7
Total	30.9	33.4	32.4	34.6	37.8	42.4

Notes
*All revenue is in current prices.
†The overseas figure is composed primarily of North American visitor revenue and was stated to be conjectural. Some revisions were made in later years to the estimation procedure.
Source: *Irish Trade Journal* and Irish Statistical Bulletin, various years, Stationery Office, Dublin.

group were, as might be expected, higher. It was estimated that this group contributed IR£9.9 million against IR£8.6 million for those visiting relatives. These figures suggest that the overall dependence on the British market was more serious than a preliminary overview revealed. The heavy reliance on poor-spending VFRs (visiting friends and relatives) acted as a constraint to the benefits which tourism could bring to the economy. In addition, the figures suggest that a more focused approach to the British market was required. Given that VFRs are largely unaffected by tourism promotional campaigns, whereas the 'pure tourist' may be, the data suggest that a more focused approach to tourism promotion be undertaken in the British market. It was unfortunate that this form of strategy was not undertaken and the poor performance of the British market was later to be documented in NESC (1980b). Subsequent reviews undertaken in the early 1990s failed to uncover such a focused approach being undertaken.

The performance in relation to the Six Counties (Northern Ireland) was also rather poor in the period 1955–1960, both in respect of visitor numbers and revenue. Between 1955 and 1960 total receipts from the Six Counties declined from IR£11.9 million to IR£11.1 million (about one-fifth of tourist revenue from Northern Ireland was contributed by 'excursionists', i.e. cross-border visitors who returned inside 24 hours). A breakdown of the statistics into the three categories of 'tourist', 'visits to relatives' and 'business' reveals that while the latter two categories remained fairly static in the period 1955–1960, revenue from the strictly 'tourist' category showed a decrease from IR£8.2 million to IR£7.1 million. The drop in expenditure was attributed to the border conflict but other factors were also at work.

Cross-border traffic declined from 2.09 million (1955) to 1.32 million (1958) (these figures include day trippers) and improved from 1959 to reach 2.3 million in 1960. Legislative changes introduced in the late 1950s played a not insignificant role in the improved performance. First, the abolition of the triptych[18] requirement for south-bound cars proved a major bonus to cross-border movements. The second major reason for the stimulus to growth came with the reform of the licensing laws for the sale of drink which extended evening opening hours and Sunday opening. This meant that public houses in the South were open for some considerable time after they had closed in the North, and led to a very considerable increase in cross-border trips to adjacent public houses in the South. So important was this factor that the decline in revenue which eventually set in again in 1965 could reasonably be explained by the relatively sharper rise in the prices of drink and tobacco in the South.

Despite the improvements in tourist numbers towards the end of the 1950s this trend was not accompanied by a commensurate increase in revenue. Revenue attributed to the strictly tourist category in cross-border traffic showed an increase of 20 per cent in the two-year period 1958–1960 despite an increase of 75 per cent in tourist numbers which demonstrated evidence of a tendency towards diminishing average expenditure in the period. The situation in relation to Ireland's participation in US tourist traffic to Europe, both in regard to numbers of visitors and their expenditure, is given in Table 2.3.

The table demonstrates that Ireland's proportion of US visitors to Europe in the six years under review remained practically constant at around 10 per cent. The share of expenditure was about four times less than the share of visitors, fluctuating between 2 and 2.5 per cent in the six-year period. The figures demonstrate that the average expenditure of the US visitor to Ireland was substantially lower than in other European countries at the time. While casual observation may have attributed this to shorter average length of stay the data at the time indicated the opposite to be the case with an average length of stay of 12 days in 1959, substantially higher than in other countries. The explanation is due to the fact that a much greater proportion of US visitors to Ireland had family ties. These visitors typically stayed with relatives for the most part and their expenditure was consequently lower but the length of their stay was relatively long (approximately one month) which pushed up the average figure for length of stay of US visitors as a whole.

Despite this factor the average length of stay of the US visitor without family connections was still longer in Ireland than in most other European countries. This appeared to have been counteracted by poor average per capita expenditure. The reason for the low expenditure was attributable to the relative cheapness of accommodation and catering facilities (even in the higher and more expensive grades) and the absence of traditionally big expenditure activities and facilities, e.g. night-clubs and casinos to be found in other countries at the time.

Table 2.3 US visitor numbers and expenditure in Europe and Ireland, 1955–1960

	Number (000)	Number (000)	Irish share of total numbers	Spend* ($million)	Spend* ($million)	Irish share of total revenue
	Europe	Ireland	(%)	Europe	Ireland	(%)
1955	482	43	8.9	430	8	1.9
1956	521	51	9.8	473	11	2.4
1957	556	55˙	9.9	483	12	2.5
1958	637	61	9.6	560	13	2.3
1959	705	70	9.9	604	14	2.3
1960	832	80	9.6	704	16	2.3

Note
*Prices are in current terms.
Source: US Department of Commerce (1960).

IMPROVEMENTS TO THE ACCOMMODATION STOCK

The problem of suitable accommodation, particularly for visitors from the US had been addressed in the Christenberry report but the legislation to lever additional accommodation had proved very cumbersome. It was only with the Tourist Traffic Act of 1957 that the situation began to improve when many of the previous administrative complexities were removed. In mid-1958, grants to cover 20 per cent of the construction costs of new bedrooms and one-third of the cost of central heating in these were introduced. Subsequently, a depreciation allowance amounting to 10 per cent per annum of the capital cost incurred on or after 1 January 1960 was granted for tax purposes. Improvement grants, relating to the installation of private bathrooms and central heating in existing accommodation were also available, covering 20 per cent of the capital cost. The effect of these measures was a significant expansion in the quantity and quality of accommodation from the late 1950s onwards. The number of bedrooms in hotels and guesthouses rose from 16,000 in 1957 to 26,000 in 1968 and the number of rooms with private bathroom increased from 800 to 8400 in 1968 (Kennedy and Dowling, 1975: 144) Despite the generalized improvements to the accommodation stock it was to be some years before the product development side of the market was tackled with any degree of commitment.

CONCLUSIONS

It has been demonstrated that tourism was a very important element of the national economy throughout many of the years under review. It is also evident from the review that tourism did not receive the attention commensurate with its contribution to the national economy. The resistance of some members of Dail Eireann to tourist development was particularly pronounced in the late

1940s when tourism made a significant contribution to the balance of payments. The situation changed somewhat in the 1950s with the establishment of Bord Failte and the passing of legislation which dealt with the development of the sector. Despite the apparent change of attitude to the sector the analysis suggests that the approach to tourism development was still somewhat ambivalent. The administrative technicalities of the legislation and the attitude displayed by the Department of Finance to tourism certainly seem to have acted as a severe constraint to tourism development. Combined with a particularly Irish attitude to service industries (which often emphasized servility) and a prevalent belief that that there was little Government could do to influence tourism served to compound these difficulties. Lynch (1969) aptly summarizes this viewpoint:

> It would be quite wrong of course, to use hindsight in criticism of individual policies; but especially after 1948 there was a long delay in effectively creating a satisfactory organisation for the promotion of tourism, even though that industry could be shown to be third in importance in the list of sources of external income. There seems to have been a belief that a competitive tourist industry could have established itself spontaneously. (p. 195)

As suggested previously the establishment of Bord Failte was certainly a step in the right direction yet the legislation and finance available to the organization was relatively conservative, given its brief. In addition, expansion of the sector was also retarded due to institutional restrictions, such as the ban on foreign coach tours, which was aimed at preserving the monopoly of the national transport authority (CIE) and which was not removed until 1957. The lack of suitable car-ferry facilities was also a constraint and was not tackled until the 1960s. The next chapter examines trends in the 1960s and 1970s.

NOTES

1. A good discussion of Dependency theory is provided by Palma (1978).
2. See Chairman's address to the Killarney Tourist Association Annual General Meeting, 12 December 1947, in Department of An Taoiseach file (National Archives of Ireland, D/T S13087 B).
3. For full text of the Minister's response see *Memorandum for the Government – The Tourist Industry*, February 1950, Department of An Taoiseach (National Archives of Ireland, D/T S13087 B).
4. The comments of Pozzi were reported by the Minister for External Affairs in *Memorandum for the Government – Tourism and E.C.A. Aid*, 27 July 1950. For the full text see Department of An Taoiseach file S13087C (National Archives of Ireland, D/T S13087 C).
5. The Irish Hotels Federation had been established in 1938 to represent the views of hoteliers. The Federation continues to act as a lobbyist for the industry.
6. The full text of the Minister's response entitled *Memorandum for Government – The Tourist Industry*, 5 January 1952, is a good example of the conservative approach to tourism development. For the full text see Department of An Taoiseach file S10387D (National Archives of Ireland, D/T S10387 D).

7. *Ibid.*
8. Cafferky made these remarks in the Dail in the debate on the Second Stage of the Tourist Traffic Act 1951, Second Stage, 28 February 1952. (See column 1342 of Tourist Traffic Act 1952.)
9. *Ibid.* columns 1353–1357.
10. *Ibid.* column 1339.
11. Copies of The Irish Tourist Bulletin are to be found in Department of An Taoiseach file 5647a, National Archives, Dublin.
12. This point was made by Deputy William Norton, Minister for Industry and Commerce during the second stage of the Tourist Traffic Act debate, 9 February 1955 (See columns 130–142 of Dail Debate (Stationery Office, 1955).)
13. *Ibid.* See columns 50–60.
14. See Arthur. D. Little Ltd (1994).
15. The data provided are in current market prices.
16. These figures come from *The Irish Trade Journal* and Irish Statistical Bulletins for the years under review.
17. These points were made by the Minister for Industry and Commerce in a *Memorandum for Government – The Tourist Industry*, 5 February, 1950. For full text see the Department of An Taoiseach file S13087B (National Archives of Ireland, D/T S13087B).
18. The triptych was a requirement for all south-bound cars from the north of Ireland. Essentially, there were two elements to the triptych. First, was the administrative burden of having to apply to the Southern Government if one wished to travel from the North, in essence the triptych was a permit that was displayed on the car window. Secondly, if one did not have triptych the car was not insured. This latter restriction had the effect of curtailing cross-border traffic.

3 Development of Irish tourism, 1960–1980

CONTEXT

Having suffered a severe economic recession in the latter part of the 1950s, Ireland enjoyed a sustained period of growth during the First Programme for Economic Expansion, 1958–1963[1]. This programme coincided with and was part of a more outward-looking economic policy stance by the Irish Government that relied heavily on attracting foreign multinational companies to establish manufacturing bases in Ireland. The programme also heralded a more interventionist stance by the public sector in many aspects of Irish economic life with the establishment and/or strengthening of the powers and responsibilities of Government agencies with tasks to support sectoral and general economic targets. Tourism was one sector to receive increasing attention because of its important contribution to the balance of payments (where deficits in the 1950s imposed severe constraints on policy choices) and its potential for employment generation.

This chapter examines the performance of the Irish tourism industry as the small economy (now more open than previously) grappled with the problems of late development from its peripheral location in the 1960s at a time when world and European tourism was expanding rapidly; this is followed by a review of developments in the following decade as the Northern Ireland troubles and high inflation rates impacted significantly on the trend rate of growth of Irish tourism; the oil-induced recessions early and late in the decade also constrained the expansion in overseas tourist numbers and related expenditures while accession to the EU in 1973 opened up new opportunities for business and conference travel.

1960s: DECADE OF GROWTH

The First Programme for Economic Expansion grew out of the crisis of the late 1950s and, although motivated by a spirit of pragmatism, it represented the arrival of Keynesian macroeconomic thinking and policies in Ireland. Most importantly, was the role staked out for the public authorities in the planning process. The increased prominence afforded to public sector bodies and

Government participation in the economy led to a more proactive policy stance in relation to tourism. The manifestation of this approach was to be found in the significant legislative measures adopted throughout the 1960s in relation to tourism development. Between 1960 and 1970 the emphasis within tourism was on two areas, first, the development of accommodation to meet growing demand and, second, to develop a tourism infrastructure in terms of amenities and facilities required by tourists holidaying in Ireland/ The legislative measures, levels of investment and performance are evaluated below.

Legislative changes 1960–1970

The movement towards a more positive stance on tourism development came with the passing of the Tourist Traffic Act in 1961. It had three main purposes:

1. to make available to Bord Failte over the following seven years a sum not exceeding IR£5 million, which roughly meant an annual outlay of about IR£700,000 per annum. The previous maximum annual limit had been established at IR£500,000;
2. to increase from IR£3 million to IR£5 million the amount which Bord Failte could guarantee loans for hotel and tourist resort development;
3. to remove the limit of IR£75,000 yearly which represented the sum that Bord Failte were permitted to pay by way of interest on loans for hotel improvement and building purposes.

The changed circumstances of the early 1960s, with signs of improved economic performance and a general mood of optimism are echoed in the Dail debate dealing with the 1961 Act. Most Dail deputies welcomed increased expenditure on tourism. If there was any thought permeating the debate it was that Ireland should concentrate more on the British tourist than tourists from other parts of the world. This sentiment was expressed through the view that Bord Failte was more concerned with luxury accommodation than that required by the average British visitor. The Minister for Transport and Power rejected this claim emphasizing that Bord Failte made no distinction between different forms of accommodation as the grants available were standard bedroom and reconstruction grants.

The need to introduce a new Tourist Traffic Act in 1963 was seen as evidence of strong investment growth by the hotel sector. The major purpose of the 1963 Act was to increase to IR£1.5 million the fund of IR£0.5 million introduced under the 1959 Act, for the disbursement of grants by Bord Failte for the development of holiday accommodation/ Under the Bord Failte grant schemes, cash grants were available towards the cost of providing additional hotel bedrooms either by way of constructing new hotels or by additions to existing hotels. Grants of 20 per cent were also available for general improvement works in hotels such as the provision of central heating, the conversion of bedrooms into bed/bath units and other structural improvements. Two new grant schemes had been introduced in 1962, under which 20 per cent grants were made available for the construction or improvement of accommodation for staff and for the provision of entertainment facilities for guests, for example, recreation rooms, tennis courts and so on. The major effect of the incentives offered was to increase the volume of accommodation substantially. The total number of registered rooms in hotels and guest houses increased from 16,642 in 1958 to 19,630 at the beginning of 1963. The net effect of the success of the schemes was that the original fund of IR£0.5 million was exhausted by the beginning of 1963. While the bottleneck in accommodation had been alleviated it was still felt necessary to improve the accommodation base. The additional IR£1 million was seen as a necessary commitment to continue the significant investment of the previous four years. During the Dail debate on the Act the Minister supported the argument for the extra funding in the following manner.

> The hotel industry is more active and enterprising today than at any time in the past. The fact that the IR£500,000 grant provided in 1959 has been exhausted is an indication of the rise in investment of the industry because the Bord Failte grants, limited to 20 per cent of approved works, must be matched at least four-fold by hoteliers' own spending. In fact total investment in hotel development has been running at more than IR£1m each year. (Dail debate, 2 July 1963, of the Tourist Traffic Act 1963)

While the sentiments of the Minister were generally endorsed by Dail deputies the concern over the lack of lower grade accommodation was again expressed. Accommodation in the lower two grades, C and D, showed a decline for a number of reasons such as some businesses closing down, or establishments improving their accommodation and moving into higher grades. While welcoming the overall developments some deputies felt that the lack of provision of lower grade accommodation could affect the British market. It was felt by some that the legislation favoured the bigger investor to the exclusion of the small operator.

Tourist Traffic Act 1966

The improved performance of tourism in the early years of the 1960s led to a greater recognition of the contribution of tourism to the national economy. In order to recognize and improve upon the contribution of tourism the 1966 Act was introduced to tackle some emerging issues. The major purpose of the Act was to provide for the registration of caravan sites and camping sites and the continuation of a scheme of Ministerial guarantees in respect of loans raised for the construction or improvement of holiday accommodation. This Act also contained provisions for the future financing of the various statutory functions of Bord Failte.

The Tourist Traffic Acts, 1939, 1952 and 1957 had provided for the registration by Bord Failte of certain categories of holiday accommodation, namely, hotels, holiday hostels, youth hostels, holiday camps and motor hotels or motels. The effect of the legislation was that no person could describe or advertise any premises as an hotel or guest house unless the premises were registered in the appropriate category with Bord Failte. To secure registration, premises had to comply with standards prescribed by Bord Failte/ With the increase of motoring and caravan holidays in the mid-1960s it was felt appropriate that an initiative in this area was required. Previous to 1966 little progress had been made in the provision of caravan sites to a standard comparable to the best sites in Britain and on the Continent. It was felt that an essential step towards the raising of standards of facilities and operations would be the introduction of a system of inspection and grading. It was also hoped that the provision of such facilities would attract camping visitors from European countries where camping holidays were very popular.

The 1966 Act also made some minor amendments to the previous Tourism and Traffic Acts. The 1952 Act had restricted guarantees for loans raised for the provision of amenities and services to works related to particular tourist resorts. With the creation of the regional tourism organizations in 1964 and the growing popularity of motoring tourism, developments in tourism were now occurring in places other than those which had traditionally been regarded as resorts. The 1966 Act gave formal recognition to this development by extending the guaranteed loan scheme to tourist enterprises even though they may not have been in a recognized tourist resort or associated with a particular hotel. The scheme of guaranteed loans had been initiated under the 1952 Act for five years. The period was extended by two further periods of five years by the Tourist Traffic Acts of 1957 and 1961. The 1966 Act authorized the continuation of the scheme until 1972.

A significant element of the 1966 Act related to the future financing of the statutory functions of Bord Failte. These functions had previously been paid out of funds voted annually by the Oireachtas in the form of grants-in-aid to the Bord. In 1966 the statutory limits applicable to the three main divisions of the Bord's activities had been reached. The three functions related to the major resort development scheme, the scheme of cash grants for the development of holiday accommodation and the general function of increasing tourism to Ireland. Accordingly, the Act contained enabling financial provisions related to all three functions

The resort development scheme had been inaugurated under the Tourist Traffic Act of 1959, which provided for the payment to Bord Failte within a 10-year period of sums not exceeding in the aggregate IR£1 million for the disbursement of grants for major tourist resorts. From this fund a grant scheme had been operated by the Bord to enable such essential schemes as basic site development, provision of promenades, parks and other recreational activities to be undertaken. The major resorts and resort areas selected by Bord Failte for development were Galway/Salthill, Killarney, Bray, Dun Laoghaire, Tramore, Skerries, Kilkee, Youghal, Ballybunion, Lahinch, Arklow, Greystones, West

Cork, County Donegal, Achill Island, Dingle Pensinsula, River Shannon and Lakes. The scheme was carried out by Bord Failte in consultation with the local authorities and local interests. One of the major conditions of the scheme was that there should be a minimum local contribution of 20 per cent.

The progress of the resort scheme was slow in the first four years of operation but accelerated in 1964–1965 and the limit of IR£1 million had almost been reached by 1966. In addition, the development of the Shannon waterway had not been included among the original areas to be developed and the subsequent addition of the Shannon had absorbed some of the initial fund. As a result, the 1966 Act provided for the raising of the existing limit on the resort development fund from IR£1 million to IR£3.25 million, an increase of IR£2.25 million, of which IR£1.5 million was in respect of the completion of works underway with the remaining IR£0.75 million to be devoted for a second resort programme. The 1966 Act also increased grant monies available for holiday accommodation. The 1959 Act had specified an amount not exceeding IR£0.5 million which had subsequently been increased to IR£1.5 million by the 1963 Act (Stationery Office, 1963). While there had been significant investment and provision of new accommodation it was felt necessary to increase still further the accommodation base and the Act increased the amount which could be provided for holiday accommodation from IR£1.5 million to IR£3 million.

The 1966 Act made one very important change to the funding arrangements for Bord Failte. Apart from the special funds for accommodation grants and for the development of major resorts, the cost of administration and general activities of Bord Failte had been met from an annual grant-in-aid. From this grant-in-aid the Bord were required to meet the cost of overseas publicity and advertising and a wide range of activities, including improvement works at minor resorts, access works and other improvements at places of historic or other special interest, assistance towards developing angling tourism and other sporting attractions, assistance to hotel staff training schemes, grants to meet interest on loans for accommodation and resort development and promotional work in connection with festivals and international conferences.

Prior to 1961, this grant-in-aid was subject to a limit of IR£0.5 million in any year but this limit was removed by the Tourist Traffic Act, 1961, and replaced by the provision of a global sum of IR£5 million, the intention being that for a limited period the level of state spending on the development and promotion of tourism would be substantially increased. It was indicated at the time that, on the basis of annual provisions related to the then current requirements, the sum of IR£5 million might be expected to meet requirements for a period of seven years. The increased activity during the early 1960s had changed the circumstances and it was necessary to modify the objective of allocating the IR£5 million over a seven-year period. Increased interest grant commitments, resulting from the improved rate of investment by the hotel industry in the development of holiday accommodation, made it necessary initially to reduce the period to six years and the annual grants-in-aid to Bord Failte up to and including the financial year 1963–1964 were allocated on the basis of a six-year period. The grant-in-aid for 1964–1965 had, however, been increased very substantially to allow Bord Failte to initiate a programme of increased activity, particularly in overseas publicity and marketing. The increased publicity was deemed necessary due to the growing competition in international tourism and with due regard to the importance of tourist income in the national economy and particularly because of the formidable target of doubling tourism income (1960–1970) which had been established in the 'Second Programme for Economic Expansion' in 1964 (Stationery Office, 1964). As a result of the above activity the statutory maximum had more or less been reached by 1966 and the new Act established a new mechanism to deal with the grant-in-aid to Bord Failte. It was felt by the Minister that it would be inadvisable to set down a definite limit on the amounts to be expended on tourism as the figure would vary depending on the success or failure to approach the targets established for tourism. In this context the 1966 Act provided for the deletion of the existing limit of IR£5 million contained in the 1961 Act and did not substitute any new limit. Henceforth, the amount to be provided to Bord Failte in any year would be determined by the Minister for Transport and Power and the Minister for Finance and would be included in the annual estimates. While some deputies were sceptical of this new arrangement the Minister assured the Dail that the estimates related to Bord Failte could be debated in the normal manner.

Tourist Traffic Act 1970

The Tourist Traffic Act of 1970, was introduced at the time when the impact of the 'troubles' on Irish tourism was still a little unclear. This Act had two main elements. First, it doubled the financial provision for holiday accommodation from IR£5.5 million to IR£11 million, particular attention was given to the development of holiday cottages. Secondly, the Act increased the membership of the board of Bord Failte from seven to nine members. During the Dail debate on the act a number of deputies expressed dissatisfaction with the performance of Bord Failte. In a spirited defence of Bord Failte, the Minister for Transport and Power expressed the view that Bord Failte had made a considerable contribution to the development of the economy since 1952 and it was unwise to criticize the organization for a decline in tourism numbers that was outside its control. He also suggested that the need to introduce the additional finance for holiday accommodation was due testimony to the success of Bord Failte. The Minister went on to report that the IR£5.5 million expended between 1963 and 1970 on holiday accommodation had levered an additional IR£31 million of investment from the private sector. In relation to the increased membership of the Board of Bord Failte, the Minister argued that this initiative was been undertaken to add particular private sector expertise. In general, the Minster reported that he was generally happy with the performance of the tourism promotional agency and alluded to the growth of tourism income in the 1960s to substantiate the argument[2] (Stationery Office, 1970) The general arguments on the effectiveness of Bord Failte became a recurrent theme in subsequent years and the accountability of the organization came in for serious review in 1994 (see Chapter 9).

INVESTMENT IN PRODUCT DEVELOPMENT

The provision of additional public funds to develop the tourist industry, which had begun in the late 1950s was significantly enhanced by the legislative changes that occurred in the 1960s. Two priority areas, accommodation and resort development, were seen as sufficiently important to warrant special attention. The significant state investment in the development of tourism during this period is presented in Table 3.1.

The data presented in Table 3.1 show significant investment in the tourism industry in the 1960s through a number of state led schemes operated by Bord Failte. Between 1960 and 1970, IR£6.36 million was invested in accommodation representing 47 per cent of the total outlay of IR£13.5 million in the years 1956–1977. From 1958, grants of 20 per cent were provided towards bedroom construction in new hotels. In 1960, improvements to existing hotels were included and in 1963 staff accommodation and guest entertainment facilities qualified for grants of 20 per cent of the cost of structural works. In 1967 it was decided to increase grant levels generally while, at the same time varying them depending on location. Hotels falling within the Special Development Areas[3] qualified for higher grants; these ranged from 35 per cent of total construction costs of a new hotel in a remote area to 50 per cent of the costs of bedroom

Table 3.1 Direct capital expenditure by the state on tourism development, 1960–1970* (IR£000s)

Year	Accommodation	Interest grants	General development	Major resorts	Special holiday accommodation
1960	63	22	62	32	
1961	118	67	61	62	
1962	267	129	50	85	
1963	252	182	104	130	
1964	323	238	131	297	
1965	355	321	139	351	
1966	500	421	69	257	
1967	695	491	148	184	23
1968	788	501	284	336	83
1969	1498	514	337	405	87
1970	1500	400	522	400	76
Totals	6359	3286	1907	2539	269

*Current prices.
Source: Bord Failte, Reports, Audited Income and Expenditure Accounts, various years.

construction in areas where there already was accommodation. At the same time, outside the Special Development Areas, grants were increased to 25 per cent of total construction costs and 40 per cent of bedroom construction costs. The increased availability of pump-priming finance stimulated significant investment and report 51 of the NESC (1980b) noted 'It was recognised in the early 1970s that there was an oversupply of hotel accommodation and no new commitments were entered into'.

Interest relief of IR£8.6 million was provided by the state to developers of tourism accommodation in the years 1955–1977. From a slow start in the mid-1950s the scheme had a significant impact from about 1964 and the 1960s evidenced a total outlay of IR£3.3 million. In the early years of the 1970s a significant proportion of the total outlay was expended, tapering off to a relatively small outlay of IR£123,000 in 1977. Almost all of the expenditure during the period went to the hotel sector.

The Major Resorts Fund, introduced in 1958 was an attempt to upgrade resorts and resort areas. This fund operated by Bord Failte required the collaboration of local authorities, local development companies, associations and clubs. Originally, 17 resorts were chosen with two more being added in subsequent years. The General Development Fund, originally introduced in 1955 was principally concerned with sign-posting and angling development. In 1965 it was extended to encourage investment in ancillary activities. Grants were made available towards the provision of amongst others, equestrian, deep-sea angling, entertainment and golfing facilities. Expenditure from the fund increased significantly as a result.

The Major Resorts Fund had a statutory limit of IR£4 million and was expended between 1958 and 1975. Expenditure in the 1960s represented 65 per cent of the total outlay. The relatively small 'Special Holiday Accommodation Fund' was directed towards encouraging Farmhouse and Town and Country Home development in the Special Development Areas, and the total outlay between 1966 and 1977 was IR£866,000 of which IR£269,000 was allocated in the late 1960s.

The provision of additional finance for the development of tourism in the 1960s enabled the provision of facilities and amenities for visitors and the domestic holiday market and obviously enhanced the overall tourism product. The NESC in a comprehensive report in 1980 concluded that the grant schemes, originally intended as a pump-priming exercise had generally been successful though the report did also conclude 'with the passage of time, what was started as a means of stimulating an underdeveloped tourism sector has become accustomed practice and is considered at this stage by many within the industry to be an inviolate part of tourism development policy' (NESC, 1980b: 103).

INNOVATION IN PRODUCT DEVELOPMENT

Innovation in product development is a crucial element in the international competitiveness of the tourism industry. The quality and delivery of new and innovative tourism products can play an important role in attracting the ever more mobile international tourist. In order to maintain and improve competitiveness it is vital that destinations continually re-appraise the product being offered and where necessary introduce new products in tandem with changing market demand and consumer preferences. During the 1960s a number of innovative projects were developed in Irish tourism, particularly in the Shannon region and are worthy of further consideration.

Bunratty Castle, one of Ireland's most popular visitor attractions was developed as a tourist amenity in the late 1950s and early 1960s. The development of the castle was a joint initiative between Lord Gort (the owner of the castle), the Office of Public Works (OPW), Bord Failte and the regional industrial development agency, Shannon Development. The castle was opened to the public in 1960. A medieval banquet was developed in 1962 as part of a Shannon tour programme. The tour programme was an attempt by Shannon Development to entice transit passengers at Shannon airport to spend some time in Ireland. The initial pilot project of 1962 was marketed as a 'Free Day in Ireland'. The tour incorporated a short tour of county Cork and Limerick to give visitors a sufficient glimpse of Ireland to whet their appetites for a longer stay at some future date. The perceived success of the pilot project led to the introduction of a 'one-day tour' in 1963, priced at US$15. The culmination of the tour was a medieval banquet at Bunratty Castle (Share, 1992). The outcome was seen to be extremely positive, with 30,000 tour visitors participating by 1966. The medieval tour subsequently developed in cooperation with Coras Iompar Eireann (CIE), the state-owned transport company, into two-, three- and four-day tours involving other areas such as Connemara and Killarney and constituted an exciting development for Irish tourism. In tandem with these developments a folk park was developed in the grounds of Bunratty Castle by Shannon Development. Visitor numbers to the folk park increased from 29,100 in 1963 to 72,500 in 1970.

The apparent success of the Bunratty project led those associated with it to develop a number of other innovative tourism ventures in the 1960s. In 1965, the main mover behind many of the projects, Brendan O' Regan,[4] proposed the establishment of 'Cottage Courts'. It was intended that these would be groups of five to six tourist cottages with one central cottage to handle reception, entertainment and dining facilities. It was intended that the cottages would be in traditional style, following the favourable experience with the folk park. By 1967 the 'Cottage Court' idea had matured in to the proposal for a 'Rent-an-Irish-Cottage' (RIC) scheme. The broad objectives of the scheme were two-fold:

- to meet the growing demand for accommodation around Shannon Airport; and
- to stimulate village development in poorer areas.

Rent-an-Irish-Cottage was established as a limited company in 1968 and had some significant success in the early years. Subsequent administrative problems arose with the scheme in the 1970s and 1980s and Shannon Development subsequently sold off its share to private interests in the early 1990s. Nonetheless, the scheme still exists today and is an example of the phase of tourism innovation that began in Shannon in the 1960s.

While the developments at Shannon during the 1960s had a number of failures, probably inevitable during a period of experimentation, it is noteworthy that many of the innovations that were developed during this period are still operational today. What is probably more significant is that the level of innovation that occurred during this period does not appear to have been harnessed in subsequent years It is noticeable that the Bunratty product is very similar today to what it was 20 years ago and numerous tourism developments in subsequent years do not appear to have the same level of innovation, generally new variants of an old theme are developed rather than something 'new'.

Tourism performance

During the period 1960–1969 tourism exhibited a strong growth pattern in the number of visitors to Ireland. This growth had been anticipated in the First Programme for Economic Expansion (1959–1963), where it was explicitly recognized that Ireland had the potential to benefit from the accelerating growth in world tourism. The aforementioned tourism investment was seen as an important element in meeting the demands of tourists, particularly in relation to accommodation. In tandem with the expectation that tourism performance would improve, the Second Programme for Economic Expansion aimed at doubling total income from tourism between 1960 and 1970 in constant 1960 prices. The final outcome was that total tourism revenue (which includes carrier receipts and excursionist revenue) did increase by 47 per cent in real terms. Before the political instability began in Northern Ireland the registered growth to 1969 was 52 per cent. Figures 3.1 and 3.2 illustrate the constituents of the growth.

The data presented in Figure 3.1 shows that out-of-state visitor numbers grew considerably from 1.37 million in 1960 to 1.75 million in 1970 (28 per cent increase), having peaked at 1.94 million in 1969 before the 'troubles' began. A further analysis of the data reveals that 'total overseas' numbers had grown from 941,000 in 1960 to 1.45 million in 1970, a growth of almost 55 per cent. The more modest growth exhibited in 'out-of-state' numbers to 1970 occurred due to the massive drop in numbers from Northern Ireland as a result of the outbreak of the 'troubles' in 1969. Notwithstanding this setback the performance from Northern Ireland had been rather poor in any case and visitor numbers in 1969 were just slightly greater than the 1960 level.[5] In contrast, the performance of all other markets was rather buoyant during this period. Visitor numbers from North America increased from 69,000 in 1960 to 258,000 in 1970, albeit showing a slight decrease from the high of 267,000 recorded in 1969. The number of British visitors increased by 28 per cent to 1970. This growth was boosted by British currency restrictions on travel outside the 'sterling area' (which included

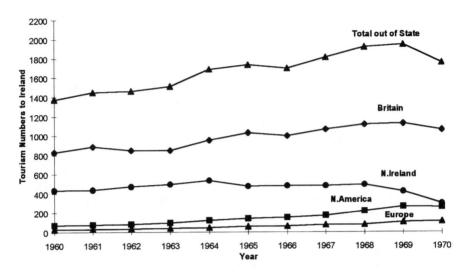

Figure 3.1 Total out-of-state visitors (thousands) 1960–1970 (other overseas visitors are included in the out-of-state visitors but are not shown in the figure. The numbers were generally quite small in this period.) *Source*: Derived from Bord Failte (1987)

Ireland at the time) towards the end of the decade and numbers peaked at 1.125 million in 1969. The European market, which had been relatively neglected by promotional activity exhibited particularly strong growth during the 1960s. Beginning from a low base of 25,000 the number of European visitors had increased to 110,000 by the end of the decade. The performance in revenue terms is detailed in Figure 3.2.

In real terms the revenue from out of state visitors increased by 21 per cent during the 1960s. While revenue growth from Britain of 2 per cent was rather disappointing, the performance of North America and Europe, with 222 per cent and 344 per cent growth, respectively, was very encouraging. Consequently, the performance of these markets had alleviated the reliance on the British market as an earner of foreign exchange. While the decade had begun with 59 per cent of foreign exchange earnings being based on the British market the decade ended with that reliance being reduced to little less than 50 per cent. What was less encouraging was the overall trend in per capita spend. In real terms this had declined from IR£324 in 1970 to IR£306 in 1970 (1993 prices). This decline in real per capita spend that emerged in the 1960s continued through the 1970s and 1980s and was only finally arrested in the early 1990s.

1970s: SURVIVAL IN THE FACE OF ADVERSITY

The sustained expansion of Irish tourism during the 1960s was halted in the early part of the 1970s particularly from the principal source market of mainland

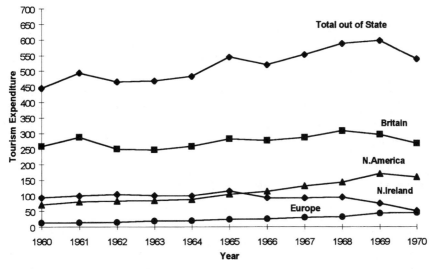

Figure 3.2 Tourism revenue (in IR£ million) by source markets 1960–1970 in constant 1993 prices (revenue does not include carrier receipts and excursionists). *Source*: Derived from Bord Failte (1987)

Britain (or other foreign tourists markets using that route to Ireland). Ostensibly the reasons were the increased violence in Northern Ireland from 1969 and the subsequent burning of the British Embassy in Dublin in 1971, which represented an angry and highly emotive response to the 'bloody Sunday' deaths in Derry in that year. Clearly the perception that Ireland was no longer a 'safe' tourist destination coupled with the media image of a nation expressing strong anti-British feelings encouraged British tourists to look to alternative destinations/ One would have expected this to impact more on the 'pure' tourists rather than the significant group of VFRs (visiting friends and relatives) which formed the bulk of British tourists to the Republic (see Bord Failte, 1973). Ironically, the relative importance of VFRs fell over the period 1972–1976 from 52 to 37 per cent of overseas visitors while the general category of tourist increased from 38 to 52 per cent The experience of these early years of the 1970s highlights the impact, adversely or otherwise, of special factors or particular events on the fortunes of tourist destinations in subsequent years.[6] This can make it extremely difficult to gauge the effectiveness of country-level marketing campaigns and also can lead to much wasted resources in advertising and promotion spend which can be negated by one or two terrorist incidents.[7]

Tourism acts in the 1970s

The 1972 Tourism Traffic Act served to amend and extend the Tourist Traffic Acts, 1939–1970. Similar to the 1970 Act, this Act increased the upper limit of grants to Bord Failte from IR£3.25 million to IR£4 million for the development of major tourist resorts. The financial provision for holiday accommodation was also increased from IR£11 million to IR£13 million. While the 1972 Act extended the amount of grant money for the development of holiday accommodation the main function of the 1975 Act was to introduce a new tourism development fund, from which advances could be made to Bord Failte towards the cost of capital works other than holiday accommodation. As a means of financing development work, the new tourism development fund was to replace the major resort development fund. Development work was defined by the Act as follows:

- being capital in nature;
- in the opinion of the Bord will develop tourism;
- not work for the development of holiday accommodation.

In response to calls from Dail deputies[8] for the development of inland areas rather than the more traditional seaside resorts, together with a growing concern for the environment

> Good environmental quality is all important ... Unspoiled surroundings are becoming increasingly scarce ... The pressure on existing resources is such that the quality which attracts the visitor is being eroded. The Bord are concerned that this erosion needs to be halted. (Stationery Office, 1975: 22 October)

a tourism conservation policy was introduced in conjunction with the new tourism development fund. This policy was based on the idea of designated areas. Moreover, a zoning strategy was also implemented aimed at stimulating a balanced mix of facilities within an area. This strategy differed from that previously pursued in that more areas, in particular inland areas, were to benefit from grant schemes. Only 19 resorts had previously been targeted for development.

A second element of the 1975 Tourist Traffic Act was to increase from IR£13 million to IR£16 million the amount payable to the Bord for the giving of grants for holiday accommodation. However, with the realization of the importance of the environment, emphasis was to switch from providing additional accommodation to improving the range and quality of holiday accommodation.

The main feature of the 1979 Dail debate (on the Tourist Traffic Act of that year) was the oil crisis and the problems it posed for the tourism and hotel sectors. The Minister of the day was accused of not tackling the immediate problems of the industry. For instance the voucher scheme (introduced for tourists to overcome petrol restrictions) was deemed to be flawed in that tourists had only limited access to these vouchers. Because of the oil crisis, hoteliers were experiencing great difficulty in repaying loans. The 1979 Act did not offer any relief, such as subsidized loans or interest rate payments, to hoteliers experiencing the difficulty. The purpose of the 1979 Tourist Traffic Act was to increase the amount to Bord Failte from IR£16 million to IR£25 million for the development of holiday accommodation and to increase from IR£4.75 million to IR£10 million the grant aid for development work. While there was a general welcome for the increased amounts given to Bord Failte, again several features of the Act were criticized by Dail deputies. Some called to make cities eligible for grants. Another criticism was that assistance was confined to hotel bedrooms. Deputies feared that lower standards would prevail in other parts of the hotel and therefore asserted that grants should be extended to all aspects of hotel business and not just bedrooms.

Therefore, while emphasis in tourism in the 1960s was on the provision of additional accommodation, in the 1970s the range and quality of accommodation and facilities became more important. The performance of the industry is considered next.

Tourism numbers from principal overseas markets, 1970–1980

The numbers of overseas and Northern Ireland (NI) tourists together represent the international dimension of Ireland's tourism industry. The balance consists of domestic tourism. It is recognized that there were significant data deficiencies in the official tourism statistics which, apart from being subject to sampling errors (being based since 1972 on the annual Survey of Travellers by Bord Failte), suffered also from the difficulty of tracking cross-border movements of both tourists and excursionists. The margin of error in domestic tourism estimates is reckoned to be much wider though like many statistical series this margin may be consistent over time and thus enable trends to be analysed reasonably accurately. These data deficiencies have been addressed in a number of publications and it is not proposed to repeat the discussion here.[9] A revision of the earlier estimates of numbers and expenditure data was carried out by Bord Failte and the Central Statistics Office (CSO) so that there is a reconciled and therefore consistent series published since 1968.[10] Bord Failte has published a series covering the period since 1960, though prior to 1978 (when the CSO first conducted its annual survey of visitors – the Passenger Card Enquiry Survey) there is less confidence in the accuracy of the data. The series is used throughout this book as a basis for the analysis conducted. While the numbers of tourists moving between origin and destination countries may be associated with widely differing levels of expenditure they are used extensively to track the varying importance of international tourism to given destinations. The movements to Ireland in the 1970s are presented in Figure 3.3 from the principal origin zones (see also Table A1 in the Appendix).

The addition of NI tourists (though not excursionists) gives the total out-of-state tourists for the decade and provides an interesting basis for comparing the differential impact of the 'troubles' on various markets. Apart from the difficulty with the accuracy of the cross-border tourist flows their inclusion as 'international' tourists may be misleading in that the holidays taken in the Republic are more akin to domestic than foreign holidays for residents of Northern Ireland, at least in terms of the influencing factors and relative ease of access. Throughout the 1970s the numbers of tourists from NI continued to expand at

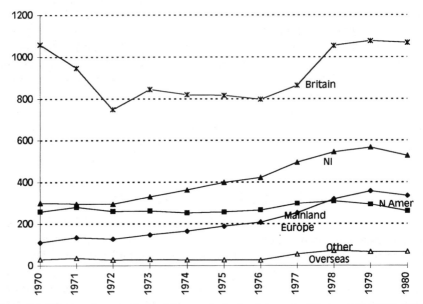

Figure 3.3 Tourism flows to Ireland from principal origin zones (thousands), 1970–1980.
Source: derived from Bord Failte (1987)

a steady pace of almost 6 per cent per annum, even though total out-of-state tourist numbers declined to 1975 but expanded thereafter by 6 per cent annually. The numbers of all out-of-state tourists to Ireland was 28 per cent higher in 1980 compared with 1970, which reflects an annual increase of 2.5 per cent.

Turning to the trends of overseas tourists to Ireland the decade divides into two halves for most zones with declines in the first half being reversed for the 1975–1980 period (Table 3.2).

The exception was the strong and sustained growth in numbers from mainland Europe of almost 12 per cent annually, a market which was clearly less affected by the NI 'troubles'. The most dramatic fall in numbers was experienced from Britain (1970–1975) while there was a sustained average annual increase of almost 20 per cent from the 'other overseas' zone (Australia, New Zealand,

Table 3.2 Annual average percentage change in numbers of overseas tourists to Ireland by principal origin zones, 1970–1980

	Britain	North America	Mainland Europe	Other overseas	Total overseas
1970–1975	–4.2	–0.2	11.3	–1.3	–2.2
1975–1980	5.5	0.3	12.3	19.1	6.1
1970–1980	0.1	0.1	11.8	8.4	1.7

Source: Derived from Bord Failte (1987).

South-east Asia) from 1975 to 1980 although from a low base of c. 30,000 tourists in 1970. Tourist numbers from North America were almost stagnant throughout the decade which represented a dramatic reversal of the significant annual compound increases of 14 per cent in the 1960s. Ireland's share of the US market to European destinations fell throughout the 1970s, from 8 per cent (1970) to 6 per cent (1980). Overseas tourists to Ireland also increased much less rapidly than to other European countries during the 1970s with the result that Ireland's share of these European arrivals' market fell from 1.6 to 1.2 per cent and of total world tourists from 1.1 per cent (1970) to 0.8 per cent (1980). In terms of the distribution of overseas tourists to Ireland, Britain's share declined from 73 to 62 per cent by 1980, North American from 18 to 15 per cent while that of mainland European increased from 7.5 to over 19 per cent. These changes occurred when overseas tourist numbers to Ireland showed an average annual increase of only 1.7 per cent from 1970 to 1980.

Thus, overall it was a decade in which Ireland's expanding international tourism sector was halted in its tracks and went into reverse until 1974 but expanded thereafter. The combination of the NI 'troubles' and the oil-induced recession of 1973–1975 were important factors in explaining the slow down which was observed.[11] In addition, the rapid expansion of keenly priced package tours for mass tourism to Europe's sun destinations of the Mediterranean militated against the relatively more expensive Irish destination in which price inflation in general and in tourist goods was much higher than in other northern European countries (excluding Britain).[12] The improvement in economic growth rates throughout the OECD countries in the latter half of the 1970s assisted the resumption of growth in overseas tourists to Ireland though there was a decline from 1979 to 1981 (related to the recession caused by the second international oil crisis in 1979). Crucial components of the profitability of the industry are the expenditure levels of overseas visitors which are now examined for the 1970s.

Expenditure patterns of overseas tourists, 1970–1980

Though tourism had been a relatively neglected industry compared with the extensive range of subsidies transferred to the agricultural and industrial sectors, its contribution to the balance of payments was of immense importance to Ireland. Both the expenditures on goods and services while overseas visitors were holidaying in Ireland together with the payments to Irish carriers (sea and air) to access the island were a significant part of the invisible exports from Ireland, a point highlighted by Kennedy and Dowling (1975) particularly during the 1960s.[13] Excluding foreign passenger receipts of Irish sea and air carriers the tourism and travel share of total exports of goods and services ranged from 11.5 per cent in 1970 to 5.9 per cent in 1976. Part of the decline over this period was influenced by the expansion of exports of the manufacturing sector and agriculture which enjoyed a relative boom in the years following EU entry in 1973. While the numbers of tourists have frequently been the policy target the economic benefit of overseas tourism is much more sensitively reflected in the expenditure per tourist and the aggregate expenditure derived from all out-of-state visitors. This has become even more important as questions of 'carrying capacity' and 'environmentally sensitive' tourism development are raised and need to be addressed. The expenditure trends in real terms are presented in Figure 3.4 (and in Table A2 of the Appendix).

With the exception of visitors from the European mainland all other zones registered annual average decreases in real expenditures in the first half of the decade of more than 1.5 per cent. There was some recovery in all markets in the 1975–1980 period with the exception of North America where real expenditures declined even more dramatically (−4.3 per cent per annum) (see Table 3.3).

Real expenditure growth by the mainland European visitors averaged 11.2 per cent annually throughout the decade. These differential trends had a dramatic effect on some market shares. For example, mainland Europe accounted for just over 9 per cent of the overseas market share of expenditure in 1970, a share which increased to almost 24 per cent by 1980. The corresponding proportions for North American expenditures were 33 (1970) and 22 (1980) per cent. British tourists accounted for the lion's share of the Irish overseas (and out-of-state) tourist markets though this proportion of the overseas market declined from 55 to 49 per cent and from 50 to 43 per cent of the out-of-state market. In the previous section it was noted that the UK accounted for over 60 per cent of overseas tourist numbers which highlights their lower average spend compared with other country markets.[14]

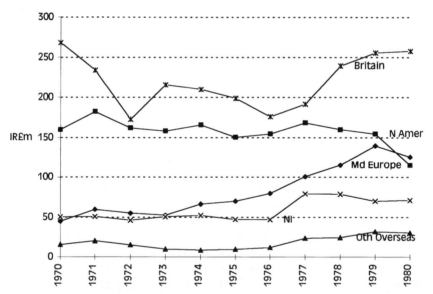

Figure 3.4 Real expenditures by tourists to Ireland by principal origin zones, 1970–1980 (in 1993 prices). *Source*: Derived from Bord Failte (1987)

Table 3.3 Annual average percentage change in expenditures by tourists to Ireland, in real terms, 1970–1980

	UK	North America	Mainland Europe	Other overseas	Total overseas	NI	Total
1970–1975	–4.3	–0.5	10.1	–6.3	–1.7	–0.7	–1.6
1975–1980	5.3	–4.3	12.4	26	4.3	8.5	4.7
1970–1980	–0.1	–2.3	11.2	7.4	1.2	3.8	1.4

Source: Derived from Bord Failte (1987)

Finally, if the change in expenditures in real terms is expressed as a percentage change in 1980 over the base year of 1970, we find that the North American expenditure declined by 25 per cent while that of mainland European increased by over 190 per cent, though admittedly the latter is related to a much smaller base. Total expenditure was up 12 per cent for overseas visitors and by over 15 per cent for out-of-state with the difference accounted for by a strong recovery in the Northern Irish market over the interval 1975–1980.

If we compare Ireland's share of UK spending on foreign holidays in 1968 with that of 1977 we find a rather dramatic reduction from 22.3 to 8.8 per cent. Ireland's share of US travel expenditures in Europe declined from 3.2 per cent in 1968 to a low of 1.9 per cent in 1972 but recovered subsequently to over 4 per cent by 1977 (NESC, 1980b). The trends in international tourist receipts were much stronger in other OECD countries during the 1970s where they increased by an annual average of 6.5 per cent while Ireland's corresponding growth in real terms was only 1.2 per cent for overseas tourism expenditures. Thus, Ireland clearly lost international market share of tourist receipts over the decade of the 1970s.

CONTRIBUTION TO THE ECONOMY

The combination of the reduction in real terms of the expenditures by out-of-state tourists and the development of other sectors of the economy meant that tourism's relative contribution to the economy declined during the 1970s. The overseas tourism receipts represented 9 per cent of total exports and 37 per cent of invisible exports on average during the 1970s though both proportions declined consistently throughout the decade. The importance of the sector relative to trade data and to GNP is shown in Table 3.4. Foreign tourism receipts almost halved from 13 to 7 per cent as a proportion of total exports between 1970 and 1980 while the relative reduction as a proportion of invisible earnings was considerably less, declining from 41 to 32 per cent. These data include Irish carrier receipts for overseas tourists which represents approximately 16 per cent of total expenditure by foreign tourists.

Table 3.4 Relative importance of foreign tourism receipts in the Irish 'export' tourism sector, 1970–1980

	Foreign tourism receipts* as % of:		Foreign tourism receipts
	total exports†	invisible earnings	as % of GNP
1970	13.1	41.2	5.3
1971	13.0	43.8	5.1
1972	10.0	37.6	3.8
1973	9.1	35.8	3.8
1974	8.8	35.1	4.1
1975	7.9	33.3	3.7
1976	7.2	32.3	3.7
1977	7.4	35.7	4.0
1978	7.3	36.4	4.1
1979	7.4	36.0	4.1
1980	6.9	31.8	3.9

*Includes carrier receipts.
†Of goods and services.
Source: Derived from Bord Failte (1987) and Irish Statistical Bulletin, various issues.

Foreign tourism receipts are expressed as a proportion of GNP. In estimating the economic impact of these receipts, appropriate multiplier values are applied which allow for direct, indirect and induced expenditures to determine the foreign tourism income generated.[15] Henry (1990–1) and Deane and Henry (1993) outlined the methodology used and applied the same to the expenditure data in two more recent years, i.e. for 1989 and 1992. Based on an input–output model of the economy the authors derived what appear to be plausible multiplier values which were close to unity. Earlier estimates of export tourism multiplier values appeared to exaggerate the impact of the sector on the economy with estimates of 1.8–2.08 for some 1960s and early 1970s studies as reported in NESC (1980b). Norton (1982), using a Keynesian model of the economy, calculated an export tourism multiplier value of 1.09 (corrected to 0.8 on changing some of the assumptions) for 1976. Other economists, e.g. O'Hagan and Mooney (1983) and Bradley *et al.* (1981), estimated values closer to 0.5. It is true that the tourism export multiplier values for the expenditures of foreign tourists while in the country are little different from those of domestic tourists but the payments to Irish sea and air carriers generates lower multiplier values because of their above average capital intensity and greater propensity to import in terms of the indirect expenditures by these carriers.[16]

While not absolutely accurate it is reasonable to adopt multiplier values close to unity for export tourism which suggests that the impact on the economy of the sector averaged 4 per cent of GNP during the decade having been as high as 5.3 per cent in 1970.[17] Domestic tourism would augment this impact by 1–1.5 per cent of GNP without taking into consideration the import substitution effects of home holidays, which would further boost its impact.

Employment effects

Employment represents another way of reflecting the importance of the industry to the economy and covers those directly employed in tourism on a year-round or seasonal basis and indirectly employed through the purchases of goods and services from other sectors of the economy. A further component is reflected in the induced employment arising from the purchases made out of the incomes generated directly and indirectly in tourism. This applies principally to export tourism since the initial stimulus represents a net inflow of incomes to the economy whereas with domestic tourism the incomes generated in the sector are based on incomes already earned in the economy. It is only where domestic tourism is a diversion from holidays abroad that one could legitimately include the induced employment arising from this source. Government support for the industry is often designed to support employment creation though estimates can be difficult to determine. NESC (1980b) noted that about 26,000 people were employed in the tourism sector (direct employment) and another 20,000 on a seasonal basis, in 1977. Their figures were based mainly on CERT manpower surveys. A high proportion were employed in the hotel sector and it was observed 'Given that the primary economic objective of Government is directed towards job creation, it would seem desirable to promote a tourism that attracted the type of visitor who was willing and able to use hotel accommodation' (p. 135). Indeed the dominance of the hotel sector in shaping Irish tourism policy has been quite significant over the years.

Total tourism-related employment was estimated to be about double the numbers directly employed, which led to projected employment of 74,000 in 1977 (NESC, 1980b: 70).[18] Indeed some of the tourism estimates of the late 1970s were almost as high as those officially agreed for the late 1980s when tourism numbers were significantly higher. In the absence of official employment data, Bord Failte produced its own set of figures based on input–output tables for the economy. A critical determinant of the estimates related to the recycling of Government tax revenue generated from the expenditures of tourists. It was assumed that such revenue from out-of-state tourists was entirely respent and supported jobs which were deemed to be part of tourism employment. There was a good deal of confusion and little consensus on the true employment figure dependent on the tourism sector (foreign and domestic) at the time. Much of this confusion was cleared up in the 1980s following the report of an inter-departmental committee established to provide reliable data and a consistent series (see Minister of Tourism and Transport, 1988).

Whatever about the measurement problems, the sector was an important generator of employment even if much of this employment was precarious, i.e.

temporary, seasonal and part-time. This precariousness was exacerbated by the generally poor conditions of employment, the lack of a career structure, the dominance of family-owned enterprises in the core hotel and catering sectors, and an over-reliance on Government to promote and develop the industry. Approximately 5–6 per cent of all those at work were dependent on tourism, either directly or indirectly. The industry was losing market share of international and European tourism although it had recovered from relative stagnation during the first half of the 1970s. The next section examines briefly developments on the supply side of Irish tourism during the 1970s.

SUPPLY-SIDE ASPECTS

On the supply side, although accommodation facilities continued to improve, there was only limited investment in tourism product and infrastructural development. The state supports for the industry since the 1950s were largely confined to resort development and grants for accommodation, both of which schemes were winding down in the mid-1970s. The quantity of hotels increased by 10 per cent from 1968 to 1972 when there was also a net increase of approximately 5000 hotel bedrooms or 25 per cent of the 1968 stock. Over 90 per cent of the increased expenditure on bedrooms received grant aid. The long-term expansion of the industry would be severely constrained without a higher rate of investment specifically geared to raising the quality of the Irish tourism product, which was critically assessed in a 1973 publication by Bord Failte.[19] The failure to develop the core tourism product, other than through substantial Government subsidies, partly reflected the scale problem in Irish tourism and the low return on investment. Public investment is also a vital dimension of tourism development given the 'public goods' nature of many of the amenities enjoyed by tourists and in which individual private investors could not be expected to invest.

In line with the decline of the real value of non-domestic tourism expenditures, the accommodation stock contracted during the 1970s. This decline was reflected in both the number of units available and the total number of rooms in these units. For example, there were 10 per cent fewer hotel rooms available in 1979 compared with 1973 and a higher relative decline in the number of units. The guest-house sector suffered an even greater decline. These data refer to registered accommodation only. Information is not as readily available on the bed and breakfast sector of the market which has shown substantial growth through the 1980s.

Subventions to the industry, through Bord Failte, increased significantly from 1969 to 1972 but declined thereafter though the grants for accommodation increased again from 1976 onwards. Amounts for subventions for capital projects were generally small and thinly spread over this period. Ireland's attractive scenery and friendly people were the prime assets on which the industry was built and insufficient investment was undertaken to ensure the tourism ' product' itself was being enhanced. Indeed it was another decade from 1980 before serious attempts were made to develop and enhance the tourism product in line with a more strategic approach to tourism development. Such an approach was made possible through the generous financial transfers available from the EU's Structural Funds to Ireland as a peripheral region of the European Union.[20]

One other dimension of capacity worth noting is the load capability of the air and sea carriers. These did not appear to constrain the volume of visitors coming to Ireland though prices were somewhat contentious for air travel, according to NESC (1980b: 182). Access transport is a critical dimension of the development of island tourism. Given both the price sensitivity of tourists to the overall holiday price and the impact of alternative package tours to several 'sun' destinations, an efficient and competitively priced access transport service is vital for the development of the industry. This point is returned to later. Slightly over 50 per cent of visitors were using the air carriers to gain access to Ireland in the 1970s. Given the scale problem with scheduled services and the amount of investment/commitment required, it can lead to a situation of some inflexibility in responding to the needs of an expanding tourism sector. To this end charter services can frequently represent the most flexible short-term response to emerging markets.

CONCLUSIONS

The demand experience of the 1960s in Irish tourism combined steady expansion in numbers of overseas tourists, with those from Europe and North America increasing more rapidly than those from Britain. Real revenues increased in tandem though real expenditure per capita declined. All variables dipped downwards towards the end of the decade in response to the onset of the 'troubles' in Northern Ireland, a feature that continued to depress tourist flows in the first half of the 1970s, particularly from the dominant market of the UK. The main emphasis on the investment side was on providing subventions in the form of grants and interest subsidies to increase the accommodation stock and special aids for resorts (mainly seaside).

The problem in the 1970s was that the core tourism product was not being developed, promotional policies were geared to the traditional ethnic and VFR markets, there was heavy reliance on the traditional characteristics of beautiful scenery, friendly people and a relaxed easy going style of holiday. Policy design and delivery were largely left to Bord Failte and there was no clear strategic focus on how the industry should develop. The economic environment was not as benign as two oil crises (and associated recessions) and rapid price inflation, combined with the successful packaging and marketing of alternative destinations, reduced Ireland's market share of international tourism. Trends improved somewhat towards the latter part of the decade though the mainland European market performed strongly throughout averaging over 10 per cent annual growth. Tourism product innovations which featured strongly in the 1960s were conspicuously absent in this decade of survival. /

NOTES

1. Recorded economic growth was 23 per cent for the duration of the programmme (1959–1963), the target was only 11 per cent.
2. During his contribution the Minister provided a figure of IR£44 million as being the tourism income for 1960. Revisions to the data in subsequent years show that this figure was overstated by IR£2.5 million. For full text of the Minister's speech see Dail debate on Tourist Traffic Bill 1970, columns 1982–2010.
3. The areas were defined by the Central Development Committee and covered the western seaboard counties together with West Cork, Roscommon, Cavan, Monaghan and Leitrim.
4. Brendan O'Regan was appointed Comptroller for Sales and Catering at Shannon Airport in 1943. Due to arrangements agreed with Government in the late 1950s the Comptroller was given wider functions to include the development of transit traffic, tourism and airfreight. O'Regan proved himself to be a very innovative developer of projects and was involved with many new initiatives for tourism and industrial development over the next three decades. He was appointed Chairman of the newly formed Shannon Free Airport Development Company in 1959 and was instrumental in the development of the Shannon region.
5. The growth in numbers to 1965 was probably due to the initial effects of the abolition of the triptych requirement for south-bound cars introduced in 1959. In addition, the change to the licensing laws introduced in the South in 1959 allowed far more liberal opening times than in the North. The relatively sharp rise in excise taxes on drink and tobacco that applied in the South from 1965 could plausibly explain the decline in numbers that ensued from that time.
6. These may be Government induced events such as the UK's decision to restrict the amount of currency moved outside the sterling area in 1967 which increased the numbers of visitors to Ireland from that market in 1968, or much later the impact of the Gulf War in 1991 on US and other travel to and within Europe; some commentators have linked the staging of international sporting events and country participation to subsequent travel decisions as for example in the expansion of Italian travel to Ireland following the 1990 World Cup finals held in Italy in which Ireland participated. These special factors may reinforce or work against the more influential general demand factors (incomes, relative prices, etc.), e.g. in the 1973–1975 period, the oil-induced international recession would have had a significant bearing on tourist flows.
7. Indeed this latter possibility discouraged the Northern Ireland Tourist Board (NITB) from engaging in any serious marketing efforts in origin countries for a number of years (see Wilson, 1993).
8. Elected members of the national parliament (the Dail).
9. For example, see Clark and O'Cinneide (1981) for a particular discussion on the tourist flows between the ROI and NI and Barry and O'Hagan (1972) for problems

encountered in measuring the flows of tourists from Britain as part of their study of demand determinants of British tourists to Ireland; O'Hagan and Waldron (1987) provide a more detailed analysis of data deficiencies in a number of EU countries including Ireland, and summarize the methods of data collection used by both the Central Statistics Office and Bord Failte. Indeed the accuracy of international tourism data generally, especially of receipts and expenditures, has been questioned and shown to give quite divergent results even when measuring similar variables. For a discussion on this see Edwards (1992: 279–291).

10. However, the the statistics published by the Irish Central Statistics Office (CSO) do not conform to the international conventions on measuring tourist flows as set down by the World Tourism Organization, i.e. the CSO publishes visitor numbers and revenues and not tourist numbers and revenues as per the WTO definition of staying visitors (the balance being made up of excursionists).

11. It has been argued that the slow-down in Irish tourism growth began in the late 1960s but had been masked for a number of years by the imposition of exchange controls on British tourists, which restricted the amount of British currency they could take outside the 'sterling area'. This had the effect of diverting more tourists from this source market to Ireland from 1967 to 1969 in line with the substitution effects within international tourism (Britons diverting from non-sterling to sterling area countries outside the UK) and between domestic and international tourism (Britons diverting to domestic holidays in the UK). For further discussion of the impact of these restrictions see O'Hagan (1972), Institut du Transport Aerien (1970) and Oliver (1971).

12. See NESC (1980b: 45) for comparative data on this aspect of international tourism; the point in the text refers to the inflation rates in these countries and Ireland and not to the absolute levels of prices. Ireland was still regarded as a relatively cheap destination though this advantage was being eroded. In economic terms it had the hallmarks of an 'inferior' good where lower incomes induced by the recession encouraged British visitors to substitute the relatively cheaper holiday in Ireland (including access costs) for more expensive destinations.

13. See in particular Chapter 8 (in Kennedy and Dowling, 1975) on 'Invisible Exports' which tracks the changing importance of Irish tourism in terms of receipts on the external current account and its relative share of UK and US overseas tourism expenditures.

14. This reflects the lower average expenditures of UK tourists to Ireland, a point referred to by Steinecke (1979) in his linking of Irish emigration to the social class profiles of these tourists. Far lower proportions of UK tourists to Ireland were from the AB and C1 social classes than those coming from North America, mainland Europe or other overseas.

15. A proportion of recycled taxes generated by the tourism expenditures is sometimes included in the determination of tourism income though as we note later there is no economic rationale for doing this.

16. Norton (1982) makes reference to this while Deane and Henry's (1993) article shows estimates for multiplier values based on carrier receipts which are less than 70 per cent of other foreign tourism receipts. For a brief summary of the Irish literature on export tourism multipliers see Deegan and Dineen (1992).

17. Though tourism may decline in relative importance as an economy grows (as Ireland's did during the 1970s) the declining relative importance of the tourism sector noted here was a combination of a poorly performing sector and a growing economy.

18. Though it was recognized in the report that this estimate was probably exaggerated as it was based on the high multiplier estimate of 1.8.
19. This publication (Bord Failte, 1973) set out to review the overall product policy of Irish tourism and signalled a clear developmental role for Bord Failte; ironically, many of the deficiencies identified and improvements needed were not attended to in any kind of an effective manner until the EU's Structural Funds were made available several years later.
20. See Chapters 7 and 9 for a fuller discussion on the EU impact on Irish tourism.

4 Performance of the Irish tourism industry since 1981

INTRODUCTION

The belief that tourism has a central role to play in Ireland's economic development and, by extension, in attempts to reduce unemployment levels gained credence during the 1980s. The performance of Irish tourism in the latter part of the 1980s has been quite remarkable by comparison with the record of the previous 20 years. Building on this, new policy instruments have been applied to the sector (notably the EU Structural Funds) and tourism has a higher profile than previously. The sector is no longer regarded as a residual one whose fortunes rise and fall with those of the macroeconomy or whose growth is largely dependent on the goods producing (agriculture and manufacturing industry) sectors of the economy. Such interdependencies do exist, of course, as one should expect in a developed and increasingly integrated economic system, but oftentimes the causes and effects run in both directions. An expansion of international tourism receipts stimulates output and employment expansion in the manufacturing sector, often giving rise to higher net gains than an equivalent expansion in receipts for manufactured exports. This results from the low import content of tourist expenditures[1] and the relatively greater labour intensity in the sectors which are stimulated into producing greater output, e.g. clothing, craft goods though not the food sector which is relatively capital intensive..

Although international tourism is forecast to expand by 5 per cent per annum over the next 10 years (Edwards, 1992), Europe's already dominant share of the world tourism market is declining (down from 72 per cent of international tourist arrivals and 57 per cent of receipts in 1960 to 60 per cent and 48 per cent, respectively, in 1993). This will make it all the more difficult for Ireland to increase its market share as the European tourism industry competes to do likewise in the broader world context. Besides, much of Ireland's tourism growth in recent years has been from continental European countries which does not represent net gains to the EU industry but rather a redistribution within the Union. This may ultimately set limits to the extent to which EU Structural Fund transfers will be available to support the industry in Ireland.

This chapter examines the performance of the Irish tourism industry since the early 1980s both in terms of changing visitor profiles, numbers of tourists and expenditure effects; this is followed by a more detailed analysis of the economic impact of overseas and domestic tourism in terms of the impact on Irish GNP and on direct, indirect and induced employment dependent on the sector; a brief outline of the balance of payments impact is provided followed by a summary of the principal performance trends to 1994.

IRISH TOURISM OUTCOMES

Before examining tourism outcomes in Ireland it is instructive to set the Irish industry in the appropriate international context. International tourism is one of the few global growth industries and in 1992 accounted for 420 million tourist arrivals and $180 billion in earnings. The numbers of arrivals were 70 million in 1960 and 285 million in 1980. While world tourism increased relatively rapidly in the 1960s the rate of growth has decreased in successive decades. Ireland's share of world tourism arrivals has declined since 1960, falling from over 2 per cent to less than 1 per cent in 1990 while her share of world tourism receipts has more than halved from 1.4 to 0.5 per cent over the same interval. While Europe is still the dominant global region for tourism in terms of both destination and origin countries its share has been declining, particularly relative to south-east Asia. Although Ireland's share of European tourism increased from 1988 to 1990, this share has declined significantly over the 30-year period from 1960 to 1990 – the growth in international tourist arrivals to Ireland was 150 per cent compared with Europe's growth of 420 per cent. Indeed, if Ireland had maintained her share of world or European tourism there would have been between 7.1 million and 8.2 million international tourists in 1990. In the absence of appropriate planning, the geographical and seasonal distribution of this volume would certainly have caused severe problems of congestion.

Compared with relative stagnation in the 1970s, the total number of overseas visitors to Ireland increased by 119 per cent over the period 1981–1994, i.e. from 1.680 million to 3.679 million (see Figure 4.1).

Much of this growth took place in the latter half of the period. The annual average growth rates for specific sub-periods are shown in Table 4.1.

The acceleration in overall growth rates is noted in the latter years of the decade with the compound average annual 15 per cent growth rate target[2] (equivalent to a doubling of numbers over five years) being almost achieved over the three-year interval, 1988–1990. The dramatic replacement of North American by mainland European visitors is evident in this period and right up to 1993 when the 'European' share reached 27 per cent compared with the North American share of 13 per cent. It is noteworthy that North American visitors exceeded those from mainland Europe in each year from 1982 to 1988 during which time they averaged 350,000 visitors annually; the dramatic upsurge in European visitors since then is illustrated by the 1994 data when 988,000 visited Ireland, exactly double the number from North America. While various factors

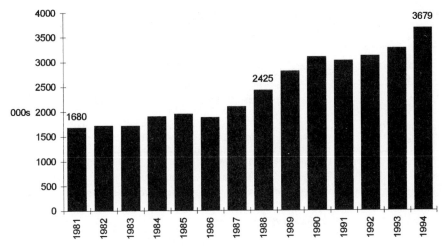

Figure 4.1 Overseas visitors to Ireland, 1981–1994. *Source*: Derived from Tourism Facts 1981–1994 (Bord Failte Eireann, Dublin)

Table 4.1 Annual average percentage change in overseas visitor numbers to Ireland by country/zone of origin, 1981–1994

	1981–1985	*1985–1990*	*[1988–1990]*	*1990–1994*
UK	−1.1	10.1	[10.4]	3.4
Mainland Europe	4.6	17.5	[35.5]	7.3
N. America	17.6	1.4	[4.0]	2.8
Other areas	14.0	8.6	[20.0]	6.4
Total	3.5	9.9	[14.4]	4.4

Source: Derived from CSO, Tourism and Travel, and Tourism Facts (Bord Failte Eireann, Dublin) 1981–1994.

can explain the growth in tourism from mainland Europe, e.g. cheaper access fares and more convenient charter air services, the turn away from sun destinations, environmentally attractive location and effective marketing campaigns, it seems also as if Ireland was suddenly 'discovered' by a sizeable number of Italian and Spanish tourists (almost quadrupled between 1986 and 1991) in addition to increased numbers of visitors from the more well-established German and French markets.

An additional indicator of the changing importance of Irish export tourism is given by its relative shares in the principal country markets. Four main origin countries are chosen which together accounted for 80 per cent of Ireland's overseas tourists in 1990 – UK, USA, Germany (Federal Republic) and France (see Table 4.2).

Table 4.2 Ireland's share of outbound tourist numbers from the UK, USA, Germany and France, 1981, 1985 and 1990 and relative market growth, 1981–1990 (in per cent)

	1981	1985	1990	1981–1990 Market growth	Growth to Ireland
UK*	7.2	6.3	7.5	169	174
USA*	1.4	1.7	1.8	123	163
Germany (FR)†	0.3	0.3	0.5	146	206‡
France†	0.4	0.4	0.8	124	227

*Based on data from 13 leading OECD country destinations.
†Based on data from 14 leading OECD country destinations.
‡Exaggerated somewhat because the base year was relatively depressed for outbound tourism to Ireland.
Source: Derived from OECD (1992).

Ireland forms a small part of the country markets shown, Britain excepted, and the table does reflect the growth of Ireland's market share in the latter part of the 1980s, a trend which reversed a 20-year decline. Britain is still the principal market for overseas holidays in Ireland although its share declined from 62 to 55 per cent between 1981 and 1994. Ireland is Britain's fifth largest market for overseas tourism (1990). Comparisons with a number of popular European country destinations (Greece, Portugal, Italy, Spain, UK) show that Ireland had

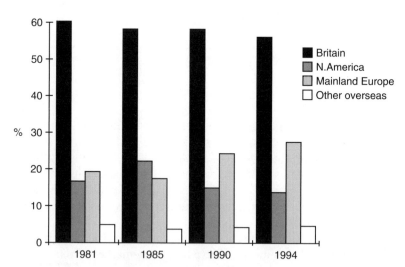

Figure 4.2 Changing shares of overseas tourism visitor numbers to Ireland, 1981–1994.
Source: Derived from CSO, Tourism and Travel, and Tourism Facts, various years (Bord Failte Eireann, Dublin)

more rapid growth in foreign visitor numbers since 1985 and particularly since 1988. Another measure of changing market shares of overseas tourists to Ireland is shown in Figure 4.2 which highlights the growing importance of the mainland European market, and the dominant though declining share of the market from Britain.

Demand factors in Irish tourism

The strong performance of Irish tourism, particularly noted above in the latter part of the 1980s, has not been rigorously analysed and, indeed, very little of an empirical nature has been written on the demand factors in Irish tourism. One of the few studies examined expenditure by British tourists to Ireland and is quite dated by now (see Barry and O'Hagan, 1972). More recently, Walsh (1994) developed a model of international demand for Irish tourism from Ireland's principal overseas markets, i.e. Britain, USA, Germany (Federal Republic) and France over the period 1968–1992. The main independent variables, which largely explained the changing demand for holidays in Ireland from these markets, were:

- real disposable income in the four origin countries;
- relative prices in the origin countries and the destination country (Ireland); and
- relative prices in the principal substitute destinations for outbound visitors from the origin countries.

The relative prices were adjusted for exchange rate variations between the relevant currencies. The dependent variable was the number of overseas visitors to Ireland from each of the country markets.

The results of this analysis showed the explanatory variables were uneven in their impact in the origin markets included in the model. Real per capita disposable incomes were found to be particularly strong in explaining outbound US tourism to Ireland and also from France – high income elasticity measures were found for both markets, i.e. increases in real incomes were positively associated with increased numbers of tourists from the USA and France to Ireland. In the case of the UK and Germany real incomes were not found to be significant factors explaining tourism demand to Ireland. For the UK visitors to Ireland, the high proportion of VFRs dominate the visitor flows and, since these are largely non-discretionary visitors, they are less responsive to real income changes; while in Germany the real income levels and volume of foreign holidays are at such a high level already that income changes are perhaps less important than time availability as an influence on overseas holiday-taking.[3] Indeed the model specified for Germany gave the poorest explanatory results of all four countries suggesting key explanatory variables were missing.

UK visitors were particularly sensitive to prices in substitute markets and to exchange rate movements while the inflation rate in Ireland (lagged one year) was an important factor in the demand levels from France. Weather conditions, as measured by the Poulter Index,[4] were significant only in the case of France also. The impact of a number of 'disturbance factors' (used as dummy variables[5] in the model) was notable, i.e. the Northern Ireland (NI) troubles on UK and French visits (but not from the US or Germany) while the 1979 oil crisis particularly affected the outbound travel from the USA.

In tourism demand analysis, the use of a multivariate framework helps to capture the relative importance of different explanatory variables and can be used to do this over an extended period. In a paper by O'Riain (1992) on modal competition on the Irish Sea from 1960 to 1990, the variations in numbers travelling to/from the UK were examined and found to be directly related to terrorist incidents connected with the NI troubles. While the main thrust of his paper was on inter-modal competition and the distribution of travellers between sea and air carriers, the linking of passenger-traffic volumes to any one variable can lead to conclusions and decisions which are too narrowly based.

Walsh (1994) used a trend variable to capture changing tastes and the general international trend towards higher demand for overseas travel, i.e. to test whether, when real incomes and relative prices are held constant, there is a long-term upward (or downward) trend towards more holiday-taking in Ireland. This was not found to be significant for any of the markets studied which was not altogether surprising since Ireland has clearly not shared proportionately in the global expansion of tourism. Two key independent variables were omitted from the model through data deficiencies – the cost of travel to the destination market (Ireland) and marketing expenditures in the origin countries. Travel costs may have been particularly critical to the US market as they tend to form a higher proportion of the cost of long-haul holidays. The absence of marketing expenditures (both absolute and relative to competing destinations) by origin country is a serious deficiency from a policy perspective as the considerable emphasis on marketing spend in the national tourism campaigns pre-supposes a major impact on travel destination choice.[6] It is especially difficult to incorporate some of the less tangible variables in holiday destination choice, e.g. the natural beauty of the Irish countryside, friendliness of the people, clear air and uncongested roads, although the fact that these change imperceptibly from year to year diminishes their explanatory power. However, some trends could have an impact, such as the turn away from sun destinations, growth of 'green tourism' and special events (Italia '90, Eurovision triple success).

Categories of tourists

It is customary in tourism surveys, especially at national level, to categorize tourists according to their reason for visiting particular destinations if only to get an idea of the market segmentation prevalent and to plan marketing strategies accordingly. Ireland is no exception to this and it is no surprise in a country with such an extensive tradition of emigration to find a sizeable proportion of visitors with ethnic connections to the country.[7] Ireland is unique in this regard in international tourism terms as it has the highest proportion of VFRs (visiting friends and relatives) in its overseas tourism mix than any other country in the world (for example, almost one-third of UK visitors to Ireland were VFRs in 1994 compared with slightly less than one-sixth of North Americans). Indeed it is precisely because of the strong ethnic dimension that the tourism industry has performed remarkably well, even during years of quite adverse circumstances connected with the political situation on the island. The initial upturn in visitor numbers in the mid-1980s was due to an increase in VFRs from a buoyant UK economy encouraged by cheaper air fares on the routes.[8] By contrast, the expansion of tourists from mainland Europe was dominated by those in the 'pure' tourist category.

There has been a greater diversification of the geographical mix of tourists from 1988 to 1994 which suggests a clear maturation of the industry and the attraction of a more discerning category of tourist – more discretionary and thus more mobile in terms of destination choices than the ethnic or, more particularly, the VFRs. The growth rate of tourist numbers by purpose of visit is presented in Table 4.3.

The VFR category is quite important to the Irish tourist trade where the proportion varied between 32 and 41 per cent of overseas visitors and averaged 37 per cent in the 1988 to 1990 period, although it fell to a 24 per cent share in 1994. The sustained growth in 'pure' tourist numbers (i.e. those coming principally for holiday purposes) is noted from 1985 to 1990 with particularly dramatic growth in the years 1988–1990. This coincided with the strong growth in mainland European visitors noted in Table 4.1. VFRs continued their steady growth throughout the decade but expanded at a less than proportionate rate since 1985, a trend which continued into the 1990s. Economic conditions in the UK would have influenced these trends also. Ireland appeared to be gaining market share among non-ethnic tourists which could be critical to the longer

Table 4.3 Average annual percentage changes in visitor numbers to Ireland by reason for journey, 1981–1994

	1981–1985	*1985–1990*	*[1988–1990]*	*1990–1994*
Business	−1.8	11.8	[7.6]	5.8
'Pure' tourist	5.1	10.9	[28.0]	2.0
VFRs*	5.7	8.3	[7.3]	4.4
Other	−3.0	8.4	[−0.8]	10.4
Total	3.5	9.9	[14.4]	4.4

*VFRs = Visiting friends and relatives.
Source: Derived from CSO, Tourism and Travel, various years and Bord Failte survey data.

term development of the sector. In terms of the relative importance of those coming to Ireland principally for holidaying purposes, these increased from 39 per cent of overseas visitors in 1981 to 41 per cent in 1994.

Irish tourism expenditures

The critical determinant of the economic importance of the tourism sector is not so much the numbers of visitors but rather the expenditure generated by these visitors. Expenditure by domestic tourists has a similar impact where their Irish holidays represent a substitution for foreign destinations – in effect having an import substitution effect. The revenue receipts from foreign visitors to Ireland have shown significant fluctuations over an extended time span. The pattern in the 1980s was one of continued fluctuations to 1986, partly due to the international recession and dollar exchange rate changes. A steady improvement in real terms was experienced from 1986 to 1991 (Table 4.4). The replacement of higher-spending North Americans by lower-spending mainland European visitors did not lead to overall revenue reductions because of the sustained growth in visitor numbers.

Numbers and real revenues increased modestly and evenly (+4.4 to 4.5 per cent per annum) in the interval 1990–1994, though there was a stronger

Table 4.4 Tourism revenue* from out-of-state visitors to Ireland, 1981–1994

Year	IR£ million†	Annual % change
1981	747.9	–
1982	732.3	−2.1
1983	730.6	−0.2
1984	774.1	+6.0
1985	847.2	+9.5
1986	774.0	−8.6
1987	841.6	+8.7
1988	958.4	+13.9
1989	1093.5	+14.1
1990	1218.1	+11.4
1991	1258.0	+3.3
1992	1236.1	−1.7
1993	1359.5	+10.0
1994	1455.2	+7.0

*Total expenditure (excluding international fares) plus passenger fare receipts of Irish carriers from visitors to Ireland.
†In constant 1993 prices.
Note: Includes expenditures by visitors from Northern Ireland.
Source: Stationery Office (1985), and Tourism Facts (Bord Failte, various years).

performance in revenue terms in 1993–1994, pushing up average expenditures per head. The shift towards higher-spending tourists on average optimizes on the benefits of tourism to the economy. Surprisingly, an increase in North American visitors in 1992 over 1991 of 17 per cent was accompanied by a fall in revenues generated in real terms from this source. Such dramatic swings show how volatile the market is and how difficult it can be to anticipate demand changes from year to year. Since 1987 the real growth rate of more than 9 per cent was maintained until 1990 and, following two lean years, resumed again in 1993.

Estimates of domestic tourism revenues (home holidays and other non-business trips) varied from 33 to 55 per cent of foreign revenue over the interval from 1981 to 1992. On this basis domestic tourism generated between 25 and 30 per cent of total revenue from tourism since 1984, although it was somewhat higher at 35 per cent in the early part of the 1980s.[9] Total foreign tourism expenditures (or revenues) may be segmented into payments to (Irish) carriers and spending on accommodation and other tourist goods in the economy. These may be augmented by domestic tourism expenditures to measure the total initial impact of the sector and its contribution to economic growth. The volume growth in tourism revenue is shown in Table 4.5 for recent years together with its principal components.

The proportionate contribution of foreign revenues to total tourism revenue growth is highlighted in the table. Rising real incomes in Ireland have led to increased expenditure on tourism products by Irish residents, both at home and overseas. The impact on the domestic market of this is clearly seen in the table which shows the substantial increase in home holidays, causing particularly strong increases in domestic tourism revenue from 1988 to 1993. This was partly caused, in 1991, by the diversion away from other international tourism destinations prompted by the Gulf War situation.

The expenditure patterns of tourists from different countries of origin show interesting variations which are influenced by average length of stay, socio-

Table 4.5 Annual average growth in Irish tourism revenues (real terms),* 1981–1994 in per cent

	Out-of-state	*Irish carriers*	*Total foreign receipts*	*Domestic tourism receipts*	*Total tourism revenue*
1981–1985	4.0	0.8	2.6	−4.2	0.6
1985–1990	8.0	6.0	7.5	5.4	6.9
[1988–1990]	[12.2]	[14.7]	[12.7]	[11.1]	[12.3]
1990–1994	5.7	0.4	4.5	10.5†	6.3

*1993 prices.
†The basis for estimating domestic tourism was altered in 1992 which means that comparisons with earlier years are not strictly valid.
Source: Derived from Tourism Numbers and Revenue, 1980–1994 (Bord Failte Eireann, Dublin).

economic class, age and purpose of visit (business, pleasure), and type of holiday (package, individual). Contrary to popular belief, long-haul visitors from North America have a shorter average length of stay compared to mainland Europeans (Table 4.6). This may be partly explained by the tendency among North Americans towards touring Europe as part of a package tour which includes Ireland.[10] While still the highest daily spenders among the principal origin countries shown in the table, American visitors are now on a par with France and Germany in terms of the numbers of tourists required to generate a specific revenue target. The nominal increase in average expenditure per tourist has been much less from the North American market than the European countries since 1981, where the rate of increase has been greatest from French tourists.

The consumer price index increased by 88 per cent over the interval 1981–1993 so that real expenditure per tourist fell in two of the five leading overseas markets, more or less kept pace with inflation among low-spending British visitors and increased in the two key growth markets of France and Germany. These trends have important implications both for monitoring the performance of the industry, assessing the best market segments to target and in strategically positioning the future direction of Irish tourism where the objective to hold and build market share in the high-income European countries is worth considering as one key priority.

The average real expenditure per tourist has not been increasing since the early 1980s which may have been due in part to the quality of the tourism product which was available. This outcome may also explain the preoccupation in policy circles with increasing numbers in order to boost revenue generation from overseas tourists. Figure 4.3 illustrates the changing average real expenditures per tourist by broad origin zones.

Table 4.6 Expenditure indicators and duration of stay variations among visitors from the leading tourism generating countries to Ireland, 1981–1993

	Average expenditure index 1981=100	Average daily expenditure	Tourists per IR£1000 expenditure	Average length of stay
	1993	1992 (IR£)	1993	1981–1992 (days)
Britain	191	20	4.8	11.6
North America	175	36	2.3	10.7
France	227	33	2.7	12.6
Germany	225	25	2.3	15.5
The Netherlands	175*	23	4.4	13.8
Italy	na	30	2.2	12.1

*1992.

na = not available.

Source: Derived from Bord Failte (1987), Tourism Facts, 1992, 1993 and data on country tourism profiles from Marketing Division, Bord Failte.

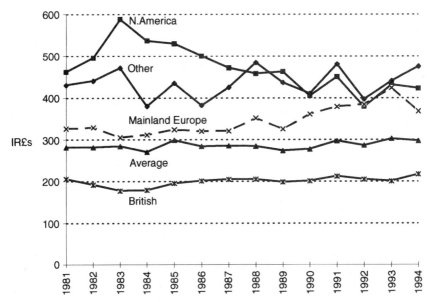

Figure 4.3 Average real expenditure by overseas tourists to Ireland by principal country markets, 1981–1994 (in 1993 prices). *Source*: Derived from sources in Table 4.6

The figure clearly illustrates, within the relatively constant average real expenditure of approximately IR£300, the convergence of average expenditures from the non-UK market sources reflecting primarily the declining spend of the North American tourist contrasted with the steadily rising average spend of the mainland European tourist. The segmentation of the Irish international tourist market into the British (low spending) and the relatively affluent non-British markets is also notable. As with other sectors (agriculture and manufacturing) of the Irish economy at earlier stages of Irish economic development, the excessive dependence on the British market may operate to constrain the economic potential of the tourism sector. Britain accounted for 55 per cent of Irish overseas tourism revenue in 1970, a figure which had fallen to 48 per cent by 1980 and to 41 per cent by 1994; in the latter year 55 per cent of all overseas tourists were British based. Thus, dependence on the British market has been falling especially in revenue terms.

Should the trends towards higher volumes of low-spending tourists be sustained it would mean ever increasing numbers of tourists would be required to maintain a given real expenditure target. Apart from the environmental consequences, this highlights the need to develop marketing strategies which are targeted at higher-spending segments of the market such as those linked to particular sports (e.g. golf, angling) or special interest holidays (e.g. conferences) or at segments which would generate longer stay holidays or the second holiday market. Both of the latter require continued investment in product improvement and development and improved/cheaper access to the country. These points are returned to later.

IMPACT OF TOURISM ON THE ECONOMY

Tourism expenditures are spread over quite a number of sub-sectors in the economy which have varying propensities to import and varying labour productivity rates. These latter values influence the full impact of tourism on GNP and employment respectively. Initial tourism expenditures are heavily concentrated in the services sector (retail trade, hotels and transport) while (in Ireland) approximately 12–14 per cent of total tourism GNP is reflected in output in the goods producing sectors of the economy. To determine the full impact of tourism expenditures on GNP it is necessary to estimate the indirect purchases made by sub-suppliers to the prime 'tourist' providers. In essence, this is the intermediate demand for the goods and services supplied to tourism enterprises. This includes purchases of food and drink, craft and souvenir goods, and any other goods or services supplied to hotels, guesthouses, transport services and the variety of tourist amenities in the country.[11] The principal sectors which benefit from the indirect expenditures are food and drink, retail trade, internal transport, business services and other market services. Such expenditures are deemed to be dependent on the direct purchases by tourists and as such the value-added generated is considered part of tourism's contribution to the GNP of the economy. An additional impact arises from the respending of incomes generated in hotels and other tourist suppliers and in the sub-supply firms, i.e. the induced spending. The sum of direct, indirect and induced spending is used to measure the impact of tourism on Ireland's GNP.[12]

The total impact of the tourism expenditures gives an estimate of the tourism multipliers which have been calculated for Irish tourism in recent years by Henry (1990–1) and Deane and Henry (1993) for the years 1989 and 1992, respectively. The input–output (I–O) approach is recognized as providing a reliable basis for estimating both the GNP impact of tourism expenditures and the corresponding employment impacts, since the baseline work of Archer (1977), who convincingly applied the I–O methodology to the tourism sector. Norton (1982) estimated export tourism input–output multipliers for Ireland for 1976 and estimated the impact of this tourism revenue on GNP, the exchequer revenue, the balance of payments and employment. His results (an overall export tourism multiplier, defined as the ratio of the incremental change in GNP to the incremental change in international tourism receipts, including carrier receipts, of 1.03) contrasted sharply with the then prevailing view which suggested much higher multipliers, e.g. Murray (1977), Byrne and Palmer (1981), NESC (1980b) and Kennedy and Foley (1977) used multipliers of 1.8 and upwards in estimating the impact of export tourism on the economy at the time. Bradley *et al.* (1981) estimated a much lower multiplier of 0.5 which Norton (p. 49) argued was probably an underestimate because of too high a value assumed for the marginal import propensity of the sector in 1977. Norton considered his own estimate to be too high and suggested a value closer to 0.8 to be more accurate. O'Hagan and Mooney (1983) considered some of the methodological problems in using multipliers and analysed the impact on the economy of relaxing the assumption that no supply constraints exist (it is an essential tenet of the concept of the multiplier that spare capacity exists in the economy). They found that the 1976 export tourism multiplier of 0.86 (at factor cost, equivalent to Norton's 1.03 at market prices) was reduced to 0.59 where domestic supply constraints were deemed to exist in the agricultural sector. They concluded that appropriate export multipliers for Irish tourism were 0.6 or less, especially given the openness of the economy – in effect concluding that every additional IR£100 million of foreign tourism expenditure increases GNP by IR£60 million.

In converting the GNP impact into employment estimates a critical factor is the degree of capital intensity in the tourism sector, including sub-suppliers and other sectors benefiting from the induced spending which arises. Deane (1987), among others, refers to the relatively low capital intensity of the sector and thus the strong link between increased expenditures and employment, although Norton (1982) argued that the capital intensity of tourism was similar to that of the rest of the economy and was probably higher when the relatively capital intensive international carriers are included. The acute seasonality of the Irish tourism industry adds to its capital intensity as measured by the average capital to labour ratio since plant utilization rates are close to zero for much of the year. The jobs in manufacturing which are dependent on tourism are, of course, subject to the capital intensities in that sector and the extent of employment growth will be critically dependent on the productivity gains which accrue there. Productivity gains are much more difficult to achieve in the services sector so that increased output can be more directly associated with employment gains. Henry's I–O analysis for 1989 and 1992 suggest that average labour productivity arising from tourism's GNP contribution is broadly equivalent to that of the economy as a whole though variations are found within individual sub-sectors.

Impact on GNP

Table 4.7 summarizes some of the results from more recent work and shows multiplier values for four years since 1978, although the estimates for that year and 1982 are more tentative than those for the two more recent years. Data refer only to the impact of foreign tourism revenues and exclude carrier receipts and domestic tourism impacts.

Thus, the impact of foreign tourism receipts on Ireland's GNP is measured by the multiplier of approximately 1 in recent years, having declined from the admittedly tentative estimate of almost 1.3 in 1978 and the exaggerated estimates for the late 1970s noted above, some as high as 1.8. Although it is difficult to tell from the data, the reduction over the intervening years has been due possibly to a number of factors – greater import leakages in the first round 'direct' expenditures

Table 4.7 Foreign tourism expenditure in Ireland, estimated GNP impacts and derived weighted average multipliers, 1978–1992, for selected years

Year	Aggregate expenditure (1) IR£million†	GNP impact Direct (2) IR£million†	GNP impact Direct+ Indirect+ Induced (3) IR£million†	GNP normal impact multipliers* Direct	Direct+ Indirect+ Induced
1978	215.9	128.1	276.3	0.59	1.28
1982	355.0	211.5	437.9	0.60	1.23
1989	751.0	473.5	747.6	0.63	1.00
1992	949.0	485.9	972.2	0.51	1.02

*GNP normal impact multipliers: Direct = (2)/(1); Direct + Indirect + Induced (Total) = (3)/(1).
†Current prices.
Source: Henry (1990–1), Deane and Henry (1993) and estimates derived from data provided by Henry, based on earlier I–O tables and on his unpublished report for Bord Failte in April 1993 'Estimated GNP and Employment Impact of the Irish 1991 and 1992 Tourist Trade'.

(noted for 1992) and greater import propensities also by the 'sub-supply' goods producing sectors. Higher indirect taxation might also explain the reduction in the multiplier values observed. Based on these estimates the contribution of foreign tourism receipts to GNP in recent years is approximately the same as the value of these receipts, i.e. a multiplier of approximately 1 which is quite plausible.

To get the full picture of the impact of tourism on the economy one would need to take account of the impact of the international carrier receipts (which tends to be lower because of the greater capital intensity of the output from this sub-sector compared with the general 'tourism' sector and the greater marginal propensity to import by the carriers) and of domestic tourism (which has a lower impact because no induced effects are included since the household income which generates this spending has already been earned within the Irish economic system).[13] An issue of some contentious debate over the years has been the extent to which the recycling of Government revenues generated from tourism spending should be included as part of the GNP generated by the sector. Clearly to include all tax revenues generated from tourism expenditures implies a balanced budget hypothesis which is quite an unlikely scenario. Deane and Henry (1993) assumed (arbitrarily) that 30 per cent of tourism tax revenues respent within the economy could be counted as part of tourism's GNP contribution, with the Government included as part of the economy's inter-industry matrix. This gave rise to the GNP multipliers for 1992 as shown in Table 4.8 (bottom row).

In the absence of this partial recycling the GNP multiplier for international or export tourism to Ireland was very close to 1 in both years while for domestic

Table 4.8 Normal GNP multipliers for Irish tourism, 1989 and 1992

	International tourism		Carrier receipts		Domestic tourism	
	1989	1992	1989	1992	1989	1992
Direct	0.670	0.512	0.664	0.343	0.631	0.505
Direct+Indirect	0.786	0.786	0.735	0.531	0.811	0.799
Direct+Indirect+Induced	0.995	1.024	0.962	0.690	–	–
+Government recycling (full)	1.357	1.395	1.349	0.982	–	–
+Government recycling (30%)	1.104	1.136	1.078	0.778	–	–

Source: Based on Henry (1991), Deane and Henry (1993), Table 1 and on data supplied by E. Henry.

tourism was close to 0.8. There was greater variation in the estimation of the GNP multiplier for carrier receipts which varied from 0.69 to 0.96. Applying the average of these multipliers to Irish tourism revenues gives a reasonable estimate for the proportion of GNP arising from tourism since 1981, though clearly one would have less confidence in the results for the early part of the period covered. The relevant averages of the multipliers are:

	(including 30 per cent recycling)	(including no recycling)
International tourism	1.120	1.010
Carrier receipts	0.928	0.826
Domestic tourism	0.805	0.805

Figure 4.4 shows the changing relative importance of tourism in Ireland's GNP since 1981 (based on zero tax-recycling)

Foreign tourism's contribution to Irish GNP stabilized in the early 1980s at about 3.5 per cent of GNP, but increased steadily from 1987 onwards to 4.7 per cent in 1994.[14] The sector expanded much more rapidly than overall GNP over the five-year period from 1987 to 1991. Domestic tourism's share of GNP has varied from 1.7 per cent in the early 1980s and declined to one per cent in 1986 but recovered strongly to stabilize at 1.8 per cent in the mid-1990s. One must be very cautious about interpreting the importance of domestic tourism both in terms of displacement of other forms of expenditure and in the accuracy of the measurement of the extent of it. Indeed, there may be a case for excluding it completely from the measurement of tourism performance since the only addition to GNP arises where there is substitution of domestic for foreign holidays, a form of import substitution. The extent to which this occurs is not known as there is no survey evidence available on the issue. However, Deane (1987) does point out that even though domestic tourism expenditures are a

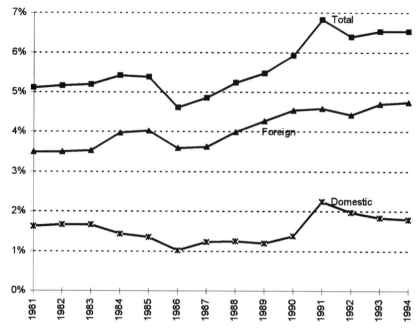

Figure 4.4 Estimates of tourism GNP to total Irish GNP, 1981–1994. *Source*: See text for tourism product estimates, GNP data from Stationery Office, National Income and Expenditure, various years

substitute for other forms of expenditure they may have a greater impact on GNP because of the lower propensity to import compared with, say, expenditure on consumer durables or other goods many of which are imported. He refers also to the regional redistributive effects of domestic tourism which assists the relatively poorer parts of the country disproportionately. Even if we believe domestic tourism cannot be ignored, the accuracy of measurement is an important issue particularly when a considerable amount of employment is attributed to it.

Henry's (1991) paper on the input–output model of the economy for 1989 showed export tourism having a higher GNP multiplier than transport, food, drink and tobacco, paper and printing, clothing and footwear, textiles and chemicals. This finding is not unrelated to the very low propensity to import generated from tourism, which for export tourism was estimated at approximately 10 per cent of direct expenditure in 1989 and 1992. In terms of direct contribution to GDP (rather than GNP) the net output of tourism was greater than the drink and tobacco, textiles, and clothing and footwear sectors. Within the European Union tourism is relatively more important in Ireland than all members with the exception of Spain, Greece and Portugal (1992 Eurostat data in CEC, 1995a).

Tourism employment

A primary reason for the Government's interest in the tourism sector arises from its potential to generate employment opportunities, particularly at a time when the output/employment ratios in the goods producing sectors are so unfavourable and because unemployment is such a major problem in Ireland. Labour intensity is higher in parts of the 'core' tourism sector (apart from the carriers) itself though of course many of the indirect employment effects arise in more capital intensive manufacturing industries. Estimates of employment in Irish tourism have been subject to a good deal of discussion with no clear and unambiguously determined data set available and agreed upon. Work by the interdepartmental committee[15] on the topic suggested that the 'proportional' method of estimating tourism employment was probably the best available since it had an intuitive appeal (employment estimated in proportion to the output generated), was clear and cheap to produce and had a sound theoretical/methodological base in input–output analysis. Surprisingly, the methodology was not used to produce a systematic and consistent series in official circles. The void was filled by a few 'experts' who came up with a plausible set of estimates largely based on the detailed work of Henry. Employment estimates (supplied by Henry) for the years shown in Table 4.7, using the same methodology and relating to foreign tourism receipts only, were as follows.

	Direct (1)	Direct + indirect + induced (2)	Ratio multipliers (2)/(1)
1978	18,295	35,966	1.97
1982	17,341	33,302	1.92
1989	25,190	38,879	1.58
1992	23,302	44,171	1.90

With the exception of 1989, these data suggest that for every full-time equivalent job arising directly from foreign tourism receipts in Ireland, one additional job is created elsewhere in the economy. Employment arising from carrier receipts and domestic tourism (as well as the 30 per cent 'recycling', if included) augments the employment numbers to give the total employment dependent on the sector of 86,000 in 1992 – international: 52,500; carriers: 9500; and domestic: 24,000. The methodology applied by Deane and Henry (1993) to estimate tourism employment numbers for the period 1978–1993 and which have, to a large extent, been adopted as 'official' figures, was used to retrospectively estimate employment data from 1981. Assumptions were made about average productivity gains over the period which reduced the employment impacts to some extent though the indirect and induced employment arising in the goods-producing sectors was only 12.5 per cent.[16] Employment is related to the expenditures in each of the main categories – international, carriers (adding a proportion for recycling) and domestic. The results are presented in Table 4.9 and compared with other estimates of tourism employment assembled from a variety of sources (column 7).[17,18]

The exclusion of the tax-recycling effects reduces the estimated tourism-dependent employment by approximately 8 per cent. To put the employment estimates in context these are related to total employment in the economy from the annual labour force estimates (Table 4.10). Employment in tourism is related both to total employment and to services sector employment in Ireland.

Employment dependent on tourism has been rising steadily since 1986, from 4.2 per cent to 7.5 per cent (1994) of the total at work; it has also increased as a proportion of the more rapidly growing services sector, accounting for one in eight services sector jobs in 1994.[19] Tourism's contribution to the recovery in employment in Ireland over the interval from 1987 to 1994 has been substantial when it accounted for 35 per cent of the net employment increase and over 37 per cent of the corresponding increase in services employment.[20] Ireland's reliance on tourism as a source of employment growth in recent years has far outweighed the relative importance of the sector in terms of overall employment. This disproportionate contribution is a function also of the failure of other sectors to expand in employment terms and to the lower productivity growth rates experienced in direct tourism services. The latter would lead one to expect

Table 4.9 Employment in Irish tourism by principal segments, 1981–1994

Year	Out-of-state	Carriers	Total foreign	Domestic	Total	Other estimates	(6) excluding tax-recycling
(1)	(2)	(3)	(4)	(5)	(6)	(7)	(8)
1981	30,982	7797	38,778	17,211	55,989	55,900	51,771
1982	30,594	7298	37,892	17,130	55,022	60,500	50,919
1983	30,656	7030	37,686	16,714	54,399	61,000	50,335
1984	32,386	7354	39,740	13,463	53,203	60,200	48,931
1985	35,655	7717	43,372	13,530	56,902	65,000	52,259
1986	32,531	6943	39,474	10,413	49,888	55,600	45,676
1987	37,182	7049	44,231	13,351	57,582	61,600	52,893
1988	42,096	7596	49,692	13,756	63,448	67,600	58,203
1989	46,391	9194	55,585	13,944	69,529	73,700	63,660
1990	51,935	9759	61,694	16,553	78,246	83,000	71,761
1991	53,641	9766	63,406	27,259	90,666	90,700	84,025
1992	52,440	9532	61,971	24,051	86,022	86,000	79,550
1993	59,099	9178	68,277	23,014	91,290	91,000	84,213
1994	63,056	9441	72,497	23,568	96,065	–	88,580

Source: See text and (for column (7)) Tansey Webster and Associates (1991); other estimates derived from Deane and Henry (1993), Minister of Tourism and Transport (1988) and Stationery Office (1994).

Table 4.10 Employment in tourism as a proportion of total and services sector employment in Ireland, 1981–1994 (in thousands)

Year	Total at work	Employed in services	Employed* in tourism	Tourism employment to: total employment	services sector employment
1981	1146	587	51.8	4.5	8.8
1982	1146	598	50.9	4.4	8.5
1983	1124	604	50.3	4.5	8.3
1984	1103	603	48.9	4.4	8.1
1985	1079	602	52.3	4.8	8.7
1986	1081	606	45.7	4.2	7.5
1987	1080	616	52.9	4.9	8.6
1988	1091	626	58.2	5.3	9.3
1989	1090	618	63.7	5.8	10.3
1990	1126	643	71.8	6.4	11.2
1991	1134	656	84.0	7.4	12.8
1992	1139	668	79.6	7.0	11.9
1993	1146	692	84.2	7.3	12.2
1994	1181	712	88.6	7.5	12.4

*Column (8) Table 4.9.
Source: Derived from Labour Force Surveys, 1994 and earlier years; (CSO,1988); Tansey Webster and Associates (1991); Deane and Henry (1993); Minister of Tourism and Transport (1988); and Stationery Office (1994).

that increased revenues would lead to higher employment gains in tourism though the experience from 1987 to 1994 indicated marginally greater labour productivity gains in tourism GNP than the average for the economy.[21]

Balance of payments effects

The employment effects of tourism are essentially incorporated in the contribution of the sector to GNP, representing a share of the net output so created. In effect it reflects a particular distribution of the value-added which is biased towards a better return for labour inputs.[22] A further dimension of the economic importance of tourism is its contribution to total and services exports though again this does **not** represent an additional benefit over and above that arising from the overseas tourism revenue generated and the payments by these visitors to the international carriers. It can, of course, be a very useful source of foreign exchange particularly when there is pressure on the balance of payments. Foreign tourism receipts, as measured by the tourism and travel credit balances in the balance of payments, accounted for almost one-third of invisible exports over the 12 years from 1981 to 1994 inclusive (see Table 4.11).

Table 4.11 Impact of tourism and travel receipts on total exports, invisible exports and on the current account balances in Ireland, 1981–1994

Year	*Tourism and travel receipts on current account*			*Impact on current account balance*
	IR£m	*% Total X*	*% Inv X*	
1981	417	6.9	32.3	R.D.
1982	476	6.8	33.1	R.D.
1983	520	6.3	34.7	R.D.
1984	591	5.6	33.2	R.D.
1985	685	5.9	33.9	R.D.
1986	649	5.8	33.3	R.D.
1987	731	5.8	33.3	R.D.
1988	842	5.7	32.5	DtoS
1989	983	5.6	31.5	R.D.
1990	1131	6.4	31.0	DtoS
1991	1218	6.5	30.6	DtoS
1992	1230	6.0	30.9	I.S.
1993	1366	5.8	33.4	I.S.
1994	1497	5.5	32.6	I.S.

*R.D., reduced deficit; D to S, deficit turned into surplus; I.S., increased surplus.
Source: CSO, National Income and Expenditure, Stationery Office, Dublin, various years.

These receipts formed an average of 6.1 per cent of total exports (merchandise and services). These low proportions are depressed because of the inflated values for merchandise exports arising from the practice of transfer pricing by multinational companies based in Ireland. These exports have much higher import contents than many indigenously produced traded goods. The tourism sector itself has a much lower import content than many internationally traded goods. Tourism was Ireland's fifth largest export sector in 1990 being exceeded in order of magnitude by machinery and transport equipment, manufactured goods classified chiefly by materials, chemicals and related products and food and live animals (EIU, 1991).

The final column in Table 4.11 provides another indicator of the relative importance of the tourism and travel sector in contributing to the current account of the balance of payments. This shows that in eight of the 14 years since 1981 the earnings from travel and tourism reduced the deficit on current account, while in three of these years it had the effect of converting a deficit into a surplus. In 1992–1994 its impact was to increase the current account surplus. This stabilizing effect of international tourism has been noted in quite a few countries (e.g. see O'Hagan and Waldron, 1987).

Other economic impacts

A further aspect of the economic impact of tourism is the contribution to the Exchequer mainly from the taxes arising from the expenditure of overseas tourists. The recycling of tax revenues generated from out-of-state tourists, on the assumption of a 'balanced-budget' hypothesis, is not a plausible scenario in the Irish context as such revenues are more likely to be used to reduce the size of the budget deficit and thus reduce the Exchequer borrowing requirements. In purely Exchequer accounting terms, any additional income source will reflect a broadening of the tax base and thus reduce the burden of taxation elsewhere in the economy. Given the excessive rates of income tax which have dominated the Irish fiscal debates in the 1980s, the significant growth of foreign tourism receipts since 1987 contributed to a reduction of this burden in no small way. By providing an inflow of foreign currency, these receipts are used indirectly to reduce foreign borrowings, which further reduce the tax burden to fund debt interest.[23]

SUMMARY REVIEW OF PERFORMANCE, 1981–1994

The performance of Irish tourism since the mid-1980s has been impressive relative to the remarkably weak performance of the previous 15 years. However, the improvement in tourist arrivals (from 1987 to 1990) masked a rather worrying trend in Irish tourism. Ireland's share of both world and European tourism receipts has been consistently lower than its equivalent share of tourist arrivals. This may be due to the fact that almost 55 per cent of overseas tourists come from Britain who are traditionally low spenders and come from lower socio-economic groupings than the norm from other origin countries. In addition, there has been a long-term decline in the real inflation-adjusted spending per foreign tourist; by 1984 such spending fell to its lowest level since 1961. Since then it has increased by over 20 per cent to the 1994 level though these recent improvements, while encouraging, would need to be sustained over several years to arrest the long-term decline.[24]

The principal outcomes since 1981 were as follows:

- following an erratic first half of the 1980s Irish tourism increased its overseas market share for the first sustained period in almost 20 years;
- specific targets to double foreign tourist numbers over the five-year period from 1987 to 1992 were roughly on target for the first three years but fell short of the ultimate 1992 target by 26 per cent or over 1 million fewer overseas tourists;
- there was a significant shift to mainland European country visitors towards the end of the 1980s while visitor numbers from North America remained relatively static, i.e. their numbers declined in relative terms though there was some recovery in 1994 (up 17 per cent on 1993) which was not unrelated to the 'peace process';

- the 1994 revenue figure (foreign tourism revenue less carrier receipts) was over 120 per cent in nominal terms and more than 80 per cent in real terms above the 1987 figure though a comparison with 1981 showed an increase (in real terms) of this revenue in 14 years of only 115 per cent;
- employment increased by 26,500 over the five-year interval (1987–1992) which was ahead of the 25,000 target set;
- there was a significant improvement in the tourism product over the period principally due to the EU Structural Funds and the significant increase in investment in Irish tourism under the Operational Programme for Tourism, 1989–1993, and its successor, the 1994–1999 OP.

The question is often raised as to why Irish overseas tourism performed so well in the latter part of the 1980s particularly when the Government's allocation (through Bord Failte) for tourism promotion and development had been cut back in real terms especially since 1985.[25] Indeed, the success of Irish tourism during this period is often attributed (in official terms) to the first OP for Tourism though the latter had no real impact until well into the 1990s. There is a widely held belief also that increased marketing expenditures lead directly to increased numbers of tourists (often within the same season) without recognizing the myriad and complex factors which influence such a decision of destination choice.[26]

Three factors suggest themselves as possible explanations for the revival in Irish tourism fortunes.

1. Changing trends in the international tourism market place with a shift towards alternative tourism including 'green' tourism and a movement away from previously popular sun-spots for health and environmental reasons.
2. Liberalization of air fares particularly on the Irish–UK routes (though there is still a long way to go for an 'open skies' policy in Europe).
3. Investment supports by the Government with the aid of the EU's Structural Funds which included some marketing support measures.

The first two factors may just as easily work adversely against the further development of the sector as fashions change and airlines seek to survive through rationalization which may inevitably imply less competition. However, the third factor represents a unique opportunity to overcome some of the deficiencies of Irish tourism and particularly of the Irish tourism product and to positively develop the sector to the year 2000. The next chapter examines the regional dimensions of Irish tourism.

NOTES

1. The low propensity to import (c. 10 per cent), compared with manufacturing, arises because of the nature of tourism services, which generally require less imported inputs

for service provision and because of the strong bias in expenditures by foreign tourists in Ireland on home-produced goods. The indigenous ownership structure in hotels and other sub-sectors within tourism, with well-established linkages to other sectors in the economy, also helps reduce the import content that would arise where foreign ownership is the norm. An exception arises in the case of the international air (and sea) carriers with heavy fuel import expenditures.

2. This target was set for the increase in overseas tourist numbers to Ireland in the Programme for National Recovery (Stationery Office, 1987); both numbers and real expenditures were targeted to double and 25,000 additional jobs were to be sustained by these expansions.

3. Tourism expenditures are influenced more by real income changes than are tourism numbers to a given destination as other studies have shown (Barry and O'Hagan, 1972). This arises at high incomes as tourists raise their expenditure in response to income increases rather than tourist nights, given time constraints, while income reductions may not lead to holiday cancellations but rather reductions in expenditure possibly accompanied by shorter stays. Some of these hypotheses require further testing. However, it was not possible to incorporate a tourism expenditure variable into the model used by Walsh (1994) due to data deficiency problems.

4. The Poulter Index is a recognized international composite index used to measure weather conditions; the index represents mean temperature, rainfall and sunshine duration, during the popular summer months of June, July and August, and the data are available for Ireland from the Meteorological Office, Dublin.

5. The limitation of using dummy variables is that they are a crude instrument and fail to capture the changing impact of a problem like the NI troubles which were not a single once-off event but rather a prolonged series of incidents over a number of years with some particularly severe incidents from time to time (see Chapter 8).

6. Country marketing campaigns are frequently based on simplistic bivariate relationships both in terms of cause and effect, without sufficient empirical understanding of the underlying factors, e.g. the impact of the Gulf War on US travel to Europe/ Ireland was assumed to be significant, while the subsequently increased marketing expenditure in the US market was deemed to be an appropriate response in the belief that there was a direct link between this spend and the decisions of US tourists to visit Ireland. Marketing expenditure decisions continue to be made in the absence of a solid research base to guide the decision making process; a case in point is the Irish Government's decision to allocate an additional IR£3 million to promote Ireland in the US market in 1994, a decision which had been prompted primarily by pressure from the industry which convinced the Government to move in this direction. Responses like this to such effective lobby groups does not necessarily lead to the best allocation of scarce resources, given the expedient nature of the decision and the process used.

7. A recently observed development has been the holding of weddings of previous emigrants in Ireland influenced by both the ethnic connection as well as the cheap access fares from the UK. In economic terms the impact would not be dissimilar to the revenue derived from a small international conference though the propensity to spend in the former may be much greater.

8. The upsurge in travel from Britain would have been affected also by the nature of emigration from Ireland in the 1980s (when gross outflows were close to 50,000 per annum in the last few years of the decade). These migrants included a not insignificant

number of well-qualified graduates who had the financial means to take advantage of the cheaper air fares available with the advent of the independent airline, Ryanair, on the Dublin–London route, in 1986.

9. Estimates of domestic tourism revenues are generally less reliable than those arising from international tourists; indeed from 1992 the method of calculation of domestic revenues appears to have changed so that the series from that year cannot be compared with earlier years. One needs to be cautious also in interpreting the economic importance of domestic tourism particularly whether to treat the expenditure as an alternative to other forms of expenditure on goods and services in Ireland or as a substitute for holidays abroad or for other imports. In the former case it represents a form of displacement expenditure while in the latter there is more of a net economic benefit to the economy. See O'Hagan and Waldron (1987) for a comparative analysis of domestic tourism estimates in the EU.

10. The absence of direct scheduled flights to Dublin from large east-coast US cities has been advanced as one argument for the short stay of US visitors in Ireland, given that quite a number of such visitors travel via the UK. There is no firm evidence to substantiate these arguments though the ending of the Shannon stopover in 1994 and the introduction of direct scheduled flights to Dublin will, at least, remove this alleged constraint on longer-stay holidays in Ireland.

11. O'Hagan and Waldron (1987) addressed this issue of estimating the economic impact of tourism expenditures on the GDP of European Union countries and referred to the treatment of intermediate demand particularly in the UK context. Estimates in the latter country attributed the same proportion of intermediate demand in the total economy (69 per cent) to the tourism sector though the authors point out that this proportion is likely to be considerably less because of the high labour intensity of the tourism sector which would give rise to lower intermediate demand levels. The authors conclude that, on average, intermediate demand as a proportion of final demand in the tourist-related sectors was only around half that for other sectors in the economy. This has direct implications for the employment estimates from tourism in the economy.

12. Henry (1991) used an input–output model of the Irish economy to measure the impact of tourism on GNP and employment. His approach was adopted by Tansey Webster and Associates (1991) to derive estimates of tourism's contribution to Ireland's GNP over the period 1985–1990. In addition to the direct, indirect and induced effects, a 'fourth stage' induced effect was included also which measures the impact of respending the additional taxes generated from tourism through an increase in Government expenditure. This assumes a balanced budget policy stance which is not generally considered plausible in the Irish economy context with its widespread experience of deficit financing throughout the late 1970s and 1980s. In a recent paper by Deane and Henry (1993), 30 per cent of the impact of the respending of the Government income (i.e. tax revenue) derived from foreign tourism was deemed to be a reasonable measure of the additional impact ('fourth stage' effect) on the economy both in income terms and in employment terms. This allows for the fact that this tax revenue is used for other purposes such as a reduction in the budget deficit. This assumption is rather arbitrary and GNP/employment estimates are exaggerated by the inclusion of these partial 'tax-recycling' effects.

13. There are difficulties associated with the accuracy of the estimates of domestic tourism revenues which affect the confidence one can place in the implied GNP

impacts. Estimates have varied widely in recent years both from the trend patterns, suggesting a major and sudden expansion of domestic tourism, and from the earlier data published by Bord Failte. Such variations are reflected also in the employment estimates possibly attributing greater employment to the sector than is actually the case.

14. If the 30 per cent tax-recycling is allowed for, the 1994 proportion increases to 5.3 per cent.

15. See Minister for Tourism and Transport (1988).

16. This methodology may be criticized because of the over-reliance on the I–O relationships used for 1989 and 1992 since the base models used for these two years were the I–O relationships for 1982 and 1985, respectively.

17. Though the tourism GNP and employment estimates presented here follow the convention of attributing 30 per cent of the tax revenue generated in the sector to the overall impact of tourism in the economy there is no economic basis nor rationale in the literature for so doing; consequently, the relative contribution of tourism to the economy is probably overestimated by approximately 7.8 per cent in 1993. This would reduce estimated employment arising in tourism to 84,200 from 91,300.

18. The employment estimates in Table 4.9 converge towards the end of the period (1991–1993) because an identical source is used (Deane and Henry, 1993) but differ from the estimates in that source for 1987–1990 because different estimates of domestic tourism revenues are used in the table, based on the Bord Failte series in Tourism Numbers and Revenues (Annual).

19. Though it should be noted that the employment included in tourism is not exclusively services but also includes some jobs in manufacturing through the indirect and induced effects of the purchases from these sectors.

20. Though if one takes the earlier interval, 1987–1992, the respective increases were 45 per cent and 51 per cent, indicating a slowing down of the relative tourism employment growth rates since 1992.

21. Output per head in tourism is about 6 per cent below the economy average though it enjoyed a 26 per cent increase (compared with 23 per cent for the economy) from 1987 to 1994.

22. An exception to this is the relatively more capital intensive international carriers. However, Norton (1982) questioned the notion that the tourism sector is more labour intensive than the economy average. On balance, Ireland does relatively well in terms of her ability to capture a significant proportion of the gross revenue generated by the tourism sector both because of the linkages developed with the manufacturing and other sub-supply sectors and also the limited repatriation of profits generated because of the ownership structure of the principal tourism assets. While the absence of foreign investors may be a function of the poor returns available in Irish tourism it probably also reflects the relatively slow rate of expansion of the sector thus not attracting mobile capital looking for a quick return on investment.

23. Tourism is also deemed to have a beneficial effect on less developed regions both at European and local country levels. This regional dimension is considered in Chapter 5.

24. Average expenditure by out-of-state tourists in the 1990s was over 10 per cent below the levels achieved in the 1960s in real terms though was higher than the levels experienced in the mid-1980s.

25. This begs the question as to how effective tourism promotional funds are in developing overseas demand for Irish tourism in the first instance.
26. The demand estimation model developed by Walsh (1994), and referred to above, highlights the complexity and rigour required to do an effective evaluation of marketing spend and to place it in the proper context of a multivariate framework.

5 Tourism and regional development

BACKGROUND

Tourism, by its nature and economy, is a spatially distributed industry. This arises, on the supplyside, from the dispersed location of natural tourist attractions (e.g. Cliffs of Moher, Co. Clare, Giant's Causeway, Co. Antrim) and other product developments in particular parts of the country (e.g. golf courses and interpretative centres). It arises also, on the demand side, from the residential locations of the tourists who by definition reside in other countries for international tourism and often in more prosperous regions within countries. At a European level the general movements of tourists are from the wealthier German, Dutch and other northern more-developed countries to the less-developed southern and western parts of the continent. Within Ireland the southern and western parts of the country are very popular holiday destinations for both domestic and foreign tourists although Dublin receives a larger share of foreign tourism revenue than any other region in Ireland. Capital cities are attractive in their own right and the capacity of Dublin to cater for the larger-scale tourism events such as major international conferences, the variety of entertainment forms available and the mix of historical, cultural and shopping facilities combine to enhance its appeal to the visitor. However, in relative terms tourism contributes less to regional GNP and employment in the Dublin region than it does in the relatively poorer regions of the West, South-west and North-west (see Tansey Webster and Associates, 1991; Breathnach, 1992). Brunt (1988) and Gillmor (1985) also refer to this regional bias in Irish tourism. Thus, both the supply- and demand-side factors combine to shape the spatial distribution of the tourism industry, and in turn influence the regional distribution of tourism income and employment.

The tourism sector has been identified in many local communities and less-developed parts of Ireland as a palliative for the decline in agricultural incomes and lack of industrial employment opportunities. This interest has been influenced by the structural nature of the industry in which there are low entry barriers at some levels (e.g. bed and breakfast business in the family home), low operating costs (high proportions of family labour, preponderance of female employment of an atypical (part-time, seasonal, casual) nature, small-scale capital investments, limited training required for basic provision of services) but also low returns on the investments made. Breathnach (1992) cautions against the large diversion of resources to the sector because of the precarious nature of the employment generated. However, the incomes generated, though limited, can be important sources of supplementary incomes for rural communities.[1] The sustainability of these income sources can be precarious also as the very ease of entry to the industry can cause problems for many who fail to raise their quality standards sufficiently to withstand new competitors from the immediate or more distant regions of the country.

In this chapter the regional dimensions of Irish tourism are considered. The regional distribution of visitors and revenues since 1981 are first analysed and used as a basis for estimating some of the regional economic impacts in income and employment terms; the importance of tourism's contribution to regional incomes and employment in the least developed parts of the country is noted. The regional distribution of the first round (1989–1993) of EU Structural Fund spending on the tourism sector is outlined briefly together with a prospective look at the next round (1994–1999). Local development initiatives in tourism are briefly evaluated.[2] Drawing on earlier research undertaken by the authors, the employment effects of three well-known tourist attractions in the South-west and Mid-west regions are presented. Some organizational issues are discussed in the light of the changing role and functions of the regional tourism organizations (RTOs). Finally, some conclusions are drawn on the policy and organizational aspects of tourism and regional development.

REGIONAL VARIATIONS IN TOURISM NUMBERS

The propensity of overseas tourists to visit more than a single region in Ireland is strong and this helps to geographically distribute the benefits generated by a given volume of tourists. The litmus test of benefit derived depends on the amount of expenditure in each region and the extent to which it can retain the benefits of indirect and induced expenditures, stimulated by the initial expenditures of the tourists. The changing distribution of overseas tourists in Irish regions is analysed now.

Ireland was divided into eight tourist regions, each with its own regional tourism organization, from 1964 to 1988. In line with the allocation of EU Structural Funds, 1989–1993, the number of sub-regions in Ireland was reduced to seven, through assigning counties or parts of counties to different regions. Figure 5.1 shows the old and new classifications.[3]

The numbers of overseas visitors to each region and the annual average growth rates are shown in Table 5.1.

The rapid expansion of overseas tourists to Ireland from 1987 to 1990 is masked in the table because the regions were re-classified during this interval. The average annual changes were evenly spread geographically in the 1981–1988 period with the exception of the Midlands. This is one of the least-popular/

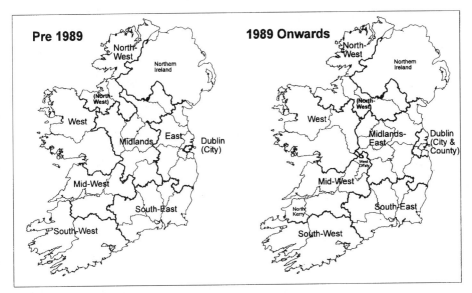

Figure 5.1 'New' and 'old' tourism regions in Ireland, pre-1989 and from 1989 onwards

Table 5.1 Regional distribution and average annual changes of overseas visitors to Ireland, 1981–1994

Region	1981 (000s)	1988 (000s)	Average annual change 1981–1988 (%)	1989 (000s)	1994 (000s)	Average annual change 1989–1994 (%)
Dublin	684	886	3.8	1146	1768	9.1
Midlands east				439	624	7.3
South-east	298	433	5.5	484	775	9.9
South-west	547	826	6.1	855	1071	4.6
Mid-west	341	532	6.6	661	807	4.1
West	361	496	4.6	778	920	3.4
North-west	205	276	4.3	410	498	4.0
East	213	336	6.7			
Midlands	161	275	8.0			
Ireland*	1680	2425	5.4	2804	3679	5.6

*Note that the numbers in each row do not add to the totals in the final row because of multiregion visiting which occurs.
Source: Derived from Bord Failte (1988b) and (1994a) and Bord Failte's Tourism Facts 1994.

least-developed tourism regions but from a low base experienced an 8 per cent average growth rate. The two regions which experienced the most rapid expansion in the 1989–1994 period were Dublin and the South-east. The latter expansion is noteworthy since traditionally it has had the strongest regional dependence on domestic tourism.[4] The West and North-west regions showed the most sluggish expansion from 1989 to 1994. Given their high relative dependence on tourism as an income source this trend is somewhat worrying. Indeed a significant 'east–west' divide has emerged over the five-year interval 1989–1994 with the three 'eastern' regions (Dublin, South-east and Midlands-east) showing growth in tourist numbers far in excess of the four other 'western' regions, 53 per cent compared with 22 per cent. Much of this divergence arises from the British and Rest of the World (Australia/New Zealand) origin markets.

Dublin and the South-west are by far the most popular tourism regions with one-third or more of all overseas visitors visiting each region. By contrast only about 10 per cent visited the 'old' North-west or the Midlands region from 1981 to 1988, while the Mid-west, West and South-east each attracted between one-fifth and one-quarter of all overseas visitors over the entire period.

Regional tourism densities provide a useful comparative basis for assessing the relative importance of tourism volumes in an area. The densities may be expressed as tourism numbers per thousand of the resident population (or per square kilometre of regional space). Average densities do not take account of the extreme seasonality of Irish tourism, which coupled with the popularity of a relatively small (though expanding) number of key attractions, can lead to congestion problems at certain times of the year. Two tourism density measures are used: one, which expresses the total number of overseas visitors as a monthly average and relates this to the resident population (per thousand); two, which takes the average of the two peak months of July and August and also expresses this in relation to the same population base. The ratio of the monthly peak season average to the average monthly figure was 1.92 to 1 in 1981 which fell to 1.86 to 1 in 1986. In other words, the monthly volume of overseas tourists in the peak season (defined here as July–August) was 1.92 times the average which would arise if the total volume of visitors was spread evenly throughout the year. The ratio fell to 1.80 in 1991 but increased to 1.86 by 1994. However, we are referring to a much greater volume of tourists in the 1990s than in the first half of the 1980s. For example, the monthly average volume of tourists per thousand of the resident population was only 41 in 1981 (and 44 in 1986) but increased to 71 and 77 in 1991 and 1994, respectively. Increases of this order of magnitude can lead to considerable congestion and swelling of the local population at popular tourism centres in the high season, e.g. in Galway. In the peak season, the respective densities ranged from 78 in 1981 to 144 in 1994. Regional variations in tourism densities are shown in Figures 5.2 and 5.3, while Table 5.2 shows the degree of variation in seasonality patterns between the different sub-regions in 1994.

The acute seasonality is noted for the West, North-west and South-west regions with a ratio greater than 2 compared with the countrywide average of 1.74 to 1. If peak and low seasons are compared the ratios would be much higher. These seasonality patterns make the problem of developing tourism in these regions all the more difficult as any investments undertaken have to contend with an even greater degree of under-utilization of tourism plant than elsewhere in Ireland. Dublin has a much more even spread of tourists throughout the year.

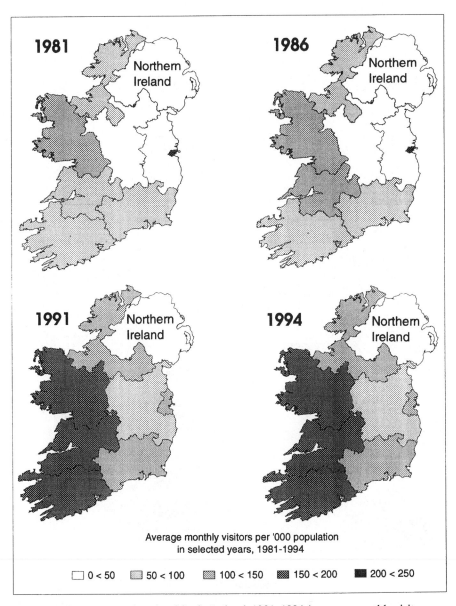

Figure 5.2 Overseas tourism densities in Ireland, 1981–1994 (average monthly visitors per thousand of the resident population) for selected years. *Source*: As for Table 5.1

The distribution of regional tourists by broad origin zones shows that while overseas tourists form almost 50 per cent of all tourists in the Dublin and Mid-west regions, NI tourists comprise a minuscule proportion of total visitors in most regions with the North-west (19–28 per cent) being a notable exception, followed

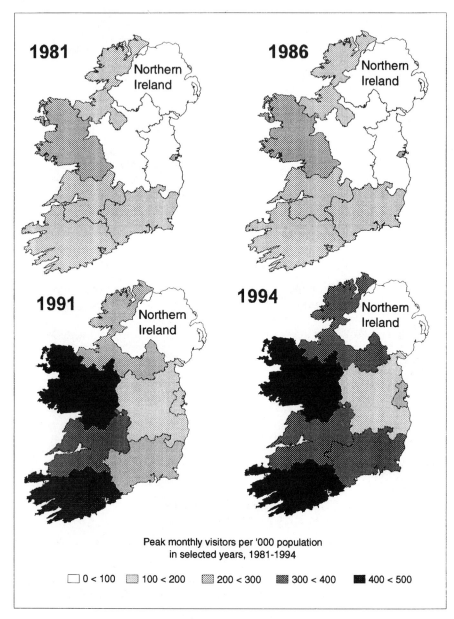

Figure 5.3 Peak overseas tourism densities in Ireland, 1981–1994 (peak season densities are the average for July–August per thousand of the resident population) for selected years. *Source*: As for Table 5.1

Table 5.2 Regional distribution of peak to average
monthly overseas tourists to Ireland, 1994

Region	Ratio peak/average
Dublin	1.68
Midlands-east	1.80
South-east	2.10
South-west	2.22
Mid-west	2.10
West	2.40
North-west	2.22
Average	1.74

Source: As for Table 5.1.

by Dublin (6–9 per cent). Domestic tourism is relatively most important in terms
of visitor numbers in the South-east, Midlands-east and South-west regions over
the period from 1981 to 1994.

REGIONAL REVENUE AND INCOME VARIATIONS

The crucial initial measure of the economic impact of tourism in a region is
reflected in the revenues generated from tourists visiting from outside the region.
Depending on the 'leakages' arising from indirect and induced expenditures, the
region will capture a greater or lesser share of the tourism income which arises.
Regional economies within a country tend to be extremely open so that indirect
benefits may accrue in large measure to firms located outside the immediate
tourism region, particularly where the local industrial structure is weak. Local
craft enterprises and other locally produced foodstuffs offset this tendency to
lose the benefits of regional tourism expenditures as do measures which increase
the local length of stay and spend through tourism product diversification, e.g.
cultural tourism, traditional entertainment, wet weather facilities and so on. The
changing regional distribution of tourism revenue in real terms is illustrated in
Figure 5.4 for selected years in the interval 1981–1994. All tourism revenue is
included and related to the changing regional population bases.

Although overall tourism revenue per head (of the resident population)
declined from 1981 to 1986 there was a steady increase in the overseas revenue
per head from IR£137 to IR£151 (1993 prices). This latter increase was recorded
in all regions with the exception of the Mid-west and North-west. Since 1986 both
overseas and total revenue per person have increased though the revision of the
method used to estimate domestic tourism accounted for a significant proportion of the increase in total revenues generated. The latter stood at IR£520 per
head of the resident population in 1994 while overseas revenue was IR£309 per
head (1993 prices). The overseas figures exclude carrier receipts which cannot

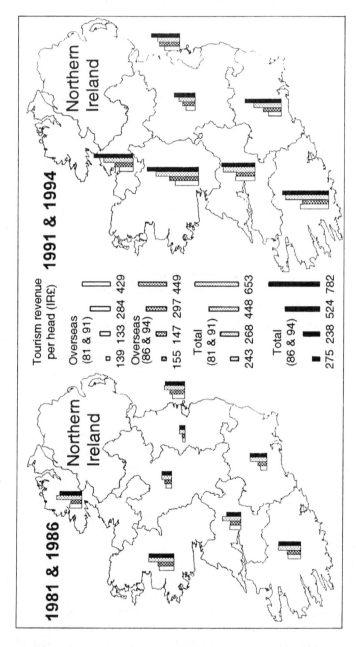

Figure 5.4 Regional distribution of real tourism revenue per head of population in Ireland for selected years, 1981–1994 (in constant 1993 prices). *Source:* As for Table 5.1

easily be attributed to individual regions. The regional revenue variations are shown in ratio format in Table 5.3 for the years in question.

The revision of the regional boundaries has affected the ratios to the extent that five of the eight 'old' regions (including the four 'western' regions) had ratios of average overseas tourism expenditure per head of population above the national average in 1986, while only three of the seven 'new' regions (including only two 'western' regions) were in this category in 1994. The South-west and the West regions were consistently well above the country average throughout the period although they had declined, while the North-west showed a significant relative decline to 1991 but recovered somewhat thereafter. This latter observation reflects no more than the revisions to the boundaries in which two low-priority tourism counties (Cavan and Monaghan) were added to the more 'touristic' counties of Donegal, Sligo and Leitrim. The convergence noted in Table 5.3 above reflects a shift in the distribution of the benefits of overseas tourism away from the more dependent 'western' regions of the country towards Dublin and its contiguous regions, with likely adverse consequences for the regional distribution of income.[5]

The disaggregation of tourism revenues for each region shows that domestic and Northern Ireland (NI) revenues go some way towards offsetting the imbalances in the distribution of overseas revenues. In the interval from 1981 to 1988, NI and domestic tourism revenues declined in real terms. The North-west had almost 36 per cent of NI revenues in 1981 which declined to 32 per cent in 1988, although it had only approximately 7 per cent of total national tourism revenue over this period. Although the South-west region had the largest share of domestic tourism revenues (23–26 per cent), the South-east region was more heavily dependent on this source of tourism revenue than any other region in 1981 (63 per cent of its total) and second highest in 1988 (over 45 per cent).[6] Table 5.4 shows changes in regional tourism revenues from 1981 to 1988.

Table 5.3 Ratios of overseas tourism spending per head of population in Irish regions in selected years, 1981–1994

'Old' regions*	1981	1986	'New' regions*	1991	1994
Dublin	141	155	Dublin	89	102
East	30	32	Midland-east	55	62
South-east	74	96	South-east	76	90
South-west	149	138	South-west	169	131
Mid-west	127	114	Mid-west	117	93
West	166	163	West	140	146
North-west	140	116	North-west	83	90
Midlands	65	73	Ireland	100	100
Ireland	100	100			

*For the county composition of 'old' and 'new' tourism regions, see Figure 5.1.
Source: As for Table 5.1.

Table 5.4 Irish regional tourism revenues* in 1981 and annual average changes from 1981 to 1988 by broad origin zones

Region	1981 IR£ million				Annual average % change 1981–1988			
	Overseas	NI	Domestic	Total	Overseas	NI	Domestic	Total
Dublin	101.0	18.2	66.2	185.4	6.9	−4.1	−6.3	1.5
East	34.6	6.2	37.4	78.2	6.0	−0.8	5.3	5.2
South-east	38.0	2.4	67.9	108.3	5.0	1.9	−3.2	−0.1
South-west	106.8	5.8	96.1	208.7	4.2	0.6	−4.0	2.2
Mid-west	53.6	1.9	45.3	100.8	3.6	4.0	−2.4	1.0
West	65.1	8.1	51.0	124.1	3.5	−2.9	0.3	1.9
North-west	40.0	25.0	27.6	92.7	1.2	−3.6	0.0	−0.5
Midlands	32.0	2.3	24.6	58.8	7.3	−1.5	−1.2	4.0
Ireland	472.8	70.1	415.1	958.0	4.8	−2.7	−1.5	1.8

*In constant 1993 prices and excluding carrier receipts.
Source: As for Table 5.1.

The East and Midlands regions showed the largest annual average revenue increases from 1981 to 1988 although the base revenues in 1981 were the lowest of all the regions, accounting in aggregate for only 14 per cent of total tourism revenue then. Turning to the more recent period, Table 5.5 shows that the revenues generated from both overseas and domestic tourism were shared (if unevenly) throughout the regions while NI tourism continued to show considerable volatility with the South-east, South-west and West experiencing declines in real revenues from this source.[7]

The 1989–1994 period covered and extended beyond the first round of the EU Structural Fund spending on the Irish tourism sector. While the benefits of this

Table 5.5 Annual average changes in Irish regional tourism revenues,* 1989–1994, by broad origin zones

Region	Annual average % change, 1989–1994			
	Overseas	NI	Domestic	Total
Dublin	10.1	6.6	16.3	11.2
Midlands-east	7.9	14.3	13.4	10.0
South-east	14.3	−7.1	12.1	12.5
South-west	7.5	5.7	13.0	9.8
Mid-west	2.4	−8.0	7.6	4.3
West	2.3	−6.6	10.5	4.3
North-west	6.5	9.8	17.0	10.3
Ireland	7.3	4.6	12.5	8.9

*In constant 1993 prices and excluding carrier receipts.
Source: As for Table 5.1.

spending will extend well beyond the immediate period in which it occurred, it is noteworthy that the increased expenditures from overseas visitors continued throughout the four years although was more dramatic in 1989–1990 when few of the benefits of the EU funds could have been effective. While all regions shared in the revenue increases, the West and Mid-west regions benefited least over the period 1989–1994, experiencing average annual growth rates of only one-third of the best performing region (the South-east).

Focusing on the overseas tourism revenue only for the period since 1981, Figures 5.5 and 5.6 show the overall trends. The relative loss of market share for the three western regions of the Mid-west, West and North-west has been persistent since 1981.

While the removal of the compulsory Shannon 'stopover' in 1993 for all transatlantic flights has been argued as a reason for the more recent relative decline in tourism in the Mid-west and other western regions, it is clear from the trends noted above that there are more fundamental and long-term factors accounting for the loss of market share. One can only speculate about the underlying causes of the differential regional changes. Four possible causes are: first, the changing mix of international visitors with a substitution of European for North American visitors – the former are not drawn to the traditional west of Ireland tourist attractions to the same extent as the latter; second, the ease of access and points of access on the east and south-east coasts has enabled the adjoining regions more opportunities to 'capture' the passing tourist traffic – the South-east region particularly benefited from the growth in numbers of British tourists in the recent 1989–1994 period; third, Dublin has become quite a fashionable tourist destination in its own right and the growth of short-stay/ weekend breaks, together with cheap access fares, has helped it capture a growing share of overseas tourists to Ireland; four, the innovative tourist products of the 1960s and 1970s which built on the innate attractiveness of the western

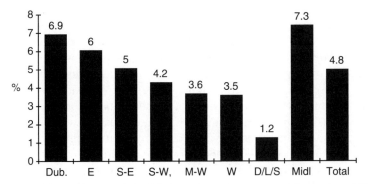

Figure 5.5 Annual average growth (%) in real overseas revenue by region, 1981–1988 (Dub, Dublin; E, East; S-E, South-east; S-W, South-west; M-W, Mid-west; W, West; D/L/S, Donegal–Leitrim–Sligo; Midl, Midlands). *Source*: Derived from regional tourism data in Bord Failte publications

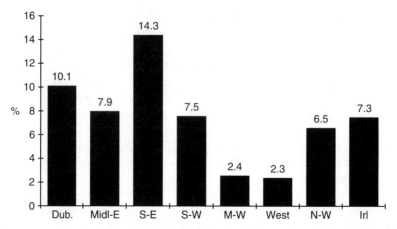

Figure 5.6 Annual average growth (%) in real overseas revenue by region, 1989–1994 (Dub, Dublin; Midl-E, Midlands-east; S-E, south-east; S-W, south-west; M-W, Midwest; N-W, North-west). *Source*: Derived from regional tourism data in Bord Failte publications

parts of Ireland may no longer have the same appeal for the modern-day tourist, who is more discerning, likes variety, is more activity focused and budget conscious. The danger of complacency and failure to recognize changing market trends, and to effectively respond to them, might also explain the regional differences.[8] The changing distribution of tourism revenues suggest that the expectation that tourism will improve the regional distribution of incomes within Ireland may be misplaced, a point which the distribution of EU Structural Funds for tourism failed to address in any meaningful way.

Tourism as a regional income source

In the input–output (I–O) model developed by Henry (1993a), it was estimated that approximately half the additional income generated from overseas tourism spending accrued to 'front-line' tourism enterprises (accommodation, restaurant, retail and transport firms) while the other half was diffused throughout the economy. Those less developed regions, such as the West and North-west, are unlikely to capture as significant a share of the additional income generated from direct tourism expenditures because of weak industrial structures and less developed linkages than more developed and integrated regions.

Full scale inter-regional I–O models would be required to capture the regional income impacts of tourism but such models have not been developed systematically for all Irish regions. Some attempts have been made to develop ad hoc I–O models for specific regions or sub-regions or to use other estimated multiplier values for specific tourism projects (see Brady Shipman Martin, 1983; O'Cinneide and Keane, 1988; and Deegan and Dineen, 1992).

Based on the estimated tourism expenditures in each of the regions and the estimated tourism multipliers, it is possible to come up with some reasonably plausible measures of tourism income for Irish regions. Using the I–O models and multiplier estimates determined by Henry (1990–1) for 1989 and by Deane and Henry (1993) for 1992, regional tourism income estimates were made for these two years.[9] The regional incomes dependent on the carrier receipts were assumed to be confined to four regions: Dublin, South-east, South-west and Mid-west, based on the locations of the major airports and ferry-ports. Tansey Webster and Associates (1991) used an allocation which was adapted here and confined the incomes generated entirely to these regions. Indeed, it is (perhaps naively) assumed that all tourism incomes (direct, indirect and induced) are retained in the regions in which the initial direct spending occurs and no allowances are made for the potentially greater leakages which arise in the less-developed regions of the economy.[10]

Regional incomes were estimated as proportions of total GNP as published in the National Income and Expenditure accounts (CSO, 1993). The proportions used are based on the NESC (1980a) report on the distribution of personal incomes by county, subsequently updated to 1984 in an unpublished work.[11] Thus, the same regional income distribution applies to 1989 and 1992 although regional income per person may differ because of population movements since 1984. The resulting regional tourism incomes are presented in Table 5.6 and related to regional incomes for 1989 and 1992. The final column of this table shows the (identical) variation in regional incomes per person for both years.

The relative importance of tourism income in different regions is clear from the table with the 1992 data showing that the West, North-west and South-west

Table 5.6 Regional distribution of tourism incomes in Ireland and index of regional per capita incomes, 1989 and 1992

Regions	Tour Y* 1989 (IR£m)	Tour Y 1992 (IR£m)	Reg Y 1989 (IR£m)	Reg Y 1992 (IR£m)	Tour Y/ Reg Y 1989 (%)	Tour Y/ Reg Y 1992 (%)	Index of Reg per capita Y 1989 and 1992
Dublin +East	541.8	670.5	10127.4	12201.7	5.3	5.5	111.8
South-east	98.9	159.2	2173.3	2617.8	4.5	6.1	90.2
South-west	232.0	374.3	3332.0	4013.4	7.0	9.3	99.7
Mid-west	136.5	165.5	1865.5	2246.9	7.3	7.4	95.5
West	168.8	223.0	1592.5	1918.1	10.6	11.6	87.0
North-west	89.9	122.3	1111.7	1339.0	8.1	9.1	85.0
Midlands	77.2	90.8	1958.6	2355.9	3.9	3.9	86.7
Ireland	1345.0	1805.5	22,161.0	26,693.0	6.1	6.8	100

*Current prices, Y = income.
Source: See text.

regions derive more than 9 per cent of regional income from this source. The data confirm that tourism as a source of income is much greater in the relatively less-developed and poorer parts of the country, notably the West and North-west, where average incomes are approximately 86 per cent of national and only 77 per cent of average incomes in the Dublin-east region. Similar biases were noted in earlier studies such as that of Gillmor (1985), who noted that coastal resorts and urban centres had a disproportionately high share of tourism activity within regions; he suggested that the carrier entry points to the east of the country helped to redress the spatial imbalance (biased towards western parts of Ireland) in tourism incomes to some extent. NESC (1980b) also highlighted the regional impact of tourism as did Deane (1987). O'Cinneide and Walsh (1990–1991) examined the role of tourism in national and regional development and, using essentially a supply-side approach, assessed the spatial impact of tourism which is clearly more important in less developed parts of Ireland. They referred also to the artificial advantages enjoyed by the western regions arising from the (then) compulsory stopover in Shannon and the influx of tourists associated with it. Hannigan (1994) is more sceptical about the contribution of recent Government policy towards tourism in redressing regional imbalances and rather sees the recent EU-stimulated growth as exacerbating the expansion of tourism in traditional tourist areas. Apart from the South-west region, which benefits enormously from tourism, a continuation of existing trends in the distribution of tourism incomes and investment will continue to help the more-developed regions and may thus contribute to an overall weakening of the regional distribution of income. The problems these regions experience in development terms is their inability to attract a proportionate share of manufacturing industry. Tourism has a limit to its potential to solve the endemic economic problems of the western regions of Ireland.

EMPLOYMENT IMPACTS AT REGIONAL LEVELS

With limited employment opportunities and an apparent ease in creating direct employment in the tourism sector in response to increased revenue flows it is not surprising that policy-makers have focused on tourism as a sector with potential to create and distribute employment regionally. A proportionate method is used to relate regional tourism revenues (converted to incomes) to regional employment estimates, allowing for the composition of the underlying revenue sources (domestic, foreign, carriers) and for productivity changes over time.[12] It is further assumed (perhaps too strongly) that the direct, indirect and induced employment so generated are based in the regions where the revenues arise. Between 45 and 52 per cent of total tourism employment was concentrated in the Dublin and South-west regions throughout the period from 1981 to 1994. Figure 5.7 shows the changing relative importance of tourism employment as a proportion of total employment in the eight 'old' tourism regions.[13]

The period divides into three sharply contrasting sub-periods, from 1981 to 1986 (when tourism employment declined in absolute and relative terms in each region), 1986–1991 (when tourism employment increased dramatically in all regions with the most rapid expansion in the West and Mid-west regions) and 1991–1994 (when employment growth rates were positive though low and strongest in the Midlands, South-west and Dublin-East). One in eight of those employed in the West in 1994 was dependent on tourism while approximately 10 per cent of regional employment in the North-west and South-west was similarly dependent. Absolute employment estimates for selected years and the annual average changes for the three sub-periods are shown in Table 5.7. The substantial employment expansion in tourism in all regions is clearly shown in the five-year period, 1986–1991. Much of this expansion occurred prior to the full impact of the EU Structural Fund investments from 1989 to 1993 though obviously some projects had come on stream. The east–west divide in real tourism revenue terms did not translate very obviously into differential employment changes though some of the 'eastern' regions (East and Midlands) recorded relatively stronger employment growth rates from 1991 to 1994.

Regional employment in tourism may be relatively important because other sectors of the regional economy are doing much worse or conversely, tourism may experience a declining share of regional employment because the rest of the economy is buoyant. The Irish economy experienced declining employment

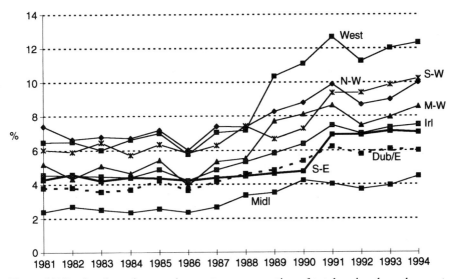

Figure 5.7 Regional tourism employment as a proportion of total regional employment in Ireland, 1981–1994 (using the 'old' regions with Dublin and the East combined as one region). *Source*: As for Table 5.1 and based on methodology used in Deane and Henry (1993) for aggregate employment; Census of Population, 1981 and Labour Force Surveys used for regional employment estimates

Table 5.7 Regional tourism employment and annual average changes of tourism employment in Ireland, 1981–1994, various years

	1981	1986	1991	1994	Annual average % change 1981–1986	Annual average % change 1986–1991	Annual average % change 1991–1994
Dublin	14,561	12,548	26,879	27,891	−2.6	16.5	1.2
East	3641	3909	2838	3365	1.4	5.0	5.8
South-east	5025	4756	8205	8221	−1.0	11.5	0.1
South-west	10,230	9119	16,152	17,575	−2.1	12.1	2.8
Mid-west	5179	3889	8329	8637	−4.6	16.5	1.2
West	5861	5284	11,288	11,609	−1.9	16.4	0.9
North-west	4482	3511	5811	6079	−4.0	10.6	1.5
Midland	2775	2660	4523	5202	−0.8	11.1	4.7
Ireland	51,771	45,676	84,025	88,580	−2.3	13.0	1.8

Source: As for Figure 5.7.

for the first half of the 1980s when tourism employment declined in most regions. The expansion of tourism employment in the late 1980s coincided with overall employment expansion, while recent gains (1993 onwards) occurred in a context of relatively rapid overall employment growth. It is interesting to compare the relative contributions of tourism employment growth in each region (Table 5.8).

While tourism contributed about two-fifths of the net increase in employment in total from 1986 to 1994, it made a disproportionately large contribution to net regional employment change in two of the seven tourism regions shown (West and Mid-west) and was equivalent to all of the net employment gains in two further regions (South-east and North-west). Although the Dublin-East region has the largest share of tourism employment in Ireland (35 per cent) it accounted for only one-fifth of total employment growth from 1986 to 1994, a reflection of the growth of other sectors there.

Table 5.8 Tourism's contribution to net employment changes in Irish regions, 1986–1994

Region	Tourism employment change, 1986–1994	Total employment change, 1986–1994	Tourism employment change/total employment change (%)
Dublin–East	14,799	70,477	21.0
South-east	3465	3400	101.9
South-west	8456	15,500	54.6
Mid-west	4748	2300	206.4
West	6325	2500	253.0
North-west	2567	2500	102.7
Midland	2542	3838	66.2
Ireland	42,902	100,515	42.7

Source: As for Figure 5.7.

The implications of these changes for the employment structures of the western regions of Ireland are potentially very serious as there clearly appears to be an excessive reliance on the tourism sector to generate employment growth. Ironically the failure to develop the industrial base of the western regions, especially the West and North-west, has contributed to the development of the tourism sectors there with heavy reliance on returned emigrants and their families. While some of the employment in tourism arises in other sectors of the economy and is of reasonable quality, much of the direct employment (about 50 per cent of the total) comprises precarious employment forms – part-time, seasonal and casual – with limited career paths and prospects for progression.[14] There is a dominance of low-skill and low-wage employment and, while this can form important supplementary income and employment opportunities for those involved, it is questionable if it forms a sufficiently robust economic base for developing a peripheral economy which can offset development failures in other sectors of the economy. With limited alternative employment opportunities in these regions the choice can frequently be a stark one between poor quality jobs or no jobs at all although the strategic policy preference for a tourism industry which puts a premium on quality may critically influence eventual outcomes.

EU STRUCTURAL FUNDS AND THE REGIONS

Tourism was targeted as one of the key sectors for support under the first (and second) rounds of EU Structural Fund transfers to Ireland as part of the redistribution measures agreed in the process of adjustment to the Single European Market. It was the first time the industry achieved such a priority in national development programmes and provided considerable access to resources which could be used as part of a product development and marketing strategy for the industry. There was also a strong emphasis on training for the industry. The contribution of the EU transfers to the overall development of Irish tourism are considered in Chapter 7; here we focus on the sub-regional dimensions only.[15] The first Operational Programme (OP) for Tourism briefly discussed the notion of major and regional tourism centres with minimum levels of facilities in terms of accommodation, restaurants, entertainment services, transport linkages and visitor information sources. Figure 5.8 shows the location of the principal tourism centres, regional centres, theme towns and the (national and international) airports in the country.

The financial package outlined in the two OPs for Tourism referred to three funding sources: EU, Irish Government and the private sector. There was some attempt in the first Community Support Framework (CSF)[16] agreed between the EU Commission and the Irish Government to distribute the overall expenditure across all OPs throughout the sub-regions of the country on a basis which approximated to the population distribution. The EU Commission were pushing strongly for a greater role for the sub-regions in the allocation of resources in the first CSF (agreed in 1989) but this was resisted by the Irish Government

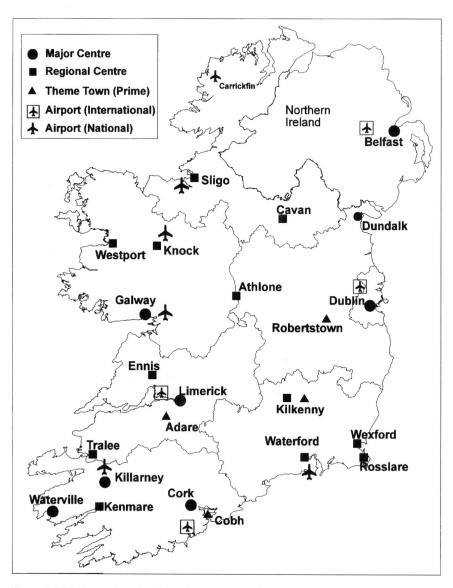

Figure 5.8 Major and regional tourism centres, theme towns and airports in Ireland.
Source: Department of Tourism and Transport (1989) and Bord Failte

which eventually conceded a largely discursive/consultative role for the sub-regions. Some technical assistance was provided to evaluate the impact of the first round of the Structural Funds in each of the seven sub-regions though the impact of these evaluations on the second CSF appears minimal.

In the CSF which was agreed in 1994, a more structured role was assigned for newly created Regional Authorities with access to the National Monitoring Committee, which oversees the implementation of the overall programme of Community support.[17] The Tourism OP is one of a number of sectoral programmes and there is no clear application of the OP with any kind of specific sub-regional objectives. There was neither an attempt to re-distribute investment in favour of the less-developed parts of the country nor to develop tourism in those sub-regions where it was least developed according to Hannigan (1994). He pointed out that during the first OP for Tourism, investment in the industry mirrored quite closely the overseas distribution of tourism revenues with the result that traditionally strong tourism sub-regions (e.g. the South-west) benefited while the weaker sub-regions (North-west and Midlands-east) did less well proportionately. However, his conclusions are not supported by the data in Table 5.7, although he included Business Expansion Scheme (BES)-funded projects in his analysis and these are more likely to be biased towards the better developed tourism centres. The sub-regional distribution of total investment under the first and second OPs and their relation to 1993 foreign revenues are shown in Table 5.9.

The proportion of tourism expenditure has increased dramatically in favour of the Dublin area in the second OP while all other sub-regions with the exception of the North-west have suffered proportionate declines. It should be noted, however, that planned tourism expenditure is almost doubled for the second OP, 1994–1999. A number of large-scale projects in the Dublin area accounts for this relative shift in resources, e.g. a National Conference Centre capable of attracting large international conferences. When the expenditure under the OPs is related to foreign tourism earnings in the sub-regions it can be seen that the South-east and Mid-west were most favourably treated in the first OP, and these were not the highest earning regions. Planned expenditure under the second OP continues to favour the South-east while the least developed of all tourism regions, the Midlands-east, is favoured the most in terms of expenditure per 1993 foreign tourism earnings.

Evaluation of regional impact of OP for Tourism

There is no real rationale advanced for the particular regional distribution which emerged. If the Tourism OP was being used to improve the distribution of income and employment opportunities on a geographical basis then it would be more appropriate to focus investment expenditure on the West and North-west sub-regions. Such a strategy might not be consistent with getting the best return on the resources available which could be obtained through focusing on investments in the more popular tourist destinations.[18] The ESRI (1993) noted that though there were no explicit regional targets in the first OP for tourism there were "allusions in the programme documentation to the job creating potential of tourism in the less favoured areas of the country" (p. 38). They were critical of the wide spreading of projects in the first OP rather than the alternative

Table 5.9 Sub-regional distribution of investment under the first and second OPs for Tourism in Ireland – proportions and related to foreign tourism earnings, 1989–1993 and 1994–1999

Sub-region	OP 1989–1993 expected (%)* [1]	OP 1994–1999 expected (%)† [2]	[1] £s per £100 1993 foreign tourism earnings [3]	[3] in ratio terms: average = 100 [4]	[2] £s per £100 1993 foreign tourism earnings [5]	[5] in ratio terms: average = 100 [6]
Dublin	16.0	26.9	19.4	56	56.2	94
South-east	13.0	11.0	58.2	167	84.7	142
South-west	18.0	15.2	33.0	95	47.7	80
Mid-west	15.7	12.1	49.1	141	65.1	109
West	12.5	13.2	29.0	83	52.7	88
North-west	12.5	7.9‡	46.6	134	45.3	76
Midlands-east	12.5	13.7§	47.5	136	101.3	169
Ireland	100	100	34.8	100	59.8	100

*Outturn, in prices adjusted for inflation changes 1989–1993.
†Planned, in 1994 prices.
‡Refers to the Border sub-region which comprises the North-west region plus Louth.
§Refers to the Midlands-east sub-region minus Louth.
Note: data in column [5] are adjusted for the North-west and Midlands-east to take account of the 'new' regional boundaries.
Source: Derived from Stationery Office (1994).

of "a strategically focused series of significant interventions". For the second OP they suggested a greater focus on those tourism regions which are likely to give the best returns, i.e. the South-west, West and Dublin. Fitzpatrick and Associates (1994) took issue with this in their prior appraisal of the draft OP for Tourism, 1994–1999, although there is a greater emphasis on large scale projects in the latter and on a few very large strategic projects, particularly in Dublin. Indeed the Dublin region is likely to gain a double dividend under the second OP since over a quarter of the expenditure has been allocated there and the 'leverage' of private sector funds is likely to be much more effective there than in less developed regions. The boom in hotel investment in the capital since 1994 is further evidence of this impact and the achievement of significant scale economies in Irish tourism may be possible only in this large urban context.

In the SIS (1992) evaluation for the EU Commission the argument for spreading tourism investment was based on the need to relieve congestion in the more popular destinations through a greater geographical spread of tourists (within and between regions) in the interests of ensuring better long-term income and employment outcomes.

This regional equity versus economic efficiency argument is not easy to resolve and the spreading of the funds throughout the country might have had more to do with political clientelism than with setting strategic objectives for the tourism sector and spreading the benefits of tourism development to less-developed areas. There is a problem with the 'fuzziness' of thinking in Government planning circles in this regard as there is a form of aspiration for using tourism development to assist regional income and employment distribution but very little follow through in implementation to realize this aspiration. Either the aspiration should be dropped or placed on the agenda as a key strategic objective of the OP and relevant indicators used to measure performance against target. It would be foolish to abandon the key role of tourism in aiding the less developed parts of Ireland.[19]

RURAL TOURISM

There has been a growing interest in recent years throughout Irish rural communities in examining alternative opportunities for development in the light of the reform of the EU's Common Agricultural Policy (CAP). The 1994 GATT agreement will put further pressure on farm incomes and employment in the medium to longer term. The EU Commission has produced a number of position papers on the future of rural society and on rural tourism but probably of most significance has been the introduction of the LEADER programme in 1992.[20]

The precise meaning of rural tourism can be elusive. It has been used interchangeably though erroneously with farm tourism and agri-tourism, both of which have connotations of taking holidays in farmhouse accommodation or on farms. Rural tourism is a broader concept and refers to all tourist activities in a rural area, i.e. the entire tourism product of the area. Although it can exist through the initiatives of individuals responding to the opportunities presented to them, the various efforts to intervene and promote the concept in Ireland has revolved around rural communities through their leaders. This community participation, which does not automatically emerge but very often has to be nurtured and encouraged, is a vital component of the more successful rural tourism initiatives in Ireland.[21] This emphasis on the development of local resources for the benefit of the local community aligns this form of tourism with the 'green' or 'soft' tourism classifications or as a form of 'alternative tourism' which respects the environment; the scale of activities tends to be small also and many of the products are in keeping with a benign use of local resources in such activities as hill walking, horse riding, cycle trails and the like. The community involvement can be most effective in providing services such as co-operative marketing which would not be cost effective for individual operators or in providing local forms of 'public goods' such as training for those new to the industry.

Keane and Quinn (1990) present a useful account of the principal issues involved in rural tourism and rural development and include an evaluation of the Ballyhoura (Co. Limerick) community experience. Ballyhoura Failte Society was set up in 1986 as a local tourism co-operative and formed to develop tourism in the local community. It is frequently cited as one of the best examples of rural tourism development in Ireland. Local community dynamism was tapped by energetic community leaders who saw that an integrated approach would bring best results. They adopted a systematic approach to the development of the local tourism product, emphasized training as an important dimension and sought to package holidays in niche markets for the area. Although the impact in terms of income and employment terms was not very large when the evaluation was carried out, the model did represent a basis for maximizing the contribution of rural tourism to an area's economic well-being. The tourism accommodation base was enlarged considerably in terms of bed and breakfast facilities generating useful supplementary income for families and independence for farm wives hitherto dependent on their husband's farm earnings (O'Connor, 1995, 1996).

The Ballyhoura experience contrasts sharply with earlier attempts to develop rural tourism in Ireland dating back to the 1960s. Farm tourism had limited impact and became largely driven by the provision of accommodation without either linkages to the way of life in rural areas or as part of integrated packages of rural tourism products. Very few farmers became involved (partly because farming itself was more lucrative in the years following entry to the EU in 1973) – some estimates put the proportion as low as 0.2 per cent – and they required quite high occupancy rates to justify the investment in a minimum of three bedrooms dedicated for tourists.[22] Another form of tourism in rural areas was the Rent-an-Irish-Cottage schemes which were pioneered in the Shannon region by Shannon Development in the 1970s (Share, 1992). These were clusters of self-catering cottages, built in a traditional thatched roof style, whose occupiers had little interaction with the local communities and were effectively run by independent private companies. They lacked the community dimension of rural tourism both in terms of resource inputs and benefits accruing (Keane and Quinn, 1990).

Byrne *et al.* (1993) also stress the importance of a holistic approach to rural tourism development which embraces community involvement. They refer to the re-distributive function of rural tourism, which is another key objective, but frequently the benefits may not flow to those most in need. This is often because lower income households do not have the matching resources to take advantage of any funding supports which may be made available. The case of north-west Connemara is used to support their conclusions.

LEADER I programme

The EU's LEADER I programme was developed in response to the decline of agriculture and the search for alternative forms of development. It was primarily a 'bottom-up' approach to local economic and social development. It has been instrumental in mobilizing quite a number of rural communities throughout Ireland in taking a fresh look at the possibilities for local development and in providing resources to support local initiatives. Figure 5.9 shows the distribution of the 17 LEADER I areas covering 61 per cent of the land area of the Republic of Ireland.

About 44 per cent of the projects funded under LEADER I were in rural tourism which claimed more than 50 per cent of the IR£70 million funds allocated under the programme.[23] It was particularly beneficial to communities already mobilized and eager to exploit opportunities in their local areas. Ballyhoura (Co. Limerick) is a case in point which received funding under the programme and was provided with much needed resources to further develop and market its unique tourism products.

Approximately 35 per cent of all funded projects were in accommodation. This provided alternative 'public' funding for accommodation to promoters or 'industry entrants' as Bord Failte had ceased to provide grant aid for such purposes for a number of years. Other frequently supported projects included amenity improvement, culture, heritage, equestrian, golf and fishing. Employment in rural tourism projects was only 34 per cent of the total generated under LEADER I compared with 51 per cent of planned expenditure. There was a high incidence of atypical employment in LEADER-funded projects generally and this was even higher in the tourism projects, given the seasonal nature of the industry. The benefits of the LEADER I initiative lay not so much in the net employment gains (difficult though these were to measure) but in the more qualitative improvements through 'capacity-building' in rural communities. Kearney *et al.* (1994) identified tourism as a sector which was particularly suitable for interventions to correct market failure, especially where local communities took some form of 'ownership' of the resource development process. Individuals may be slow to invest in marketing measures to promote an area for which the direct returns may be questionable but communities could internalize such costs and mount area-based marketing campaigns. Rural tourism development was described as being a 'potent vehicle for local development, economic recovery, social progress and conservation of the rural heritage'.

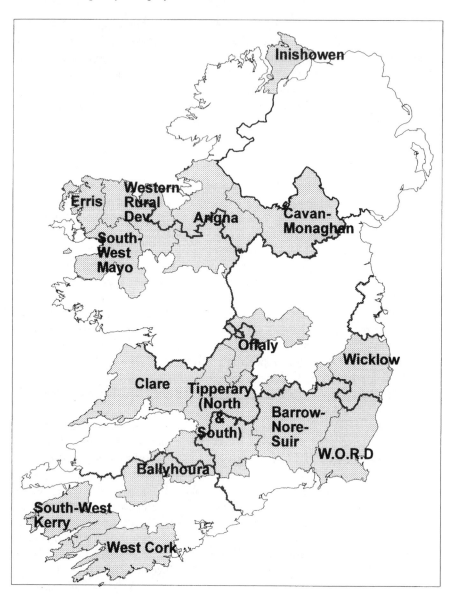

Figure 5.9 Distribution of LEADER I areas in Ireland

There were some interesting examples in the LEADER areas of initiatives which arose from the programme, e.g. two groups prepared strategic tourism plans for their areas, training courses were seen as being particularly effective in the 'capacity-building' process and in developing a more professional approach to the business and a co-operative marketing strategy in another area to overseas markets had the potential to minimize 'displacement' effects of funded projects. The ease of entry to the tourism industry, especially supported with public funds, can lead to believing that a lot of activity equates with net improvements in the outputs of the sector. This may be far from being the case since non-funded operators may find their businesses depleted. Thus, a focus on professionalism is important as a differentiating factor for new entrants.[24]

The difference between LEADER and other development initiatives (such as Farm Tourism) lay in the 'animation' and 'facilitation' efforts or components of the programme. There was more focus on the process and the confidence building in the rural communities selected, with the funds providing the necessary 'lubrication' to launch and stimulate tourism (and other) projects (Kearney *et al*,. 1994). Keane and Quinn (1990) concluded that there was a very fragmented approach to the development of rural tourism in Ireland. The mistrust between local communities and state agencies was part of the problem. The lack of support from Bord Failte, which only belatedly (Bord Failte, 1988c) gave official support to this marginalized aspect of Irish tourism, did not help those seeking to promote development at the local level.

Conclusions on rural tourism

In assessing the role and importance of rural tourism in the context of Ireland's tourism industry, it can be classified as a specialist tourism activity, with the possibility of exploiting niche domestic and overseas markets where 'alternative' tourism is in demand. It has a marginal though important contribution to make to regional income distribution in areas of the country which have under-developed tourism resources and are not on recognized tourist routes. To some international tourists it represents the essence of Irish tourism – the beautiful countryside, the clean air, the friendly people, the relative solitude. It can be effective also in securing a greater geographical spread of tourists. Local spin-off effects in food supply and craft industries may arise. To fully exploit its potential requires strong community support, an integrated product development and marketing strategy, adequate public resource supports at the critical early stages and a professional approach to the management of the sector and its component parts. Much can be learned from 'best practice' in this field and the LEADER I programme was notable primarily for its qualitative rather than quantitative outputs.

EMPLOYMENT EFFECTS OF TOURISM PROJECTS

The local or regional impact of tourism can be measured in the employment effects of prime tourist attractions. Many of these, especially in the heritage and historical fields, are well established in national and regional tourism centres (see Figure 5.8 above), though quite a number of new centres were funded under the first Operational Programme for Tourism, 1989–1993 (Department of Tourism and Transport, 1989). Interpretative centres of various kinds have been developed over the years, with greater or lesser degrees of authenticity. The numbers of fee-paying visitors are a critical basis for determining the viability of such ventures and the likely profitability of any ancillary activities. The composition of these visitors between domestic (local/elsewhere in Ireland) and overseas can provide insights into the origin of the flow of funds arising from the centres and, with other data, enable local and national employment multiplier effects to be estimated. The prime fee-paying visitor attractions in Ireland for two recent years are shown in Table 5.10.

While the visitor numbers and their revenue spend at the attractions are a critical determinant of their commercial viability, the employment impacts extend beyond the direct employment generated at the sites. Indirect employment arises from the secondary or 'upstream' activities of those supplying goods and services to the facilities. Induced employment effects result from the re-spending of incomes generated by those directly employed at the facilities and in the sub-supply firms in the immediate locality or elsewhere.[25] Import leakages will detract from the potential employment impact though these tend to be low for traditional tourist attractions where visitors (especially overseas) prefer to purchase locally produced craft and other goods. Spending by tourists on associated activities (local accommodation, shops, restaurants) may be attributed partially to the existence of some key facilities; the proportions attributed would require visitor surveys to determine their motivations for visiting an area and how important the particular facility impacted on this decision and on their length of stay.

Table 5.10 Major fee-paying visitor attractions in Ireland, 1990 and 1993

Name	1990 visitors	1993 visitors	% change 1990–1993	Location
1. Dublin Zoo	442,064	671,966	+52.0	Dublin
2. Book of Kells	na	321,134	–	Dublin
3. Bunratty Castle and Folk Park	272,000	268,552	–1.3	Clare
4. St Patrick's Cathedral	na	238,000	–	Dublin
5. Blarney Castle	na	211,575	–	Cork
6. Fota Wildlife Park	158,618	201,070	+26.8	Cork
7. Muckross House and Gardens	163,949	189,309	+15.5	Killarney
8. Rock of Cashel	146,621	180,737	+23.3	Tipperary
9. Waterford Crystal	61,899	175,369	+283.3	Waterford
10. Kilkenny Castle	127,043	146,556	+15.4	Kilkenny
11. Newgrange	132,005	139,741	+5.9	Meath
12. Powerscourt Gardens	140,065	133,000	–5.0	Wicklow

na = not available.
Note: rankings are based on 1993 visitor numbers.
Source: Bord Failte (1994b).

Employment impact of three visitor attractions[26]

This section draws on and augments previous work undertaken by the authors on the employment effects of three visitor attractions in the Mid-west and South-west of Ireland. Two of the three attractions are listed in Table 5.10 (Bunratty Castle and Folk Park and Muckross House and Gardens, which had the third and seventh highest number of fee-paying visitors, respectively, in 1993). The third facility is Aillwee Caves in Co. Clare which had 120,000 visitors in 1993. The study was conducted in 1990 and was based on accounting and visitor data for 1989 which were used to estimate the employment effects. A sample survey of 300 visitors (100 to each facility) was conducted in the 1990 peak season to provide a basis for estimating how much of their spending on associated activities could be attributed to the presence of the tourist facility in the respective areas. Table 5.11 summarizes the characteristics of the three facilities which reflect an interesting 'product mix' for the visitor: one is a country period or 'manor' house (Muckross) located on the Killarney National Park with well-preserved gardens which overlook the lakes of Killarney; the second is an underground cave complex (Aillwee Caves) in the Burren district of Co. Clare, while the third is a specially constructed 19th century folk village and medieval castle complex (Bunratty).

A critical question is to determine the difference which the facility makes to the level and type of employment in the local area or region in which it is based. The gross employment arising from direct, indirect and induced expenditures in addition to the attributable expenditures does not take account of the diversion of expenditure from other facilities or on other goods and services either in the immediate areas or elsewhere in the country. Such diverted expenditures merely

Table 5.11 Characteristics and data on three visitor attractions, 1989

	House	*Caves*	*Park*	*All*
Location	Major tourist centre	Off main tourist route	On tourist* route	West of Ireland
Facilities	House, gardens	Underground caves	Folk park and castle	Tea-room, shop
Admission charges†	21	43	47	
Shop sales†	55	33	45	
Tea-room sales†	24	24	8	
Visitor numbers (% foreign)	144,000 (52)	104,000 (53)	264,000 (70)	
Ownership	Public	Private	Public	
Season	Year round	March–October	Year round	

*Eight km from Shannon International Airport.
†Per cent of gross revenue.
Source: Derived from Table 9.2 (p. 140) in Deegan and Dineen (1992).

lead to employment 'gains' which displace other employment leaving a smaller net increase. The smaller the area the lesser is the potential displacement while at a national level all the employment may be considered as displacing employment elsewhere in the country giving rise to a zero net increase.[27] Thus, gross and net employment impacts are estimated with the latter providing a much sharper guide to the extent to which there should be Government funding for tourism projects.[28]

Methodology used [29]

The primary data used for this study consisted of the accounting information supplied by the management at the three tourism projects. The audited accounts and information from management enabled estimates of the full-time equivalents (FTEs) to be made while key invoice data on all purchases made during 1989 were used to record the amount, sector and location of the supplier (within 50 km of the sites or further afield). While there are some problems with using invoice data,[30] these enable reasonably accurate estimates of the employment effects of first round purchases to be derived. To make similar estimates for second and subsequent rounds would require invoice data from suppliers further down the supply chain; in any event these are likely to be much less than the first round impacts. Imports (3 per cent or less at the House and the Park, 15 per cent at the Caves) are netted out as they contribute nothing to employment either locally or elsewhere in Ireland.

The proportional method is used throughout whereby average output or sales (net of indirect taxes) to employment ratios are applied to the expenditures estimated.[31] Ideally, marginal ratios should be used when measuring the additional impact of a tourist facility. It is assumed also that spare capacity exists in the economy to accommodate any increased demand requirements from these facilities. Given Ireland's relatively high unemployment rates this is not too heroic an assumption to make although one might not always find suitably skilled labour for specific short-term needs and the physical capacity at the 'tourism sites' may be limited in the short run.

The induced employment was estimated primarily on the basis of the respending of incomes earned by those directly employed at the three sites in addition to the incomes generated in the sub-supply manufacturing and services firms, both local and non-local. Again, only first round income spending is included.[32]

Results

There was a total of 99 FTE persons employed directly at the three facilities while the indirect employment amounted to 11.8 FTEs in services and 12.6 in manufacturing. Over 90 per cent of the indirect manufacturing employment was located elsewhere in Ireland while almost 50 per cent of services employment was generated locally. The principal services' sub-sectors from which purchases were made were wholesale and retail distribution (58 per cent of total services

Table 5.12 Gross employment effects of the three tourist facilities – house, caves and park, 1989

	Local	*Non-local*	*All*
Direct	99	–	99
Indirect	6.53	17.89	24.42
Induced	14.02	2.61	16.63
Totals	119.55	20.50	140.05

Note: employment expressed as full-time equivalents.
Source: Revision and updating of Table 9.4 in Deegan and Dineen (1992).

expenditure at the house). Repairs and maintenance accounted for 28 per cent of services' expenditure at the caves while publicity and advertising accounted for a corresponding 21 per cent at the park. The only employment estimated for the distribution sector was that in the wholesale and retail firms themselves and their propensity to import would affect any second or subsequent round employment effects in the economy. The indirect manufacturing employment was mainly in clothing (51 per cent) followed by crafts (27 per cent). The proportion of indirect to direct employment in the local areas was approximately 8 per cent, rising to almost 25 per cent when purchases elsewhere in Ireland are taken into account. Thus, there is a mistaken view that the spin-off benefits from indirect employment will be generated in the tourism areas themselves.[33] For manufacturing, the distribution of the indirect employment benefits are likely to follow the sectoral pattern of industrial location rather than any regional distribution, with the exception of the food and drink sector where over 75 per cent of the supplies were sourced locally. The induced employment effects augment these results by 14.2 (local) and 2.6 (non-local) FTEs, having a greater impact in the local economy because of the first round purchases of the direct employees. Table 5.12 summarizes the results of the gross employment impacts of the three facilities.

There are 120 jobs in the local economy dependent on the tourist facilities with an additional 20 in the rest of the economy. These are gross jobs and take no account of displacement effects either locally or nationally.

Net employment

Employment that arises from expenditures which were diverted from other goods and services in the local areas (or from elsewhere in Ireland) displaces this existing employment. This latter employment would have continued to exist in the absence of the facilities. The geographical limits of an area will influence the amount of displacement which occurs. At the local level, any spending diverted from other facilities or economic outlets in the area represents displaced employment in the sense that the jobs exist at the facility rather than in the alternative outlets; expenditures which are diverted from other parts of Ireland, e.g. by domestic tourists, supports additional employment in the local area but from a total economy perspective is displaced employment.[34] Foreign tourist spending leads to additional employment and no displacement at either the local or national levels.

The nature of the visits to the facilities (tour groups passing through the area, excursionists visiting from within the area or from outside, foreign tourists based in the area who are attracted by these and other facilities) influence the measurement of displacement. A survey of 300 visitors to the three sites (100 at each) gave some indication of the motivations for the visits made. It was assumed that domestic visitors based in the local areas, either residents or tourists, generated full displacement for their expenditures while foreign visitors were assumed to generate no displacement. Data on visitor profiles from the management at the three sites also helped to arrive at a measure of the amount of displacement, which differed between the sites. The smaller the area the less is the displacement likely to be. Local displacement effects were deemed to average 19 per cent while total economy displacement was found to average 38 per cent. These proportions reduce the gross employment gains from the three facilities by 23 (local) and 53 (total economy), thus giving rise to net employment numbers of 97 in the local area and 87 for the country as a whole, including the local area. While the gross employment data suggest that there are 41 additional jobs (20 locally) arising because of the expenditure generated at the tourist facilities, the net impact of the facilities is to generate less employment in total than is employed directly, reducing to 88 per cent when total economy displacement effects are taken into account.[35]

The foregoing analysis does not take account of employment in associated activities which benefit from the attraction of tourists to the sites. Some attempt was made to determine the attribution factor for the latter by means of the visitor survey and the direct expenditures in the local area (see Deegan and Dineen, 1992: 150). The respondents were asked about their reasons for visiting the areas and how critical the existence of the facilities were in these decisions. The proportions which considered the facilities to be the primary influence on their decision to visit were 21 per cent at the house, 44 per cent at the caves and 67 per cent at the park. Annual expenditure estimates were made using the survey results and the total numbers of visitors to the three facilities in 1989, and sales/employment ratios were then used to estimate the attributable employment arising from this source. Gross employment arising from these was 103 FTEs while the corresponding net figure was 83 (locally) and 64 (nationally). Indirect and induced effects from the attributable expenditures were not estimated. Even allowing for this omission, the additional impact from attributable expenditures is quite substantial and represents an extra net employment increase of almost 75 per cent of the net direct employment generated. Table 5.13 summarizes the outcomes.

Table 5.13 Gross, net and attributable employment effects of the three tourist facilities – house, caves and park, 1989

	Local	Non-local	Total	Attributable
Gross	119.5	20.5	140	103
Net	96.5	(9.5)	87	64*

Note: Employment expressed as full-time equivalents.
*Eighty-three net locally.
Source: Revision and updating of Table 9.4 in Deegan and Dineen (1992).

Conclusions on employment effects of tourist attractions

The analysis above raises some important policy issues for tourism development at regional and national levels.

1. Since the generation of employment is a critical objective of much tourism development and many local initiatives are designed around projects not unlike the facilities included in the impact analysis (in concept if not in scale) the question of recognizing and quantifying displacement effects should be central to any funding decision.
2. It is important also to distinguish between the local and national impacts of tourism projects–the displacement effects are clearly much less in the case of local impacts.
3. Project funding might vary also according to whether projects are complementary or competing; if the latter then displacement will be greater and should attract lower levels of public funding, other things being equal. Complementary projects, apart from having less displacement effects, could have the benefit of enhancing the overall attractiveness of a region beyond the marginal benefit of one additional project and thus attract proportionately more public funding.
4. Another factor in considering the effects of displacement is the varying labour intensities of the sectors involved. Displaced employment may be in sectors of lower labour intensities (with higher import contents in the goods supplied) than the tourist attractions at which employment expands so that there is a net overall gain for the local and national economy.

The analysis suggests also that quite modest employment gains arise from the indirect and induced expenditures, suggesting about 40 additional jobs for every 100 employed directly at the tourist attractions.[36] The main impact appears to come from the employment dependent on the associated spending in the areas of the attractions. The amount of the latter is critically dependent on the attribution factor applied and its accuracy. The results reported above suggest that total employment from this spending was as much as the direct employment at the facilities themselves. This highlights the local economy benefits possible from popular tourist attractions and the need to recognize these wider benefits in deciding on levels of investment support from public resources. Displacement effects will also need to be factored in as the associated spending and specific additionality to individual projects may not always be clear but rather arise from the general attractiveness of an area for tourists.[37] If every new project claims the same additionality effects in an area there will clearly be an exaggerated estimate of the impact of tourism investment there.

There are some further policy issues which impinge on the investment decisions for tourism projects.

1. Some impacts are immeasurable such as the impact which preservation of the 'national heritage' might bestow on future generations.
2. Improving the range of facilities in an area may make it more attractive to inward industrial investment thus creating extra income and employment which might not otherwise occur.
3. The nature of direct jobs in tourism (such as at the attractions) may be quite precarious (part-time, seasonal, casual) and give a misleading impression of the value of investment in the sector. This highlights the importance of indirect and induced employment which can frequently be of better 'quality'.
4. Finally, it should be noted that additional tourist expenditures may not always create extra employment if some sectors of the economy experience under-employment, or where the extra demand is met from productivity increases or from higher imports.

TOURISM ORGANIZATION AT THE REGIONAL LEVEL

Tourism organization in Ireland has been regionalized since 1964 when the regional tourism organizations (RTOs) were established by Bord Failte in partnership with local authorities and industry representatives in each of the regions. The purpose of the RTOs was to bring the delivery of Irish tourism closer to the communities which benefited from the development of the sector and which bore the costs of any adverse impacts of tourism. Contributions were provided from the local authorities in each of the original eight regions in addition to financial support from the primary businesses at the core of local tourism, i.e. hotels, other accommodation, transport firms, leisure centres and others. These local sources of funding were important as they had the effect of generating a degree of local ownership and hence commitment to the practice of tourism organization at a regional level. The RTOs were essentially the regional branches of Bord Failte and, by virtue of the high grant-in-aid level from the Bord, were obliged to implement Irish tourism policy at a regional level. Bord Failte typically had only one member on the Management Committees (later replaced by Management Boards) of each RTO. Established as companies limited by guarantee the RTOs recruited their own directors and staff from outside the Bord Failte organization, though some personnel were subsequently transferred (or 'promoted') to posts within the Bord.

The primary function of the RTOs was to promote tourism in their regions and to assist the Bord in overseas promotion as required, to provide information centres (Tourist Information Offices) and services to tourists and to act as an initial filter for applications for funding supports to tourism enterprises. This latter part of their functions became critically important in the implementation of the first Operational Programme for Tourism, 1989–1993.[38] RTOs also administer grants on behalf of Bord Failte though in these instances act only as 'conduits' for the transfer of funds.

The eight original tourism regions were reduced to seven in 1988 (see Figure 5.1 above). Shannon Development always had a function in developing tourism on a regional basis arising from its remit to generate passenger traffic through Shannon Airport. It existed alongside the Mid-west RTO from 1964–1987. The latter was abolished in 1987 and its functions transferred to Shannon Development which from 1 January 1988 was given a broader role to promote and develop tourism (and industry) in the extended Mid-west region, now including west Offaly and north Kerry. While this changeover removed unnecessary duplication of services (some of which was seen as healthy local 'competition' between agencies), a more critical negative effect has been the breaking of the industry link through removal of direct board level representation and the implied 'ownership' of the regional tourism development process.[39] The local authorities no longer contribute to tourism development in the Mid-west region through this mechanism, unlike the practice in other regions.

Turning to the other six RTOs, these have become less reliant on Bord Failte for funding over the years and this has shaped different approaches to tourism promotion and development at local levels. The changing income sources are shown in Table 5.14.

The proportion of revenue from the Bord declined from 68 to 31 per cent, with membership subscriptions and commercial sales making up the shortfall. The Bord Failte subvention fell from 11 to 8 per cent of its total operational grant over the 10-year interval. While this reduction might be due to a lack of commitment to the regional dimension of tourism or to rivalry between the Bord and RTO management, as Pearce (1990) suggested, the cost savings to the Bord were important (when its own budget was being cut) and the new commercial climate signalled alternative sources of income as the way forward for the funding base of the RTOs.[40] This has meant that the more popular tourism regions and more efficient RTOs could gain most from commercial ventures. This is borne out by the data on incomes received for 1993 when Dublin, the South-west and West RTOs received 25–27 per cent of their income from Bord Failte, while the South-east (35 per cent), Midlands-east (42 per cent) and North-west (47 per cent) were much more heavily dependent on the Bord in this respect.

Table 5.14 Income sources of Regional Tourism Organizations in Ireland, 1989–1993*

| | 1983 | | 1986 | | 1990 | | 1993 | |
	IR£ million	%	IR£ million	%	IR£ million	%	IR £million	%
Bord Failte	2.34	68	2.34	55	1.56	36	1.70	31
Local authorities	0.44	13	0.52	12	0.47	11	0.58	10
Membership	0.22	6	0.29	7	0.35	8	0.56	10
Commercial sales	0.46	13	1.10	26	1.93	45	2.71	49
Total income	3.47	100	4.25	100	4.31	100	5.55	100

*Excludes Mid-west RTO for 1990 and 1993; it is not possible to determine, from Shannon Development annual reports, the tourism grant allocation to the agency nor the commercial income received from tourism activities.
Source: Derived from data supplied by Bord Failte and direct from the RTOs.

Changing role and structure of RTOs

In the initial phase of Irish tourism development in the 1960s the sector was expanding rapidly though the accommodation and product bases were very underdeveloped. Regionalism and regional development were very much in vogue in the 1970s and the structures to deliver on policy objectives in tourism were similar to those set up for industry, the health services and some public utilities. Pearce (1990) noted a change in the relative importance of the RTOs in the early to mid-1980s as more emphasis was directed towards national marketing campaigns and the RTOs appeared to be less important players in tourism development. Deane (in NESC, 1980b), while recognizing the important information service function of the RTOs, was quite critical of their role because of their limited powers to make things happen, the inherent rivalry and local political pressures which affected their operational independence and effectiveness and the limited resources made available to them. Even were they to be supplied with sufficient resources, he questioned the unnecessary duplication which arises as regions vie for an increasing share of the domestic tourism market and argued that Bord Failte could more effectively deliver such regional policy objectives from a national perspective.

The first OP for Tourism restored the roles of the RTOs, in partnership with Bord Failte, to a prime developmental function supported by significant EU and matching national resources. In undertaking this function, of evaluating and advising on which projects to support, the RTOs' intimate knowledge of the local tourism scene was important though conflicts of interest could arise in being both promoter and funder of particular projects.[41] The EU Commission was also quite keen to include a sub-regional dimension – Ireland was treated as one Objective 1 region for Structural Fund purposes – in many of their programmes and the regional tourism organizational structure in place was very appropriate to deliver on this. The Commission subsequently softened its approach in the light of the rebuffs to over-interference in national affairs expressed in the initial Danish referendum rejecting the Maastricht treaty proposals; the principle of subsidiarity re-asserted itself which for 'regionalists' in Ireland usually stopped at the level of the national Government, noted for its centralist approach to managing the nation's affairs.

The 1987 targets to double Irish tourism numbers, increase revenue by IR£500 million and raise tourism related employment by 25,000 within five years led to a clarification of the role of the RTOs as viewed by Bord Failte (1988c). Essentially the RTOs were there to assist the Bord to achieve these targets through a variety of functions including visitor servicing, product and facilities' development, improving and monitoring standards, assisting the marketing efforts and continuing on the path towards greater commerciality including investment and direct operation of tourism facilities. Neither integration of the RTOs into Bord Failte nor centralization of their functions was considered desirable while the relationship would change to one based less on control and more on performance. Structural changes were proposed whereby each RTO would develop a two-tier structure of a Regional Council (with all tourism interests represented) and a Management Committee of nine members (local authorities, tourism interests and Bord Failte) to direct the ongoing work of the organization. The funding arrangements were to change also with a phasing out of the general grant-in-aid over five years and payment of fees to the RTOs based on services provided and/or work carried out on an agency basis for the Bord.

Plans were announced in 1992 to establish county enterprise partnership boards with the objective to 'promote and assist integrated socio-economic development, in particular by means of enterprise creation and development leading to increased employment through ... providing a local focus for tourism which plays a major economic role in rural counties. The Government have in this context decided to transfer RTO staff to the local county level'.[42] The Tourism Task Force, primarily a private sector ad hoc committee established by the Minister for Tourism, Transport and Communications to advise on tourism strategy and development, cautioned against abolishing the RTOs without equally effective regional co-ordinating mechanisms in place (Stationery Office, 1992).

The transfer (to county level) was later reversed in 1993 and alternative County Tourism Committees (CTCs) were established which would operate as sub-committees of the RTOs and whose membership would be drawn from local authorities, various tourism interests, executives of the RTOs and other staff representatives. The Management Boards of the RTOs include the chairpersons of the CTCs. The CTCs were to be involved in the 'hands on' development at county/area level and attempt to stimulate, assist and co-ordinate 'community and rural based enterprise projects in the tourism sector in order to maximize job creation'.[43] The CTCs would also prepare county tourism plans, focus on initiatives to improve the local tourism environment and assist in the development and promotion of tourism. They appear to overlap considerably with the LEADER area groups both in terms of function and target groups but differ through having a link to the statutory organizations in the tourism sector.

Future role of RTOs

The RTOs make an important contribution to the development of Irish tourism though at times relationships between them and Bord Failte have been strained. Their main strength lies in their knowledge of the operation of tourism at regional and local levels, their wealth of experience in providing information and other services to incoming tourists and the participation by the industry itself at board level. The latter derives from the contributions made by industry operators to the funding of the RTOs in each region which provides an element of autonomy and flexibility to act in the interests of the local industry. Revenue generation from services to tourists also helps move the RTOs closer to self-funding much of their activities, particularly in the more successful tourism regions. The fact that other organizations have been established to support local development, such as the County Enterprise Boards and the County Tourism Committees, and that these and other programmes have targeted tourism as a key sector for development, such as LEADER and INTERREG, can lead to lack of coherence in the manner in which the industry is developed at regional level. It can also mean also that the considerable expertise of the RTOs is not properly utilized in the drive to access grants and other forms of support available for tourism projects as the alternative organizations with direct access to public funding choose to develop their own expertise. To avoid such fragmentation, the RTOs should be accorded a stronger participative role in all forms of regional tourism development within the context of moving towards more self-reliance through its revenue raising and membership activities.

CONCLUSIONS

Several aspects of the regional dimensions of tourism in Ireland have been examined – the performance and economic impact of the industry at a regional level, the distribution of the EU Structural Funds, the nature and importance of rural tourism, the employment effects of local tourism projects and the organizational arrangements for tourism development at regional level.[44]

Tourism has undoubtedly an important contribution to make to regional development though one which may be as much a function of the failure of alternative strategies as the comparative advantage which the sector offers. Caution has been expressed about too great a reliance on tourism as the engine for growth in less-developed regions since it has limits related to the environmental impacts (and the carrying capacity of some popular regions), the precarious nature of employment and the indirect and induced effects of first round spending may be found disproportionately in other more-developed regions.[45] This latter point was clear from the analysis of the employment effects of the tourism projects reported above. The changing regional organizational structures and functions were discussed in the last section and the concluding points focus on these.

One has to seriously question the motivation for and likely impact of the changing regional organizational structures in Irish tourism. There is no apparent rationale for the formation of county level committees other than the fact that the counties exist as administrative units and that there may be political motives for formally involving local authority representatives in the development of county tourism. However, it seems an unnecessary further layer of bureaucracy which could lead to more duplication of effort and waste of resources as well as pressure to fund more and more small scale projects with each county and area unit demanding its 'quota'. It was precisely this problem that was criticized in the evaluation report of the first OP for tourism by the ESRI (1993). The success of the LEADER I initiative may have been a factor in the new emphasis on local development but voluntary community effort on a spontaneous and selective basis is hardly a rationale for a formal statutory institutional measure throughout the country. The RTOs themselves may be partly to blame for their lack of influence on the emerging structures. Caught between their responsibility to Bord Failte (although their funding base suggests they should have far more autonomy), and their local client base, which may have considered they were not appropriately serviced, as well as being undermined by the new initiatives such as LEADER and the County Enterprise Partnership Boards, the RTOs have failed to assert their unique contribution to the development of Irish tourism. They do not have a place on the National Tourism Council (except through the Bord Failte representation) and have been relegated to an advisory role in the evaluation of projects under the second OP for Tourism.

The question of scale is an important one in Irish tourism[46] and one which can only be overcome if a sufficient number of key projects or tourism centres are effectively developed. The fragmentation in regional organizational structures, roles and spheres of influence suggest an opportunity for coherence and effectiveness in developing tourism at an appropriate scale is being lost.

NOTES

1. The successes and limitations of rural tourism initiatives are discussed in Keane and Quinn (1990), Quinn and Keane (1991) and in Kearney *et al.* (1994).
2. These have expanded in recent years particularly stimulated by the EU's LEADER I programme focused on rural development and, more recently, the County Enterprise Boards. The operation and impact of the LEADER I programme is discussed later in this chapter. The County Enterprise Boards were established in 1993 in each county and county borough to assist start-up enterprises through the provision of small loans and grants for seed capital and related purposes.

3. These changes made it difficult to analyse continuous series of data from 1981 to the present though, where possible, the entire period's data were expressed in terms of the 'old' regions particularly in estimating regional tourism income and employment proportions.

4. This (and the West) were the two regions which did not change county boundaries in the re-classification of regions in 1989 and this more recent growth rate of 9.9 per cent may be compared directly with the 5.5 per cent average from 1981 to 1988.

5. The average of the squared deviations fell from 4.1 in 1991 to 2.0 in 1994 confirming significant convergence; the more rigorous test of the ratios of variance gave a measure of 2.03 (1991 vs 1994) which is significant at the 10% level (using the F-ratio test).

6. Reference was made above to the difficulties with the estimates for domestic tourism and hence the volatility which the data throw up can be large; for example, Dublin experienced a decline from 16 to 7 per cent of total domestic tourism revenues from 1981 to 1988 for which there is no obvious explanation.

7. The gains in domestic tourism revenues seem inordinately high over this period but the reasons for this may be methodological rather than real.

8. There is a serious lack of research in Ireland on changing international demand trends for inbound tourists and a certain naiveté in attributing causation to the trends observed; filling this information gap is an essential requirement to develop any realistic strategies to support tourism as part of regional development.

9. Overseas tourism revenues for each county (or part county) were used to estimate regional revenues based on the 'old' regional classifications in 1989 and 1992. The 'old' regions were used for the regional income and employment estimates because it was possible to make some reasonable estimates of the regional incomes and employment drawing on earlier studies (e.g. NESC, 1980a) on personal incomes by county and on the Labour Force Survey data presented for the so-called planning regions. Planning regions are co-terminus with the 'old' tourism regions with the exception of the North-east, which does not exist as a separate planning region. NI and domestic tourism regional revenues were estimated on the basis of the 1988 distributions in the 'old' regions. Foreign and domestic multipliers were applied (from Table 4.8).

10. The study by Deegan and Dineen (1992) on the microeconomic effects of tourism projects showed substantial outflows beyond the immediate region in the indirect spending emanating from the projects. However there are no systematic data on the extent to which these leakages occur. A similar point applies to the regional distribution of tourism-dependent employment which is analysed later in this chapter.

11. We follow the approach used by Tansey Webster and Associates (1991) here to derive estimates of the 1989 and 1992 regional incomes. He drew on Ross' unpublished work for 1984 and we also assumed the same proportions of regional income distributions existed in 1989 and 1992 as in 1984. The North-east region is divided in two with counties Cavan and Monaghan included with the Midlands region and county Louth included with the East region. The North-east regional income estimate is split in direct proportion to the countys' share of 1991 regional population and allocated accordingly to the two adjoining regions.

12. We are indebted to both Brian Deane and Eamonn Henry for access to the methodology used for their estimates of total tourism employment, 1989–1993 (Deane and Henry, 1993); this was used to make retrospective estimates for the years

1981–1988 and prospective estimates for 1994. The proportionate method simply distributes regional employment in tourism in proportion to regional tourism revenues.

13. See Table A3 in the Appendix for the data on which Figure 5.7 is based.

14. Breathnach (1992) noted this and argued for a more balanced form of development. The poor image of the industry among those making career choices has been highlighted in a recent report conducted by the National Centre for Tourism Policy Studies, University of Limerick, for CERT (1996).

15. Ireland was classified as a single Objective 1 region, in common with Portugal and Greece, for purposes of Structural Fund transfers under the European Regional Development Fund (ERDF). These Objective 1 regions were defined generally as having GDP per capita below 75 per cent of the EU average and higher than average unemployment rates.

16. The Government (of Ireland) first submits its strategy to develop the economy using EU and national Exchequer resources and indicates the contributions from the private sector; this is presented in the form of a national development plan (see Stationery Office, 1989, 1993) to the EU Commission which then develops a Community Support Framework. The latter forms the basis of an agreement between the Commission and the national Government on the transfers to be executed for the duration of the programme. It is on the basis of the CSF that the sectoral operational programmes are then drawn up indicating the mix of programmes and the delivery mechanisms to be employed to meet the objectives set out in the framework document.

17. The principle of subsidiarity has asserted itself more effectively in the discussions leading up to the second CSF in the light of the political climate in some countries (e.g. Denmark) which considered the EU Commission had meddled too much in national affairs; thus concessions to a sub-regional dimension were made only at the behest of the national Government.

18. It should be noted that the Tourism OPs accounted for a mere 3.5 per cent of the total expenditures (actual or planned) under the CSFs so that on its own it would have a limited impact on overall regional income distribution.

19. The report on the west of Ireland by Euradvice Ltd (1994) placed important emphasis on tourism as part of the strategy for survival of the West region; unfortunately, as so often happens in reports of this nature, it primarily took a supply-side approach to tourism development and assumed there would be little problem in attracting tourists once the investments were undertaken. There is far too little attention in Ireland focused on the changing trends on the demand side of the international tourist market as the starting point for tourism investment in the regions and at local level. The poor performance of the western relative to the eastern regions in tourism revenue growth since 1989 highlights the danger of complacency in monitoring international tourist trends and the need to develop strategies to capitalize on them.

20. See CEC (1988b, 1990); LEADER is an initiative of the EU Commission to assist rural communities adjust to changes in the CAP and prepare for a future in which a lesser proportion of rural income will derive from agriculture. LEADER stands for Liaison entre action de Developpement de l'Economie Rurale (links between actions for the development of the rural economy).

21. For example, in Ballyhoura, Co. Limerick which is discussed in Keane and Quinn (1990) and in Feehan (1992).

22. This was required to qualify for grants from Bord Failte and to become officially registered; of course, there has been a thriving unregistered tourist accommodation business in rural Ireland for many years. Though this was a source of aggravation for their registered competitors and Bord Failte, which sought to improve and monitor standards in the sector, the unregistered sector has had an important role to play in years of excess demand through enlargement of the available capacity. There is little evidence to suggest the quality of the unregistered accommodation is inferior though many pay less in taxes which causes resentment.

23. See Kearney *et al.* (1994) for an evaluation of the LEADER I programme; the main commentary above on the impact of LEADER I derives mainly from this report.

24. Over 80 per cent of those involved in funded tourism projects under LEADER I had no previous experience of the sector.

25. These concepts are identical to those used above in analysing regional employment impacts; they are employed in the present analysis at the microeconomic level of the tourist enterprise and its impact at the local level and further afield.

26. For details of the context and methodology used and the initial results of the analysis conducted, see Deegan and Dineen (1992). This section draws on the latter for much of its structure while updating the results of the original 1990 study and developing some of the conclusions.

27. This ignores diversion from spending in other countries, which represents either import substitution or additional export earnings (in the case of foreign tourists).

28. While full-time equivalent (FTE) employment numbers are estimated, distinctions are not made between the quality of different forms of employment arising either at the facilities themselves or in the supply chain firms or other tourism service firms in the country. This is a deficiency which could be rectified only in a more detailed study.

29. The approach used in the study is not dissimilar to that used by Johnson and Thomas (1992) in their study of the Beamish Museum in north-east England; in this book they report on many of the technical aspects encountered in their analysis while our summary in the text focuses primarily on the results.

30. Detailed in Deegan and Dineen (1992: 145).

31. In this update of the original study the Census of Industrial Production, 1989, (CSO, 1992) was used for gross output to employment ratios in the five key sectors from which purchases were made – food and drink, clothing, paper and printing, crafts and miscellaneous. The Census of Distribution, 1988 (CSO 1991) was used to provide estimates of employment in the wholesale and retail sectors. Estimating other services' employment is more problematical since detailed establishment level data are not published; recourse was made to the data from the annual Labour Force Survey and National Income and Expenditure publications by the CSO to provide estimates; recourse was also made to the continuing work of Henry (1990–1 and 1993b) on updating input–output models of the Irish economy and to measure the impact of tourism, including some private communications with Henry. The result was that many of the original estimates of the employment effects of services' inputs were revised for this publication.

32. For details of the sources used in deriving these calculations and how some of the methodological problems were overcome, see Deegan and Dineen (1992: 148).

33. There is little work done to establish the spatial distribution of indirect employment arising from tourism; these microeconomic studies merely point to the fact that it would be naive to conclude that the regional distribution of the indirect employment

from core tourism activities is necessarily located in the same areas. This does not mean that the expansion of tourism in other regions would not benefit a specific region though the extent to which it might would relate to the structure of local industry and how geared it might be to the needs of tourists.

34. In this analysis domestic holidays which are substituted for foreign holidays represent a form of import substitution and thus do not lead to displaced employment either locally or nationally. The substitution effects and the proportion of expenditure involved are not quantifiable without direct survey evidence. The above analysis also assumes that the employment intensity of sales in the diverted activity is the same as at the tourist facility leading to an equivalent amount of employment displaced. See Johnson and Thomas (1992: Chapter 4) for a fuller discussion.

35. Johnson and Thomas (1992) found that the displacement effects were much greater in their reference area of north-east England reducing the net impact of the Beamish Museum to only 34 per cent of the direct employment arising at the facility itself.

36. These micro-level results are significantly below the economy wide results reported in Chapter 4 above which indicated that employment from indirect and induced tourism expenditures was almost as large as the direct employment generated in the sector (except for 1989 when the reported figure was 58 jobs for every 100 direct jobs). These values refer to the impact of foreign tourist expenditures, ignoring carrier receipts and domestic tourist expenditures, while the microeconomic results presented in this section ignore only carrier receipts.

37. Further surveys are needed to test some of the hypotheses suggested by the commentary, e.g. what factors influence visitors' decisions to visit an area?, is there an optimum size of tourist area beyond which capacity constraints will generate negative tourism externalities?, to what extent do residents substitute domestic for foreign holidays?

38. This role is still important under the new Operational Programme, 1994–1999, though less so because the final decisions on project support are made by two independent management boards appointed by Government rather than by Bord Failte or Shannon Development as previously, when the RTOs did initial screening of applications for the 'Bord'.

39. A regional tourism consultative forum was set up in the Mid-west but it has no more than an advisory role. An internal Shannon Development review of its operation revealed serious doubts, among industry representatives and tourism operators, about the relevance of the forum to their needs.

40. Indeed this more commercial approach to the development of Irish tourism was also signalled in the recent Arthur D. Little Ltd (1994) review of Bord Failte where the consultants indicated the need for less 'hand-holding' of the maturing industry by the Government and a greater role for the industry itself in shaping and developing its future expansion.

41. A point emphasized by Arthur D. Little Ltd (1994) in advising on a less decisive role for Bord Failte, and by extension the RTOs, in the grant allocation process for the second OP for tourism, 1994–1999.

42. From Government press release, 1 October 1992.

43. Government press release, 1993 (precise date unknown).

44. There is limited focus in this chapter on supply side aspects of regional tourism. For a comprehensive if slightly dated summary of these see O'Cinneide and Walsh (1990–1991). More recently, some unpublished studies on the regional distribution

of accommodation supply highlights the continued investment in some western regions at levels not supported by the shifting real revenue bias towards the eastern part of the country; this may ultimately cause over-capacity problems unless there is a closer focus on changing demand trends.

45. Here we have ignored the potentially negative social, cultural or even moral factors which tourism development can bring to host communities. See O'Cinneide (1992) for a perspective on the likely negative impacts of tourism development on Gaeltacht communities and Crick (1989) for an international perspective on tourism development in less-developed countries. On a more positive note, Keane *et al.* (1992) examine some of the organizational and business structures required to ensure host communities can reap optimum benefit from tourism development; they developed their conclusions from a case study of island tourism development.

46. A study of innovations in Irish tourism found that many of the smaller operators had a poor record in innovation (Shannon Development, 1990); innovative ideas and the implementation of same were far more common among the larger hotels and tourist businesses. Innovation in the Irish tourism sector will be critical to the maintenance of market share in the medium term; however, the development of organizational structures at a county level will militate against the development of projects at an appropriate scale.

6 Tourism and the environment

INTRODUCTION

The emergence of environmental issues to the mainstream public policy debate is among the most notable developments of the past 25 years in the developed market economies. Concern for the environment is no longer considered the province of a small number associated with the 'alternative movement' of the 1970s but rather an issue of importance to the average voter.[1] The expression of this interest in the environment is to be found in the electoral success of green candidates and parties in Europe and elsewhere across the world. There is a growing view that economic development strategies may need to be rethought and perhaps substantially revised if further degradation of the global environment is to be averted. Particular concern relates to global warming and economic activities that contribute to deforestation and increased consumption of fossil fuels. International expression of concern related to these issues is to be found in the Brundtland report (World Commission on Environment and Development, 1987) and most recently in the United Nations Conference on Environment and Development (Halpern, 1993) The UNCED conference reflected the status which the environment now receives in that it was the largest gathering of world leaders for a global summit on any issue. The UNCED also reflected a sense of seeing the planet, perhaps for the first time, as a single environment. While the number of delegates at the UNCED made decision-making virtually impossible there was at least general agreement on the broad concept of 'sustainability' which had previously been proposed by Brundtland. Briefly this means 'to ensure the needs of the present without compromising the ability of future generations to meet their own needs' (World Commission on Environment and Development, 1987: 43). Understandably, this concept has received broad-based support, unlike many other environmental issues. There are perhaps two main reasons for this. First, as Solow[2] has remarked 'The less you know about it the better it sounds and secondly it is generally regarded as a near impossible concept to be against'. There is also some truth in the criticism 'that it has come to mean whatever suits the particular advocacy of the individual concerned' (Pearce *et al.*, 1989).

It is the difficulty in operationalizing the concept of 'Sustainability' that now lies at the core of the environmental debate. While it may yet prove difficult for policy-makers to operationalize the concept the plethora of environmental legislation over the last 20 years suggests that a generalized view of pessimism is also inappropriate. During the last 20 years there has been a mushrooming of pollution control laws, regulations, environmental bureaucracies and public and private spending on environmental protection. Evaluation of the state of the environment by the OECD (1990) indicates that this evolution has had some successes and some failures, with modest progress overall. The inclusion of the concept of 'Sustainability' in the Maastricht Treaty and the Community's Fifth Environment Action Programme[3] in tandem with Community directives on the environment ensures that at the very least the environment will continue to play a major role in international debate. Of increasing importance to the debate will be the advocacy of market mechanisms to tackle environmental impacts. Market mechanisms, which include incentives, penalties, tradeable rights and environmental taxes are increasingly being heralded as elements of a strategy to deliver 'Sustainable Development' and will provide the focus of great debate in the years ahead.

Tourism, perhaps more than most other economic activities relies heavily on a good quality environment to deliver a product which the consumer desires. The activity of tourism also possesses the innate capability to either protect the environment or alternatively to destroy the major asset on which it is based. This chapter will address the evolving relationship between tourism and the environment and will evaluate to what extent the development of tourism in Ireland has been in sympathy with evolving international norms.

THE TOURISM ENVIRONMENT NEXUS

The growth of international tourism in the post-war years was generally welcomed as a good contributor to foreign exchange earnings, employment and the balance of payments. The preoccupation in the industrialized world with 'rebuilding' and the dearth of awareness of environmental issues ensured that the growth of tourism went unhindered. As recent as the early 1980s the general perception of tourism was that of a 'smokeless' industry.[4] The major exception to this generalized viewpoint had come from economists and sociologists in developing countries. Having expressed their general dissatisfaction with the dependent relationship that existed between developed and developing countries in mainstream economic activities these writers turned attention to tourism in the 1980s. Outrage at the damage which conventional tourism inflicts on nature is captured in the following quote from Hong:

> Having ruined their own environment, having either used or destroyed all that is natural, people from the advanced consumer societies are compelled to look for natural wildlife, cleaner air, lush greenery and golden beaches elsewhere. In other words, they look for other environments to consume. Thus armed with their bags, tourists proceed to consume the environment in the countries of the Third World – that unspoiled corner of the earth. (Hong, 1985: 12)

While this view may seem rather extreme it is evident that the current re-appraisal of the relationship between tourism and the environment is less likely to be swayed by the simple arguments of employment and foreign exchange earnings that were so prevalent heretofore. In this regard a recent quote from the President of the World Tourism and Travel Council sums up the current situation rather well:

> As the world's largest industry, Travel and Tourism is an essential component of international trade, a major contributor to economic growth, and an integral part of life in developed and developing countries. At the same time, moving, housing, feeding and entertaining hundreds of millions of people every year has an evident environmental impact. Either we add to global problems or we adopt our practises and become part of the international solution. In reality there is no choice-we must strive for continuing environmental improvement. (Lipman, 1993: 1)

The general thrust of the foregoing suggests that the tourism industry has both the potential to contribute to environmental improvement or alternatively to destroy the asset on which tourism is built. As the world's largest industry tourism and travel is in a unique position to spread the environmental message and the means to influence the products and services provided by its suppliers. It can also contribute to the preservation of cultural and historical sites that otherwise may deteriorate in the absence of tourism development. Importantly, it can also contribute to the preservation of areas threatened with depopulation and the loss of social mores. Alternatively tourism can be developed in such a manner that can have deleterious effects on both the physical and social environment. Evidence can be quoted to substantiate either argument. The next section evaluates why the environment and tourism in particular may be subject to particular damage and identifies appropriate action that must be undertaken to avoid same.

PUBLIC GOODS AND EXTERNALITIES

The growth of the public sector in most economies across the world has emerged as a major issue of public policy debate over the last 15 years. The government share of gross domestic product (GDP) had reached 60 per cent in some countries by the late 1970s and led to a substantive re-appraisal of the role of government (Tanzi, 1986). The electoral success of governments with free-market laissez-faire policies in the UK, France and the United States at the end of the 1970s provided clear evidence of a de-scaling of government involvement in economic activity. The subsequent embrace of policies of privatization and a market-oriented approach to economic development by international agencies such as the World Bank and the International Monetary Fund has provided clear evidence of a new approach to the role of government in a market economy. While the untrammelled operation of the market has been severely criticized by proponents of government intervention it does appear as though there is now general acceptance that government intervention had become burdensome in many economies towards the end of the 1970s. In this context attention has now focused on the most appropriate areas for government intervention. Apart from policy measures designed specifically to improve the workings of the market economy, to increase competitive pressures, it is widely accepted that government intervention is justifiable in conventional economic terms in the area of 'Public Goods and Externalities.' These cases are generally specified in the literature as 'Market Failures' and it is accepted that in these situations it is appropriate for government to intervene.

Public goods

The workings of the market for private goods ensures that once the market equilibrium price has been established the goods are effectively rationed to those (some but not all) who can afford to pay the prevailing price. It must be understood that the equilibrium is simply an 'equilibrium' and there is no reason to believe that this outcome will bring forth a great outpouring of public enthusiasm. This is understandable as the equilibrium price has effectively excluded people attaining the good who would have wished to receive it at a lower price. The property of 'rivalness in consumption' also ensures that not all consumers who can afford to pay the price receive the good. Pure public goods as originally defined contrast greatly with private goods in that they possess the characteristics of 'non-excludabilty' and 'non-rivalry in consumption' (Samuelson, 1954). The property of non-rivalry ensures that provision of the good for individual A ensures provision for individual B. Similarly, the property of non-excludability ensures that we cannot exclude consumer B from enjoying the benefits of the public good, consequently there is no incentive for individual B to contribute to the costs of providing the public good. In this circumstance the combination of non-rivalry and non-excludability can lead to sub-optimal provision of public goods.

While the original example of a public good found expression in the classic example of a lighthouse signal, it does appear that there are relatively few examples of pure public goods. A more common typology relates to goods which are non-excludable but rival in consumption. In other words, rivalness in consumption separates what are now commonly called public goods from pure public goods. It is public goods of this category that have the greatest application in terms of the environment and more particularly tourism. Before the application is considered it is appropriate to deal with the issue of 'externalities'.

Externalities

There are many cases where the actions of one individual or one firm affect other individuals or firms. Instances where one individual's actions impose a cost on others are referred to as negative externalities. A simple example would include a factory churning out smoke that affects air quality. It must also be stressed that not all externalities are negative. There are some important examples of positive externalities, where one individual's actions confer a benefit on others. If one individual creates a beautiful flower garden in front of her house, her neighbours may benefit from being able to look at it. Whenever externalities exist the resource allocation provided by the market may not be efficient. Since individuals do not bear the full cost of the negative externalities they generate, they will engage in an excessive amount of such activities; conversely, since individuals do not enjoy the full benefits of activities generating positive externalities they will engage in too little of these. Thus, for example, there is widespread belief that without government intervention of some kind the level of pollution will be too high. To put it another way, pollution control provides a positive externality, so without government intervention there would be an under provision of pollution control.[5]

Approaches to solving problems associated with public goods and externalities

Governments respond to the problems of public goods and externalities in several different ways. In some cases (mainly involving negative externalities) they attempt to regulate the activity in question; thus the government imposes pollution standards for cars and imposes regulations for air and water pollution by firms. More recently, the mechanisms of the market have found favour as a means to tackle problems related to public goods and externalities. Market mechanisms, which include incentives, tradeable permits and environmental taxes have the attraction of contributing to government revenues while ensuring that industry internalizes the costs of environmental damage. Traditionally, most economists have favoured the use of fines as a way of remedying the inefficiencies associated with negative externalities. The basic principle involved is the imposition of fines (charges) for controlling externalities is simple: in general, whenever there is an externality there is a difference between the social cost and the private benefit. A properly calculated fine presents the individual or firm with the true social costs (and benefits) of their action.

While the movement to accept market-based solutions has gained significant momentum, there remains resistance to this approach. Those against the market-based approach are strong adherents of regulation, even though it may be less efficient, it is seen as being definitive. Others prefer a voluntary approach to these issues even though the weight of evidence suggest that this approach has not proved successful. The next section of this chapter will evaluate the evidence of the relationship between tourism and the environment and the extent to which the issues of public goods and externalities arise. It will also focus on what attempts have been made to tackle the emerging environmental concerns related to tourism development.

DEVELOPMENTS WITHIN TOURISM

The surge of interest in environmental issues in recent years has led to a critical assessment of the role which tourism plays in the international economy. No longer is the simple message of foreign exchange earnings and employment adequate to convince people of the appropriateness of tourism development. Whilst it is accepted that tourism can have a positive influence on environmental outcomes there is also significant evidence of severe problems associated with certain types of tourism development. One of the main problems relates to the sheer increase in volume of numbers increasing from 60 million international travellers in 1960 to over 450 million in 1991. Forecasts from the World Tourism Organization (WTO) suggests a growth rate of 4–5 per cent per annum over the 1990s and a growth rate of 3–4 per cent per annum between 2000 and 2010 (WTO, 1991). Growth of this magnitude has and will continue to have environmental repercussions and requires significant monitoring and the use of the best available management tools to avoid significant deleterious effects.

From the Lake District in England to the Acropolis in Athens, from the Kenyan game parks to Bhutan, tourism has taken its toll. The result has been pollution, danger to wildlife, deforestation, strains on local resources, damage to historical monuments and deleterious effects on local culture. The Parthenon is reported to have been eroded more in the last 25 years than in the previous 2500. Examples abound of inappropriate developments in Spain, Turkey and in many less-developed countries throughout the world. Even though attempts have been made to prevent the environmental damage, the lure of tourism revenue for many poor and underdeveloped countries has, not surprisingly, proved irresistible.

The reason why much of the development has resulted in undesirable outcomes relates to the existence of public goods and externalities in tourism. A region whose comparative advantage depends on outstanding natural beauty may attract too many tourists, leading to congestion, overcrowding, pollution and the destruction of the environment which formed the basis for the area's competitiveness. Similarly, this can occur and has occurred with ancient build-ings, footpaths, cliffs and waterways. Where property rights are well defined the private markets can easily solve such problems by charging a price, thus excluding those unwilling to pay and using some of the income to maintain the asset. The destruction of natural resources and the pollution of the environment have proceeded apace because those responsible do not bear the costs directly. This is because substantial parts of the tourism market are based on common property such as scenery, coastlines and mountains. The traditional view of pure public goods possessing the characteristics of non-excludability and non-rivalness suggests that beautiful views are available to all and one person's consumption of a view does not spoil that of another. In other words, parts of the tourist market are characterized by property rights which are ill-defined, unenforceable or not worth policing and enforcing. While there is obviously certain merit in this view it is increasingly obvious that the tourism market pertains to many situations where there is the existence of non-excludability but rivalness in consumption. This line of argument suggests that when many people congregate at some point to observe some beautiful landscape that this can actually detract from the enjoyment. The following passage from McNutt and Rodriguez aptly demonstrates the implication of moving from non-rivalness to rivalness in consumption:

> The public good in this typology is characterised as non-excludable and rival. In other words rivalness in consumption is the distinguishing feature between a public good and a pure public good. The good could be described as a common good in the absence of any rival behaviour between citizens; some examples include air quality, frontier land and outer space. Rivalous behaviour, however, converts the common good into a public good as [say] frontier land is zoned, air quality control becomes necessary and space stations are constructed. Once property rights are established the good eventually becomes an excludable and rival private good. (McNutt and Rodriguez, 1993)

The authors go on to give an example of a congested bridge (a rival and non-excludable good) where the problem is resolved by the imposition of a toll, suggesting that the good becomes a rival and exclusive private good. The application of this analysis to tourism development is deemed particularly pertinent. An analogy could be drawn as to the different stages that a country will pass through in terms of its tourism development, from collective good to overcrowding at a particular stage to another stage where the government may decide to exclude particular tourists and restrict certain tourist-related activities. An element in this approach may be the strategic targeting of tourists who exhibit evidence of being 'price inelastic' and 'income elastic'.

Appraisal of progress

The 1994 report of the World Travel and Tourism Environment Research Centre (WTTERC) has aptly described the challenges which the industry faces and the progress that has been made to date. The report begins by stating 'the key challenge for the Travel and Tourism industry is to ensure that the way travellers are moved, accommodated, fed and entertained is compatible with and, if possible enhances the environment' (WTTERC, 1994). The review shows that a number of companies have already started to examine the impacts of their operations on the environment and established how improvements can be made but warns that the industry is unlikely to become truly sustainable until environmental issues are incorporated into the decision-making process of every travel and tourism company and until every corporate leader becomes committed to sound environmental management. The review goes on to suggest that 'this is not as unrealistic as it may seem at first; more and more companies are recognizing that good environmental practice is usually good business practice, bringing prosperity to the company, to the destination and the environment' (WTTERC, 1994a). Internationally, the arguments in favour of using market instruments for environmental protection are extensive and impressive but are primarily confined to the academic literature. In one sense the debate has become polarized between those who favour the market and those who prefer regulation. This is not helpful as the two approaches should not be seen as mutually exclusive. The possibility of success with market-based solutions is influenced to a great deal by a regulatory environment that permit activities to occur without prescribing that they must.

Market mechanisms for natural resource management first became popular in New Zealand when applied to fisheries management in 1983. A total allowable catch was set and within that a system of individual transferable quotas – a tradeable property right – was established. As Plimmer remarks 'this was useful in establishing the proposition that economic instruments do not necessarily replace regulation. Rather, they can permit a regulated intent to be achieved in a flexible, effective, and incentive based manner'(Plimmer, 1994).

The preliminary success with a market-based approach in New Zealand led to the 'New Resource Management Act in 1991'. This Act focused on the effects of activities on the sustainable management of resources rather than on controlling the activities themselves. The Act requires planners and managers of natural and physical resources to consider a wide range of means for achieving their sustainable goals. It specifically permits economic instruments. Already, there have been a number of examples where this novel approach has been applied to tourism. While it is too early to give a considered view, the early indications suggest that this market based approach may offer some very interesting and useful mechanisms to tackle problems related to tourism and the environment. Some examples will be considered to provide a useful insight.

Examples of market mechanisms in action

Tradeable rights in travel and tourism

Plimmer reports that the clearest application of economic instruments to travel and tourism in New Zealand's natural areas is in tradeable rights. Concessions to operate – a form of property right – in national parks and other conservation areas may be approved on a tradeable basis. This means that recipients, if ready to move on, can sell their permit for the best price on the open market. The incentive element in this is clear; the operator has the maximum incentive to improve the facility, reinvest and maintain the surrounding environment in pristine condition in order to achieve the optimum return at sale time.

The case of The Waitomo Glow-worms caves provides a good example of market incentives in action. Carbon dioxide (CO_2) from the breathing of human visitors was threatening the glow worms and consequently severe restrictions on the numbers of visitors appeared desirable. However, instead of prescribing maximum numbers of visitors per day, as a classic regulatory approach would suggest, the permit fixed an acceptable CO_2 level for the air within the caves. This gives the permit-holder a financial incentive to engage in wise management of the resource. By scheduling tours carefully, spreading route patterns throughout the caves, closing off parts of the caves for different times of the day, and other techniques, the operator can increase the number of visits, i.e. increase revenue and still maintain acceptable air quality. As Plimmer observes 'This approach does not abandon regulation but replaces 'command and control' with a flexible technique backed by a market incentive. All the parties involved benefit: the caves and the glow-worms are protected, the visitors 'experience is enhanced, and the operators business flourishes' (Plimmer, 1994).

Economic instruments for visitor management.

In national parks and related areas, price differentials have been introduced for hiking tracks. As well as reflecting variations in standards of accommodation, these encourage a better regional dispersal of visitors by the higher pricing of popular attractions and a better seasonal spread by heavy discounting of fees in the low season. The increased use of such market instruments can provide an alternative to the threat of rationing related to popular attractions

SUMMARY REVIEW OF PROGRESS AND PERFORMANCE

This section of the chapter has reviewed the evolving relationship between tourism and the environment. It has demonstrated that the arrival of the environment to the top of the political agenda will subject tourism to a much greater degree of scrutiny than heretofore. While the industry can claim, with reasonable justification, that it contributes to the environment the sheer numbers of tourists now requires a positive response from the industry if environmental degradation is to be avoided. While the use of environmental instruments is well rehearsed in the academic literature it needs to be distilled to the general populace in a more user-friendly fashion. Early adoption of market-based approaches in New Zealand seems to offer some scope for optimism. Results appear to suggest that people respond well to incentives. However, the extension of market solutions, in New Zealand and in other countries, is likely to progress steadily and with caution. The merit of flexibility is often more readily accepted by the operator as being good for business than by the environmentalist as being good for conservation; many groups will need to be satisfied that the new techniques are superior to existing or potential regulation.[6] Increased knowledge and adoption of market mechanisms should contribute to a lively debate in the years ahead. The remainder of this chapter will evaluate the evolving relationship between the environment and tourism in Ireland and will *inter alia* comment upon any new approaches adopted to tackle emerging problems.

ENVIRONMENTAL POLICY FOR IRELAND

International evidence suggests that concern for the environment is often directly related to the stage of economic development and industrialization which a country has experienced. Among Europeans, the running has been made by the West Germans and the Dutch.[7] As McDonald remarks 'They, after all, had seen the future and realised that it didn't quite work out as well as expected. Progress in the sense of unrestrained economic growth, also meant pollution and environmental degradation and the more a country was industrialised, it seemed the greater it developed a constituency for environmentalism' (McDonald 1990). In this context, the rather late embrace of the environment as an issue of serious concern in Ireland is understandable. Ireland is generally perceived to be a latecomer to the process of industrialization and therefore has not been subject (at least until recently) to the strains imposed on the environment by industrialization. Until very recently, sustained public concern for the environment was confined to a small minority. Regularly, in surveys of EU Member States, Ireland came out at the bottom of the league on environmental awareness. Those involved in the environmental movement were usually dismissed as cranks and malcontents.

Over the last four to five years this situation has changed quite considerably. Recent changes in population distribution, increased urbanization, rapidly changing land use policies and increased industrialization have all contributed to a greater awareness and concern for environmental issues. In terms of concrete action the most important catalyst has been the necessity to comply with directives on the environment emanating from Brussels. The following section will address the evolution of environmental policy in Ireland and will *inter alia* discuss the implementation of European Union directives on the Environment.

Evolution of policy on the environment

While sporadic interest in the environment is to be found in academic literature from the 1960s it is only since the 1980s that a concerted environmental movement is discernible in Ireland. In a review article on 'The physical environment' published in 1982, Convery concluded that it was 'difficult to judge the overall trends in environmental quality *vis-à-vis* water, air, wildlife, wetlands, and our structural endowment and natural areas. This partly reflects difficulties inherent in measurement but it also reflects the absence of a systematic data gathering and publishing capability, although there are a number of agencies involved in some aspects'. While Convery accepted that an impressive array of legislation had been enacted in relation to planning, water pollution control and the preservation of wildlife he felt the system was not achieving the success that might be expected. The system was too heavily dependent on the threat of legal sanctions to encourage compliance with regulations. Convery suggested 'This is the Achilles heel of the Irish environmental management system. Our post-colonial cultural and social traditions and attitudes mean that the enforcement process is not seen to have the legitimacy and popular sanction which such a system enjoys in most other North European countries. This has an adverse effect on the thoroughness and enthusiasm applied by enforcers to their task and diminishes the social opprobrium with which breaking the law is associated' (Convery, 1982). A similar view is suggested by McDonald 'We are a wild and untameable people. There is no consensus here on the need for rules and regulations of any kind about almost anything. That is why it is so hard to sustain a planning system ... Rabid individualism rules the day'. He goes on 'This is the main reason why the countryside is littered with bungalows and those who do not get permission by hook, through the normal planning process, can get it by crook through their friendly local councillor by tabling a section 4 motion. We excuse it all by saying that it is at least partly due to our post-colonial mentality – but that excuse is wearing a bit thin after nearly 70 years' (McDonald, 1990).

The first serious attempt by government to address the emerging concern for the environment is to be found in the 'State of the Environment Report' published in 1985. The report had been commissioned by the Minister for the Environment in 1982 and was the first national report which attempted to document how the process of economic development had impacted on the environment. While the report was extremely important in focusing attention on the environment it was inconclusive in many areas due to the dearth of appropriate information. The report specifically recommended 'a need for periodic reports so that progress on implementation of environmental policy can be measured. Such reports would make people more aware of the importance of the environment in the overall quality of life, of the needs of the environment, and of the actions that are being taken to ensure that total quality is preserved and improved' (State of the Environment Report published in An Foras Forbatha, 1985).

Throughout the 1980s a number of international incidents contributed to increased attention on environmental issues. The Chernobyl and Bhopal disasters along with major incidents of oil spillage such as the Betelegeuse received mass media coverage. Electoral success of green candidates internationally suggested the environment had finally arrived as an issue of major importance. The Irish general election of 1989 reflected this international concern for the environment with the election of the first green candidate to the Irish Parliament.[8] The Programme of Government agreed by the coalition parties in July 1989, reflected the general movement to environmental awareness in the country. In particular, the Programme stated 'A new office for the protection and improvement of the environment on a similar basis to the existing offices for Trade and Marketing, Science and Technology, Horticulture and Food will be established under a Minister of State' (Programme for Government, 1989). In subsequent months the environment was to receive significant attention due to vigorous work undertaken by the new Minister and Junior Minister responsible for the environment. In addition, the Irish Presidency of the Community in the first six months of 1990 stressed environmental issues as being paramount to the future development of EC policy. The further greening of the Irish government is to be found in the establishment of an environmental information organization (ENFO) in September of the same year. ENFO is funded through the Department of the Environment and is responsible for disseminating information on the environment to the Irish public. A considered review of events would suggest that 1990 was the first year in which environmental concerns rose to the top of the political agenda in Ireland. The following section will evaluate to what extent the rhetoric has been translated into practice.

The influence of European Union directives on the environment

Ireland became a member of the European Community in 1973 and as a result has been subject to European legislation on the environment since that date. Many of those involved with environmental issues in Ireland would argue that European legislation has been far more influential in determining positive action on the environment than any initiative of the Irish Government. While generally accepting this proposition, there are some who argue that EC directives also have the added problem of standardization to the level of the lowest common denominator (McDonald, 1990). Notwithstanding this point, there is general acceptance that directives emanating from Brussels have proved to be a powerful instrument in persuading the government to take action on the environmental front because they are a yardstick against which things can be measured.

EU legislation on the environment is mostly in the form of directives – this means that the EU outlines, often in quite specific terms, the objectives to be achieved but leaves it to the individual member state to legislate itself as to how it will achieve those objectives. In Ireland, environmental protection functions have typically been distributed across several statutory bodies. The Department of the Environment (DOE) has overall responsibility for drafting and implementing environmental policy but is increasingly devolving responsibilities to the newly formed Environmental Protection Agency (EPA). The EPA, first proposed in 1990, was subject to substantive debate in the Irish Parliament and was finally established in July of 1993. Under the aegis of the EPA, integrated pollution control (IPC) licences are to be issued to most categories of polluting industry and the agency is currently undertaking a State of the Environment Report which will be published in late 1995. Responsibility for wildlife and landscape conservation is undertaken by a branch of the Office of Public Works (OPW) while development control, strategic planning and some aspects of pollution control are local government responsibilities. As the EPA becomes better established it is expected that it will play a major role in integrating many of the processes currently operated individually by these agencies. To date the EPA has not involved itself in tourism issues.

Progress on implementation

In recent years there has been significant progress in introducing new legislation related to the environment. Unfortunately, implementation has not been so successful. A review of implementation of the European Union's Fifth Action and Policy Programme 1993 undertaken by Convery suggests that progress has been slow. Only in the area of smoke emissions in Dublin has significant progress been made. In other areas Convery reports that the generalized situation is as follows 'Objectives have been set, the most cost effective mechanisms for achieving same have been identified, but the financial resources and political will to take effective action have yet to be mobilised. Generally, no implementation has been tried' (Convery, 1994). In general, while some progress has been made there appears considerable scope for future action. While the new Programme for Government agreed in December 1994 devotes substantial attention to the environment it remains to be seen whether this will translate to positive action.

TOURISM AND THE ENVIRONMENT

The previous sections of this chapter have outlined that the embrace of environmental issues is a relatively new phenomenon in Ireland. Tourism, however, does provide an example of a sector where, at least in theory, the environment has always received particular attention. Numerous statements by industry interests and government agencies continually refer to the environment as being of fundamental importance to the success of the industry. The remainder of this chapter will evaluate the policy which has evolved relating to tourism and the environment.

Historical development 1922–1980

While we have already established that tourism was understandably not a priority of the new Free State Government in 1922 it is interesting to note that the newly formed Irish Tourist Association (1925) viewed the environment and scenery as the foremost asset of the tourism industry. Numerous references to the beautiful scenery, friendliness of the people and relaxed atmosphere in Ireland featured regularly in the early bulletins of the organization. As early as 1926 a review article by Curran in *Studies* focused attention on the virtues of Ireland as a tourist destination and the attributes which the country possessed. It is also interesting to note that he was, even then, sceptical of certain developments which he saw as being detrimental to the environment and as a result to the development of a tourist industry. The following brief excerpt will give a good view of these sentiments:

> Ireland is the richest country of Western Europe in the remains of antiquity, whether in sepulchral tumuli which make of the Boyne another Valley of Kings, or in the uncounted profusion of stone and ring forts, or in the prehistoric gold ornaments

of our Dublin Museum to which Sir Arthur Evans finds a rival in Athens alone. Excelling in the decorative arts, our people developed national variations in architecture in the sixth, ninth, eleventh, thirteenth and eighteenth centuries which scattered over the countryside, are silent witnesses to its history. This complex of natural beauty, art and history is our inheritance to be used wisely, to be wasted, or to be defaced. We are doing all three in unequal measure. Consider Dublin, its streets were nobly planned and its architecture distinguished, preserving even in its decay something of dignity and reserve. But with the social disintegration of the nineteenth century big business and shop-keepers got their untrammelled way, and a pretentious, tatterdemalion disorder set in. They thought bad manners meant good business, and entered upon an ostentatious rivalry which forbade neighbourly building and broke up the harmony of the street. There followed the blatant publicity of outrageous facade advertisement, street hoardings, sky signs and posters, an orgy of waste which defeats its object. (Curran, 1926).

The quotation serves two purposes. First, it suggests that concern for the environment was a live issue as far back as 1926. Secondly, it shows that the concerns which are often portrayed as new to today have been current for a long period. The most recent dismay over the shop fronts and neon signs in O'Connell Street in Dublin is very similar to the views of Curran, expressed many years previously. While numerous statements by politicians and tourism industry lobbyists continued to stress the environment in the intervening four decades virtually no policy action was taken which could reasonably be construed as relating to the tourism environment nexus. The Christenberry report and the early pronouncements of Bord Failte did place significant emphasis on the environment but were more aspirational than anything else. Given the generalized view that Ireland was relatively clean and unspoilt this does not appear surprising. The beginnings of an integrated approach to tourism planning and the environment in Ireland are to be found in a number of reports that were undertaken in the late 1960s and early 1970s. Given the prevailing views on the environment these reports can now be seen as very far-sighted.

The basic approach adopted in these early studies was an attempt to match supply (the resources) with potential demand (the market). This basic approach to tourist planning in Ireland was first formulated in a study of Co. Donegal in 1966 (An Foras Forbartha, 1966). In this study a method was devised whereby resources and people could be directly compared using the idea of 'capacity'. The effects of a number of possible tourism development policies were set out in a manner which could be readily comprehended. As Mawhinney and Bagnall (1976) concluded 'The capacity of the resources was devised to ensure both the continued existence of their intrinsic qualities and the quality of recreational experience offered to visitors'. This approach to tourism development was extended to a study of the Beara Peninsula in County Cork in 1968 (An Foras Forbartha, 1968). The study attempted to demonstrate how a major policy of tourism development, which was most in accord with sound landscape planning objectives for the area, was also the best in terms of the economic benefits brought to the area. The National Coastline Study commissioned jointly by Bord Failte and An Foras Forbartha (1972, 1973) also made a significant input to the integrated planning of tourism and the environment. The aim of the study was to ascertain the 'best use' of the coastline, and to provide a framework within which all future public investment would be planned and private investment encouraged. The study took into account the other uses of the coastal area – agriculture, forestry and industry – to ensure that recommendations for best tourist use were part of a context of best general use. The basic work on determining the 'best use' of different parts of the coastline lay in establishing the capability of the various coastal resources to support a range of different uses. This in turn was set in the context of current use, physical characteristics, local social and economic need and conservation considerations; from this a best use, or range of optimum uses, was established. An important input was information about the tourists, and the nature and spatial pattern of their activities. A national strategy for the development and conservation of the Irish coastline was prepared, together with regional strategies which were available to guide national and regional agencies in tourism development.

Throughout the 1970s a number of important reports were published which continued to stress the importance of the environment and the necessity for appropriate planning if unwise developments were not to occur. Foremost among these were the tourism plans produced by Bord Failte and the 'Shannon Study', concluded in 1975 (Bord Failte and Office of Public Works, 1975).

Lack of appropriate institutional arrangements

The integrated planning of tourism outlined by numerous reports in the 1970s required appropriate institutional arrangements which were sadly lacking. Consequently, little affirmative action was taken. The National Economic and Social Council Report of 1980 on 'Tourism Policy' summarized the prevailing situation very accurately (NESC, 1980b). While the general thrust of the argument relates to the heterogeneous nature of tourism it also serves to illustrate why so little had been implemented of the numerous reports relating to tourism and the environment:

> It might be thought that the co-ordination of tourism policy would be a matter over which Bord Failte, as the national authority, would have a large measure of control. In practice this is not so, particularly in respect of development policy. The reality is that the great proportion of development work is undertaken by organisations external to the control of Bord Failte and consequently, there can be no assurance that what gets done is in sympathy with tourism policy ... The result is that only by coincidence will all tourism interest be going in the same direction at the same time ... There remains an industry in which potential areas of conflict are many, yet no satisfactory mechanism for resolving such conflict exists.

In a subsequent chapter of the report the following was noted

The environment is central to the type of tourist product that Ireland offers. The existing range of tourist products such as golf, fishing and sailing are closely related to it and depend upon its quality. Currently there is an abundant supply of this natural component of the tourist product. However, the quality is vulnerable and has been eroded. If current trends continue, a further decline in the quality of the product is almost certain and this will, in time, reduce the capacity of Ireland to attract discretionary visitors. (NESC, 1980b)

Developments 1980–1988

The inadequacies of tourism policy underlined by the NESC Report of 1980 were not tackled in the ensuing years of the 1980s. In some respects the rather far-sighted approach entailed in many of the reports of the 1970s seems to have been abandoned in the early 1980s. This may be explained by a generalized focus within the country on economic issues as the public finances and unemployment became severe constraints. In a context of poor economic performance it has not been unusual for environmental concerns to be overlooked. The Government did, however, publish a White Paper on Tourism Policy in 1985. Among other things it stated 'The environment is of primary importance to the overall tourism product. The economic and employment benefits of tourism would be severely eroded if environmental conditions were permitted to decline. Careful management of the environment is therefore an economic necessity as well as a social issue' (Stationery Office, 1985: 32). The document contained many such laudable aspirations but was woefully inadequate in terms of policies to achieve same.

In the absence of a comprehensive report on the evolving relationship between tourism and the environment the industry itself commissioned a report in 1985 which was published in October of 1986 (ITIC, 1986). While the report was written mainly from the perspective of available environmental resources for tourism rather than the effects of tourism on the environment it did highlight some major areas of concern. Specifically, the report dealt with issues in the rural and urban environment, from 'bungalow blight' in scenic beauty spots to dereliction in cities. A wide range of measures was proposed in the report to deal with these and other problems. Unfortunately, very few of these measures have been implemented to date. The report also emphasized that while appropriate legislation existed in many circumstances to prevent environmental damage there was very poor enforcement. The institutional framework was found to be totally inadequate and the report recommended the establishment of a co-ordinating agency as a fundamental requirement if the quality of the environment was to be protected. The study also pointed out that there were only five qualified planners working in the Department of the Environment at the time.

Renewed interest in tourism emerges

Throughout the first half of the 1980s the performance of tourism was unimpressive and was relatively neglected by government. While the White Paper of 1985 could be described as the first general statement of government policy for tourism it significantly downplayed the role of public expenditure in financing promotion and capital development schemes. The stated aim was 'to provide a framework within which individuals can undertake new tourist enterprises' (Stationery Office, 1985). This viewpoint and policy stance was to change dramatically in the ensuing years. The election of a new government in 1987 and the publication of 'The Programme for National Recovery' (Stationery Office, 1987) identified tourism as a sector with considerable employment potential. In later years this policy commitment continued to grow with 'The Programme for Economic and Social Progress' and 'The National Development Plan'. The Report of the Tourism Task Force in October of 1992 emphasized the importance which the government now attached to tourism. The rationale for the increased focus on tourism can be traced to the relatively poor performance of industry, long-term decline of agricultural employment and the emergence of an endemic unemployment problem. Of utmost importance to the momentum was the availability of European Structural Fund monies which could propel the ambitious investment outlined in the various planning documents. While the increased emphasis on tourism led to a plethora on tourism, the main emphasis was placed on job creation and the environment received only the normal aspirational platitudes. The increased funding available to tourism from 1989 to 1993 represented the biggest injection of funds the industry had ever received and the environmental effects of same are just beginning to be evaluated. The results presented below suggest that far greater attention should be placed on the environment in the Operational Programme 1994–1999 if some serious mistakes are not to be repeated.

THE OPERATIONAL PROGRAMME 1989–1993 – ENVIRONMENTAL IMPACT

Over the period of the first Operational Programme some IR£380 million was expended on tourism. Of this amount, roughly 53 per cent was funded by the EU, 30 per cent by the private sector and the remaining 17 per cent by the Irish Exchequer. If one includes the amounts spent on other EU programmes such as INTERREG and LEADER the total amount of investment is estimated at IR£450 million. The foreword to the new Operational Programme 1994–1999 describes the performance of the first programme as follows: 'The Operational Programme (OP) for Tourism 1989–1993 has been a major success. The ambitious strategic targets for the development of Irish tourism at the outset of the programme have been substantially met' (Stationery Office, 1994: 1). Independent reports on the OP by a number of organizations were generally positive about the OP but nonetheless highlighted some serious inadequacies that needed to be addressed. Interestingly, the focus of these reports was on economic issues. The Government did not see fit to commission a report dealing with how the OP had affected the environment.

Structural funds and the environment

In 1992 An Taisce[9] undertook an interim report dealing with the relationship between the Operational Programme and the environment. Interestingly, this work was funded by the World Wide Fund for Nature and not by the Irish Government. The report was extremely critical of the philosophy behind the Operational Programme and suggested 'The targets and strategies in the current plan place too much emphasis on the exploitation of Irish scenery, heritage and culture to achieve short-term economic targets' (An Taisce, 1992: 24). Of particular concern was the development of tourism through a product based approach which was seen to place the environment in a secondary position. The lack of attention to the effects of the programme on the environment is neatly summarized in the following passage:

> A clean and unspoilt environment is listed as one of the strengths of Irish tourism but the targets and strategy identified by the programme do not appear to take full account of the fact that (a) our relatively unspoilt environment is largely due to our low level of economic development and peripheral location in relation to the rest of Europe, rather than as a result of a conscious planning philosophy or particularly well developed environmental legislation. It is therefore especially vulnerable to change following increased pressures, and (b) features which are essential to tourism can be destroyed by tourism itself. (An Taisce, 1992: 24)

Private sector projects

The report details particular reasons why private sector projects funded under the OP and subject to an environmental checklist may still be harmful to the environment. The reasons were listed as follows:

• the overriding objective of the OP is to maximize economic return from tourism through employment creation and foreign earnings generation;
• significant inadequacies in the environmental impact assessment procedure;
• limitations in the planning procedures, for example, the fact that certain developments, such as golf courses and marinas, are exempt from the requirement to obtain planning permission; and
• the absence of adequate management strategies and the lack of guidelines for new leisure projects (An Taisce, 1992: 22).

The report suggested that these inadequacies had and would continue to contribute to environmental degradation. The OP had identified a particular niche market for golf and integrated leisure facilities which the report suggested could lead to severe damage to the environment. In addition, many of the proposed developments in relation to marinas were also seen as being ill-advised. Before outlining the extent to which this prognosis has materialized the public sector involvement in the OP is analysed.

Public sector projects

Under the public sector sub-programme, projects could be undertaken by Bord Failte or the Office of Public Works (OPW), or, in the case of the Mid-west region, by Shannon Development as the relevant tourism authority. At this time the OPW had autonomy over the implementation of its own section of the programme, and its projects were not subject to the environmental checklist included in the OP. As a result, projects being undertaken by the state sector did not require planning permission and were subject only to a consultation process. The report argued that 'Consequently, the opportunity for public involvement in the process is limited to making submissions on any environmental impact assessment which may be required, and there is no appeal process'. It was argued that such a system led to the many controversies that arose in relation to interpretative centres.

The emergence of problems

Interpretative centres

he most controversial element of the OP has been in relation to the decision of the OPW to construct visitor/interpretative centres at Luggala, County Wicklow, for the Wicklow National Park, at Mullaghmore, County Clare, for the Burren National Park and at Dun Chaoin, County Kerry, for the Great Blasket Island National Historic Park. The controversy has resulted in court actions with numerous claims and counter claims about the suitability of the aforementioned sites. While there are numerous definitions of 'interpretation' the general objective is defined as being 'to increase visitor awareness of the significance of a site and the desire to conserve it' (Aldridge, 1974). Interpretation in its true sense, therefore is a laudable concept which deserves universal support.[10] The controversy in Ireland is derived largely from an inherent conflict between tourism development as a commercial enterprise and interpretation as an art form with conservation as its primary objective. Colleran argues that the main driving force behind the provision of interpretative facilities in Ireland has been, 'undoubtedly' a commercial one as exhibited in the contents of the OP (Colleran, 1992).

The point at issue in the controversy is not the need for interpretation (although some would question this) or the ability of the OPW to provide true interpretation in the sense defined earlier. The controversy relates solely to the respective sites chosen by the OPW for the proposed centres. It is recognized by many environmentalists that excellent visitor facilities have been provided by the OPW at the longer-established National Parks at Glenveagh, Connemara, and at Glendalough, County Wicklow. In these cases, however, visitor facilities were provided within an existing infrastructure. In the case of the new National Parks, the proposed visitor centres are being sited in more remote areas without existing services or infrastructure. The concern that has been voiced by many people is whether, by locating the interpretative centres in vulnerable areas, the

OPW risks adversely affecting their primary function of conservation. Colleran suggests that this concern was 'exacerbated by the fact the OPW does not require planning permission for developments of this nature and by the perception that planning considerations, which would have to be taken into account by private developers, were not adequately addressed by the OPW prior to its decision on site location'. The environmental impact assessment studies commissioned by the OPW for all three sites did not assuage the misgivings of those who were objecting. These studies were initiated only after considerable pressure and were deemed to be too limited in their brief.

The proposed centre at Mullaghmore for the Burren National Park reflects the concerns related to all three sites. The Burren comprises an area of about 200 square miles of karst limestone pavement and escarpments which are unique in Ireland and Europe. The area around Mullaghmore is generally accepted as one of the least spoilt and most representative of the Burren. The proposed location for the centre is at the periphery of land currently held in state ownership and was chosen because it affords a magnificent view of Mullaghmore and Lough Gealain and provides immediate visitor access to the pavements and turloughs. In the context of the Burren as an entity, however, the site chosen is not at the periphery and is, in fact, in a relatively undisturbed wilderness area where the indigenous population is served by narrow winding lanes and minor roads. Objectors to the development argue that the siting of a major visitor facility at the location chosen would totally transform the wilderness character of the area and suggest that appropriate park management practices would focus visitor pressure away from, rather than encourage visitor access to, such an area. This suggestion is very much in accordance with the world-wide tendency to locate interpretative centres in a visitor management zone at the periphery of National Parks. An Taisce and other concerned parties have strongly urged the abandonment of the development of these centres and suggest relocating them in adjacent towns.

It must be stressed that there is not unanimous objection to the construction of the site at Mullaghmore. A majority within the local community and the wider north County Clare community are in favour of the centre being completed. In the area nearest to the centre site (Corofin town and rural settlement near to the site) this support is overwhelming, with about 95 per cent of people declaring themselves to be in favour of the centre as planned. In an area of endemic unemployment and emigration the centre is seen as a possible boon to local employment. Moles (1993)[11] has noted that 'those against the centre are viewed with massive suspicion' probably due to the feeling that outsiders are meddling in local affairs. In many ways the issues pertaining to all three sites go beyond the narrow sectional interest and raise the fundamental issue as to who has the property rights to the area. The question arises as to whether the local populace should have a greater right in this issue than environmentalists in Dublin or further afield. Those against the site argue that the endowment of future generations is being eroded while proponents in the local populace are understandably concerned with the immediacy of employment for local residents.

The issue of the interpretative centres has certainly pushed the relationship between tourism and the environment to the centre of the policy debate. Recent changes in the planning regulations require that the OPW must subject their plans for new developments to the relevant local authority. While this has generally been welcomed it is not seen by many as an adequate measure to forestall developments such as Mullaghmore. The Local Authority will still have the power to grant approval which many environmentalists feel is unsatisfactory. Environmentalists argue that there is a need for overall management plans for areas, as a whole entity, to be devised. It is argued that, such large units would represent a mosaic of intensively conserved areas – monuments, reserves, even National Parks; agricultural and forestry land. In the absence of such a plan it has been proposed that all developments should be deferred.

At the time of writing the Boyne Centre is virtually completed. The new Government has deferred a final decision on Luggalla and Mullaghmore,[12] possibly because of the considerable investment already made and the risk of alienating supporters of the centres. It seems likely that some form of compromise will have to be devised.

Golf courses

Golf is considered one of the most important attributes Ireland possesses in the encouragement of special interest holidays. Bord Failte estimated that about 130,000 tourists played golf in Ireland in 1992 with some 60,000 of these being influenced by golf to visit Ireland. With the support of the Operational Programme for Tourism, 1989–1993, a large increase in golf course development occurred throughout the country. Bord Failte has played a critical role in the development of new courses which often received assistance through the Structural Funds. The Bord individually assesses each application in relation to its location, environmental and economic impact before recommending funding from the EC. Until 1994 it was not necessary to acquire planning permission to initiate a golf course. While it was stated policy of Bord Failte to consult other agencies, such as the Wildlife Service of the OPW, it appears as though this was often overlooked. An Taisce[13] has shown that a number of the new courses developed over the period of the OP have inflicted considerable damage on sensitive eco-systems.

History/culture product

In 1992 Bord Failte produced a strategy document entitled 'Heritage Attractions: A Strategy to Interpret Ireland's History and Culture for Tourism'. The document explicitly recognizes that:

> There is, inevitably, a risk that, in promoting interpretation as a most potent visitor management initiative, commercial forces may override conservation considerations. Having recognised the risk the strategy document outlines guidelines for project approval:
> • Visitor centres should not be built just for the sake of it, at sites where proper access and an explanatory plaque may be all that is required.

- Great care must be taken that, when developing visitor centres in wilderness areas, the very wilderness attraction of the area is not eroded.
- Development of commercial centres or of 'visitor attractions' masquerading as commercial centres should not be permitted in the vicinity of sites located in undeveloped areas.
- New buildings near heritage sites, for the purpose of visitor attractions, or otherwise, must not spoil the setting of the site. (Bord Failte, 1992)

While recognizing that many fine-quality heritage centres have been developed throughout the country it is also obvious, that, in the drive to market Ireland's history and culture product the above guidelines have sometimes been ignored. The demolition of the lock-house in Killaloe provides a clear example of short-term gain in terms of tourism revenue and job creation taking precedence over a more sustainable, long-term development based on conservation. Colleran relates the development as follows:

> The strategy of the local development committee was to develop the town as a 'Waterways Theme Town' in which navigation of the Shannon would be the major focus. The lock-house, built approximately 150 years ago on a small man-made island between the canal and the river was initially identified as the ideal choice for a visitor/interpretative centre. However, as development plans proceeded, it became evident that the tiny lockkeeper's cottage, with its small rooms and narrow staircase, could not accommodate the proposed use of information centre, interpretation area, restaurant, etc. The building was, consequently, demolished and a new, enlarged structure capable of satisfying these requirements was constructed in its place. The result was that the one building which embodied the navigation history of Killaloe and, which, in a unique way,would have interpreted the navigation theme for visitors, was destroyed in order to create an artificial 'interpretative centre which would act as a 'honey pot' for short-term commercial gain. (Colleran, 1992: 585)

The example above illustrates the need to carefully monitor 'history and culture tourism' product developments. If careful control is not exercised, the availability of significant funding can result in developments which, in seeking to develop 'history and culture tourism product' may actually undermine the basis of a sustainable tourism industry in Ireland and, in the process, erode or destroy elements of national heritage. These concerns and others related to the environment are likely to become more pronounced as significant investment is undertaken in the second Operational Programme for Tourism, 1994–1999.

THE OPERATIONAL PROGRAMME 1994–1999

Confident in the view that the last OP was a significant success the new programme was launched in the latter part of 1994. The major programme details are discussed at length in Chapter 9. The focus here is on the relationship between the new programme and the environment.

The link with the environment

While the environment is an integral part of the tourism product it receives only scant attention in the 130-page Operational Programme document. In essence it receives only a 14-line paragraph. It reads as follows:

> Ireland has a deserved reputation as a clean and relatively unspoilt Country. This Programme intends to maintain and enhance that reputation by ensuring a proper balance between the needs of the environment and sustainable tourism development. The compatibility of State-owned tourism-related developments with good environmental practice will be secured through the widened scope of domestic planning law. The strategic emphasis on improving Irish tourism's seasonality profile is consistent with sustainable development, and it is further envisaged that a substantial proportion of EU assisted investment in physical developments in this programme will enhance existing tourism infrastructure or will convert existing structures to new or improved tourism facilities. A good dispersal of EU tourism funds across the eight sub-regions is again envisaged, so as to minimise capacity problems in individual areas. Progress on the consistency between tourism developments and the principle of sustainable development will be continually monitored as part of the programme (Stationery Office, 1994: 9)

The above statement, while laudable in intent is very weak on specifics. While endorsing the principle of 'Sustainable Tourism' it offers little in terms of explanation as to how this laudable objective will be achieved. The emphasis placed on domestic planning law is rather worrying given the poor implementation of such to date and the controversies which have already arisen. Interestingly, the statement does acknowledge that environmental problems have already occurred due to capacity constraints but suggests this can be solved by dispersal of visitors across the sub-regions and also by an attempt to tackle seasonality. This approach to the environment is considered to be inappropriate for a number of reasons.

First, the objective of spreading funds thinly throughout the eight sub-regions has been shown to be sub-optimal by the ESRI[14] report on the last round of spending. It is seen to lead to poor return on investment and offers no guarantee of environmental protection unless accompanied by appropriate management techniques. Such an approach is absent from the document.

Second, the emphasis on seasonality as a means of tackling environmental problems is also seen to be rather superficial. While a better seasonal spread of visitors would undoubtedly alleviate some problems there is little in the document which suggests an appropriate strategy. The problem of seasonality has been an issue in Irish tourism for many years. It received attention in the First and Second Programmes for Economic Expansion but little concrete action has occurred since the An Tostal campaign of the early 1950s and the 'June Holiday Plan' of Bord Failte in 1962. Deane in the NESC report of 1980 concluded 'Overall, however, there has been no major commitment of marketing resources aimed at promoting the seasonal pattern of demand' (NESC,

1980b: 120). Subsequent analysis in the 1980s has focused on seasonality but little has occurred in terms of concrete action. It must also be stressed that the prevailing emphasis on seasonality has usually been concerned with increasing the numbers of tourists to Ireland rather than alleviating the problem of too many tourists during a particular month, causing environmental pressures. The general purpose has usually been to focus on seasonality in order to tackle the poor profitability of the industry.

The 1994–1999 OP document acknowledges that Irish tourism is particularly seasonal with 30 per cent of visitors arriving in the peak months of July–August in 1993. The Programme aims *inter alia* to increase tourism numbers and to achieve a better seasonal spread of tourists by 1999. The objective is to have 75 per cent arriving outside the peak in 1999 as against 70 per cent at present. The document does not outline what effect the implied extra numbers will have on the environment but suggests the seasonality objective can be met by better promotion of the off-season by appropriate fiscal incentives which give better aid rates to the promotion of new markets and also for off-season promotion. Deegan (1994) has argued that these incentives are unlikely to achieve the objective and has suggested that a bolder initiative should have been taken which would have placed the bulk of marketing resources in the off-season. At first glance this might appear a risky strategy but may not be for two reasons. First, the experience of other countries in marketing the shoulder months is that it simply increased numbers in the peak. Second, there are many untapped markets in Europe amenable to such an approach which have to date been relatively ignored by the authorities.

The overall emphasis within the OP on the environment is deemed inadequate. The mistakes made in the first OP in relation to public and private sector projects have scarcely been acknowledged and little administrative change has occurred which can ensure they will not be repeated. The emphasis on seasonality obscures the fact that the country will absorb significant extra tourists if the plan is successful and is in itself flawed. Even if the Programme itself is flawed Ireland may still attract additional visitors[15] due to the buoyancy of international demand. The Programme has not considered the adoption of market-based or other approaches to solve the problems associated with additional visitors. The current problems at particular tourist venues associated with too many visitors is being ignored and will undoubtedly affect the qualitative aspects of a visit to Ireland.

CONCLUSIONS

The relationship between economic development and the environment has received considerable international attention in recent years. Ireland, as a relative newcomer to industrialization has not faced the pronounced effects of environmental change which some of our more industrialized neighbours have grappled with in recent years. Consequently, awareness of environmental issues and appropriate legislation lags many of our European counterparts. Even where legislation exists, it is not implemented with the rigour one would expect. Membership of the European Union has forced the government to accept regulations enacted in Brussels which many see as a very positive element of involvement in the EU. Some would argue that little would happen in the absence of the European Union directives.

Tourism across the globe is accepted as a fundamental element in the growth of the services sector, with the potential to create many new jobs in the years ahead. It is also accepted that the growth of tourism numbers poses a considerable environmental threat that requires immediate action. In the international arena we observe the experimental use of market-based solutions to environmental problems and although in their infancy are expected to contribute part of the solution. In a more general sense the goal of 'Sustainable Development' will require many new initiatives which will require the co-operation of the public and the private sector. Many issues remain to be resolved but the early warning signs are evident and are too serious to be neglected.

Governmental emphasis on tourism in Ireland is a relatively new phenomenon. While tourism has always been identified as having potential by Irish Governments of the past it is only recently that commensurate monies has been allocated to the sector. In fact numerous government statements in recent years would suggest that the development of Ireland in future years is inextricably bound up with the success of policies related to products associated with Ireland's image as an environmentally green country.[16] Tourism in particular falls into this category. While Ireland certainly possesses a comparative advantage in these areas it should be remembered that this is more by accident than design. Our relatively clean and unspoilt environment is due to an absence of heavy industrialization (not for the want of trying) and rather poor policy for tourism which spanned many decades. It has certainly not been due to any great foresight in relation to planning legislation and implementation.

Towards the latter years of the first OP a number of problems arose in relation to tourism developments. While there have been some attempts to tackle these concerns through legislative actions there remains some outstanding concerns. First, the implementation of legislation on the environment has been historically poor in Ireland. In addition, the fiscal system has often worked in favour of demolition of culture and heritage rather than its preservation. Poor incentives to maintain old buildings and a plethora of tax-breaks to erect new buildings is seen to have contributed to the decline of much of the built environment (Dowling and Keegan, 1992). Second, there is no evidence of any attempt to undertake a study which would ascertain the 'carrying capacity'[17] of the environment in relation to tourism. Third, there has been no attempt to date to seriously consider market-based or other approaches to environmental problems associated with tourism problems.[18]

Tourism by its nature contains the seeds of its own destruction. Promoting a country or region as 'quiet and unspoilt' obviously can lead to an influx of visitors which destroys the original attractiveness of an area. Ireland is such a place. It is a relatively small country which already attracts more visitors than inhabitants.[19] Those visitors are generally attracted here by the unspoilt countryside and friendliness of the people. Already there are signs that the influx of tourists in certain places at certain times is undermining the attractiveness of visiting the country. This will affect repeat visits and the general willingness of visitors to holiday in the country. In this context it is a matter of urgency that appropriate policies be formed which can allow an orderly development of tourism.[20] Such a policy will take cognisance of the demands of our tourists, which have generally been neglected to date. The erection of numerous heritage centres, interpretative centres and theme parks may actually undermine the reason for a visit rather than enhance it. The requirement to preserve the environment may require the development of a policy which focuses on a market-based approach and the attraction of income-elastic tourists.[21] Too often policy decisions have been guided not by a vision of the future based on the common good but rather, are reactions to pressure from powerful groups to serve their own interests. Failure to confront these issues can only lead to the destruction of the environment and the failure to create sustainable jobs which the government so badly requires.

NOTES

1. For a more detailed discussion see De Kadt (1990).
2. See Solow (1993).
3. The European Union's Fifth Action and Policy Programme came into effect in 1993. For details see CEC (1992).
4. For further discussion of this viewpoint see Butler (1980) and Mathieson and Wall (1982).
5. A detailed discussion of these issues is provided by Deegan (1991).
6. In some cases of course the opposite may apply. If the operator paid no charges previously for pollution emissions it is likely than any market-based approach that will impose costs will be vigorously resisted.
7. It is interesting to note that parts of Ireland, particularly the west coast now have significant numbers of German and Dutch immigrants. These people have come to Ireland to escape the environmental problems associated with their home countries. In general they have been very staunch defenders of the environment.
8. In the election of 1989 Roger Garland was elected to the Irish Parliament.
9. An Taisce is a voluntary organization concerned with issues related to the environment. Established in 1946 by Lloyd Praeger the organization now has 6000 members. Corporate membership is currently about 200 members. The organization attains funding through a membership fee. Total fees in 1994 were IR£78,000. The organization produces commissioned work for international bodies concerned with environmental issues.
10. There are some however who dispute the need for certain types of interpretation. An interesting discussion of this matter in relation to Ireland is provided by O'Toole (1994).

11. In an interesting article Moles provides a very different perspective on the controversy. He suggests *inter alia* that it is extremely difficult to assess accurately the effects on the environment of the centres due to the dearth of information. He also suggests that environmental damage may occur, even in the absence of the centres being built. For a detailed discussion see Moles (1993).

12. The new Fine Gael/Labour/Democratic Left Coalition Government (December 1994) has already expressed a keener interest in the environment than its predecessor. Interestingly,the responsibility for National Parks and Monuments has been taken away from the OPW and transferred to the Department of Arts Culture and the Gaeltacht. It is too early at the time of writing to predict the outcome of this development.

13. See Mitchell (1992).

14. The ESRI report (1993) suggested that such an approach was driven more by political expediency than the returns which the projects could generate.

15. The only work of note on this issue in Ireland has been undertaken by O'Hagan and Duffy (1994). The work relates to access and admission charges to the National Museum. It seems likely that work of this nature will extend to tourism in the not too distant future.

16. A good example of this thinking is provided in the Culliton report (1992).

17. An excellent review of the issue of capacity is provided by Johnson and Thomas (1994).

18. A new unit to study market-based solutions to environmental problems was established in the ESRI in 1994. To date the emphasis has been on environmental issues associated with industry.

19. The example of the effects of tourism in the Aran Islands presents an interesting microcosm. It may prove insightful of the effects tourism could have in Ireland. For a detailed discussion of the Aran Island experience with tourism see Keane *et al.* (1992).

20. In this context the joint project between An Taisce and An Bord Failte dealing with Protected Landscapes is to be welcomed. The findings and recommendations of the pilot project will be available in late 1995.

21. This policy essentially means targeting tourists who are high spenders. This approach may be particularly relevant to Ireland. For a more detailed discussion see Deegan and Dineen (1993).

7 Irish tourism – the European Union dimension

INTRODUCTION

Ireland was formally accepted as a member of the European Economic Community (now the European Union) in 1973. Membership of the European Union places certain fiscal, monetary and legislative constraints on the Irish Government but in general membership is seen as positive by all political parties and the electorate.[1] In fact, in every year of membership Ireland has been a net recipient of funds from the grant agencies of the Union. In the early years of membership the immediate benefits were to the agricultural sector but as time elapsed European funds have been used for investment in infrastructure, education and *inter alia* for the pursuit of social policy. In recent years the tourism sector has received substantial funding from the European Union. This chapter evaluates the evolution and role of tourism policy within the European Union (to the extent that one exists); the contribution of EU aid to the development of Irish tourism; the importance of tourism to the economies of Member States, and analyses the recent performance of Irish tourism relative to other Member States. It concludes with an evaluation of the future role for the EU in tourism policy.

THE ROLE OF THE EUROPEAN UNION IN TOURISM

The European Union Commission[2] has been slow to develop a tourism policy. Given the bigger issues that the EU has had to consider, it is perhaps not surprising. Different views exist about the role, forms and extent of intervention by national governments, let alone supra-national organizations, like the EU, intervening in the economies of Member States. At one extreme there are interventionists who believe that governments should intervene strategically, via state agencies, state ownership and subsidies, throughout an economy at industry and firm levels, because of market imperfections. At the other extreme there is the laissez-faire approach, which expounds that every economic activity should be left to the marketplace (Akehurst, 1992). While it is not intended to argue the merits of these arguments in any detail the following sections of this chapter suggest that the importance of tourism to the European Union economies warrants some form of clear policy statement which to date has been absent.

The slow emergence of tourism as an issue of concern within the Union is supported by both the dearth of concrete actions in the tourism sector and also by the poor institutional arrangements established over the years. It was not until 1980 that a commissioner was given specific responsibility for tourism, originally within the Transport Directorate (DGVII), subsequently becoming part of Directorate General XXIII (Enterprise Policy, Distributive Trades, Tourism and Co-operatives). Fitzpatrick, in a comprehensive report for the European Parliament has argued that the situation of tourism within DGXXIII is far from satisfactory (European Parliament, 1993). He suggests that the Commission has effectively chosen to operate without a coherent tourism policy: 'Rather than centralising tourism in its own Directorate General, the Commission has opted to allow DGs such as VII(Transport) and DGXI (Environment, Consumer Protection and Nuclear Safety) to formulate tourism-related policies based on their primary areas of responsibility'. The tourism unit within DGXXIII is responsible, among other things, for ensuring co-ordination. This arrangement is deemed inadequate for a number of reasons. First, the resources available to DGXXIII are tiny relative to a DG such as XVI (Regional Policy–European Regional Development Fund) and consequently can have little influence over policy design. Secondly, notwithstanding the Tourism Unit's lack of resources, formal consultations only take place when a proposal is drafted. Thus the tourism unit has no impact on the thinking behind a proposal and it is unlikely that tourism will have played anything other than a minor role in policy formation.

In the absence of a specific tourism-related policy within the Union, action in the tourism sector has arisen from the activities of particular DGs whose policies impact upon tourism and through periodic resolutions and regulations of the European Council. Further to the appointment of a Commissioner responsible for tourism in 1980 the Community's first report on tourism appeared two years later. Objectives of the 'Community Action in the Field of Tourism' (CEC, 1984a, 1986) include:

- facilitating tourism within the community;
- improving the seasonal and geographic distribution of tourism;
- making better use of financial instruments;
- providing better information for the protection of tourists;
- improving working conditions in the tourist industry;
- increasing awareness of the problems of tourism and organizing consultation and co-operation.

Further statements and decisions on Community policy continued to be developed throughout the 1980s. In general the decisions can be classified under three related headings: information, quality of services and promotion. The Commissioner for DGXIII, in a speech marking the inauguration of the European Year of Tourism[3] in Dublin in January 1990 (Cardosso e Cunha, 1990), asked whether the Community has a role in tourism policy that goes beyond the control of state aid and competition policy within member states. In affirming this he argued for:

- the marketing of Europe as a whole and the importance of ensuring that the product 'Europe' is a consistent, high-quality product;
- integrated information and reservation systems;
- co-operation between Member States' governments, national tourist boards and the tourist industry, with the Community as a partner of national governments.

According to Akehurst the 'designation of 1990 as European Tourism Year could have been regarded as a belated realisation of the economic, social and political importance of tourism, but it can also be seen in retrospect as one further manifestation of a developing EC tourism policy' (Akehurst, 1992). While the recent publication of a 'Green Paper' on tourism (CEC, 1995b) suggests that there may be some merit in this argument it is far more likely that the designation of 1990 as the 'Tourism Year' was an attempt to boost awareness of tourism in the lead up to the development of a single European market by 1992 (CEC, 1988a). Specifically, the objectives of European Tourism Year were to:

- prepare the coming of the large area without internal frontiers, using the integration role of tourism to advantage;
- promote greater knowledge of cultures and lifestyles by citizens of Member States, especially the young;
- stress the economic importance of the tourism sector in the completion of the internal market;
- promote a better distribution of tourism over time and location, the staggering of holidays, alternatives to mass tourism and new destinations;
- promote increased awareness of the importance for tourism of a high-quality environment;
- promote intra-Community and international tourism in Europe and improve the freedom of movement for travellers.

While the fund allocated to the programme for the 'European Tourism Year' was very disappointing (a meagre 5 million ECUs)[4] and certainly limited the effectiveness of the programme, the designation of the 'European Tourism Year' can be seen as an important policy departure. Given that the Treaty of Rome does not confer competence for tourism the Council Decision to launch the 'Tourism Year' can be seen as the first Community action in the area of tourism. The results of the year,[5] together with the views of the European Parliament and the Council's deliberations in 1990 and 1991, led to a proposed 'action programme'.[6] The discussions had taken note of a wide range of views on the Community's role in promoting tourism, and a lack of co-operation between operators, both public and private. The industry appeared to be very fragmented compared to other sectors and its competitiveness was falling. The action programme to run from 1993 to 1995 eventually adopted was therefore aimed at developing tourism by promoting exchange between the various parts of the industry, and by co-ordinating tourism activities within the Commission and the Member States. A certain degree of emphasis was placed on legislative measures to improve or safeguard the rights of the tourist in a number of ways. These included:

- making it easier to cross the Community's internal frontiers;
- developing tourism with due account to the environment;
- improving tourists' protection as consumers.

In 1992 the Community spent 5.642 million ECU on tourism, of which 0.75 million was for promotion. There were three priority objectives:

- improving statistical knowledge of tourism
- developing tourism with due account to the environment
- promotion of Europe as a tourist destination, especially in the USA and Japan.

In 1993 the European Commission budget provided 7 million ECU out of the total 18 million ECU for the whole action plan.[7] The main aim was to stress the importance of cross-border co-operation and the initiatives to improve tourist information. A major effort was also made to develop transnational forms of cultural tourism and the development of cultural routes which is continuing.[8] Shortly before the Commission's proposals for the action programme were published, the Economic and Social Committee (ESC) issued an own-initiative opinion calling for such a programme, and while welcoming the plan suggested the programme adopted by the Council was narrower than that originally proposed by the European Commission. The ESC has since called for the 1996 Intergovernmental Conference to consider giving tourism a legal basis in the new Treaty which will be developed by the Conference. This subject was also covered by the Green Paper published in 1995 which will be discussed in the latter sections of the chapter.

FUNDING OF TOURISM PROJECTS

While a general macro-policy in relation to tourism at EU level is still emerging the specific funding of tourism projects at a micro-level has assumed increased importance in recent years. Funding of tourism through Structural Funds is more a facet of the Community's regional policy than tourism policy and this element of funding received a major boost with an overhaul of the Structural Funds in 1988.[9] The following details the funding of tourism projects through the European Regional Development Fund (ERDF) and identifies the importance of the fund as a contributor to tourism development in Ireland.

European Regional Development Fund (ERDF)

The ERDF was established in 1975, two years after the first enlargement of the Community, as the central instrument in developing a Community regional policy (CEC, 1985). The purpose of the ERDF is to 'contribute to the correction of the principal regional imbalances within the Community by participating in the development and structural adjustment of regions whose development is lagging behind and in the conversion of declining industrial regions' (CEC, 1984b), a role explicitly recognized in the Single European Act. This goal has been pursued by making grants available for investment in infrastructure, and to help finance directly productive investment in industrial, craft industry and service activities to create or maintain jobs. Access to advice on marketing, management, and innovation is also provided to firms, particularly small- and medium-sized enterprises and to local and regional authorities.

While there have been many changes to the funding mechanisms within the ERDF it is possible to categorize two distinct periods for analysis. The first period covers the period of ERDF funding from 1975 to 1988 and the second encompasses the changes to the funding arrangements by virtue of the requirements of the Single European Act.

Distribution of ERDF funding 1975–1988

Between 1975 and 1988, throughout Europe, 429.7 million ECU were channelled into specific tourism projects primarily from the ERDF. This, however, represented only 1.9 per cent of all ERDF project grants. The vast majority of grants were used for major infrastructural investments and industrial projects (Pearce, 1992). Table 7.1 below shows ERDF funding patterns from 1975 to 1988.

From 1975 to 1988 grants for projects from the ERDF totalled 22,723 million ECU, some 93 per cent of all ERDF commitments for this period (the remainder

Table 7.1 Distribution of ERDF project grants, 1975–1988 (million ECU)

	All project grants	*Tourism grants*	*% Tourism*
Belgium	175.00	20.20	11.50
Denmark	166.34	2.50	1.50
France	2540.19	18.30	0.70
Germany	830.35	23.00	2.80
Greece	2184.16	21.90	1.10
Ireland	1156.88	10.30	0.90
Italy	7753.90	8.20	1.00
Luxembourg	14.69	1.60	10.80
The Netherlands	233.28	5.30	2.30
Portugal	1082.04	11.30	1.00
Spain	1958.72	0.70	0.03
United Kingdom	4627.42	232.50	5.00
Total	22,723.00	429.70	1.90

Source: Pearce (1992).

essentially going for programmes with a negligible amount for studies). The two major recipients were Italy and the UK, which together accounted for over half of all project grants during this period (Pearce, 1992). Significant sums also went to France, Greece, Spain, Ireland and Portugal. The relatively poor priority received by tourism is reflected in the low spending on tourism projects, 1.9 per cent of all project grants. Interestingly, over half the tourism project grants went to projects in the UK, while Italy received 19 per cent. In addition, of the major recipients of ERDF finance the UK also had the highest percentage allocation to tourism (5 per cent), although in relative terms it was exceeded by the smaller Member States, Belgium (11.5 per cent) and Luxembourg (10.8 per cent). The cumulative allocation of tourism grants to each Member State exhibits different features over the period 1975–1988, although there was a general increase from 1984 in tandem with tourism specifically being identified in the 1984 ERDF regulation as being one of the sectors for exploiting the potential for 'internally generated development'. The inclusion of tourism as a specific regulation within the ERDF was a reflection of a changing attitude to tourism within the Community. A Commission document of 1986 noted the following:

> It is generally agreed that tourism can be particularly beneficial in the present difficult employment situation. It is a labour intensive industry, and its continuing expansion offers a valuable counterbalance to the unemployment which is devastating other sectors and the less favoured regions. (CEC, 1986)

The changing status of tourism within the Community is demonstrated by the nature of allocations over the period. The single largest allocation to tourism projects occurred in 1985, with subsequent patterns being influenced by the entry of Spain and Portugal. The UK and Italy, together with the former Federal Republic of Germany, made consistent applications for funding over the period. France, on the other hand, allocated 56 per cent of all funding in 1988. The Netherlands and Ireland received no tourism grants until 1983 and 1984, with 80 per cent of all appropriations in Ireland being granted in 1988 (Pearce, 1992). Portugal has made consistent applications since joining the Community. While the different country allocations reflect year of entry and the prevailing emphasis on tourism within the Community it is worthwhile emphasizing that the ERDF finance increased considerably from 257.6 million ECU in 1975 to 3684 million ECU in 1988.

ERDF funding in Ireland

The foregoing has shown that Ireland only began to use ERDF funding to finance tourism development in 1983. Of the 1156.88 million ECU which Ireland received between 1975 and 1988, only 0.9 per cent were specific tourism grants. Table 7.2 below contrasts the investment in Ireland with other European members during the period.

Table 7.2 Distribution of ERDF assistance by types of tourism project, 1975–1988

Type of project	EC (%)	Ireland (%)
Infrastructure	32.4	18.9
Accommodation	6.4	–
Leisure complexes	10.6	–
Port facilities	9.2	22.3
Winter sports facilities	2.5	–
Other sports facilities	4.2	–
Thermal resorts	3.1	–
Museums/historic centres/restoration	11.7	24.0
Cultural and visitor centres	5.8	34.8
Conference centres	9.0	–
Other	5.1	–
Total	100.00	100.00

Source: Pearce (1992).

The striking feature of the above table is the amount of expenditure Ireland allocated to projects of an infrastructural nature. Basic infrastructure and port facilities accounted for 41 per cent of all expenditure. In addition, Ireland devoted the remainder of expenditure to projects with a cultural/historic theme. The expenditure on cultural and visitor centres at nearly 35 per cent of the total expenditure is a reflection of the new-found emphasis being placed on 'Culture' as an integral element of Irish tourism. The growth of expenditure in this area in subsequent years has led to criticism which is explored in greater detail in Chapter 9. Notwithstanding these reservations there can be no doubt a lack of adequate funding in the years 1975–1988 did in fact impede the progress of Irish tourism. Hurley *et al.* (1994), in a review article suggested that the dearth of investment over these years contributed to a decline in both the quality and quantity of visitor facilities. The review also points to the steady decline in the amount of hotel accommodation. For example, there were 806 hotels in Ireland in 1972, but by 1978 the number had dropped to 707 and by 1985 to only 643, with the number of grade A hotels almost halved over the period. While a decline in the number of establishments was cause for concern a more worrying issue was findings of a Price Waterhouse survey (1987) which revealed a relatively high level of customer dissatisfaction with both the price and quality of the accommodation available to tourists visiting Ireland.

REFORM OF THE STRUCTURAL FUNDS

The entry into force in 1987 of the Single European Act brought a considerable shift in Community policy as a whole, and structural assistance in particular. The

Single Act stressed the importance of the large frontier market in 1992, the strengthening of economic and social cohesion, faster progress in research and technology, the development of social and environmental policy and monetary integration. The Structural Funds have a key role to play in the strengthening of economic and social cohesion and, accordingly, the Single Act provided for a reform to increase their efficiency and to co-ordinate their assistance, both between themselves and with the existing financial instruments. These reforms were set in train by a series of regulations which came into force on 1 January 1989.[10]

Major changes to funding and funding mechanisms

As the Community looked to foster greater economic links within Europe, it soon became apparent that the traditional mechanisms for allocating funds and the volume of finance available were inadequate to cope with the objectives of the Single European Act. Instead of the previous approach of providing funds on a project by project approach in response to specific requests channelled through national departments and ministries, a radical new system was introduced:

> The reform is based on certain principles such as the concentration on priority objectives, the doubling of resources by 1993, a decentralised programme approach instead of a project based approach, partnership between the Commission and national, regional and local authorities, greater co-ordination between all instruments and improved and simplified management, assessment and monitoring rules. (CEC, 1991a)

Under the new system, Community Support Frameworks (CSFs) are drawn up by the EU for each Member State, introducing the Community's structural action for that member under defined objectives. Each CSF defines the sectors, including tourism, to which the funds shall be directed. Assistance under a CSF is then provided predominantly in the form of operational programmes. The following section outlines the development of tourism within Ireland under these new arrangements[11] but before analysing the Operational Programme for Tourism it is important to put developments in context.

The emergence of a focus on tourism

The first sign of a renewed Irish governmental focus on tourism came with the publication of a White Paper on Tourism Policy in 1985 (Stationery Office, 1985). This was the first attempt in many years to clarify governmental thinking on tourism in a focused manner and to specify the broad objectives of policy. The White Paper was rather vague but did place job creation high on the agenda as the desired outcome of tourism development in Ireland. The policy objectives were to be refined into more specific targets in both the 'Programme for National

Recovery' (Stationery Office 1987) and the 'National Development Plan 1989–1993' (Stationery Office 1989a). While the tourism sector was receiving far greater attention than heretofore it must be stressed that the attention to the sector was more a reflection of the poor performance of the manufacturing sector to create employment and also to the long-term decline of agricultural employment. In addition the growth of the labour force had led to an endemic unemployment problem in the latter half of the 1980s.[12]

The focus on tourism as a sector that could alleviate unemployment dovetailed nicely with the availability of Structural Funds for tourism development. These funds represented the most important source of finance that had ever been made available to the sector. Adopting the year 1988 as a base, very ambitious targets were established for the forthcoming five years. Strategic emphasis was placed on developing a new and improved product base, including weather-independent facilities, expanded and more focused marketing and training. The demand-side targets established projected the number of visitors and expenditure by those visitors to double over the period 1988–1992. The 'Operational Programme for Tourism 1989–93' (Department of Tourism and Transport, 1989) adopted these targets and provided some formalized objectives as to how they would be achieved.

THE OPERATIONAL PROGRAMME FOR TOURISM 1989–1993

In the period 1989–1993 it is estimated that some IR£450 million (about 557 million ECU) was invested in tourist facilities, training and marketing in Ireland. The bulk of this investment (IR£380 million or about 470 million ECU) was supported through the Operational Programme for Tourism. Table 7.3 shows that the initial investment targets for EU co-funded expenditure under the programme were exceeded.

Of the IR£380 million invested, approximately 53 per cent was funded by the EU, 30 per cent by the private sector and the remaining 17 per cent by the Irish

Table 7.3 Total co-funded investment achieved by the tourism Operational Programme, 1989–1993

IR£million	Programme targets	Forecast/outcome	Target/outcome (%)
Product development	263.4	278.7	106
Marketing	23.0	48.3	210
Training	49.2	52.1	106
Technical Assistance	0.3	0.7	233
Total	335.9	379.8	113

Source: Operational Programme for Tourism 1994–1999 (Stationery Office, 1994).

Exchequer. During this period all ERDF project grants to Ireland amounted to IR£1387.3 million, of which tourism grants accounted for £157.6[13] million (11 per cent). For purposes of comparison the breakdown of expenditure is presented in Table 7.4 below in the same format as Table 7.2.

While comparison with the period 1975–1988 is rather difficult due to the late investment of ERDF expenditure in tourism in 1985, the table gives some indication of changing priorities in the period 1989–1993. The most notable change is the sharp decline of investment in port facilities, from 22.3 per cent to a little under 1 per cent. The second major change is to be found with the investment of funds into sporting activities, a priority under the Operational Programme. Finally, the allocation of 37 per cent of funds to museums, historic centres and for restoration is indicative of the emphasis placed in the Operational Programme on one of the unexploited assets of Irish tourism. While the appropriateness of the expenditures will be analysed in more detail in Chapter 9, it is sufficient to note that the investment of ERDF monies has played a major role in improving the physical plant of the tourism sector in recent years. The Irish tourism industry, with its predominantly local ownership and a preponderance of small units was not able, alone, to generate sufficient capital to refurbish, improve and expand its stock of accommodation, amenities and facilities without outside assistance. Finance provided on a project by project basis had proved inadequate and, longer term, more integrated planning with funding from the European Community as well as the Irish public and private sectors was required to achieve the targets established for tourism adopted in the National Development Plan. It is also important to note that the changes to the

Table 7.4 Distribution of ERDF assistance by types of tourism project, 1975–1988 and 1989–1993

Type of project	Ireland 1975–1988 (%)	Ireland 1989–1993 (%)
Infrastructure	18.9	19.9
Accommodation	–	–
Leisure tourist complexes	–	9.4
Port facilities	22.3	0.9
Winter sports facilities	–	–
Other sports facilities	–	13.2
Thermal resorts	–	–
Museums/historic centres/restoration	24.0	37.0
Cultural and visitor centres	34.8	–
Conference centres	–	3.3
Other	–	16.3
Total	100.0	100.0

Source: Pearce (1992) and Department of Tourism and Transport (1989).

ERDF by virtue of the Single European Act made it possible that much greater investment took place in tourism than heretofore.

THE IMPORTANCE OF TOURISM WITHIN THE EUROPEAN UNION ECONOMIES

Tourism involves many millions of individuals as both providers and consumers of a wide range of services. As a tourist, each individual moves outside his/her usual location and acquires benefits which are cultural, aesthetic and recreational, and which generate economic rewards for those offering them. In Europe the exact economic importance is difficult to assess, but it has been estimated to represent an average of 5.5 per cent of GNP[14] in the EU.

Employment associated with tourism activity is also extremely difficult to estimate but conservative estimates place this in the region of nine million jobs in the EU, or about 6 per cent of the total number of jobs in the Union. Figure 7.1 shows the relative importance of European Tourism in the international marketplace.

For many years, Europe has been the primary tourist destination world-wide. In 1994, it accounted for roughly 60 per cent of international arrivals. However, it is now clear that this market share is undergoing a constant process of erosion, and that competition from developing areas is growing steadily.[15] Europe's share of the world market in terms of arrivals fell from 72.5 per cent in 1960 to 59.6

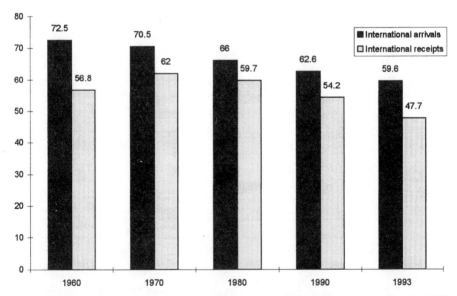

Figure 7.1 Europe's changing share of world tourism, 1960–1993. *Source*: Eurostat 1995 (CEC, 1995a)

per cent in 1993. The major shift has been to the Far Eastern and Pacific regions, whose share increased from 1 per cent to 14.1 per cent. The American continent has also lost out with its market share declining from 24.1 per cent to 20.5 per cent over the period. While the decline of the European market share has been continuing since 1960 it is noticeable that the erosion took place at a much faster rate in the period 1990–1994 than in the preceding decade 1980–1990. While in the 1980s the market share diminished at 0.3 per cent annually, the latter four-year period evidenced an average yearly decline of 0.75 per cent. While the preliminary statistics for 1994 suggest an improved performance the long-term trend is for Europe to face increasing international competition.

The most worrying aspect of the data presented in Figure 7.1 relates to receipts. Up until 1990 the share in receipts was declining at a slower rate than arrivals, demonstrating that tourist spending in Europe was increasing more than proportionally with respect to other areas. However, in the period 1990–1994, European tourism's share decreased more in terms of receipts than arrivals (6.1 per cent), meaning that tourists in Europe increased their spending capacities less than proportionally to those in other areas (CEC, 1995a). This phenomenon is indicative of the new situation that European tourism is confronting: the greater spending capacity that international tourists have always shown in Europe, with respect to other areas, has in recent years no longer been borne out by the facts. If European tourism is to arrest this trend it must place greater emphasis on improving the quality of product available and also aggressively target high-spending tourists for longer stays in the country of destination. The not insignificant contribution of tourism to national economies presented in Figure 7.2 suggests that this task be embraced as a matter of priority.

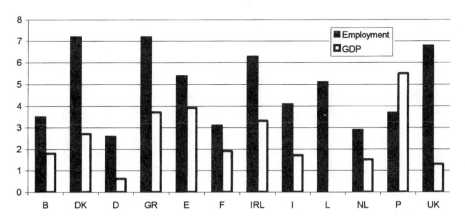

Figure 7.2 Contribution of international tourism to the national economy in the Member States (employment data are for 1991 except DK and D (1990), B (1989), GR and IRL (1987) and F (1986). GDP data are for 1992 except BLEU, GR, and P (1991)). *Source*: CEC (1993)

The latest comparable figures collected by Eurostat and presented in Figure 7.2 suggests that tourism occupies a fairly important position in Member States' economies, particularly in southern Europe. Income from international tourism accounted for 5.5 per cent of GDP in Portugal, 3.9 per cent in Spain and 3.7 per cent in Greece. The comparable figure for Ireland was estimated to be 3.3 per cent but this is probably somewhat low.[16] At the other end of the scale, international tourism in Germany accounted for only 0.6 per cent of GDP. Tourism is an even more important creator of jobs, accounting for 7.2 per cent of all jobs in Greece and Denmark, 6.8 per cent in the UK and 6.3 per cent in Ireland. The balance of tourism in the balance of payments of Member States presented in Figure 7.3 also highlights the differing importance of tourism across the EU.[17]

The data show that the BLEU (Belgium/Luxembourg Economic Union) and three other Member States (Germany, the Netherlands and the UK) showed a deficit on their balance of tourism in 1992. Germany had the biggest deficit, at almost 20 billion ECU. Spain had the biggest surplus, at 12.8 billion ECU followed by France (8.6 billion ECU) and Italy (3.9 billion ECU). The data show a small net balance for Ireland (0.2 billion ECU), which has steadily increased in the 1990s to reach 0.3 billion ECU in 1994. It is important to note that there has been a steady improvement for Ireland since 1980 when the net deficit was 2.2 billion ECU. Figure 7.4 concludes the picture.

Figure 7.4 shows that France was the country with the largest income from tourism in 1992, 19.3 billion ECU, followed by Spain (17.1 billion ECU) and Italy (16.6 billion ECU). Seen in relation to the total income side of the balance of payments, tourism declined in importance between 1989 and 1992 in virtually all Member States. The decline was steepest in Spain and Greece (CEC, 1995a).

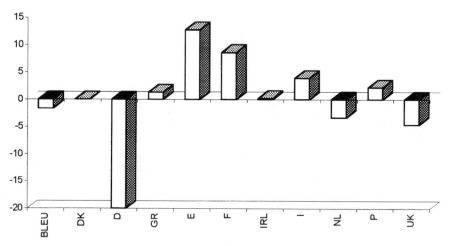

Figure 7.3 Balance of income and expenditure on international tourism, in billion ECU (1992 data except BLEU, GR and P (1991)). *Source*: CEC (1993)

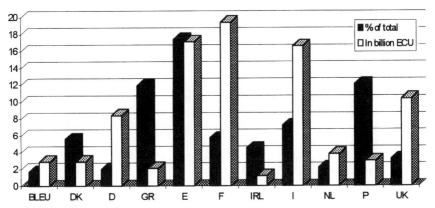

Figure 7.4 Income from tourism as a percentage of total income in the current balance of payments, 1989 and 1992 (except BLEU, GR and P (1991)). *Source*: CEC (1993)

Tourism accounted for more than a tenth of balance of payments receipts in three Member States in 1992: Spain (17.4 per cent), Portugal (12.1 per cent) and Greece (11.9 per cent) in 1991.

Tourism performance 1980–1992

Analysis of tourism data presented to date suggests that tourism is an important contributor to economic development in Europe, particularly in the poorer countries. The analysis has also demonstrated that members of the European Union have placed a greater emphasis on tourism through the use of ERDF funds in recent years. Table 7.5 outlines the growth rates of tourism earnings in EU member states and selected non-EU members over the period 1980–1992.

The data presented in Table 7.5 show that Ireland has been the best performer over the period in question, albeit with the smallest market size.

CURRENT DEVELOPMENTS IN IRISH AND EU POLICY FOR TOURISM

The Operational Programme for Tourism 1994–1999

While the causal relationship between investment in the first Operational Programme for Tourism 1989–1993 and the subsequent outcomes require further discussion in Chapter 9, the government stance on tourism as expounded in the second Operational Programme was very positive. The document outlining the new programme began as follows:

> The Operational Programme for Tourism, 1989–1993 has been a major success. The ambitious strategic targets set for the development of Irish tourism at the outset of the Programme have been substantially met. (Stationery Office, 1994)

Table 7.5 Growth of international tourism earnings in Europe, 1980–1992

Country	Average annual increase %	Market size Sterling £billion
Ireland	11.0	0.9
Portugal	10.4	2.1
Sweden	10.1	1.7
Spain	10.5	12.5
France	9.9	14.1
The Netherlands	9.8	2.8
Denmark	9.6	2.1
Italy	8.5	1.1
Norway	8.5	12.2
Switzerland	8.3	4.3
Austria	7.5	8.3
Belgium	7.3	2.3
Britain	6.4	7.9
Greece	5.6	1.9
Germany	4.6	6.2

Source: Derived from Eurostat data (CEC, 1995).

After attributing the performance of tourism to the first Operational Programme (OP) the new OP document goes on to stress that there are still some major deficiencies to be tackled. The new programme stresses the need to increase marketing spend to promote facilities developed under the first programme, an 'urgent need to improve facilities at major National Cultural Institutions, the requirement to preserve fish stocks and angling facilities to help ameliorate seasonality, the need to develop a major conference centre' and finally stresses the continuing need to upgrade training for the tourism sector. The commitment to tourism is endorsed by a significant investment programme to run from 1994 to 1999. The financial plan is outlined in detail in Table 7.6.

The financial plan shows that the EU contributions to the programme will be about 57 per cent (53 per cent 1989–1993), the private sector 30 per cent (same as 1989–1993) with the direct contributions from the national exchequer falling slightly to 13 per cent (17 per cent in 1989–1993). Figures produced under the Community Support Framework for Ireland over the period 1994–1999 estimate that Ireland will receive a total of 5620 million ECUs in Structural Fund Support. Of this, the ERDF will account for a total of 2562 million ECUs and spending on tourism will account for 354 million ECUs, or approximately 14 per cent, which shows an increase of 3 per cent on the programme 1989–1993. Figures of this magnitude demonstrate that tourism is finally receiving the attention and commitment of financial resources from government that for many years were not forthcoming.

Table 7.6 Financial plan for tourism Operational Programme, 1994–1999

IR £million based on ECU = 0.80824	Total cost	EU	National/public	Private sector
Product development	287	139	19	129
Marketing	125	51	5	69
Natural/cultural	125	94	31	–
Tourism training	110	82	28	–
Technical assistance	5	3	1	1
All Sub-programmes	652	369	84	199

Source: Stationery Office (1994: 24).

Tourism developments at EU level

The treaty on European Union, signed on 7 February 1992 at Maastricht, acknowledged for the first time that European Community action, if it is to accomplish the tasks which it has been assigned, should include measures in the field of tourism, under the conditions and according to the timetable set out in the Treaty (Article 3t). The declaration on civil protection, energy and tourism and Article N, paragraph 2 of the Treaty on European Union (CEC, 1992a) provide that the question of introducing a title relating to tourism in the treaty establishing the European Community be examined by the Conference of Representatives of the governments of the Member States to be convened in 1996 on the basis of a report to be submitted by the Commission to the Council. In order to prepare for this eventuality, Mr Christos Papoutis, Commissioner responsible for tourism, adopted a Green Paper on the role of the European Union in the field of tourism in April of 1995. The purpose of the Green Paper is to facilitate and stimulate thought on the European Union's role in assisting tourism, bearing in mind the report which the Commission is to submit to the Council by 1996 at the latest.

The Green Paper attempts to elicit views from the Member States, the Council of the European Parliament, the Economic and Social Committee, the Committee of the Regions, representative organizations, management and labour, and other bodies active in tourism at European, national and regional levels. In particular, the paper wishes these groups to state their opinions on the options set out in the Green Paper (CEC, 1995b). The options are as follows.

- **Option 1.** Option 1 or the 'zero option' is described as a 'scaling down of the present situation, whereby tourism would continue to benefit from measures under various fields of Community activity without being the subject of a specific action programme'.
- **Option 2.** The second option is a continuation of the current framework 'and level of intervention' to assist tourism and organize co-operation between Member States. In other words, maintenance of the *status quo*.

- **Option 3.** Option 3 would strengthen the Community's tourism involvement based on the provisions of the Maastricht Treaty, which significantly, acknowledged, for the first time the role of tourism.
- **Option 4.** This last option is the most contentious as it advocates an increase in the Community's role.

While the Commission is currently eliciting feedback it is impossible to be clear on the final outcome yet it is possible to make a number of observations. First, the zero option would become inevitable if the EU approves current proposals to cut its 8 million ECU a year tourism budget, leaving aid to be paid by other EU schemes. Secondly, it is apparent at this early stage that EU countries will not be in unison on the options. Reports suggest that Germany, the EU's largest tourist source, is strongly in favour of subsidiarity, believing that tourism is best handled at national level. Italy, one of the major tourism economies in the EU, favours a much more active role for the EU in tourism policy. Reaction to date in Spain has been rather mixed. At the time of writing there has not been any official or unofficial response to the Green Paper from the Irish Government. While the road to the final outcome will be long and arduous certain facts are clear. First, Europe will continue to face increased competition in tourism from Asia and the Pacific Rim countries. Secondly, the higher prices pertaining in Europe can only be justified and competitiveness maintained and improved if the quality of product is improved and thirdly, the projected growth from the present level of 315 million arrivals annually to 476 million by the year 2010 will place significant pressures on the present tourism infrastructure. Whatever the outcome of the Green Paper these issues will require urgent attention, whether that be in the form of increased subsidiarity or alternatively through the strengthening of EU policy for tourism.

CONCLUSIONS

This chapter has reviewed the slow evolution of tourism policy within the EU to the current Green Paper. It has been shown that while tourism was slow to emerge as a major concern in the Union it has become an important source of income and employment to many EU member states, but particularly the poorer countries. The use of ERDF funds to stimulate tourism development has been found as particularly important to Ireland, where the sector for many years had been denied access to finance to improve the quality of the product base. The development of discussions at EU level on the current Green Paper will demonstrate clearly the role which individual states feel the EU should have in relation to tourism policy. The eventual outcome of those discussions will determine how EU Member States face the increased challenge of competition from Asia and the Pacific Rim countries and how the increased volume of tourism numbers will be catered for in the years ahead. On these issues the long-term performance of Irish tourism and that of many other countries will be determined.

NOTES

1. The most notable exception (there were a small few) to the general consensus was the late Trinity College academic Raymond Crotty. He led a campaign against entry to the Common Market and also fronted a legal challenge against the Single European Act in the Irish Courts. For an in depth explanation of his views see Crotty (1988).
2. In essence, the European Commission which generally sets policy has traditionally been slow to develop a tourism policy.
3. See CEC (1989).
4. An ECU is a European Currency Unit.
5. COM (91) 95, see CEC (1991d).
6. COM (91) 97, see CEC (1991b).
7. For further details see CEC (1992c).
8. The first report, covering activities in tourism to the end of 1993 was published in April of 1994. For further information see COM (94) 74 (CEC, 1994).
9. The principal instruments with structural objectives are: the ERDF (European Regional Development Fund, the ESF (European Social Fund) and the guidance section of the EAGGF (European Agricultural Guidance and Guarantee Fund), together with the Community lending instruments, particularly the EIB (European Investment Bank), and the ECSC (European Coal and Steel Community).
10. Framework Regulation (EEC) No. 2052/88 (CEC, 1988c); co-ordinating Regulation (EEC) No. 4253/88 and implementing Regulations (EEC) Nos 4254/88, 4255/88 (CEC, 1988d).
11. The data provided for this section were kindly provided by a number of officials in Irish Government departments, primarily the Department of Tourism and Trade and the Department of Finance. At the time of writing it was not possible to get the information for other member states for the years in question.
12. For a more detailed discussion, see Deegan (1994).
13. We are indebted to Paul Appleby, Department of Tourism and Trade, for providing this figure and the estimates of expenditure based thereon.
14. GNP is the standard used by Eurostat for comparison purposes in official publications.
15. It must be stressed that while European market share has been declining the absolute number of arrivals has been rising considerably. This to some extent may ameliorate some of the problems associated with a declining market share.
16. There is grave doubt about the accuracy of Irish GDP figures due to the transfer pricing and accounting practices of multinational firms operating in Ireland. It is generally accepted that the figure for GDP is overstated and consequently the tourism proportion looks smaller than it actually is.
17. The analysis has not included the new member countries (Sweden, Finland and Austria) due to the lack of comparable data for the years under review.

8 Tourism in the Northern Ireland economy

INTRODUCTION

Tourism products are very similar in both parts of the island of Ireland[1] – the natural beauty of the landscapes, friendliness of the peoples, similarities in the cultures and weather conditions. While product enhancements have differed in scale under the recent Operational Programmes for tourism in both parts of the island, the thrust of these expenditures has been similar with funds invested in heritage and interpretative centres, golf courses and other tourism activity centres, though there has been greater emphasis on investment in accommodation in Northern Ireland (NI). Demand-side characteristics are similar also with significant ethnic links to the resident populations in the UK, USA (particularly Canada for NI) and further afield where the Irish 'diaspora' are to be found. NI has been particularly dependent on these ethnic markets while the Republic of Ireland (ROI) has attracted a greater share of the 'pure' holiday tourists. There is, of course, the obvious difference in terms of the geographical concentration of violence (mainly in NI) over the 25-year period up to the 1994 ceasefire,[2] though our analysis will show that the impact of the 'troubles' was by no means confined to NI tourism but affected tourist flows from overseas to both parts of the island and to internal cross-border flows also. Thus, both NI and the ROI are two very similar international tourism destinations subject to the fluctuations of external demand trends (i.e. income changes, exchange rate fluctuations, relative price movements, access constraints and costs, changes in tastes and random events) as well as to actions taken in or from the destinations which might influence choices made on holiday-taking (frequency and intensity of violent incidents and the perceived risks associated with these, marketing expenditures and their effectiveness). The fortunes of the respective tourist industries are inextricably linked, not merely because they represent key destinations for cross-border tourists, but also because the external images and influences impact quite similarly on both parts of the island. Indeed one could argue that both parts of Ireland are effectively separate parts of the one international tourism destination.

This chapter explores the major trends and influences on NI tourism with particular emphasis on similarities (and differences) between it and the ROI.

The trends and changing composition of tourism numbers are analysed initially from the 1960s, which is followed by a focus on the economic importance of tourism to the NI economy, particularly since the late 1970s; some aspects of the supply side of the NI tourism industry are examined, especially the varying accommodation stock and the range of attractions on offer; the organizational structure of the NI tourism industry and its evolution are outlined in the context of considering the various policy issues and measures used to develop the industry there; the first Tourism Operational Programme in NI (1990–1993), the INTERREG Programme (also EU) and the International Fund for Ireland provided useful supplementary funds for the development and promotion of NI tourism; the final sections consider recent developments in the sector, the likely impact of the peace process on the future of the NI tourism industry and the potential 'peace dividend' which might arise, followed by brief conclusions.

TOURISM TRENDS

Northern Ireland shared in the world tourism boom of the 1960s with average annual increases of 5 per cent (4.5 per cent in the ROI) in overseas tourists to the area. The start of the 25-year campaign of violence at the end of that decade is generally seen as a watershed interval for the fortunes of the NI tourism sector when there was a 'ratchet-like' reduction in numbers of visitors and a reversal of the earlier boom in percentage terms. The similarity in trends of overseas tourist flows is shown in Figure 8.1, which shows the sharp decline in numbers from 1969 to 1972, the subsequently slow recovery followed by the relative boom of the late 1980s and early 1990s.

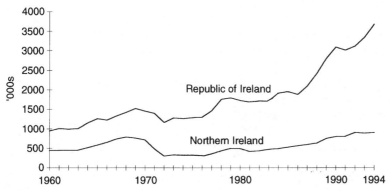

Figure 8.1 Trends in overseas visitors to Northern Ireland and the Republic of Ireland, 1960–1994. *Source*: NI Tourism Facts, Northern Ireland Tourist Board (NITB); Tourism Trends, Bord Failte, various years

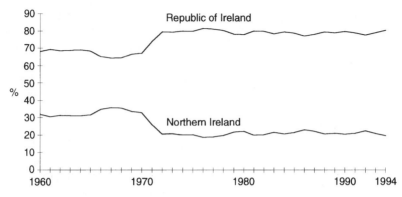

Figure 8.2 Respective shares of Northern Ireland and Republic of Ireland of overseas visitors to the island of Ireland, 1960–1994. *Source*: As for Figure 8.1

NI's share of overseas visitors to the island of Ireland stabilized at a lower level of approximately 20 per cent, from 1972 onwards, compared to the average of 33 per cent in the 1960s (Figure 8.2).

This proportion of 20 per cent persisted right through to the 1990s indicating that while the onset of violence had an immediate and more severe impact on overseas visitor numbers to the North, the variations in tourism flows were remarkably similar to both parts of the island in subsequent years. This interdependency in performance between both parts of the island is frequently overlooked in analyses which focus solely on one part of the island or the other. International tourist demand trends are critical to any explanation of tourist flows to Ireland while the negative impact of reported incidents of violence has affected the numbers of overseas visitors to both NI and the ROI.[3]

It appears from these data that both parts of Ireland are viewed as similar holiday destinations to overseas holiday-makers, with fluctuations in visitor numbers affected by similar demand variables (real incomes, relative exchange/inflation rates, access costs and convenience and products of competing destinations and negatively through the impact of shocks such oil crises, terrorist incidents in Ireland or elsewhere)

Figure 8.3 charts the year-on-year proportionate changes in overseas visitor numbers to NI and ROI for the past 35 years. While the fluctuations in numbers were remarkably similar, the peaks and troughs were more extreme in the case of visitors to NI for most of these years.[4] While one would expect this outcome intuitively in the case of the negative effects of terrorist incidents (1971–1972, 1976 and 1981) it is more difficult to understand the stronger peaking in NI for years such as 1978–1979, 1989 and 1992.[5]

In terms of numbers, the total of 2.288 million overseas visitors to the island of Ireland in 1969 (35.5 per cent or 787,000 went to NI) was not reached again until 1979 when 2.295 million visited (22 per cent or 501,000 to NI); the sustained up-

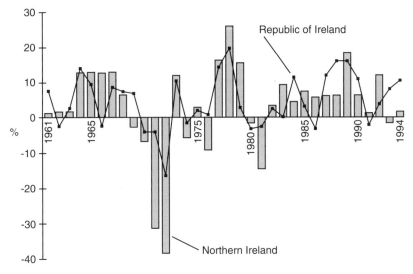

Figure 8.3 Yearly percentage changes in the numbers of overseas tourist numbers to Northern Ireland (NI) and the Republic of Ireland (ROI), 1961–1994. *Source*: Derived from NI Tourism Facts, NITB; and Tourism Trends, Bord Failte, various years

ward trend from the latter part of the 1980s led to the record level of overseas visitors to both parts of Ireland in 1994 of 4.583 million, of which 904,000 visited NI.

Referring to overseas visitors to NI, the level recorded in 1968 (of 787,000) was not reached again until 1990 when 796,000 visitors arrived there, a figure which was exceeded each subsequent year of the 1990s.

Changing tourism densities for selected years since 1981 are illustrated in Figures 8.4 (average) and 8.5 (peak season) and comparative densities for the regions of the ROI are shown also.

Seasonality is not as acute a problem in NI as in the ROI which reflects the composition of visitors to the province, particularly the low proportion of 'pure' tourists. The latter, traditionally, have a high propensity to take holidays in the peak months of the year though there are variations by nationality and age which, depending on the mix, can achieve a more even spread throughout the year. Assuming visitors are spread evenly through the peak months and throughout the year, the ratio of the peak to the year round average was 1.35 from 1991 to 1994 compared with 1.80 for the ROI. If anything, seasonality is becoming less of a problem in NI in recent years, perhaps reflecting a failure to 'grow' the pure tourist segment of the overseas market and echoing the more general problem with NI tourism which is an overall lack of tourists rather than an excess in any one season of the year. The density maps below illustrate this limited seasonality problem with NI tourism. Had the overseas tourism numbers grown in line with the targets set by the Tourism Review Group in their 1989 report

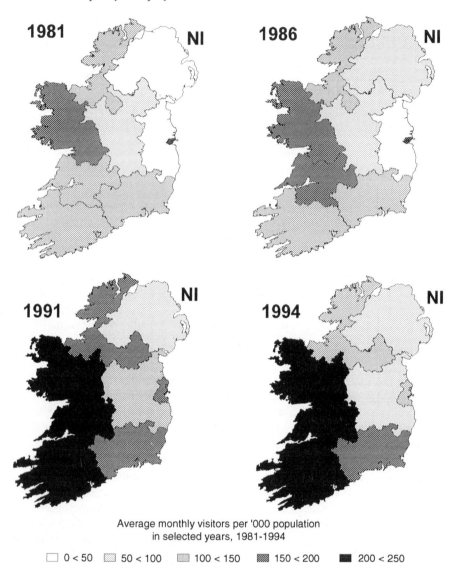

Average monthly visitors per '000 population
in selected years, 1981-1994

☐ 0 < 50   ▦ 50 < 100   ▦ 100 < 150   ▦ 150 < 200   ■ 200 < 250

Figure 8.4 Overseas tourism densities in Northern Ireland, 1981–1994 (average monthly visitors per thousand of the resident population) for selected years. *Source*: Derived from NITB, Tourism Facts, various years and Department of Finance and Personnel, 1995

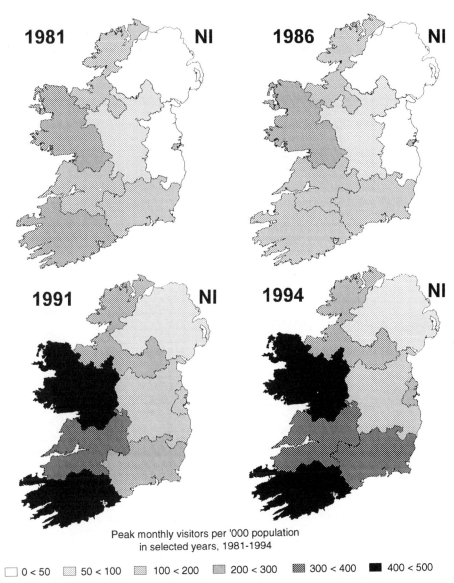

Peak monthly visitors per '000 population
in selected years, 1981-1994

☐ 0 < 50   ▦ 50 < 100   ▦ 100 < 200   ▦ 200 < 300   ▦ 300 < 400   ■ 400 < 500

Figure 8.5 Peak overseas tourism densities in Northern Ireland, 1981–1994 (peak season densities are the average for July–August per thousand of the resident population) for selected years. (Note: visitor estimates for July–August for 1986, 1991 and 1994 are estimated as per cent of the totals for the 3 months of July–September.) *Source*: As for Figure 8.4

(DED, 1989a), seasonality problems might have arisen; the dramatic increase in numbers of visitors since the 1994 'ceasefire' is likely to cause more seasonality problems given that pure tourists are anticipated to form the bulk of this increase.

Origin of visitors to NI

The principal source markets for tourists to NI are Great Britain, the ROI, mainland Europe and North America. There is an overwhelming dependence on the British market which accounted for over 88 per cent of all overseas tourists in the 1960s, a proportion which slightly declined to less than 80 per cent in the 1990s. The peak pre-'troubles' volume of visitors of 687,000 from Britain in 1968 was not surpassed again until 1990 when over 700,000 visited. North America had

Table 8.1 Visitors to Northern Ireland by origin countries/zones, 1960–1994

Year	Great Britain	North America	Mainland Europe	Other overseas	Total overseas	Republic of Ireland	Total out-of-state
			(000s)				
1960	388			52	440	200	640
1965	511			72	583	321	904
1969	674			92	766	300	1066
1970	634			80	714	263	977
1971	417			72	489	181	670
1972	254	20	13	14	301	134	435
1973	279			58	337	150	487
1974	266			52	318	169	487
1975	270			57	327	202	529
1980	403	44	27	19	493	217	710
1981	343	33	24	21	421	167	588
1982	352	40	28	15	435	277	712
1983	377	52	29	17	475	390	865
1984	405	43	30	18	496	412	908
1985	419	63	28	22	532	331	863
1986	453	47	35	27	562	262	824
1987	480	57	33	26	596	347	943
1988	512	52	39	30	633	297	930
1989	612	56	56	25	749	342	1091
1990	610	67	85	34	796	357	1153
1991	650	51	74	31	806	380	1186
1992	726	60	86	30	902	352	1254
1993	704	70	82	33	889	373	1262
1994	708	77	87	32	904	390	1294

Note: some of the figures for the early years of the 1960s are interpolated.
Source: NITB, Tourism Facts, various years and NITB (1981).

been the second largest origin market until the late 1980s.[6] However, the surge of interest among mainland Europeans to holiday in Ireland (both NI and ROI) has led to the substitution of mainland Europe for North America as NI's second largest overseas origin market since 1989. Since 1990 over 80,000 Europeans visited NI each year with the exception of 1991, while the numbers of North Americans never exceeded 70,000 until 1994 when 77,000 visited. Table 8.1 shows the broad distribution of visitors to NI from the main origin markets since 1960.

The ROI rivals the UK mainland as a major source of demand for the NI tourism market though it too was affected by the onset of the 'troubles' in the early 1970s. Pre-'troubles' visitor volumes from the ROI peaked at 352,000 in 1968, less than half the number of visitors from Great Britain in that year; this was surpassed again in 1983 when the ROI's share of the NI out-of-state totals exceeded that from GB for the first time (45.1 vs 43.6 per cent). Apart from 1983 and 1984 this relative share was not sustained, although visitor volumes from the Republic held above the 1968 level throughout the 1990s. Continuation of the 1994–1995 'peace process' will sustain and probably increase the relative importance of this origin market, currently stabilized at about 30 per cent of all out-of-state visitors to NI (Table 8.2).[7]

The long-term decline in the relative importance of the mainland UK (i.e. GB) market is noted, which in any case is dominated by business and VFRs rather than pure tourists. This is offset by the stronger and more recent growth in mainland European visitors which accounted for approximately 7 per cent of the total during the 1990s. Together with North American and other overseas visitors, these constituted 15 per cent of the total NI market in 1994 and the ability to 'grow' this segment of the overseas market in the future will critically determine tourism's contribution to the Northern Ireland economy and the

Table 8.2 Relative shares of Northern Ireland tourism market* by origin country/zones, 1960–1994 (selected years)

Year	Great Britain	ROI	North America	(%) Mainland Europe	Other overseas	Total other overseas†
(1)	(2)	(3)	(4)	(5)	(6)	(7)
1960	60.6	31.3				8.1
1970	64.9	26.9				8.2
1980	56.8	30.6	6.2	3.8	2.7	12.7
1990	52.9	31.0	5.8	7.4	2.9	16.1
1994	54.7	30.1	6.0	6.7	2.5	15.1

*All out-of-state visitors.
†Aggregate of columns (4), (5) and (6); for 1960 and 1970 also includes North American and mainland European shares.
Source: Derived from sources as in Table 8.1.

Table 8.3 Annual average percentage changes in visitor numbers to Northern Ireland, 1960–1994, for various periods

	Great Britain	ROI	North America	% Change Mainland Europe	Other overseas	All overseas*	All out-of-state
1960–1970	5.0	2.8				5.0	4.3
1970–1980	−4.4	−1.9				−3.6	−3.1
1980–1990	4.2	5.1	4.3	6.0	6.0	4.9	5.0
1990–1994	3.8	2.2	3.5	0.6	−1.4	3.2	2.9
1986–1990	7.7	8.0	9.3	24.8	5.9	9.1	8.8
1986–1994	5.7	5.1	6.4	12.1	2.1	6.1	5.8

*All except ROI visitors.
Source: Derived from sources as in Table 8.1.

success of its tourism policy. The growth rates of the different origin markets are presented in Table 8.3 which confirms this strong and recent growth from the European mainland, although from a rather low base.

The persistent decline from all market sources is noted for the 1970s while there was consistently strong growth in all areas from 1986 to 1990, particularly from the European mainland. This coincided with similar strong growth from this origin market to the ROI, confirming the importance of the linkages between the tourism markets on both parts of the island and emphasizing the significance of international demand trends in explaining the changes in Irish tourism.

Thus, there is a strong geographical bias or dependency in the NI tourism industry with, in effect, almost 85 per cent of total external visitors from what are effectively two quasi-domestic markets – GB and ROI. Seeking to lessen this dependency is a major challenge for both the industry and public agencies charged with responsibility for the sector. An alternative perspective on the nature of the industry and its demand side problems can be acquired from an analysis of the reasons for visiting NI. These are now considered.

Purpose of visit – the NI experience

There is a sharp contrast in the proportions visiting NI for pure holiday purposes in the late 1960s compared with the period after 1970. These declined from a high of 36 per cent in 1967 to a low of 8 per cent 10 years later.[8] Business and particularly VFRs have been the mainstay of the tourism industry in the province during the 1970s and 1980s. Both groups are less sensitive to the perceived security risks associated with visiting NI. Business trips tend to vary in line with economic conditions though increased as a proportion of total visits from less than 20 per cent in 1983 (during a recession) to a steady 30 per cent a decade later (see Figure 8.6).

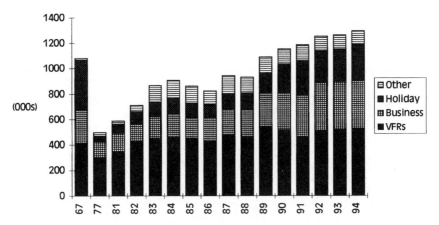

Figure 8.6 Visitors to Northern Ireland by purpose of visit, 1967, 1977 and 1981–1994. (Note: 'pure' tourists are those in the 'holiday' category.) *Source*: Derived from NITB (1982, 1993a, 1994) and NITB Tourism Facts, various years

Put in perspective, business traffic more than doubled while total visits increased by 25 per cent in the interval 1984–1994. This highlights the importance of business-related tourism in the overall promotion of NI as a tourist destination. The lessening of terrorist activity from the high levels of the 1970s also encouraged a greater level of normal business travel though it would be difficult to quantify this.

There has been significant recovery also in the pure tourist traffic from the low of 1977 to almost a quarter (276,000) of total visits in 1994 (a seven-fold increase compared with the overall expansion for all tourists by a multiple of 2.25). The corresponding proportion for pure tourists in the ROI is approximately 45 per cent.

This market segment is seen as crucial to the future of the NI tourism industry and several reports and strategy documents have alluded to this over the years.[9] Clarke and O'Cinneide (1981) commented on the difficulties of attracting these tourists to NI in the height of the troubles in the 1970s. They noted the problems of the NITB which essentially adopted a defensive strategy as reflected in such campaigns as 'Ulster is still in business' in the early 1970s. Marketing efforts were low key because of the seeming futility of expending resources on campaigns which could be negated by single atrocities.[10] There was an attempt to focus on the domestic holiday-maker through the promotion of home holidays, although the same troubles contributed to a much greater propensity among NI residents to holiday overseas or in the ROI. The de-escalation of the incidents of terrorism over a period of years gradually led to improved performance with increased volumes of tourists to the province. Figure 8.7 presents, in a crude way, the trends in terrorist incidents (here measured as recorded bombings and deaths from terrorist-related incidents)[11] and external tourist flows.

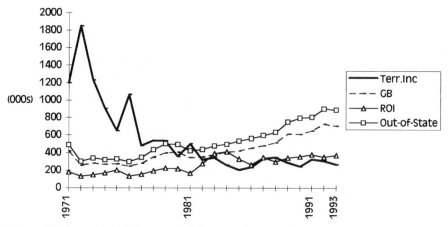

Figure 8.7 Terrorist incidents and visitor numbers to Northern Ireland by principal generating areas, 1971–1993. (Note: terrorist incidents are measured as the sum of bombings and deaths in each year; the tourism visits are measured in thousands on the value axis while terrorist incidents are measured in units on the same axis.) *Source*: Derived from data in DKM Economic Consultants (1994) and NITB, Tourism Facts, various years

The series move in predictable directions; visitors from the ROI seem more sensitized to the fluctuations in the terrorist incidents than those from GB or all out-of-state, particularly since 1981. This is probably a function of proximity to the events in NI and the greater media attention these get in the ROI.

VFRs constitute about 40 per cent of all visitors to NI, is the largest single category at slightly more than 500,000 visitors annually (1992–1994), and for part of the 1980s increased to over 50 per cent of all visitors to NI.[12] The tradition and continuity of emigration from Ireland for well over a century are key explanations for this category of tourist, which originate primarily from GB and North America. Contrary to what one might expect, the late 1980s increase in visitor flows from mainland Europe, although dominated by pure tourists, has been partially based on VFRs, reflecting the changing geographical destinations of NI emigrants.

While VFRs are not regarded as big spenders on standard tourism 'goods' they, nevertheless, make an important and reliable contribution to the tourism sector in both NI and the ROI, not least because of their contribution to international carrier receipts. Travel patterns of VFRs also help ameliorate seasonality problems. Although less sensitive to the image problems of NI they are quite sensitive, in an economic sense, to such factors as access costs, including frequency and convenience of flights. This was a major element in the commencement of the upsurge in visitor numbers to Ireland in the late 1980s, where the introduction of cheap cross-channel fares and a greater range of access points boosted traffic on the routes and encouraged more frequent visits 'home'. Cross-channel ferries were not oblivious to the changing competitive challenge presented by the airlines and responded accordingly. Although showing only a modest annual average growth of 1.3 per cent per annum from 1983 to 1992, VFRs to NI increased by over 20 per cent in 1989 compared with the previous year.

This analysis of trends in visitor numbers to NI shows heavy reliance on VFRs and business tourism while the 'discretionary' or 'pure' tourist segment of the market has shown steady expansion since the late 1970s to 276,000 visitors in 1994. The ROI has been more successful in attracting pure tourists but has a tourism industry which is also underpinned by a sizeable VFR segment and/or by visitors with ethnic links to the country. Government agencies in both parts of the island are keen to develop their respective industries through enhancing the appeal to pure tourists to visit. The trends' analysis also revealed strong dependence on the GB market in both parts of Ireland but a much greater dependence of NI on the ROI for out-of-state visitors than the reverse (30 vs 15 per cent).

Domestic holidays

Home holidays are an important part of the tourism sector though their con- tribution to the economy tends to be less significant than foreign holidays since they usually represent diversions of spending from one part of the NI economy to another and thus represent no additional source of income generation. It is only when home holidays represent a diversion of spending from holidaying abroad that their net contribution to the local economy assumes the same significance as foreign holidays. There is limited empirical evidence on the behavioural aspects of holiday-taking by NI residents and particularly on the extent of any substitution effects (home and foreign) taking place. NITB surveys have revealed that home holidays are viewed very much as second holidays (by over 40 per cent of home holiday-makers) while only 25 per cent regard these as the only or main holiday (NITB, 1993a). This low propensity to take domestic holidays may not be unrelated to the relatively poor tourism infrastructure in NI given the overall limited investment in the industry there for the past 25 years.

The pattern of home holiday-taking has been erratic over the interval 1983–1992 with total holiday trips fluctuating from 847,000 in 1983 to a low of 528,000 in 1987 and rising to 980,000 in 1988. The 1994 figure was estimated as 650,000. Self-catering is the most common form of accommodation used, i.e. caravans and camping, which account for almost half. There is comparatively low usage of commercial accommodation (19 per cent in hotels, guesthouses) and about 10 per cent are VFRs. Activities of various sorts (sporting and recre- ational) play a role in determining why and where NI residents take domestic holidays with the most popular activities being swimming, walking/hiking, fishing and attending heritage/artistic exhibitions/centres. Regionally the most popular parts of NI for home holidays are the north-east and south-west where they accounted for 60 and 72 per cent respectively of hotel room occupancy in 1993

(NITB, 1994). Not surprisingly, these holidays are seasonally very highly peaked though, because of the limited use of commercial accommodation, do not put a serious strain on the available stock. The next section examines the revenues generated from tourism and its contribution to the NI economy.

TOURISM'S CONTRIBUTION TO THE NORTHERN IRELAND ECONOMY

Although visitor numbers are important, the contribution of tourism to the economy is determined, in the first instance, not by the numbers of visitors but by the expenditures incurred by these visitors while in NI. The initial leakages through 'imports' from outside NI will reduce the impact of the direct tourism expenditures though indirect and induced expenditures enhance the total contribution which tourism makes to the local economy. Estimates of tourism multipliers are used to determine the GDP impact of tourism – these multipliers relate the total tourism output to the initial tourism spending. The level of employment dependent on tourism is a function of the employment intensity of the direct, indirect and induced outputs arising from initial tourism expenditures. Because of the difficulty of separating tourism from non-tourism outputs in typical tourism enterprises (or indeed domestic from international tourism outputs) employment estimates using a supply-side approach are too arbitrary to be relied upon. Estimates based on demand-side or expenditure data are more reliable. Though there is no definitive series of tourism GDP and employment for NI, various estimates have been made. Recent estimates indicate tourism GDP to be 1.8 per cent and employment to be approximately 11,000.[13] Both variables are well below the corresponding proportions for ROI and GB tourism, reflecting both the lack of development of the tourism sector in NI and its potential for growth given the right political conditions. It should be noted that increases in the relative importance of tourism in the NI economy are a function also of the decline in the traditional manufacturing industries (shipbuilding, textiles, shirt-making) which had been the mainstay of the economy for several decades.

Tourism revenues

Not surprisingly, tourism revenues in NI declined dramatically following the outbreak of the troubles in the late 1960s and took several years to regain the pre-troubles levels in real terms. The rate of recovery varied according to the different source markets, and generally followed the visitor trends. Revenue from Great Britain took longest to recover with the 1968 level of £96.2 million not being exceeded until 1989 when £101.1 million was generated (in 1993 prices). Revenue from the other major market – ROI – exceeded the pre-troubles level in 1983, the same year as the North American market. The main-land European and other long-haul origin markets made quicker recoveries in revenue terms probably because of their visitor profiles (young, curious, adventurous) and generally displaying less sensitivity to the social and political situation in NI. In volume terms these markets were much smaller. For all overseas visitors, revenue generated in NI through tourism activity reached pre-troubles levels in 1989 (at £132.58 million), while the following year this threshold was breached for all out-of-state visitors (whose spending reached £171 million). This contrasts with the experience in the ROI where the 1969 revenue level from all out-of-state visitors was reached again in 1978.

The worst period in revenue performance terms for NI tourism was during the 1970s when the image problems were so great that it was even quite difficult to generate enthusiasm and energy to market the province externally. The following decade halted and reversed the declines experienced and hitherto undeveloped markets (such as mainland European) emerged as important revenue generators, particularly in the pure tourist segment of the international market. Annual average changes in real revenue from the principal source markets are shown in Figure 8.8.

The chart highlights the volatility of the ROI market in revenue terms and it is noted also how this market declined in real terms in the 1987–1994 period. This was quite at variance with the overall pattern and particularly with the trend from mainland Europe which expanded in real revenue terms by 17 per cent annually, although admittedly from a very low base. While the visitor and revenue shares of the market are broadly in line for GB, there is quite a variation between the ROI and the 'other overseas markets' (North America, mainland Europe and long-haul regions such as Australasia). Between 1980 and 1993 the ROI accounted for an average of 34 per cent of visitors to NI but only 23 per cent of the out-of-state revenue, while the other overseas markets generated 24

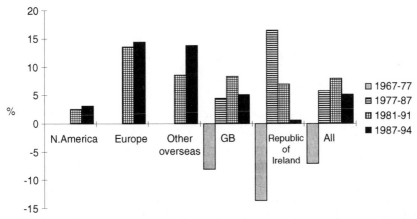

Figure 8.8 Annual average percentage change in real revenue from main source markets to Northern Ireland, 1967–1994 for various sub-periods. *Source*: Derived from NITB, Tourism Facts, various years and NITB (1982)

per cent of the revenue from 13 per cent of the visitor share. Clearly the latter are much more lucrative to the NI economy and it may make more sense to concentrate more marketing resources on these markets in an attempt to generate a better return than divert these resources to what is essentially a quasi-domestic market (in the ROI).

Focusing on the island of Ireland and ignoring domestic tourism, real revenue from out-of-state tourists had been over 20 per cent of the total in NI in the 1960s but declined to as low as 11 per cent during the 1970s. The ratio improved during the 1980s though with the relative boom in ROI's tourism in the late 1980s the proportion settled back to around 14–15 per cent in the 1990s (Table 8.4).

Some estimates have been made of the lost tourism revenues to NI arising from the troubles. These are based on alternative assumptions about a continuation of existing pre-troubles trends, tourism revenue growth at the same rate as the ROI (which for much of the time lagged behind international tourism growth) or GB growth rates, which would have been less affected, if at all, by the troubles on the island. One estimate of lost revenue was made in 1981. This assumed that, in the absence of civil unrest, the 1968 revenue level could have been sustained and with the fluctuations experienced from 1969 to 1981 the lost revenue over the 12-year interval was estimated to be over £420 million at 1981

Table 8.4 Out-of-state tourism revenues* in Northern Ireland, the Republic of Ireland and the island of Ireland, 1981–1994

Year	ROI IR£ million	ROI UK£ million†	1993 prices NI UK£ million	Island of Ireland UK£ million	NI/Island ratio
1981	543.0	434.5	79.5	514.0	0.15
1982	538.4	437.5	83.1	520.6	0.16
1983	541.7	445.4	119.6	565.0	0.21
1984	574.7	467.5	122.7	590.1	0.21
1985	635.3	523.1	116.7	639.8	0.18
1986	582.1	532.5	117.8	650.2	0.18
1987	643.7	585.1	126.2	711.3	0.18
1988	742.6	636.3	127.5	763.8	0.17
1989	829.3	718.6	166.4	885.0	0.19
1990	934.3	869.1	170.9	1040.0	0.16
1991	970.4	886.1	170.7	1056.8	0.16
1992	962.4	932.8	164.2	1097.0	0.15
1993	1082.5	1055.1	173.0	1228.1	0.14
1994	1170.7	1144.7	178.6	1323.3	0.14

*Excludes carrier receipts and excursionists' revenues.
†Average annual IR£/UK£ exchange rates used to convert ROI revenues to UK£ values.
Source: Derived from NITB, Tourism Facts and Bord Failte, Tourism Trends, various years; Central Bank of Ireland Annual Reports, 1981–1994, for IR£/UK£ exchange rates.

prices (NITB, 1982).[14] Clark and O'Cinneide (1981) made estimates of the losses in tourism revenues for both NI and the ROI using the rather optimistic assumption that the 1960–1969 trends would continue (ROI) or 1968 revenue levels would be maintained in real terms (NI). They estimated a revenue loss for NI of £280 million at current values for the 11-year period, 1969–1979, equivalent to £1163 million at 1993 prices or £106 million per year on average. This annual estimate was £42 million more than the NITB estimate which illustrates the wide variations and degree of conjecture in such an approach.[15]

Clark and O'Cinneide (1981) highlighted the problems of making such assumptions given that many other factors besides the civil unrest impacted on the sector (p. 34). These included the high inflationary pressures during the 1970s and the increased cost of energy on travel costs to more remote destinations. The alternative and much cheaper 'sun lust' holidays to southern European destinations would also have impacted on the traffic and spending volumes from GB and other northern European countries. The switch away from northern European 'cold water' resorts was part of a long-term shift in preferences which affected tourism revenues in both parts of the island. The NITB recognized some of these trends but found that where they sought to develop alternative holiday packages based on sporting and recreational activities, for example, the shortage of suitable accommodation acted as a constraint on the appropriate development of the industry.

More recently, DKM Economic Consultants (1994) estimated minimum tourism revenue losses on the assumption that the NI tourism revenues would have increased at the same rate as the ROI between 1967 and 1988. This would have given rise to a shortfall of £81 million in revenue in 1992. The ROI would have been less affected and DKM suggested the potential revenue gains under the return to normality to be of the order of 5 per cent or IR£17 million in annual revenues. These are a far cry from the kinds of estimates being made a decade ago and calls into question the value of exercises such as this. The troubles for the last 25 years have undoubtedly affected the Irish tourism industry and the 'outbreak' of peace will have, no doubt, a beneficial impact on the sector, not least because of the removal of one key element of uncertainty for tourism development and planning.

Tourism output and employment in NI

Tourism's contribution to NI's GDP has been well below that of Scotland, England or Wales and that of the ROI. Official estimates of tourism's contribution to GDP do not exist for NI though there have been a number of attempts to measure it (Horwath and Horwath, 1980, 1984; Scott and Guy, 1992) and from these and other estimates we have attempted to piece together a reasonably consistent series. Similarly, tourism employment data in NI are estimated using out-of-state tourist expenditures and that of residents taking holidays in NI, excluding international carrier receipts.[16]

One method used (from Scott and Guy, 1992) to derive GDP and employment estimates is the proportional method which relates tourism expenditure to total final expenditure and this ratio is then applied to NI's GDP and total employment. The resulting estimates are based on the notion that tourism's contribution to the economy is proportional to its contribution to total final expenditure. However, this approach does not allow for the greater labour intensity of the tourism sector. Another approach, from the same authors, is to use a 1979 Scottish input–output model, estimate the labour productivity for different sectors relevant to tourism and determine both tourism's direct GDP contribution and employment estimates based on these results. A multiplier value of 1.3 is applied to take account of employment and output generated (by tourism) elsewhere in the NI economy. This approach takes account of the relative labour intensity of tourism.

While Scott and Guy made their estimates for 1990, their input–output methodology has been applied to the tourism revenue data for 1981–1994 by adjusting the labour productivity values in line with inflation and assuming that the 1990 ratio of direct tourism GDP to revenue persisted throughout the period. Results are presented in Table 8.5.

The employment results were compared with recent NITB estimates (1990–1994), earlier estimates by Horwath and Horwath (1984) for 1981–1983 and derived employment estimates based on the proportional method for 1984–1989. These were also compared with derived estimates of tourism employ-

Table 8.5 GDP and employment impacts of Northern Ireland's out-of-state and domestic tourism expenditures, 1981–1994

Year	Tourism GDP	Tourism GDP as % of total GDP	Tourism employment	Tourism employment as % of total employment
1981	37.75	0.85	5130	0.90
1982	40.25	0.83	5037	0.90
1983	65.62	1.24	7855	1.41
1984	66.72	1.18	7605	1.36
1985	70.67	1.13	7596	1.34
1986	74.01	1.07	7694	1.36
1987	72.24	0.97	7211	1.26
1988	79.35	0.95	7549	1.28
1989	128.19	1.39	11314	1.89
1990	130.69	1.29	10539	1.72
1991	134.60	1.22	10254	1.66
1992	128.21	1.11	9414	1.52
1993	141.68	1.15	10242	1.66
1994	150.38	1.20	10871	1.76

Source: Based on Scott and Guy (1992), NITB, Tourism Facts (various years) and Department of Economic Development, NI Statistical Abstract (various years).

ment in NI assuming a similar proportionate link between tourism revenue and employment as existed in the ROI over the same period. This confirmed that the estimates in Table 8.5 on the economic importance of tourism in the NI economy, in GDP and employment, are probably upper bound estimates.[17] Thus, while tourism is growing in importance in NI, it is essentially of minor economic importance there, accounting for little over 1 per cent of GDP and under 2 per cent of civilian employment. While there is undoubted potential for expansion, given the level of suppressed demand for the last several years, a doubling of revenues and output would not greatly alter its relative economic importance.[18]

SUPPLY-SIDE FACTORS

The dominant elements of the NI tourism product are the accommodation stock (including related eating and drinking establishments used by residents as well as tourists), the transport services and private and public sector amenities.

Accommodation

The accommodation stock in NI is a key measure of the available capacity to meet any adjustments on the demand side. It also represents the main private sector contribution to NI tourism. Given the bias in external visitor terms towards VFRs, the accommodation stock effectively caters for the remaining 60 per cent of visitors, and a much lower proportion for holiday-makers. For residents of NI taking holidays in the province, there has been a shift over the past 10 years towards self-catering accommodation which requires much less capital investment than hotels or guesthouses. The shift to self-catering holidays reflects market trends elsewhere and is driven also by the lower labour and overhead costs than alternative hotel accommodation.[19] In line with the decline in visitor numbers the quantity of rooms available declined to the mid-1970s and recovered subsequently although the mix across the accommodation types changed in favour of 'other accommodation' (bed and breakfast outlets primarily) and self-catering, from hotels and guesthouses. This trend is not unique to NI. Table 8.6 shows the changing accommodation stock in terms of units available while Figure 8.9 illustrates the changing quantity of rooms available in NI for the past two decades.

The changing accommodation available has moved in line with the visitor trends although clearly with some time lags in terms of the response times involved, especially since visitor numbers have been quite volatile. Hotel units had fallen by 43 per cent between 1965 and 1993 while 'other accommodation' units increased by 27 per cent over the same period. There was a less dramatic though continuous reduction in hotel rooms available within an overall volume which surpassed the 1968 level only in 1993. Clark and O'Cinneide (1981) attributed part of the reduction in hotel (and room) stock in the 1970s to terrorist

Table 8.6 Tourism accommodation units in Northern Ireland, 1965–1995

Year	Hotels	Guest houses	Other accommodation*	Self-catering	Total units
1965	215	220	495		930
1970	147	179	797		1123
1975	144	136	488		768
1980	145	129	482		756
1981	149	135	426		710
1982	142	133	466	16	757
1983	139	123	458	21	741
1984	138	127	471	25	761
1985	136	132	538	44	850
1986	132	127	548	53	860
1987	128	129	614	58	929
1988	125	128	619	81	953
1989	120	126	618	83	947
1990	121	126	618	91	956
1991	124	135	669	121	1049
1992	125	146	675	136	1082
1993	124	146	660	176	1106
1994	124	140	619	215	1098
1995	127	151	669	275	1222

*B & B accommodation, but excludes hostels (of which there were 35 in 1995).

Source: NITB Reports, various years.

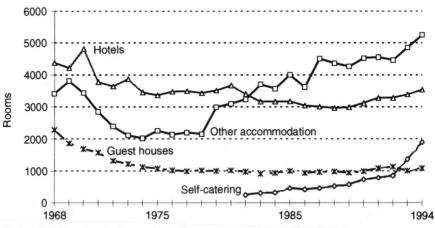

Figure 8.9 Rooms available in Northern Ireland tourism-related accommodation, 1968–1994. *Source*: Derived from NITB, various reports

attacks but also to the poor profitability associated with very low room occupancy rates over prolonged periods during the year.

Generous Government grants have been available throughout to augment existing accommodation or to build new units but this had minimal effect during the 1970s. This level of support was criticized later in the Tourism Review Group's report (DED, 1989a) in which it was argued that a dependency culture had been fostered and the private sector was unwilling to invest in tourism-related accommodation without generous state support, and, by and large, the financial institutions were not interested either. The response to poor profitability in hotels from tourism has been to diversify the businesses into catering to a far greater extent for the local market in non-tourist activities (weddings, discos and so on). The Review Group also noted the structural weaknesses in the hotel sector with many small family run businesses and only a handful of A*-rated hotels, all located in Belfast. Thus, there was a general lack of professionalism especially in the critical field of international marketing and the fragmentation in the sector had negative implications for employment and career structures. The Review concluded that the industry was inadequately prepared for any upsurge in demand, both because it was not sufficiently tourist oriented and had significant structural weaknesses (DED, 1989a). The cessation of violence in 1994 will have tested this hypothesis to a degree though an adequate supply-side response will take more than one season to be realized.[20] The years of decline and uncertainty have clearly constrained the industry's capacity to develop; the political context has further compounded the problem with the result that the NI accommodation stock was regarded to be of poor quality from an international tourist perspective. Improvements have taken place in recent years, however.

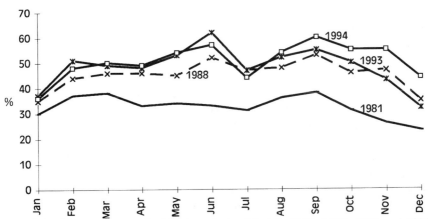

Figure 8.10 Occupancy rates in Northern Ireland hotels, 1981, 1988, 1993 and 1994.
Source: Derived from NITB Reports and Tourism Facts, 1981, 1988, 1993, 1994

Reference was made above to the varying occupancy rates in the province. This varies according to grade of hotel (positively) and to location, with Belfast and East region units experiencing better rates than, for example, the South-west scenic region of Co. Fermanagh. Less seasonality was noted also in the East regions and in Belfast. Occupancy rates have improved also over time which should impact on the profitability of the hotels (Figure 8.10).

The chart shows the noticeably higher occupancy rates in the last four months of 1994, following the ceasefire effective from 1 September. Anecdotal reports on the 1995 season have indicated extremely high occupancy rates in registered accommodation. While this is an inevitable outcome of the sudden rise in visitor numbers (dominated by visitors from the ROI and the UK), it cannot obviate the need for significant investment in improving the quality of accommodation on offer if NI is to regain a reasonable share of the international tourism market.

Transport

Transport services are another essential ingredient of the tourism product and particularly so for island destinations. This embraces the underlying infrastructure, the organization of transport services and the frequency and efficiency of access scheduled services, sea and air. Given that Belfast operates as a 'quasi-capital city' in its own right, it is well serviced by scheduled and charter air services mainly to/from destinations on the UK mainland. Direct transatlantic scheduled services have been available from NI only on a limited basis and have been boosted by the recently (1995) introduced Belfast–Shannon–Boston service operated by Aer Lingus. The main access routes to the province have been through the ROI (rail and road) or from the UK mainland (sea and air). A sufficient number of carriers operate to and from London and other UK cities to ensure strong competition and attractive prices, particularly on the London–Belfast route. The liberalization of air fares throughout Europe in the late 1980s was instrumental in diverting a good deal of NI-bound traffic from the sea to the air routes, though within totals which were relatively static. The steady rise in overseas tourist numbers to NI since 1982 (see Figure 8.3) would no doubt have been helped, especially since 1987, by the spectacular rise in similar tourists to the ROI. Many of the latter would have included an overland visit to NI in their trip to the island. Given the relatively static flows of overseas visitors via direct access routes to NI, the routes through the ROI can be the only explanation for the growth over this recent period, 1987–1990 and 1992.[21]

The Tourism Review Group (DED, 1989a) were critical of the extent to which the internal transport services and carriers failed to promote the notion of holidaying in NI, often being more interested in promoting holidays by residents outside the province. There were limitations also for the European 'wanderlust' traveller because NI railways were not part of the Eurorail system offering cheap travel; the refusal of ROI-based car-hire firms to allow cars hired in the Republic to be used in NI was a further limitation on tourist traffic from this market. It is recognized that the road system in NI is an excellent one for touring purposes but the internal public transport system is limited for the promotion of tourism. A further concern from the tourism perspective is the difficulty of arranging and the poor development of 'packages' which integrate the transport–accommodation–amenity services in such a way that intending visitors can plan vacations with ease. Specialist tour operators had not exploited this particular niche to any great extent.

Amenities

The range of amenities on offer is a third major component of the NI tourism product. Most of the historic or recreated visitor sites are publicly owned although facilities related to activity type holidays, such as golfing, can be out of bounds for tourists except under quite restrictive conditions determined by club members. NI is much less endowed than the ROI with open access type golf courses even though many of the latter have been supported by EU funds under the Operational Programme for Tourism and are thus of recent origin. Local authorities have an important role to play in the provision of tourist amenities in their areas and in encouraging tourists to visit district council areas. There are several forest or country parks and gardens, many of which have free access. The top seven attractions in 1993 attracted more than 240,000 visitors each, with the largest (Crawfordsburn Country Park) attracting an estimated 700,000. The largest fee-paying attraction in the same year was the Ulster Folk and Transport Museum with 181,000 visitors.

The Tourism Review Group (DED, 1989a) noted the soundness of the basic framework for the development of NI's competitive tourism product, while acknowledging the need for greater professionalism in both running and market-ing the facilities to an 'increasingly sophisticated and demanding tourism market'. The Group also noted that if future growth in the NI tourism industry is to be achieved the inherent product weaknesses would need to be addressed.

These weaknesses included: poor image, lack of awareness of benefits by potential visitors, fragmented industry structure and weak integration between the component product parts, limited market research resources to assist targeted marketing campaigns and a number of product gaps such as industrial tourism, wet-weather facilities, family entertainment and improved catering facilities. The Review Group concluded that NI did not offer good value for money to international tourists compared with competitor destinations. This was not an altogether surprising conclusion given the small scale of the sector, the limited growth experienced and the consequent lack of competition which restricted potential quality improvements, and, by extension, value for money.[22] Furthermore, the limited private sector investment in the sector over two decades would have had detrimental effects in raising quality standards, which contrasts with the experience in the ROI.

ORGANIZATIONAL STRUCTURES AND POLICY DEVELOPMENTS IN NORTHERN IRELAND TOURISM

Tourism development is a post-war phenomenon in most OECD countries and the organizational structures to support this in Ireland and Britain largely emanated from legislative measures initiated in the late 1940s.

Organizational arrangements

The first of the tourist boards to be established in these islands was in NI following the passing of the 1948 Development of Tourist Traffic Act (Northern Ireland). The NI Tourist Board (NITB) has been central to the development and promotion of NI tourism since then, working in conjunction with the relevant government departments (most recently, the Department of Economic Development (DED)), the local authorities and the tourism industry itself. The 1948 Act defined NITB's role to 'promote the development of tourist traffic in Northern Ireland and to encourage persons who reside elsewhere to visit Northern Ireland'. Other important functions of the NITB included the maintenance of appropriately high standards in tourist accommodation and catering through its registration and grading functions, and assistance with the provision of additional tourism accommodation and amenities through the operation of a variety of funding schemes in conjunction with the DED and District Councils.

Clark and O'Cinneide (1981) referred to the strong similarities in the organizational structures for delivery of tourism policy objectives in both parts of Ireland though the regional delivery mechanisms rely much more on the District Councils (local authorities) in NI than in the ROI. This has led to greater diversity of approach and lack of uniformity in delivery throughout NI as the energy and commitment of District Councils varied. The latter were given extensive additional functions under the Local Government (Northern Ireland) Act, 1972, which included the attraction of tourists to their areas (through holding special events and other means), the provision of tourism advisory and information services and the provision and upkeep of amenities and services for visitors.[23] Liaison with the NITB is an important dimension of the delivery of these functions if only to ensure a cohesive approach to the development of the industry. The NITB also had a funding role for the local authorities in relation to their tourism remit. Tensions between these public agencies on the appropriate approach to tourism development in NI has never been too far from the surface and a recent example was the open criticism of some (unspecified) District Councils in the 1993 NITB Annual Report (p. 7) for their public attitudes to tourist initiatives undertaken by the Board (NITB, 1993c).

The tourism industry in the ROI has had, since the 1960s, a greater participative role in the policy delivery process at regional levels through their role on the regional tourism organizations. There is not an equivalent arrangement in

NI where industry involvement is encouraged only on a voluntary/community and largely informal basis without a statutory function. Wilson (1993) was critical of the absence of any kind of consultative forum from the industry or other actors to feed back relevant information and opinions to the NITB. The Horwath and Horwath (1980) report proposed the establishment of an Ulster Tourism Consultative Council with three panels dealing with amenities, transport and accommodation. This was never established because of resistence by accommodation and amenity interests which already had effective access to the NITB, according to Smyth (1986). Smyth was critical also of the lack of coordination in the industry which he attributed to the absence of any clear policy guidelines from the DED. This void was rectified subsequently.

The organizational arrangements were such that the NITB had largely a marketing and registration function, the local authorities had a local information and developmental function while the government department assumed a policy and developmental role working through both the NITB and the District Councils. These have remained broadly intact although the report of the Tourism Review Group (DED, 1989a) recommended the dissolution of the NITB and its replacement by a much more integrated body with both a marketing and developmental function (functions to come from NITB and DED, respectively).[24] In the event, the NITB was not abolished but rather assumed greater responsibility for both development and marketing of NI tourism. This was given expression in the Tourism (NI) Order, 1992, which significantly strengthened the funding and decision-making powers of the Board, and provided it with greater autonomy also (see Buckley and Klemm, 1993). It is interesting to note that the approach adopted in the ROI in 1994, working on foot of the Arthur D. Little Ltd report on the reorganization of Bord Failte was quite the opposite – to separate its developmental role (and effectively transfer prime responsibility for it elsewhere, i.e. to the Tourism OP Monitoring Committee and especially appointed Management Boards) from its marketing role, on which it was then asked to concentrate, with particular emphasis on international marketing. Bord Failte is devoting the lion's share of its resources to its international marketing remit and has less influence on the developmental aspects of the industry today. It is questionable whether the separation or amalgamation of these two interdependent functions arises from any inherent logic on the appropriate interventions by government in a key sector of the economy (or the needs of the industry), or whether it has more to do with the competencies of the actors involved in policy delivery and an assessment of their effectiveness.[25] Although not explicitly stated, it does appear that the Government-directed tourism organizational reforms in both parts of Ireland reflect more of the latter.

Policy developments

The primary objective of attracting more tourists to NI was being successfully realized during the 1960s on foot of a global expansion of international tourism and relatively peaceful conditions in the province. The hotel and guest-house accommodation stock was limited and the private sector was not responding sufficiently to the loan facilities offered by the NITB with the result that partial grant aid was introduced in 1963, and later extended in 1972. Self-catering accommodation was included in 1978 and the supply of these units expanded significantly in the following 15 years in response to the changing market needs. During the 1970s the policy response to the downturn in tourism growth was largely a defensive one by the NITB with marketing campaigns attempting to counter the almost daily negative publicity from terrorist incidents in some years, and a greater focus on encouraging NI residents to holiday at home. Efforts largely failed on both counts. Safety considerations outweighed other positive factors in holiday decisions though it must be recognized that the alternative and much cheaper southern European sun destinations diverted considerable numbers of potential tourist away from usually more expensive north European cold-water resorts. NI residents also took advantage of these alternative destinations and demonstrated an increasing propensity to holiday abroad during this time.

The accommodation stock (particularly hotel and guest-house) declined in line with market demand and the grants on offer did little to offset this trend. Indeed, private sector investment has been generally poor in NI tourism (and mainly concentrated in accommodation). This undoubtedly reflected the poor and uncertain returns anticipated in the 1970s and to a lesser extent in the 1980s. Partially to offset this, the provision of generous grants over a prolonged period developed a 'dependency culture' in the industry which the Tourism Review Group strongly criticized (DED, 1989a).

Policy assessment in the 1980s

Tourism performance improved in the 1980s especially towards the latter half although there was a vacuum in terms of stated policy objectives until 1989 when the DED's document 'Tourism in Northen Ireland: A View to the Future' was published (DED, 1989b). Prior to this a number of studies on the contribution of the tourism sector to the NI economy were published, notably the two Horwath and Horwath reports (1980 and 1984) many of whose findings were picked up in later reports, e.g. accommodation deficiencies, improved access and better amenities. NITB, though not charged with policy formulation, had a high profile role in leading the efforts to promote the industry and in interpreting the desired policy objectives. Writing in 1986, Smyth summarized NITB's role in NI tourism which could be taken as a close approximation of (unstated) tourism policy objectives. These were as follows:

- the promotion of Northern Ireland as a holiday destination, both within the province and elsewhere;
- the encouragement of a high standard of accommodation and catering facilities by means of its registration and grading powers;

- the provision of tourist amenities both directly and through co-operation with local authorities and the DED, and
- [acting as] advisors to government and the tourist industry.

(Smyth, 1986: 125)

The direct resources made available to deliver on these objectives consisted of the modest annual grant-in-aid for the Board to deliver its marketing, quality assurance and research services together with capital grants administered in conjunction with the DED and the local authorities for both accommodation and amenities. These were augmented later in the decade through funds from the International Fund for Ireland (IFI) and the Tourism Operational Programme.[26]

The Government was taking a stronger interest in tourism. A 1984 'Discussion Paper on Tourism Development in Northern Ireland' (DED, 1984) was followed by the publication in 1986 of 'Northern Ireland Tourism – Policy Guidelines Statement' by the DED (1986). This set out a number of aspirations for the industry rather than any clear strategic vision and identified a set of targets, notably that pure holiday visitors should increase by 8 per cent a year to reach a volume of 425,000 by 1994. These policy guidelines were not supported with any increased resources allocated to the sector. However, these did point to a greater role for the private sector in shaping the future of NI tourism, a theme which was reinforced by later public policy stances in spite of the under-performance of this sector in the industry to date.[27]

Tourism Review Group

The increasing interest in the tourism sector by policy-makers led to the establishment of the Tourism Review Group in 1988 which undertook the first major review of the NI tourism industry since 1948, when the NITB was established. Comprised of representatives from the DED and NITB, the terms of reference were primarily focused on reviewing government policy towards the tourism industry. This included reviewing the role of the principal agencies, the level and effectiveness of funding and the contribution of tourism to the economy. The Review Group was asked also to make recommendations on the future strategy for the industry (DED, 1989a). The link between the media image of NI and the performance of the tourism sector was examined by the Group and particularly whether the revenues generated by the 'pure' tourists (estimated at £15 million) justified the annual government subvention provided (£6 million). This poor return begged the question as to whether much of the marketing expenditures was wasted until peaceful conditions prevail; a related question was that, given the high proportion of non-discretionary visitors, could the level of public funds allocated to tourism promotion be justified? The Group were quite emphatic that it would be very unwise to abandon the drive to attract pure tourists, which continue to come to the province in spite of the image problems. They argued for continued promotion of the sector since the returns from tourism are spread throughout the regional economy while a better return should arise from greater targeting of available funds to those receptive niche markets less sensitive to the poor image of NI.

Key weaknesses of the NI tourism industry were identified which ranged from NI's poor image, weak marketing and packaging components, the fragmented structure of the industry, product gaps and lack of competitive advantage.[28]

A strong underlying theme of the Review was the perception that the private sector had developed a dependency culture in respect of tourism development and had not invested in the industry to the desired extent.[29] The future strategy anticipated a greater contribution from this sector through direct investment in both amenities and accommodation, supported as appropriate by the financial institutions. The role of government in this context was informed by intervening only where there was evidence of market failure (communal/public goods, lack of information, presence of externalities or to overcome private sector risk aversion). The policy approach for the tourism sector was to be similar to that applied to industry and services with the critical measure being the additional visitors and revenues generated in NI from outside the province.

Thus, Government should focus on providing the appropriate context and framework within which the private sector would flourish. This would include the provision of the best regulatory framework for the industry, invest in human resource development through training provision and maintenance of high standards, stimulate new enterprises and assist firms to be more competitive, and market NI to overseas (and ROI) markets.

While the approach adopted does have a rationale in economic terms (and was clearly consistent with the then UK Government's conservative economic policies of non-interventionism) it may not have sufficiently taken account of the fragile state or stage of development of a sector essentially hanging on to survive for almost 20 years.[30] Had the Tourism Review Group taken a developmental rather than market driven stance to the sector it might well have placed less expectation on the private sector to deliver the investment required as part of the strategy outlined. Indeed the private sector failed to reach the targets set in the ensuing OP for Tourism in NI, 1990–1993, which is not altogether surprising in the light of its poor performance hitherto.

A useful outcome of the Review Group's deliberations was the clarification of the overall objectives for the NI tourism sector. The overall objective was 'to increase the overall wealth and employment creation from tourist activities in NI'. This would be achieved through (DED, 1989b):

(a) assisting local and international marketing by the industry;
(b) assisting the improvement in product quality where the private sector is constrained;
(c) ensuring tourism's needs are reflected in NI's infrastructure, and
(d) providing the best regulatory climate for strong private sector growth.

The potential of the sector for expansion was recognized and the challenge was primarily seen on the demand side to attract more external visitors to NI.

Improvements in product quality were required and linked to the need to offer 'good value for money' to tourists.

Future strategy

Arising from this analysis and identification of weaknesses, and clarification of objectives, a three-pronged future strategy was proposed:

- repackaging;
- product development;
- product excellence.

The first phase (repackaging) would focus on addressing the image problem in a professional manner, seek to integrate the various aspects of the tourism product (accommodation, transport and amenities) and focus on country, niche and specific market segments with a view to boosting visitor numbers. Joint marketing with Bord Failte was also seen as a particularly important priority in this phase.

The need for extensive product development (second phase) would arise from the initial repackaging process and be governed by the 'need to ensure the product is of the right quality and price to fit the needs of tourists'. Product development would include upgrading existing and adding new accommodation, improvement or provision of amenities, encouragement of new private sector enterprises to fill specific gaps (e.g. in evening entertainment) and improvement in access transport services and internal transport provision (DED, 1989b: 17). The focus on product development would be customer-driven and rely heavily on responses from the private sector to the market opportunities presented, while benefitting from various forms of assistance from the public sector (though now preferring 'soft' loans to grants, which emphasizes a partnership approach). The notion of indicative planning was introduced as an approach which could be utilized to provide information and guidance to private sector developers.[31]

The third phase of the future strategy – product excellence – consists of the integration of the first two approaches so that 'NI can develop particular products as centres of international excellence which could act as flagships of NI tourism'. The Fermanagh Lakelands for international watersports or a newly developed 'Gleneagles' style hotel and golf course complex were mentioned as two possibilities in this regard.[32]

The DED (1989b) report also highlighted the need for the NITB to set challenging but realistic targets, notably to increase the number of tourists to 1.6 million by 1994 (total achieved was 1.3 million) and within this to increase pure holiday visitors by 200 per cent or 300,000 (276,000 achieved). One of the more controversial proposals was the creation of a new tourist organization (NI Tourism Development Organization) in place of the NITB, and which would embrace both the product development functions of the DED and the marketing functions of the NITB. This new organization would operate under the direction of a policy design and strategic planning unit within government which would set the main policy parameters for the industry.[33]

Indicative plans, operational programmes and the 1990s tourism scene

The Tourism Review Group's report was wide-ranging and comprehensive and effectively wrote the script for the Tourism Operational Programme, Northern Ireland, 1990–1993 (DED, 1989c). The funds made available through the OP meant that the future strategy for the industry was matched with reasonable resources which could address the product weaknesses identified and develop the industry on a more professional basis. The report also had an impact on the NITB which was clearly threatened by the proposal to replace it, even if it was to be augmented in terms of scope and functions. Indeed, the first response of the NITB was to produce an Indicative Plan for NI tourism, thus meeting one of the key proposals of the Review Group (see NITB, 1990).

The Indicative Plan (IP) moved the Review Group's findings further towards the marketplace and implementation, and provided guidance on funding decisions made in the context of the OP. The IP essentially presented an outline of the areas where the public agency (Tourist Board) considered tourism investment to be appropriate and relevant. The IP focused on products with tourist potential, on the geographical distribution of tourism through identifying 'areas of opportunity' and addressed a number of issues considered to be crucial for the development of the industry.

On the accommodation front, the IP noted that only about a quarter of the province's hotel accommodation catered for tourists and there was a critical need to upgrade standards in all forms of accommodation. Under the revamped Tourist Development Scheme (TDS), the provision of assistance was to be in the form of interest relief grants or loans (although direct grant payments continued to be the dominant form of support) and would be targeted at hotels which clearly could attract additional (international) tourists and not those catering for the local non-tourist market primarily.[34]

In relation to non-accommodation tourism products, the IP identified the need to encourage the development of a limited number of 'major natural heritage attractions' and to take measures to improve the tourism potential of NI's forest and country parks. On cultural tourism, there would be a focus on supporting private and public property owners to market historic properties as tourist attractions and the NITB would encourage the development of a limited number of major projects on hitherto 'unexploited cultural heritage themes'. The criteria for the latter were international appeal, year-round operability and capability of attracting 250,000 visitors annually. Industrial heritage attractions would be also given some priority.

Activity holidays would be supported through environmentally sensitive development of the facilities linked to the natural inland water-based resources particularly on the Erne and Lough Neagh for angling, boating and other water-sports. Land-based activities such as golf would get special attention through the development of a number of new 18-hole championship courses linked to accommodation provision and capacity to market overseas as an integrated package.

Equestrian and walking products (e.g. the 'Ulster Way') were two other activities identified which had development potential. Special interest activities such as conference business, language schools, the all-Ireland National Genealogical Project and speciality tours/touring holidays would also get priority treatment.

The tourism infrastructure was identified also as playing a crucial role in NI's tourism development and one which extends beyond the remit of the tourist board and its parent department (DED) especially in relation to transport infrastructure and services. Diverse aspects include the quality improvement and monitoring of the camping and caravaning sector, the development of an electronically-based reservation system (with Bord Failte – this became known as the GULLIVER Project) and integration/improvement in the services of the network of tourist information offices throughout NI. Areas of opportunity were selected throughout the province where some concentration of resources would best realize the development potential of the sector.[35] The NITB would also play a role in developing scenic routes through rural areas and work in partnership with private and public sector bodies on worthwhile projects.

Assessment of the Indicative Plan

It seems that there would be something for everybody and every area in the Indicative Plan which would seriously dilute any effort at specialization and developments at the appropriate scale.[36] The IP also presented a list of (policy) issues for consideration by government.[37]

It is difficult to assess the contribution of the Indicative Plan other than to recognize it as a defence by the NITB of its central role in delivering tourism policy in NI and a demonstration of its understanding of the problems and opportunities in the industry. The proposal to have the NITB replaced by a new tourism development agency was shelved. Indeed the subsequent Tourism (Northern Ireland) Order, 1992 consolidated the role of the Bord and allocated to it a 'significant increase in resources both for itself and for financial assistance to the industry' (NITB, 1992). The extent to which the IP influenced the direction of development in the sector in subsequent years is not clear as significant funding from both the Structural Funds of the EU and the International Fund for Ireland (IFI) came on stream and were specifically targeted, either on the EU's individual sub-programmes or on aspects of tourism with an all-Ireland dimension. It does appear, however, that the key role envisaged for the private sector was emphasized less under the NITB while the financial transfers encouraged still further the 'dependency' culture which the Review Group had criticized. Two further 'indicative style' plans were produced in the form of corporate plans by the NITB (1992, 1995a) covering three-year periods. The first of these overlapped the first Tourism Operational Programme (OP), 1990–1993 while the 1995–1998 plan paralleled the second OP running from 1994 to 1999. The next subsection synthesizes the main elements of these measures to develop NI tourism, quantifies the diverse funding sources including the IFI and evaluates the outcomes in so far as this is possible.

Measures to support NI tourism, 1990–1999

It is evident from the various sources consulted that NI tourism was heavily underfunded in the two decades 1970–1990. The improvements in terms of increased resource allocation commenced towards the latter part of the 1980s through the IFI injections of funds and, from 1990, through the EU's first OP for Tourism and the INTERREG programme for border areas. Indeed the product development measures of the NITB, under the Selective Financial Assistance allocated, provided less funds than the IFI transfers prior to 1992–1993. It was in this latter year that the financial resources of the NITB, through its DED grant, increased by 64 per cent to £11.7 million. and was underpinned at this higher level in subsequent years rising to £13.7 million in 1995–1996 (see Table 8.7).

Table 8.7 Financial resources allocated to NITB, 1989/90–1995/6

	1989/90	*1990/1*	*1991/2*	*1992/3*	*1993/4*	*1994/5*	*1995/6*
Running costs (%*)	46.9	50.1	71.0	57.0	59.3	61.0	60.0
Promotional/programme costs (%*)	53.1	49.9	29.0	43.0	40.7	39.0	40.0
Total NITB expenditures (£ million)	3.768	5.383	5.184	8.570	8.636	8.836	9.301
Selective assistance (£ million)	1.911	2.137	1.911	3.090	3.426	3.644	4.383
Total (£ million)	5.679	7.520	7.095	11.660	12.062	12.480	13.684

*Of total NITB expenditures.
Source: Derived from, Table 6.18 of HMSO (1995).

Compared with the supports allocated to industry, trade and employment, tourism received 0.7 per cent of total expenditure in 1989, increasing to 1.5 per cent in the following two years and rising thereafter to a steady 2.5 per cent. By any standards (and particularly by comparison with the ROI) it did not appear that the tourism sector was receiving much attention from Government. This was surprising in the light of the stated objectives to 'increase the contribution which tourism makes to economic development'. It does not follow, of course, that the public sector is the only means by which this eventuality will come about and reference has been made already to efforts to secure a better performance from the private sector in developing NI tourism. Perhaps another reason for the limited commitment of UK Government public funds to tourism in the province arises from the alternative funding sources which became available through the IFI (since 1986) and the EU Structural Funds (from 1990). While the former constituted totally additional resources available for the sector, the latter did require some matching funds from the UK Government and also anticipated a private sector contribution. The INTERREG Programme also represented some additionality in funding terms although these were relatively limited at £0.3 million and £1.2 million in 1992 and 1993, respectively. Both the IFI and Tourism Operational Programme were administered through the NITB which ensured a degree of consistency across the range of interventions to the sector and eliminated any unnecessary competition which might have otherwise emerged.

The International Fund for Ireland (IFI)

Turning initially to the role and contributions from the IFI it is worth noting that tourism was merely one of the sectors and economic activities supported by the Fund. However it was considered to be a critical sector where joint efforts with the ROI could yield dividends not just in economic terms but also as part of the 'reconciliation process'. The IFI was established in 1986 as a joint North–South initiative to support economic development projects in NI and the border counties of the ROI. Projects to be supported should not be confined to one community or the other and the overt aim was 'to encourage contact, dialogue and reconciliation between nationalists and unionists throughout Ireland' (IFI, 1993). Funding was provided initially by the US government (£52.2 million), Canada (£0.76 million) and New Zealand (£0.11 million) to be followed later by Australia. The initial committed expenditure on tourism was approximately 19 per cent of the total.

Funds were made available to develop accommodation amenities (private sector only), other tourism amenities (private and public sector) and joint marketing of both NI and the ROI through support for initiatives administered through Bord Failte and NITB. The Accommodation Amenities Scheme was aimed initially at adding conference and leisure facilities to help extend the tourist season, as well as supporting an increase in the stock of hotels in NI; later this scheme embraced the development of quality small tourist hotels and self-catering accommodation. The Amenities Development Scheme (supporting projects ranging from pony trekking to marina centres) was designed to encourage additional overseas visitors to NI. Of the IFI allocation to NI over the period 1987–1994, almost half (46 per cent) was allocated to accommodation projects, 36 per cent to other tourist amenities and the remaining 18 per cent to joint marketing with Bord Failte and the NITB. The latter included joint promotions at trade fairs in London, the USA, Canada and Australia, support for a joint 'Ireland' desk at the British Tourist Authority office in London and a range of marketing campaigns in key source markets such as Britain, USA, France and Germany. The IFI also supported the establishment of a computerized reservations system used throughout tourist information offices North and South (known as 'GULLIVER'[38]) and an all-Ireland genealogy project. Over £26 million at current prices was spent by the IFI on NI tourism from 1987 to 1994; of this, almost £5 million was spent on joint marketing, over £12 million on accommodation projects and over £9 million on other tourist amenities. In the light of the limited sums advanced for product development through the

NITB, these are not insignificant sums allocated to NI tourism. Comparing the marketing and communications expenditures of the NITB, the relative IFI marketing spend (based on 50 per cent NI share) was 83 per cent in 1989–1990 although it fell to 7 per cent in 1993–1994 through a combination of a reduction in the IFI spend and a substantial increase in the NITB expenditure especially since 1992–1993.

Evaluating the IFI expenditures is difficult because no formal studies have been undertaken (to our knowledge). The funds did represent an important additional injection to the sector. The extent to which these may have led to windfall gains for the operators involved or displacement of business from non-assisted operators is conjectural though a definite possibility since the 'reconciliation' more than the 'economic' motive for support may have been paramount. The limited investment in NI tourism over the previous decade or more, particularly by the private sector, meant that the IFI resources were a welcome boost to the development of the sector which has taken on a new significance since the momentum of the 'peace process' in 1994. The IFI set out to back a large number of small projects rather than the reverse. This may have diluted the impact of the Fund and did little to encourage the development of large-scale or flag-ship projects for the sector.

Tourism Operational Programme for Northen Ireland

Another welcome boost to the resources available for the NI tourism sector derived from the EU-funded Tourism Operational Programme (OP) 1990–1993. This was part of the transfer of Structural Funds to Objective 1 regions to improve their infrastructure and competitiveness so as to compete effectively in the single market of the European Union. These funds were made available on a multi-annual basis from both the ERDF (European Regional Development Fund) and the ESF (European Social Fund). The OP was drawn up by the Department of Economic Development within the context of the Community Support Framework for NI, which was approved by the Commission in 1989 (see DED, 1989c). The funds allocated were over 44 million ECU of which 2.2 million ECU were from the ESF (for training). The programme also required some matching funding from the public sector (15.7 million ECU) and from the private sector (26.3 million ECU). The latter did not materialize to the extent anticipated. The total resources anticipated from this source (EU + public sector funds and leveraged private investment) over the four years of the programme amounted to 86.4 million ECU at 1990 prices.

The overall aim of the programme was to assist the development of the tourism industry in NI largely through implementing the strategy proposed by the Tourism Review Group summarized above (DED, 1989a, b). This required a combination of investment in tourism accommodation and amenities, training expenditures, and marketing of the facilities overseas. The private sector was to be encouraged to play a more central role in tourism development and the ultimate objectives of increasing tourism revenue and employment were

Table 8.8 Operational Programme for Tourism in Northern Ireland, 1990–1993: sub-programmes, measures and EU funding

Sub-programmes	Measures	EU funding (million ECU)	(%)*
I. Development of tourism amenities by public/similar bodies	1. Key attractions	15.6	75
	2. Heritage, culture and interpretation	6.8	75
	3. Complementary amenities	2.8	75
II. Development of tourism amenities by the private sector	1. Activity-based tourism	5.4	35
	2. Heritage and industrial tourism	2.0	35
	3. Visitor amenities including accommodation-related	0.9	35
III. Accommodation	1. Youth accommodation (voluntary/charitable sector)	2.2	75
	2. Accommodation (private sector)	2.2	15
IV. Marketing	1. NITB marketing and promotion of NI	2.6	50
	2. Marketing by other bodies in the tourism industry	1.2	64
V. Tourism support services	1. Research, development and implementation	0.1	62
	2. Other support services	0.4	51
VI. Training in the hospitality industry	1. Training in the hospitality industry	2.2	65

*Of total funding for each measure.
Source: Derived from DED (1989c).

highlighted. A summary of the six sub-programmes of the OP, the main measures in each and the EU supports proposed are outlined in Table 8.8

The bulk (57 per cent) of the EU funds were allocated for sub-programme I and were thus spent on capital projects such as interpretative centres, heritage and cultural attractions and other non-accommodation amenities.[39] While the image problems in NI will act to constrain its growth potential on the demand side, the chronic shortage of accommodation will also limit the prospect of reaching the targets set in the OP on the supply side. Clark and O'Cinneide (1991) pointed this out in their interim assessment of the OP which was undertaken primarily (for DGXVI of the EU Commission) to refine the targets and other measures used to monitor the effectiveness of the programme. The OP does not as such address the accommodation shortage (in qualitative and quantitative terms) except through its reliance on a largely private sector response both within and without the context of the Programme. All the allocated EU funds were drawn down by the scheduled dates though the total expenditures generated from the programme at 70 million ECU was approximately 80 per cent of planned. If we make the reasonable assumption that the shortfall was mainly due to an inadequate response from the private sector, the latter shortfall was of the order of 37 per cent.

No formal evaluation of the Tourism OP has been carried out either by the UK Government or the EU Commission and at this stage (1996) the follow-up programme is well under way. Clark and O'Cinneide (1991) suggested that the programme should be subject to an ex-post evaluation after two years had elapsed from the final year of implementation (1993). They also outlined a range of yardsticks which could be used in the monitoring and evaluation process, with a stronger focus on the outputs to be expected rather than the inputs (as was the tendency in the first OP proposal document). Their report has been largely ignored which begs the question as to how seriously, evaluation mechanisms are taken by Member State Governments and/or the EU Commission itself.

NI Single Programming Document

The second round of Structural Fund transfers included tourism as a sub-programme under the NI Single Programming Document (SPD)[40] which was approved by the EU Commission in July 1994. This is to run for the years 1994–1999. A significant increase in funding was secured for NI tourism with the total targeted expenditure (EU, public and private sectors) of 165 million ECU and EU contribution of 75 million ECU, representing increases of 91 per cent and 70 per cent, respectively, over the first OP for Tourism (in money terms). What is more interesting is the mix of measures proposed on this occasion with greater expenditures allocated to marketing and promotion (24.3 per cent of EU funds), training for the tourism industry[41] (22.6 per cent) and the provision of accommodation, especially that linked to other tourism activities such as golf and fishing (16.3 per cent). The investment in tourism amenities received a much lower priority than previously with 26 per cent of the EU funds earmarked compared with 57 per cent. A new measure was introduced – Conservation of the Natural and Built Environment – with approximately 10 per cent of the funding which reflects the fashionable focus on sustainable tourism as outlined in the NITB (1993b) report on the subject.

The SPD, in setting out the rationale for the continued support for tourism in NI, noted the role of the first OP as 'a major contributory factor in the continued growth of tourism in NI' from 1989 to 1993 (p. 57). This is an unfounded naive conclusion given the heavy emphasis on the development of amenities in the programme that could not realistically deliver a 'dividend' until towards or after the end of 1993. The rationale for the heavy increased expenditure on marketing (p. 61) springs from a tendency to accept at face value the view that there is a direct causal link between increased marketing spend and increased visitor numbers. It seems unfortunate that these conclusions, based as they are on practically no evaluative analyses, form the basis for the continued support of the industry and for the expenditures proposed. Nevertheless, the change of emphasis in the new programme appears to address the critical problems facing the industry. The fact remains, however, that decisions made on this basis tend to be largely subjective and deny the extensive range of techniques which may be used to ensure more efficient and effective public sector investment decisions in the tourism sector. Experience in the ROI, while based on marginally more evaluative material, differs little in essence.

RECENT DEVELOPMENTS AND THE PEACE DIVIDEND

The 1992 Tourism (Northern Ireland) Order re-affirmed the central role of the NITB in shaping the future of NI tourism. Resources made available to NITB for supporting the development of the industry were substantially increased for 1992–1993 and subsequent years (see Table 8.7). Two corporate plans were produced by NITB since then – for the three-year periods, 1992–1995 and 1995–1998[42] – and a follow up to the Indicative Plan (NITB, 1990) was published in 1995 in the form of a development strategy for the ensuing five-year period (see NITB, 1995b). While earlier plans were developed in a context where the resource back up was totally inadequate for the aspirations of the tourism planners, those developed in the 1990s had the fortunate combination of a number of significant funding sources (EU, IFI, UK Government) to back the development of the sector together with the expansive expectations emanating from the peace process started with the ceasefires which commenced on 1 September 1994.[43]

The 1992–1995 Corporate Plan of the Tourist Board re-affirmed the messages in the Indicative Plan with an emphasis on promoting the province (in co-operation with Bord Failte and the British Tourist Authority for overseas markets), on developing the product and raising quality standards in the industry, on strengthening partnerships with district councils involved in regional tourism management and improving the information services for visitors when they arrive. Both the 1995–1998 Corporate Plan and the Development Strategy to the year 2000 were written under the conditions of the so-called 'peace process' though were not radically different from the earlier plans. But there was now a greater sense of urgency about the development needs of the sector and specifically the need to enlarge and improve the quality of the accommodation stock (e.g. from 22,000 bed spaces to 41,000 by the year 2000).

This was seen as a crucial requirement to capitalize on the short-term bonanza in in-bound tourist traffic and to lay the foundations for the longer-term development of the sector.[44] More optimism also prevailed about the prospects for NI tourism and forecasts of a potential trebling of the numbers employed to 30,000 (and matching revenue growth) by the year 2000. The supply-side response cannot be confined to the accommodation sector to realize these ambitious results, as substantive improvements in the access and cross-border transport services and in the quality of service will be required if the anticipated bonanza is to be sustained. The NIEC (1995) are more sanguine about the prospects though recognize that since tourism suffered severely at the onset of the 'troubles' so now it stands to gain considerably as part of the 'peace dividend', a point echoed by Tansey (1995). Moreover, the Council recognizes that the climate for investment has changed with investors who are prepared to take a long-term perspective on the anticipated returns from tourism investment in the province. The encouragement of investment by overseas and indigenous operators is emphasized as a clear objective of the 1995 'plans'. These also signal the key role which the private sector is expected to play in delivering NI's tourism targets for the year 2000 of increased tourism revenue to £500 million, increased visitor numbers to 2.3 million (with a 'pure' tourist content of 30 per cent) and a GDP contribution of 5 per cent.[45]

The likely benefits of the 'peace dividend' have been the subject of considerable debate since September 1994 in both parts of the island. Tansey (1995) notes that the maintenance of peace will remove the biggest single obstacle to the development of Irish tourism, both North and South, and that much of the initial expansion in visitor numbers to NI might come from the ROI.[46] The NIEC (1995) liken the ending of the troubles to the removal of a non-tarrif barrier to tourism trade. This is a likely bonus for tourism in both parts of the island. The ability to offer a greater product range through the promotion of all-Ireland holidays should not be underestimated nor the opportunity to market two destinations for the price of one. The concept of 'co-operative competition', borrowed from the literature and practice of the Italian industrial districts, is relevant here. Opportunities to exploit the 'peace dividend' can be realized more fully if competition in the development of holiday packages at a sub-sectoral level complements the co-operative promotional activites at an all-Ireland level. Tansey (1995) gives a few examples of cross-border enterprise co-operation such as golf, equestrian, water-sports, cultural and historic tourism which could prove very beneficial.

While the sentiment of co-operation is to be welcomed it should not hide the fact that this will be a difficult process, especially given the tradition of limited co-operation for several decades. Teague (1993) observed that 'although there has been an upsurge in support for North–South economic cooperation, thinking on the issue remains naive and unconvincing ... new and more robust ideas are needed'. While tourism has been identified as a sector likely to gain considerably under the peace process, there appears to be an underlying view that it is a sector that can be harnessed far easier than other sectors of the economy. Official NI reports which refer to the peace dividend and the likely benefits to tourism rarely get beyond a broad assertion of a positive outcome. The impetus to develop tourism must be tempered with a sense of realism on what the sector can contribute. A rationale for co-operation has been suggested by Fitzpatrick and Associates in a report for the European Parliament (1993) whereby any joint initiative should satisfy two conditions: it should be mutually beneficial and it should lead to an increment in the level of tourism activity. Co-operative marketing initiatives especially in niche product areas can encourage more and more tourists who visit the ROI to extend their stays to include NI, which is likely to be an immediate benefit of the peace process.[47] There is also likely to be increased business from second or short break holidays from South to North, which could be particularly beneficial in the shoulder months of the season. The peace process presents an opportunity to overcome the low international demand for holidaying in NI which has restricted its development there for 25 years. The opportunities presented by these additional visitors will be missed unless there is a positive and sustained policy response to overcome the supply-side deficiencies in the quality and quantity of accommodation, in innovative product developments, in access transport and in the development of the human resources employed in the sector. The peace dividend can and must be realized partially within a NI context but more comprehensively within an all-Ireland context.

CONCLUSIONS

The international image of NI and the perceived risks of holidaying there have seriously constrained the development of the tourism sector since the late 1960s. The gradual and sustained recovery of the sector in the 1980s was not unrelated to the improved performance of tourism in the ROI, particularly since 1987 and the current, if uncertain, peace process has generated renewed confidence in the future potential of NI tourism. The demand-side constraints have seriously limited the development of the industry, given the unfavourable risk-return ratios and consequential low investment levels. To a large extent NI tourism operated with limited exposure to international tourist trends in the past quarter century. Several reports prepared since 1980 identified similar weaknesses and product gaps and suggested possible strategic initiatives to improve the performance of the sector. However, with limited resource supports, relatively little happened though the EU Structural Funds and transfers from the IFI made some differ-ence. The extreme dependence of NI on financial transfers from the British Government is a surprising context for the official approach to a far greater private sector role in developing this particular sector. Despite the plethora of reports, reviews, indicative plans and development programmes, there is still a strong dependency culture pervading the industry.

The fortunes of the tourism industry in both NI and the ROI are inextricably linked. The similarity of product in both parts of the island is not surprising but the different mix of visitors to each destination over the past 25 years has influenced the manner in which the industry has developed. With only 20 per cent of all visitors to NI classified as pure tourists (pre-1995), investors had neither the incentive nor the energy to cultivate an understanding of this market which explains why it contributes less than 2 per cent of regional GDP. The plan and prospect of increasing this relative contribution to 5 per cent by the year 2000 will undoubtedly present a challenge of unprecedented proportions to the principal actors in the industry there. While co-operation between tourist boards and governments will be instrumental in promoting an improved flow of tourists to the island of Ireland at lower cost than separate promotional efforts, competition between North and South will ultimately determine the share of this larger market as it currently does between east and west in the ROI.

NOTES

1. Northern Ireland (NI) comprises the six north-eastern counties (Antrim, Down, Derry, Tyrone, Fermanagh and Armagh) and is a politically separate entity, formally belonging to the UK and ruled from Westminster since 1921; the ROI constitutes the remaining part of this politically divided island.
2. The ending of this ceasefire in February 1996 has cast a good deal of uncertainty on the future prospects for a peaceful settlement to the conflict in NI and will undoubtedly impinge on the prospects for tourism on the whole island.
3. A number of studies/reports have examined or reported on the relationship between terrorist incidents and numbers of tourists to NI (and by extension, the ROI) since the onset of the 'troubles' at the end of the 1960s. Particular terrorist incidents or events had more dramatic impacts on visitor numbers, e.g. burning of the British Embassy in Dublin in 1972, IRA hunger strike campaign which resulted in the deaths of Bobby Sands and others in the early 1980s whereas sustained and steady campaigns of violence did not impact as strongly on visitor numbers in any given year. The DED (1989a, b) reports made brief reference to the tourism/violence links as part of the problem of image in NI tourism, a point also addressed by Wilson (1993) who was critical of the NITB's approach to marketing the province as if no violence existed; Moorhead (1991) explored relationships between the media and terrorism and how these impacted on NI tourism while Buckley and Klemm (1993) explained the decline in NI tourism in a wider framework than simply the 'troubles'. More recently, DKM Economic Consultants (1994) attempted to measure the economic impact of the NI conflict on all sectors including tourism and made some estimates of the likely growth of NI tourism in the absence of the conflict; Clark and O'Cinneide (1981) made similar estimates several years earlier.
4. Close correlations were found between the totals of overseas' visitors to NI and the ROI and the yearly percentage changes in these for the period 1960–94; the correlation coefficients for both sets of variables were 0.72, which was significant at the 1 per cent level.
5. The fact that NI is viewed as a quasi-domestic tourist destination for UK mainland based holiday-makers (who are included in the total of overseas visitors above) may explain some of this divergence with the result that the Irish punt/sterling exchange rate, adjusted for inflation rate differences, is an additional variable affecting decisions to holiday in the ROI compared with NI. This would have had no differential impact pre-1978 when both currencies were irrevocably tied to each other at parity.
6. In this part of the discussion the quasi-domestic market from the ROI is ignored, although it does provide an important component of 'foreign' earnings from international tourism.
7. The first half figures for 1995 confirm a substantial growth in the numbers of visitors from the ROI to NI.
8. Indeed the number of holiday visitors from or via Great Britain fell to 17,000 in 1972 and to a mere 7000 in 1976 (less than 5 per cent of all visitors from this market). For a further discussion of the immediate post-'troubles' start-up, see Clarke and O'Cinneide (1981).
9. See NITB Annual Reports, various years, DED (1988, 1989), and NITB (1989, 1995)
10. Wilson (1993) was critical of the general approach adopted by the NITB to marketing

the destination during the troubles; he argued that the Board hardly recognized the fact that the troubles were an issue and gave little advice to incoming tourists on how to prepare for a holiday in the area, portrayed by the media as 'high-risk' because of the record of continuous and unpredictable violence there over several years.

11. Although this may involve some double-counting, it is assumed that either or both would have most effect on influencing the discretionary tourist to visit or not to visit NI.

12. Generally, the higher the proportion of VFRs in the tourism population of an area the worse tends to be the performance of the tourism sector; there is a preponderance of Irish VFRs in the lower socio-economic groupings and hence these have a lower capacity to spend than other groupings and an even lower propensity to spend on tourist related goods than other categories of tourist products (accommodation, etc.). For further elaboration on the characteristics of Irish tourists and on their socio-economic backgrounds, see Steinecke (1979). However, more recent evidence (for the ROI) suggests that VFR expenditure is increasing relative to other groups.

13. The NITB (1995b) document quoted this figure of 1.8 per cent of GDP while the earlier report of the Review Group (DED, 1989a) gave estimates of 1.57 per cent for tourism GDP but only 4,700 employed in the sector for 1987. This latter figure was less than 1 per cent of civilian employment in NI. In a recent private communication from NITB, using the input–output method to estimate tourism GDP and employment, the figures were put at 1.2 per cent of GDP with 11,000 employed. Clearly the estimates from different sources are not consistent.

14. Equivalent to £790 million in 1993 prices or £66 million annually.

15. Their (Clark and O'Cinneide's) estimates for the ROI were for revenue losses (from visitors and carriers) of more than IR£2000 million for the 9 years, 1970–1978, or IR£224 million per annum.

16. Estimates of the ROI's tourism impact in Chapter 4 refer to the inclusion of 30 per cent of taxes generated through tourism activities as part of the 'officially accepted' tourism output and employment. The rationale for this is dubious and the implications misleading in terms of the relative importance of the sector in the ROI. For NI, no tax recycling is assumed in the calculation of GDP and employment from tourism.

17. Although the data in the table show that tourism employment more than doubled since 1981, earlier estimates by Horwath and Horwath (1984) based on 'employment due to tourism' in various sectors indicated that 9200 were employed in tourism in that year. Thus, the estimates used may be particularly sensitive to the methodology chosen.

18. In this section the focus has been on full-time equivalent employment with no reference to the quality of employment in terms of the proportion of part-time workers, its seasonal nature, or the pay and conditions of employment. It is likely that these qualitative aspects are no different than the tourism industry in the ROI with a preponderance of small and medium-sized enterprises and significant family involvement in the industry. The fact that the NI industry is smaller in scale and has not expanded as rapidly as the ROI tourism sector may have generated limited mobility opportunities there which may have negative consequences for the quality of employment. The empirical evidence on this is weak, however.

19. Predicted by Richards (1975).

20. Although the 11 per cent increase in the accommodation stock in 1995 over 1994 is non-trivial and particularly impressive was the expansion by 28 per cent in the number of self-catering units available.
21. There are no data available on the cross-border trips of overseas visitors within Ireland but the recent indications of significant movements emphasize once again the interdependence of the tourism industries, North and South.
22. Richards (1975) had earlier suggested more investment in activity-based holidays in NI – golfing, angling, fishing and boating – as a way of diversifying the product base and in anticipation of the changing market trends.
23. See Clark and O'Cinneide (1981: Appendix II).
24. The registration and grading functions of the Board were to be out-sourced and paid for by direct fees raised from the accommodation units requesting the service; similar out-sourcing was recommended and implemented for Bord Failte's role in quality assurance on foot of the Arthur D. Little Ltd report (1994).
25. Related issues on this debate concern the need for tourist board organizations to focus on their core business and not be diverted to peripheral activities which can best be handled by other bodies (public or private). The issue of cost effectiveness is relevant also for both parts of the island where the marketing expenditures may be wasted if not targeted to the truly discretionary visitor. For the ROI, Deane (in NESC, 1980b) drew attention to the poor return for the marketing expenditures by Bord Failte in the British market from where relatively few 'pure' tourists came in the 1970s; for NI, the low proportion (14 per cent) of discretionary tourists called into question the whole rationale of blanket country marketing expenditures without sufficient attention to the target/niche markets within these countries. Leslie (1991) noted the poor return in 1989 of £15 million in holiday tourism revenue in NI for a government outlay of £6 million.
26. The EU's INTERREG programme was a further funding source specifically for border regions.
27. For a fuller discussion on the role and effectiveness of planning in NI tourism see Leslie (1991).
28. See DED (1989a: Chapter 4).
29. The conditions in NI may have been quite unfavourable for high levels of investment in tourism given the likely returns (and the alternatives available) but the Northern Region of the UK has been characterized by similarly poor interest by the private sector in tourism development. This may reflect a similarity of industrial structures with a predominance of traditional large-scale industries which generate their own dependencies and may fail to generate the entrepreneurial culture more appropriate for tourism development (see Thomas, 1995).
30. It is instructive to note that a similar stance was adopted by Arthur D. Little Ltd (1994) in their review of Bord Failte in the ROI although coming from a different context. Arthur D. Little Ltd noted that countries with mature tourism sectors require less of the state support systems than those at an earlier stage of development and hence suggested a less comprehensive though more focused role for the Bord. However, the conditions for development of the sector in the ROI had been much more favourable than in NI over the previous 25 years so that the argument for rolling back the state might have been more appropriate there (ROI).
31. This consists of identifying products/product areas which ought to be developed and the likely supports which would be available from the public sector, guided by the

market-related principles referred to above – market need, market failure of some sort (why the market need is not met), net additional revenue to NI, absence of displacement from elsewhere in the province and evidence that the projects would not have gone ahead without the support provided (absence of deadweight loss).

32. The subsequent development by the Radisson Group of the hotel and golf complex at Limavaddy gave effect to this aspiration.

33. Again the contrast with the ROI is interesting where its Government moved to divest the tourist board of its developmental function and to concentrate on its prime overseas marketing function, also underlined by a belief in less 'hand-holding' of the industry.

34. Indications of the kinds of facilities which would be supported included three new 80–100 bedroom budget hotels to cater for the coach tour market and to be located in Belfast, North Antrim and Fermanagh while funds would also be available for the conversion of existing high-quality country house style hotels in the 12–30 bedroom range.

35. Among the opportunities identified were a major new central visitor attraction and international hotel development for Belfast, a major hotel, golf and leisure complex to international standard outside Belfast; priority heritage towns were selected and targeted for tourism development – Armagh, Carrickfergus, Downpatrick, Enniskillen and Derry and other special interest towns and villages were identified also (22 in total) with tourism potential; traditional seaside resorts were seen as requiring private and local authority investments to compete.

36. A similar selection of heritage towns in the ROI led to considerable diffusion of the first round of Tourism Structural Funds on numerous small-scale projects with considerable potential displacement effects for any given volume of visitors.

37. These ranged from training inputs as part of upgrading standards, support for rural tourism initiatives, need to care for the environment as part of tourism development, coping with litter and graffiti, improving the quality and choice in access transport and internal signposting and the emerging opportunities (and increased competition) in Europe within the single market.

38. By all accounts, a very unsuccessful joint venture.

39. A similar bias towards the development of the physical infrastructure of tourism was found in the ROI under its first OP for Tourism, 1989–1993.

40. See Department of Finance and Personnel (1994: 57–73).

41. And not limited to the hospitality industry as in the first OP!

42. See NITB (1992) and NITB (1995a).

43. Although the IRA ended its ceasefire on 9 February 1996.

44. The bonanza has already started with visitor numbers forecast to have increased by 17 per cent to 1.5 million in 1995, of which over 28 per cent are holiday visitors. The latter showed a remarkable growth of 56 per cent over 1994.

45. See DED (1995) for another recent official contribution on the challenges facing the NI economy in competing internationally. Tourism gets a limited mention in this report (as indeed it does in the NIEC (1995) report mentioned in the text), largely to recognize its growth potential but not in any way seeing it as a key strategic sector.

46. However, the increases recorded for the first eight months of 1995 indicated that the ROI decreased its share of holiday visitors to the province, reflecting an increase of 54 per cent (+52,000) compared to a 68 per cent rise for all holiday visitors (+126,000) over the 1994 figures.

47. For NI though not necessarily for the ROI.

9   Policy design and delivery in Irish tourism

INTRODUCTION

The relative neglect in policy terms of the Irish tourism sector for several decades, compared with agriculture or manufacturing, was partially redressed in the latter part of the 1980s. This was prompted primarily by the endemic unemployment problem in Ireland and was aided by the belief that the greater labour intensity in tourism would generate better returns in terms of job creation than competing sectors. Tourism had the advantage also of being an important export earner with relatively low import content and thus would generate more employment per IR£ million of foreign receipts. The liberalization of air-fares from 1986 onwards, particularly on the UK–Ireland routes, was a timely boost for Irish tourism. The increased policy interest in the sector 'anticipated' the availability of EU Structural Funds under the first Operational Programme (OP) for Tourism, 1989–1993. For the first time substantial non-Irish Exchequer 'public' funds were being made available to improve the quality of the Irish tourism product, to introduce new products and to move beyond the bland 'commodity' image of Irish tourism which had dominated and limited the industry for so long.[1]

This chapter outlines the policy context in which the Irish tourism industry operates, taking account of the changing organizational framework which has evolved to deliver on the established policy objectives; policy developments since the early 1980s are analysed and the main features of the two Operational Programmes (OPs) for Tourism are presented, together with a review of the first OP, 1989–1993; finally, the main policy instruments used to develop Irish tourism are briefly discussed.

POLICY CONTEXT

The approach to policy design and delivery in the tourism sector has, to a limited extent, paralleled the model for industrial policy with a state agency – Bord Failte Eireann (BFE) (the Irish Tourist Board) – formed in 1955[2] to assist the development of the industry and the promotion of Ireland as a tourist destination to overseas visitors. An additional similarity was the regionalization of policy delivery through the regional tourism organizations (RTOs), established in 1964 – paralleling the regional offices of the Industrial Development Authority (IDA) (and later, Forbairt) which were given autonomy for delivery of policy towards the small firm sector. However, tourism never received the same focus nor priority within government as the industrial sector; nor had there ever been a long-term strategic development plan for Irish tourism (prior to the OP) within which the government agency (BFE) could operate and deliver accordingly.[3] A further similarity between the approach to industry and to tourism development emerged in the manner by which the agencies (IDA for industry, BFE for tourism) assumed responsibility for policy design as well as delivery, filling the void left by the respective government departments and their ministerial leaders, a situation which has been reversed in recent years. Institutional reforms following reviews of the broader policy contexts, and the introduction of the OPs for tourism have impacted both on the agencies and the parent Government departments where there has been a redefinition of role and a refocusing of the core functions and responsibilities of the principal actors. These points are returned to below.

Clark and O'Cinneide (1981) noted the strong role played by central Government in the development of tourism in both parts of Ireland. This role has been supplemented by subsidiary local/regional tourism organizations, voluntary tourism bodies and the industry itself, although the 'dependency culture' on central Government and the main tourism promotion agency, Bord Failte, has persisted over the years. The responsibility for the tourism brief lay within the Department of Industry and Commerce for several decades up to 1977. The establishment of the Department of Transport and Tourism in that year (with the inclusion of 'tourism' in a departmental title for the first time) raised the profile of the sector at cabinet level; since then the portfolio has shifted to Industry, Commerce and Tourism (1980), Tourism, Fisheries and Forestry (1986), Tourism, Transport and Communications (1987) and, most recently, Tourism and Trade (1992).[4]

ORGANIZATIONAL STRUCTURES

In agency terms, Bord Failte has carried primary responsibility for delivery of Government objectives for Irish tourism and has used its network of RTOs to manage the process at regional level throughout most of Ireland. Shannon Development, which since its establishment in 1959 has had a mandate to stimulate passenger (and freight) traffic through Shannon Airport for the benefit of tourism (and industry) throughout the west of Ireland, was given direct and exclusive responsibility for the delivery of Government policy for tourism in the Mid-west region in 1987.[5] This was later extended to cover the Shannon Region (North Kerry plus the 'extended' Mid-west) coinciding with the launch of the first OP for Tourism in 1989.[6] The RTOs are comprised of industry as well as Bord Failte personnel and derive an increasing proportion of their operating revenue from their own resources, through sales of literature, booking charges and contributions from the tourism industry itself and from the local authorities. The balance of their budget comes from Bord Failte. The function of the RTOs is primarily operational and focused on marketing and promotion of the regional tourism product and managing the flow of tourists through their particular region. To implement the latter the RTOs operate the tourist information offices located throughout their respective regions. Bord Failte is concerned with overseas promotion on behalf of all tourism regions in Ireland and for this purpose maintain a number of overseas offices in the major origin market locations. Shannon Development maintained a number of overseas offices also in pursuit of its tourism brief, until the end of 1995 when responsibility to develop traffic through Shannon Airport was transferred to Aer Rianta, Shannon. In product development matters, the RTOs act as a filter for tourism development proposals but the primary responsibility rests with Bord Failte itself (or with Shannon Development, depending on location).[7] Pearce (1990) traced the development of the organizational structures in Irish tourism since the 1960s and noted varying tensions between the national and regional tourism bodies at different times. He acknowledged a resurgence of the role of the regional bodies in the late 1980s in the process of delivering on the policy to double tourism numbers. He also acknowledged the key role played by sectoral tourism organizations operating at the national level and the importance of their input (not always realized) to an overall strategy for the industry, e.g. the Irish Hotels Federation were instrumental in encouraging the government to adopt the policy of growth from 1988.

The organizational structures for Irish tourism essentially remained intact since the early 1950s though the functions of the key agencies have been altered in recent years. Proposed changes in the institutional arrangements were made in the 1990s, following a period of experience with the implementation of the first OP for Tourism. Before analysing these recent changes the policy objectives and instruments are considered.

TOURISM POLICY OBJECTIVES AND PROGRAMMES

The Government published a White Paper on Tourism Policy in 1985 (Stationery Office, 1985). A thorough review of the performance of the sector had been conducted earlier in the NESC (1980b) report in which several of the problems of the industry were identified but never acted upon subsequently. The White Paper was the first official attempt to clarify government thinking on tourism in a focused manner and to specify the broad objectives of policy.

The White Paper outlined the national policy objective as follows:

> to optimise the economic and social benefits to Ireland of the promotion and development of tourism both to and within the country consistent with ensuring an acceptable economic rate of return on the resources employed and taking account of:

- tourism's potential for job creation,
- the quality of life and development of the community,
- the enhancement and preservation of the nation's cultural heritage,
- the conservation of the physical resources of the country, and
- tourism's contribution to regional development. (p. 8)

Though characteristically vague, the White Paper, nevertheless, placed job creation high on the agenda as the desired outcome of tourism development in Ireland. It recognized the importance of the environment in relation to development of the sector and the role of tourism in regional development.

These broad objectives were presented in somewhat of a policy vacuum as there were no additional resources provided for implementation and no guiding government strategy to ensure that the objectives could be achieved. Bord Failte's own three-year 'planning' documents produced during the 1970s and 1980s, although not carrying the 'official' imprimateur, were similarly aspirational and without the necessary resource supports. Furthermore, there was no long-term planning context for the industry which might guide the development of the sector. In effect, tourism policy up to 1987 was essentially centred on promoting Ireland as a holiday destination and Bord Failte was charged with this responsibility. Targets were vague and Ireland was losing market share of world and European tourism. Many external factors were cited as the reasons for the poor performance of the sector over which, it was alleged, Ireland had limited control. To a large extent responsibility for policy design and delivery was left to Bord Failte which had expertise largely confined to a promotional role, although under the first Operational Programme for Tourism assumed a developmental role.

TOURISM TARGETS 1988–1992

Since 1987 a number of reports have been produced on the strategic direction for Irish tourism.[8] One of the earlier influential reports was the Price Waterhouse (1987) report on Improving the Performance of Irish Tourism, commissioned by the Department of Tourism and Transport. While this and other reports had an influence on specific policy stances taken (e.g. on access transport for cross-channel air routes, and the eventual ending of the compulsory Shannon stopover for North Atlantic flights) the most significant change in approach to the industry was the Government's setting of targets for the period 1988–1992. While the setting of these targets by government appears to have been established without prior consultation with Bord Failte, suggesting poor policy co-ordination at the time, they did have the effect of galvanizing the industry for one of its best growth periods ever.

The targets set were three-fold:

- to double numbers of overseas tourists to Ireland over the five-year period;
- to double the revenue yield from these tourists over the base year level in 1987;

- to create an additional 25,000 jobs arising from the expansions planned in numbers and expenditures.

Bord Failte responded to the targets by developing a strategy, within its existing resources, to achieve the stated targets. This strategy was set out in a document published in December 1988 (Bord Failte, 1988a), one year into the programme. It comprised a four-part strategy:

- product development in specialist activities, cultural heritage and genealogically related markets;
- competitiveness improvement with an emphasis on both price and quality;
- promotion of Ireland as an attractive holiday destination;
- distribution of Irish holiday products through appropriate channels, appropriately packaged.

These components were designed to develop both the supply and demand side of the tourism market and were reflected subsequently in the first Operational Programme for Tourism, 1989–1993. The strategy of doubling numbers and revenues was adopted by Bord Failte on a pro-rata basis for each country market. This was rather surprising and took no account of the fact that major shifts were occurring prior to 1988 in the origin markets for Irish tourism, e.g. the significant shift from the North American to the mainland European country markets was not reflected in the marketing plans prepared at the time. This highlights the approach to marketing Ireland as a tourist destination which has frequently been based on the exigencies of the day rather than any clear strategic marketing plan based on the long-term development of the industry. The increased marketing spend in the US market in the aftermath of the Gulf War in 1991 is a case in point. It has been difficult also to determine the effectiveness of particular country marketing campaigns in the absence of proper monitoring measures being used, not to mention the difficulty of assessing the impact of marketing expenditures compared with other factors influencing holiday-taking decisions. There is a question also of whether marketing expenditures are more effectively used in a pro- or counter-cyclical fashion, i.e. to maintain a presence in high-yield markets when these are doing well because of favourable economic indicators or to boost demand from poorly performing markets.[9]

Operational Programme, 1989–1993

In parallel with the target setting and implementation process the Government was gearing up for the Community Support Framework[10] through the preparation of the National Development Plan, 1989–1993 (Stationery Office, 1989a) and the subsequent Operational Programme (OP) for Tourism. For the first time, substantial resources were to be made available for the development of Irish tourism from the EU Structural Funds. The planned total spending was of the order of IR£300 million with almost IR£160 million coming from the EU in the first OP (1989–1993). The broad objectives of the OP were to accelerate the provision of necessary infrastructure for Irish tourism, to expand and diversify the product range and to increase the scale of tourism development.

This new found emphasis on tourism was linked more to the availability of funds coupled with the EU Commission's view at the time that tourism was a sector with growth potential rather than any change of direction in government thinking about the priority which the sector should receive. This has changed over the intervening period.

The OP represented a significant advance in the preparation of a strategy for the integrated development of the sector while also seizing a unique opportunity to acquire developmental resources additional to those available in the economy; it also provided the wherewithal to remedy the bland image of much of the Irish tourism product. The principal focus of the OP was on product development, investment in training and market development.

Five product themes were selected for interventions:

- specific interest (active), e.g. angling, golf;
- specific interest (passive), e.g. genealogy, language training;
- cultural, heritage and entertainment;
- leisure, fitness and health;
- business, e.g. conference and incentive travel.

There were three separate but inter-linked sub-programmes in the OP:

- sub-programme 1: public sector driven;
- sub-programme 2: private sector driven;
- sub-programme 3: training,

and a variety of measures under each to assist the development and marketing of tourism products and to support the implementation of training programmes to meet the manpower requirements of the expanding sector.

Outcomes of the Operational Programme, 1989–1993

There were some deviations from the original planned expenditures particularly between the first two sub-programmes – because the private sector take-up fell short of anticipated levels.[11] Public sector expenditures increased by 34 per cent while private sector supported expenditures were down by over 20 per cent from the planned levels. Although the initial funds allocated to marketing were low (at IR£20 million), more than double this amount was subsequently allocated to it in attempts to generate increased visitor volumes to use the new and improved facilities being made available. Although interpreted in the context of providing substantial resources to achieve the 1988–1992 targets, it was clear that the Structural Fund transfers would have minimal impact in 1990 and 1991, apart from construction jobs, and only from 1992 onwards could the effects of the higher investment levels be seen in performance terms. The OP in tourism resulted in a significant expansion in the investment made in Irish tourism with a much needed improvement in the quality and standard of the product.

The final outcomes resulted in IR£82.2 million of aid being drawn down in the case of sub-programme 1 which was almost 60 per cent more than the original target; in sub-programme 2 there was a shortfall of approximately 18 per cent (IR£66.6 million less IR£12 million), while the ESF support for training was over IR£5 million more than the targeted figure of IR£28.5 million. The total volume of investment under the OP was almost IR£380 million with the breakdown as follows: EU Commission, IR£186 million; Irish public sector, IR£65 million; and private sector, IR£128 million. The breakdown of this expenditure across the three main functions/activities was 73 per cent for product development, 12 per cent for marketing and 14 per cent for training. A small amount of £0.7 million was spent on technical assistance. Some of the key products/product categories which were developed under the programme included (from Stationery Office, 1994):

- restoration of the Ballinamore–Ballyconnell canal, linking the Shannon system to the Erne;
- 16 new theme town projects, two new literary museums and 65 houses or castles newly opened or restored;
- 27 new international standard golf courses;
- 45 all-weather health and leisure facilities.

High-quality leisure facilities have been added to the accommodation base to provide the all-weather facilities expected (although not always used[12]) by the modern tourist. Cultural and heritage infrastructures have been upgraded and a range of active interest tourism/sports facilities completed.

In addition to the OP for Tourism there were other sources of investment funds available for the development of infrastructure relevant to tourism through, for example, the OP in Water and Sanitary Services, on Peripherality and for Rural Development, as well as through the EU Commission's LEADER and INTERREG programmes.

Effectiveness of the first OP for Tourism, 1989–1993

For the first time in Irish tourism strategy there were explicit policy targets combined with a four-year spending plan to assist the development of Irish tourism, together with the necessary resources to implement such a strategy. The Department of Tourism, Transport and Communications performed a central role in the design and development of the programme in consultation with the delivery agencies (Bord Failte, Shannon Development and the Office of Public Works) and the industry. This gave the relevant government department a central role in policy formulation rather than abdicating this to the agencies as had been the *de facto* situation before then. The department was involved also in monitoring its implementation with other bodies including the EU Commission through the specially established National Monitoring Committee for the Tourism OP. Despite the elaborate plans to ensure the most efficient utilization of the resources made available under the OP there appears to have been greater emphasis in the monitoring process on ensuring the financial spending targets were met both by the Government and the EU Commission than on the 'outputs' and economic impacts derived from this spending. This inevitably led to inefficiencies. Even where other 'output' targets were used these tended to be the immediate outcomes (e.g. throughput of trainees, placement rates) rather than the potential 'structural' improvements to the industry performance (e.g. quality of service to tourists).

Bord Failte expanded its role to include a greater focus on development issues in addition to its traditional marketing function. Shannon Development and the Office of Public Works were the two other public sector bodies which received direct funding under the programme. While the OP was designed in the context of fund availability for a variety of projects and not necessarily from the perspective of taking a long-term strategic view of the industry, it represented a significant step forward in the policy formation process. It highlighted also the fallacy of designing policy without the necessary resources to support the objectives as had been the case hitherto. Furthermore, it provided a methodology and a funding base from which the long-term development of Irish tourism could be designed. The delivery agencies now had a clearer understanding of their roles in relation to tourism though this has been thrown into some disarray in more recent times, a point which is addressed below.

It is generally accepted that the Irish tourism industry performed exceptionally well in the 1988–1990 period and held these gains in the three subsequent years of the first OP. However, the two main evaluative reports on the OP (for the Department of Finance and DGXVI)[13] questioned the extent to which a causal link existed between the Structural Fund expenditures and the performance of the sector, especially since the period of rapid growth pre-dated the bulk of the expenditure draw-down. The Structural Funds are primarily a supply-side measure to improve the competitiveness of Irish tourism and to enlarge capacity. The ESRI (1993) evaluation report on the use of the funds pointed to the generation of overcapacity in two amenity areas – inland waterways and golf course provision. Referring to the Ballinamore–Ballyconnell Canal project which links the Shannon to the Erne, the ESRI suggested there ought to be greater emphasis on filling existing capacity through effective marketing strategies rather than creating more. Regarding the regional development dimension of tourism, the ESRI report noted the excessive geographical spread (and therefore limited impact) of the Structural Fund monies into numerous small projects rather than 'strategically focused series of significant interventions' (p. 38). There is a dilemma in attempting to meet both of these criticisms since attempts to overcome the scale problem in Irish tourism through investment in large-scale projects may generate overcapacity while emphasizing a geographically wide spread of projects may dilute the impact which the resources might otherwise have. Publicly funded flag-ship projects can act as catalysts to stimulate other private sector investments in ancillary activities (accommodation, restaurants, craft workshops) once the prime attractions are properly marketed.[14]

The ESRI referred to the need for a broader perspective on the development of tourism than a narrowly based industry approach (echoing the Culliton (1992) approach to development of the industrial sector[15]). They also questioned the subventions to the private sector particularly where these are intra-marginal and therefore do not need the subsidies involved, and the main beneficiaries may be local residents or (golf) club members rather than international tourists, a point also echoed in the SIS (1992) report.

Other points which were identified as requiring greater attention in the design of a second OP included (mainly from SIS (1992) and Fitzpatrick and Associates (1994)):

- the need for greater co-ordination between investments under the Tourism OP and other OPs with a direct impact on tourism amenities, e.g. the provision of access roads;
- greater integration across the sub-programmes within the Tourism OP such that, for example, training measures are consistent with the product development and marketing measures;
- more explicit linkages between investments made and the performance indicators by which these can be measured;
- training measures to take account of the increasing 'Europeanization' of Irish tourism, the new technological environment in which the industry operates and qualitative impacts as well as quantitative outputs expected;
- need for more focused training of small business tourism operators and entrepreneurs with a view to enhancing both their professionalism and innovative approach to the business;
- improvement in the project appraisal methods used in assessing applications for funds through allowing for displacement effects, qualitative assessment of promoters, effective follow-up mechanisms to compare progress with original proposals and no less stringent assessment of proposals simply because EU Funds might be regarded as 'soft' money by promoters;[16]
- insufficient attention was paid to the environmental impact of tourism investments;
- an excessive emphasis on developing the 'hardware' components of the tourist product (buildings and facilities) and, with the exception of training, insufficient attention to 'software' aspects, such as international market studies, evaluation of investments and so on.

Initially only IR£20 million was allocated to marketing expenditures but additional funds were subsequently diverted to demand-side measures of a marketing nature designed to help fill the capacity made available.[17] While one can empathize with the need to market one's products, it does seem to contradict the notion of Structural Fund interventions which are essentially supply-side measures to improve the competitiveness of the industry. Unless one takes an 'investment' approach to marketing, in which long-term market development is the goal rather than short-term promotion and advertising, then the benefits are likely to be short lived. If public sector funds are invested in tourism product developments of a substantive nature then it is difficult to justify further interventions of a marketing nature without somehow calling into question the danger of permanent subsidies. It would seem that the private sector should respond by committing its own resources to marketing expenditures. From an EU perspective, support for marketing and promotion expenditures could lead to internal competition and simply redistribute tourists around the Union, at the expense of the European taxpayer. At the very least more evaluative measures on the impact of marketing expenditures and campaigns should be introduced for specific projects and for European 'regions' (which includes ROI as a single EU 'region').

While the foregoing may appear to be excessively critical of the first OP for Tourism, this should not detract from the considerable benefits to Irish tourism of having access to such extensive resources for the first time and the enormous enhancement of the tourism product which took place during the period of unprecedented investment to end 1993.[18] Indeed, the industry was well poised at the end to take advantage of the changing international tourist trends; besides, some although not all of the above criticisms and others were taken into account in the improved design of the second OP for Tourism, 1994–1999. Hurley *et al.* (1994) pointed to the critical role of the EU's external funding in rejuvenating the tourism industry of an ailing economy. They noted the limited capacity of Ireland's fragmented and small-scale industry to generate the necessary capital to invest in further development and the limitations of the previous project-by-project funding approach. The long-term nature of the new approach embodied in the OP, combined with the partnership principle (EU, public and private sectors), provided a firmer basis for the future development of the sector. Before examining the second OP for tourism, some further organizational developments are discussed which affected the industry in the first half of the 1990s.

ORGANIZATIONAL DEVELOPMENTS IN THE 1990s

The considerable investment in Irish tourism and the greater focus by Government on its capacity to deliver on the revenue and employment targets raised issues on the appropriateness of the organizational arrangements for the sector. The implementation of the first OP for tourism did represent a new partnership between the public and private sectors in the Irish tourism policy arena and, not unlike the trend in Northern Ireland, there was an underlying perception that the public sector had too overbearing a role in the industry's development.

Tourism Task Force

The establishment of the Tourism Task Force (TTF) in February 1992 was a recognition of the importance of the private sector's contribution. It involved a form of partnership whereby the private sector was formally asked for advice on how the industry ought to be developed. Apart from the chairman, the secretary and one other member, the Task Force was composed of people working entirely in the private sector. This inevitably oriented the findings in a particular direction.

The terms of reference were to review the recent performance and future prospects for Irish tourism with particular reference to employment generation, to determine the commercial and marketing opportunities available to the industry to capture a greater share of the international tourism market and to propose creative and innovative approaches to develop the tourist market with a greater role for the commercial sector; the TTF was asked also to advise on ways to assist local communities to market their tourist accommodation and facilities (Stationery Office, 1992). Thus, there was a strong focus on marketing on the agenda set for the TTF and their brief was by no means a comprehensive one to chart the future development of the industry.

The Task Force reported in October 1992 and suggested the primary objective for the development of the sector should be to 'maximise the value-added from the optimal number of tourists' (p. i) which reflects a move away from the official preoccupation with numbers targets of the previous five years. The most far-reaching proposal (and one which has been acted on already) was an institutional one – to establish a new Tourism Council of Ireland. This would have a prime function to prepare and monitor National Tourism Development Plans and establish a system of measuring the performance of tourism. The TTF recommended that Bord Failte should operate in the context of the National Tourism Plans and its functions should concentrate on marketing and promotion as well as product development and investment; and that the new County Enterprise Boards[19] and the Regional Tourism Organizations should have a continuing role in supporting the industry below the national level.

Other points addressed by the Task Force included targeted and niche marketing strategies for specialist products (golf, equestrian, etc.), quality of product, seasonality and access, manpower and training, tax breaks for the industry and increased subventions under the next round of Structural Funds, including a proposal to dramatically increase the allocation to overseas marketing of IR£100 million.[20]

It is interesting to note the differences in approach taken by the TTF compared with the Culliton (1992) report on industrial promotion and development.

1. Culliton proposed institutional reforms of the existing state agencies active in the industrial field while the TTF proposed a new layer of co-ordination (in the form of the National Tourism Council) with a potential undermining of the role of Bord Failte and transfer of policy-making functions from its rightful place within the relevant government department.
2. Culliton stressed the importance of developing industrial policy in a broader context of tax reform, training and educational improvements, and infra-

structural measures to improve competitiveness while the TTF confined its recommendations firmly within the tourism sector and, within this, strongly focused on the marketing function.

3. The TTF report appeared biased towards a stronger voice for the industry in policy formation and a greater allocation of Structural Funds for tourism without an objective rationale for either, whereas Culliton focused less on government subventions and more on strategic, longer-term issues.

National Tourism Council

Chaired by the Minister for Tourism and Trade, the Council was established in October 1993 with a mix of public and private sector members, including those from the principal public agencies involved in developing and promoting Irish tourism. The Council's brief was to 'act as a national forum for consultation between the tourism industry, state tourism agencies and government departments, and to act in an advisory capacity to the Minister on tourism policy to be implemented by the state agencies'.[21] The Tourism Council certainly does not appear to have been assigned anything like the powers recommended by the TTF but rather is a method of formally including the industry in continuing consultation on future policy options.

The occasion of the launch of the Tourism Council was used to signal a new approach to decision-making for Irish tourism. The then Minister[22] was quoted as follows:

> We have had more than enough academic debate, reports and studies about Irish tourism. What we need now is decision-making derived from co-operation by all aspects of the industry, decision-making that is strategic, practical and sensitive to the changing winds of the international market place. (30 September 1993)

Sentiments such as these, if carried through in policy terms, could have disturbing implications for the future of Irish tourism. The Tourism Council was thus presented as an alternative forum which could somehow replace (rather than complement) an improved understanding of the nature of the continuing problems facing Irish tourism. There are still some huge gaps in the knowledge base on matters such as the effectiveness of tourism training, the impact of various marketing campaigns, the accuracy of tourism data, evaluation techniques in public tourism investments, strategic planning techniques and methods to tackle seasonality, access transport and related barriers to industry growth, which thorough research work can potentially fill. It is precisely because of the nature of the 'changing winds' in the international market place that there is a need for a solid information and research base (undertaken by the agencies as well as independently) to underpin and complement the dialogue taking place through the National Tourism Council and elsewhere. There are dangers in allowing considerable amounts of public sector funds to be unduly influenced by those with primarily private sector interests in the absence of good independent research results to substantiate particular actions. While public sector decision-making can be much improved through systematic consultations with the private sector, the essential tenets of accountability, effectiveness and efficiency in the use of the tax-payers' monies (European or Irish) must be safeguarded by the government departments concerned. Besides, private sector interests tend to be primarily short term given the nature of the constraints under which they operate whereas the public sector is better placed to take a longer term view of development. The balance of both sets of interests in the National Tourism Council, and the partnership which this implies, can be viewed as a positive development.

Although in existence now for over two years the National Tourism Council has had a low profile. In the all-important design of the second OP, 1994–1999, which has been the most significant policy initiative since the Council was established, its influence was not very evident. The government department (of Tourism and Trade) has been the central player in the design and presentation of the second OP for Tourism, and worked mainly with the public sector delivery agencies in designing it. The Council's impact appears to be a background advisory role which keeps some of the central issues on the tourism agenda and with the aid of commissioned reports makes an input to policy formulation.[23] There is no evidence that there is a more focused decision-making unit operating to drive the industry although there is a further layer of consultation in the policy design process whereby the industry now has more direct access to the Minister and departmental officials.

Reorganization of Bord Failte Eireann (BFE)

In 1994, the role of Bord Failte came under close scrutiny by government appointed consultants who were asked to review and make recommendations on the role and operations of the Irish tourist board, particularly in the light of the growth targets set by government for tourism for the rest of the decade.[24] The consultants were asked to have regard in particular to the suitability of Bord Failte's existing structures and functions in terms of strategically responding to the government's targets and the compatibility of its existing mix of functions with the priority exercise of its core roles. In regard to the interaction between the Bord and the industry itself, the consultants were requested to consider the extent to which its commercial activities are likely to encourage self-reliance in the sector and whether it is sufficiently responsive to the needs of the sector (Arthur D. Little Ltd, 1994).

Thus, fundamental questions were being asked of the Bord's capability to deliver on targets, the relevance of activities in which it had become involved, the effectiveness and efficiency with which services were being delivered and of the extent of the continuing dependence by the Irish tourism industry on the state agency. These questions were being raised against a background of, on the one hand, unease that the national tourist board had drifted somewhat from its core functions and, on the other hand, preference by government towards a greater role for the private sector in tourism development.

The consultants found that, considering the maturity of the Irish tourism industry, BFE had become involved in too may facets of the industry and should now focus primarily on the core functions of overseas promotion of Ireland as a tourist destination and consumer marketing, in both of which it had a strong competitive advantage. Regarding the services which BFE provides for the industry, Arthur D. Little Ltd recommended that BFE should play a supportive/ facilitative role for the various tourism suppliers rather than an operational one. Thus, services such as the registration and grading of accommodation, product approvals, domestic marketing and sales and the 'GULLIVER' electronic information and reservations system should be out-sourced to commercial suppliers. This would enable the industry to be more self-regulatory and take a greater share of responsibility for the maintenance of standards, all in the context of encouraging greater self-reliance within the industry. Other non-core functions such as the production of the *Ireland of the Welcomes* magazine and the organization of the annual Tidy Towns competition should either be transferred to private operators or transferred elsewhere within the public sector. Regarding the management of the Structural Fund investments for which BFE (and Shannon Development) had responsibility in the first OP, Arthur D. Little Ltd recommended that this should be retained in the second OP for public sector tourist attractions and for co-operative marketing support but advised a new approach for private sector investments. The consultants argued that project appraisal and financial viability decisions should be handed over to an independent body to encourage greater commercial reality by project promoters and to avoid the potential conflict of interest whereby BFE acted as 'project advocate, planner, sometimes initiator, and judge of ERDF funding' (p. 12). BFE would still have a role in the process regarding 'touristic value assessment'. The other important function which the Bord should continue to exercise was its information collection and dissemination service for the industry and Government and for its own monitoring and marketing functions.

In their report, Arthur D. Little Ltd (1994) also considered the organizational implications of the recommendations made. BFE had a high and growing cost base which limited the amounts available for its core functions and its marketing efforts could not be maintained without the additional resources from the Structural Funds and special allocations for overseas marketing.[25] Staff turnover had been low and there was a high average age structure in the organization with many of those in marketing without recent direct experience of the industry. While the out-sourcing of a number of functions would bring some staff with them, Arthur D. Little Ltd also recommended the appointment of an international marketing director together with the introduction of 'some new blood with recent industry experience and graduate level marketing skills' (p. 14). Thus, there was a need for rejuvenation and refocusing of the ageing organization to enable it to more effectively deliver on the Government's targets for tourism to the end of the decade.

In summary, the refocused BFE should concentrate on three core functions supporting the mission of 'supporting Irish tourism and marketing to abroad'.

1. Selling Ireland overseas.
2. Helping the Irish (tourist) industry develop.
3. Providing information for decision-making.

Since Arthur D. Little Ltd's report in 1994, there has been a gradual implementation of its principal recommendations, especially out-sourcing of non-core activities and stronger focus on overseas marketing, accompanied by a reduction in staffing levels. Independent management boards were established under the second OP to consider proposals from the private sector for funding.[26]

In principle, the stronger focus by the 'new' and steamlined Irish tourist board on its core overseas marketing function should improve its effectiveness in delivering on government targets. The changes bring it more into line with the roles of national tourist boards in more mature tourist destinations. However, it could be counterproductive for BFE to become too divorced from the product development function in Irish tourism as the latter is an important factor in attracting high-yield tourists; it is even more critical in ensuring an appropriate rate of repeat visits. It should not be forgotten that for about 20 years from 1970 there was very little product investment or development in Irish tourism with the result that efforts to attract overseas tourists were less than successful for much of the period. The potential for continued success of BFE (and Shannon Development) in Irish tourism is critically dependent on the response of the private sector to the new scenario and the extent and speed with which it becomes more self-reliant and displays the maturity implicit in Arthur D. Little Ltd's findings and the Government's faith in them.

TOURISM DEVELOPMENT, 1994–1999

The second Operational Programme for tourism (Stationery Office, 1994) was launched towards the latter part of 1994, following the earlier outline of the principal targets and emphasis in spending measures in the National Development Plan, 1994–1999 (Stationery Office, 1993). The objectives of this OP were to 'maximise Ireland's tourism potential by increasing tourism revenue, thereby creating much needed employment'. This was translated into three quantitative and two qualitative targets (Stationery Office, 1994: 16):

- increase foreign tourism receipts by 50 per cent in real terms, or to IR£2250 million by 1999 (from IR£1367 million in 1993)
- increase tourism dependent employment by 29,000 full-time equivalent persons in addition to 6000 extra construction jobs
- increase the proportion of tourists which holiday outside of the peak months of July and August, from 70 to 75 per cent
- develop and market the Irish tourism product in line with international market demands, having full regard to the need to conserve and protect the natural heritage, and

- improve service and quality in the Irish tourism product, as well as value for money.

The measures in tourism will be complemented by measures under other OPs dealing with the roads system for tourist routes and access to tourism facilities, sanitary services which will need to ensure that popular tourist areas have facilities which minimize environmental damage, and urban renewal projects which have clear tourism benefits.

Organization of the delivery of the OP was structured in five sub-programmes, with target allocations as follows.

	IR £ million
1 Natural/cultural tourism	125
2 Product development	288
3 Marketing	124
4 Training	110
5 Technical assistance	5
Total	652

The Department of Tourism and Trade is responsible for the bulk of the sub-programmes with the exception of marine tourism under 2 (Department of the Marine) and all of 1 (Department of Arts, Culture and the Gaeltacht, in conjunction with the Office of Public Works).

Table 9.1 presents the initial targets for the second OP with the corresponding targets and final outcomes of the first OP.

Regarding funding sources, the EU contribution is increased in the second OP as a proportion of the total planned investment while those of the Irish government and private sectors are reduced. The private sector's contribution is reduced from 40 to 31 per cent when the initial targets of both programmes are compared. Perhaps it was expedient to squeeze the maximum contribution from the EU although the relatively smaller contribution expected from the private sector is not consistent with the principle of encouraging greater self-reliance and responsibility by the industry for its future development. Adjustments to the investment mix show a marked shift towards marketing (from 6.7 to 19 per cent) largely at the expense of product development, which still accounts for almost two-thirds of the total outlay in the second OP. Training continues to take a sizeable proportion of the total outlay and there is a significant relative increase in expenditure on technical assistance (but from a very low base) following some criticisms of the first OP and a generally greater emphasis on evaluation by the EU Commission. It is planned, in addition to continuing evaluative and monitoring assignments, to undertake a major mid-term review of the OP at the end of 1996.

Table 9.1 Expenditure proportions in the first (1989–1993) and second (1994–1999) Operational Programmes for Tourism in Ireland

	First OP (1989–1993)		Second OP (1994–1999)
	Initial targets	*Final outcomes*	*Initial targets*
By source of funding			
EU (%)	49.1	49.0	56.7
Irish Government (%)	10.9	17.2	12.7
Private sector (%)	40.0	33.8	30.6
Total (IR£ million)	299.7*	379.8†	652‡
By type of investment expenditure			
Product development (%)	78.6	73.4	63.3
Marketing (%)	6.7	12.7	19.0
Training (%)	14.6	13.7	16.7
Technical assistance (%)	0.1	0.2	0.8
Totals (IR£ million)	299.7*	379.8†	652‡

*1989 prices.
†OP amounts inflated as per EU Commission guidelines.
‡1994 prices.
Source: Derived from Stationery Office (1993, 1994).

Proposed investments under the second Operational Programme

The investments planned under the second OP may be considered broadly under 'hardware' or 'software' measures, where the former refer to investments in buildings and tourism facilities while the latter refer to improvements in techniques, capacity-building and information dissemination activities in support of tourism development.

'Hardware' measures

Some of the main features of the second OP include under natural/cultural products:

- investment in national cultural institutions, most of which are located in Dublin, i.e. National Museum, Gallery, Library and Concert Hall;
- an integrated development programme for the Arts and the further development of Gaeltacht[27] tourism; and
- enhancement of existing national monuments and historic properties of international tourism value and the improvement of inland waterways on the Shannon–Erne, Barrow and the major canals.

Under product development, these include:

- a focus on large-scale projects such as a major national conference centre in Dublin at a cost of IR£50 million and catering for up to 2000 delegates;
- a large-scale weather-independent holiday park or holiday complex possibly developed by one of the major international leisure firms;
- enhancement of the general quality of information available to tourists through improvements in the regional tourist information offices, sign-posting, guide books and so on;
- tourism angling, with improvements in the quality of coarse and game angling facilities (expected to generate an extra 1000 jobs);
- further investment in the range of special interest holiday facilities for active and passive holidaying activities (from cycling to genealogy, golf to language learning); and
- some accommodation-related support where this is part of an integrated holiday facility (e.g. adventure sports centre with an accommodation 'add-on'); a continuation of measures from the first OP to assist conference and leisure facilities in hotels; some smaller hotels may also be eligible for assistance.

The above 'hardware' measures largely represent a continuation of the first OP with perhaps a different emphasis in terms of the scale of some of the projects. The OP contains an explicit list of indicators to measure the effectiveness of the investments undertaken, both on the supply and demand sides which will enable more precise monitoring and evaluative studies to be undertaken; it also sets out the criteria for funding, embracing outcomes such as increased overseas revenue, contribution to improved seasonality, capacity to generate repeat business and distinctive character of the projects, the latter of which could reduce the displacement effects.

However, there are a number of worrying aspects of the proposed 'hardware' measures: first, there is limited reference to the environment, arguably Ireland's most valuable tourism asset, in the 'hardware' measures mentioned in the OP; second, the 'tourism' dimension in many of the projects funded under the natural/cultural products sub-programme is quite incidental and unlikely to get appropriate attention under the Department of the Arts, Culture and the Gaeltacht, though the tourism agencies will have an input; third, additional funding of waterways and golf courses is proposed in spite of the evaluations of the first OP which pointed to the overcapacity in these facilities and concern about the marginal tourism benefits which accrue; fourth, the reliance on indicative large-scale projects with substantial private sector financing may come unstuck (if the private financing fails to materialize) and there is a danger that funds will be diverted and diffused again among a range of smaller projects (e.g. interpretative centres) with scope for much displacement effects and limited overall impact; and fifth, the proposed funding, though modest, to upgrade accommodation in the lower grades of hotels is providing an unnecessary subsidy (since there is no demonstrated accommodation shortage at this end of the market), is not addressing a product deficiency which the market itself will not correct, is likely to lead to market distortions and provide windfall gains for the hotel owners concerned.

'Software' measures

The principal 'software' measures under the other three sub-programmes are as follows.

Under marketing:

- improving the seasonal spread of visitors, through linking product developments to overall seasonality objectives and more international 'event' tourism;
- expanding air and sea access through contributing to marketing spend which (a) promotes Ireland as a tourism destination, (b) increases the load factors on existing routes, and (c) develops new capacity and routes;
- developing new country markets, hitherto under-represented in the mix of visitors coming to Ireland;
- developing product and niche markets in conjunction with the private sector, with emphasis on cooperative marketing and professionally prepared packages linking accommodation with specialist activities such as angling, golf and equestrian facilities; and
- attracting more 'high-yield' tourists, primarily through the niche marketing route.

Under training:

- training of unemployed persons and early school-leavers in the main craft disciplines in tourism, including back-to-work skills and start-your-own-business courses;
- initial full-time training of school-leavers for 'skilled professional-type courses', management courses and longer craft courses, which combine theoretical, practical and work experience training as part of the programmes;
- continuing training for those already in the industry to be organized through block-release of advanced craft and supervisory grades, together with in-company and external management development programmes designed to raise professionalism in the sector; and
- provision is made also for 'training the trainers' and for some transnational programmes which enhance language and international 'tourism awareness'.

Under technical assistance:

- a substantial increase in the allocation under this to undertake a closer and continuing review of the programme together with a major mid-term review planned towards the end of 1996.

The increased emphasis on marketing is very notable in the second OP, although very little monitoring or evaluative work was undertaken on its effectiveness in the first OP. The report on the reorganization of Bord Failte by

Arthur D. Little Ltd (1994) recommended a stronger focus by the agency on its core business of internationally marketing Ireland to foreign tourists. This shift in emphasis is already underway with a strong move to develop a unique 'Ireland' brand in the existing and emerging markets. Private sector involvement is deemed to be a key dimension of any integrated approach adopted and, given the past record of not really knowing how effective marketing expenditures are, it is critical that new strategies should have integral evaluation methodologies included to ensure the most effective use of the public funds involved. This should also apply at publicly funded individual project level. The causal link between increased marketing spend and greater numbers of overseas tourists has never been established with any degree of credibility for the Irish market. Evaluative mechanisms should focus not just on the total spend and its distribution across various origin countries but should also appraise the most effective media to use in attempting to reach desired targets.[28] The investment in human capital is an essential ingredient to raise and maintain service quality in the tourism industry.[29] The focus on tourism training is a continuation of the first OP (though much enhanced in scale) and reflects an emphasis on ensuring an adequate supply of well-trained personnel for the new tourism products available in the context of the market growth anticipated. The main delivery agency is CERT (Council for Education, Recruitment and Training for the Hotel, Catering and Tourism Industry) now brought under the aegis of the Department of Tourism and Trade. CERT's close links with the industry enables it to fulfil its placement function and the OP emphasises its demand monitoring role, the importance of European language training and facilitation of career progression through various levels of training.

While the 'shopping list' of training initiatives appears comprehensive, the weaknesses of the first OP are not really addressed. The 'output' measures are essentially 'input' measures to the industry in terms of throughput of trainees and placement rates without regard to the ultimate quality measures which should emerge.[30] The industry is asked to assume very little responsibility for training (IR£0.3 million out of a total of IR£110 million!) which again is at variance with the avowed objective of greater self-reliance. There is a weak emphasis on assisting existing or potential tourism entrepreneurs on how to start and run tourism businesses (apart from the unemployed who are least likely to have the necessary capital resources).

The increased allocation to technical assistance is a welcome development and should enhance the quality of the OP particularly since quite a range of supply- and demand-side indicators are included in the OP, and may be used as the benchmark for evaluation.

Concluding remarks – Second OP for Tourism

It is interesting to note that tourism numbers no longer feature in the government's stated targets for the sector but there is a revenue target and a jobs target associated with this. This is more in keeping with (a) the objective of achieving an optimal number of tourists while attempting to maximize the revenue returns from them, and (b) the concept of sustainable tourism. Measures to secure a more even distribution of the flow of tourists throughout the year are also consistent with a lower level of environmental damage especially at the more popular attractions. The allocation of funds to a small number of major projects, such as the National Conference Centre, does meet some of the criticisms of the first round of Structural Fund transfers about spreading the available monies over a vast range of projects and thus having a very limited impact in individual areas. However, there is an insufficient number of such projects and it is difficult to see what impact another large injection of funds in the culture and heritage field will have on the already dense coverage of heritage centres and the like. The advantage of the larger projects is that scale economies can be achieved and the underutilized capacity in other segments of the industry should benefit also (hotels, carriers and so on).

The project appraisal criteria, while more fully set out in the second than the first OP for Tourism, do not explicitly emphasize the essential need to correct for market failure. The policy instrument used to support tourism development is almost exclusively a cash grant, transferred to private promoters involved in projects. There is always a dilemma for the policy-maker in attempting to decide whether such grants are really necessary and, if so, the level at which these should be pitched. The key is to establish the level of grant-aid which is just required to enable the project to proceed so that in effect the project would not go ahead without the grant-aid. The intervention should be designed to correct for market failure, where the price–cost ratios and profit expectations are so unfavourable that private operators will not assume the necessary risks. Other factors of relevance, which are stressed in the second OP, include the need to take account of possible displacement effects and the additionality in terms of the increased overseas revenues which projects will generate.

POLICY INSTRUMENTS IN IRISH TOURISM

The range of policy instruments used in Irish tourism has been dominated since 1989 by the financial subsidies (or cash grants) administered through the two Operational Programmes for Tourism.[31] The magnitude of these transfers far exceeded earlier grants and subsidies to the industry. The latter were marginal in impact and focused mainly on individual tourism enterprises for expansion in accommodation and related facilities or on amenities in the public domain which were also key tourist attractions in their own right, e.g. Bunratty Castle, Co. Clare and Muckross House, Killarney. The Office of Public Works had a key role in maintaining the quality of some of these amenities through its annual grant-in-aid while Shannon Development and some Regional Tourism Organizations invested in the development and operation of tourist amenities as going concerns.[32] Local authorities also became involved in tourism development both through their contributions to the RTOs and their investment in urban renewal and development schemes which had tourism spin-offs. Prior to 1989, the major subvention to Irish tourism came through the annual grant-in-aid to Bord Failte, the bulk of which was spent on operational costs of the organization and marketing of Ireland as an international tourist destination. The balance of their budget went on a variety of expenditures including accommodation and non-accommodation grants,[33] brochures and other publicity materials, subventions to the RTOs, accommodation inspection/grading and other services.

The other major source of funding for Irish tourism arises from the fiscal incentives introduced to stimulate investment in the industry. It is important to point out that tourism was rarely targeted specifically with fiscal measures but many of these measures initially introduced for manufacturing were later extended to tourism enterprises. There were two principal sets of measures:

- (accelerated) capital allowances; and
- relief for investment in corporate trades (namely, Business Expansion Scheme (BES) funding).

(Accelerated) capital allowances

These were an effective means of reducing the cost of capital or the capital requirements to establish a tourism business, which served to overcome a potential entry barrier to certain types of tourism markets. Hotel investments which qualified, for example, could secure an immediate write-off against profits tax of up to 100 per cent (from 1977 to 1988) of qualifying capital expenditure such as the construction costs of a premises. Accelerated capital allowances applied to hotel investments up to 1988 but were reduced then and eliminated in 1992. The Commission on Taxation[34] was critical of the use of this provision even if it was perceived as appropriate for tourism policy (Stationery Office, 1984). It was argued that it was too blanket an approach and failed to take account of the type and location of accommodation provided. Their preference was for direct financial transfers on the grounds that the funds could be directed to where they were needed and could be operated flexibly.

While there may be some merit in this argument it is worth noting that the delivery costs of financial transfers are much greater, requiring an elaborate structure of project evaluation and assessment, monitoring and reporting. Furthermore, there is little evidence that the eventual results are better than market-induced outcomes, even if the latter may be somewhat distorted by the fiscal incentives and the rent-seeking behaviour of the beneficiaries.[35]

Urban Renewal Scheme

The Urban Renewal Scheme (URS) is another example of an incentive scheme, involving the use of accelerated capital allowances and other reliefs such as property rates' exemptions and double rent reliefs for tenant firms, which benefited tourism indirectly. The primary objective of the URS was to revitalize derelict inner city areas in the main urban centres of Dublin, Cork and Limerick. Several forms of trade qualified for the reliefs as long as these were located in the designated areas. This included many with a 'tourism content' such as shops, cinemas, theatres and restaurants, although 'industrial buildings' (incorporating hotels) were excluded since these qualified for accelerated capital allowances in 1986 irrespective of location.[36] The incentives had a strong property-based 'guarantee' for the risk-takers which stimulated a significant flow of funds to the various schemes, though information on the cost in terms of tax foregone is not readily available and may be considerable. While the urban centres were not noted tourist 'Meccas' at the outset, the ability to target specific parts of the cities, e.g. the Temple Bar area of Dublin, generated significant tourism spin-offs in later years, as did the general improvements to the urban landscapes in other cities. Urban tourism is growing in importance as 'living' city areas have become attractive to visitors. The URS did address some of the earlier criticisms of blanket coverage of reliefs in that targeted zones could receive special treatment and generate investments which might not otherwise occur. There is a problem in evaluative terms of determining what proportion of the investments are simply diverted from other parts of the urban centres to take advantage of the tax reliefs available.

Renewal Scheme for traditional seaside resorts

In principle, the introduction of the pilot scheme for seaside resorts is an extension of the URS to a number of designated resort towns which has been the mainstay of Irish (domestic) tourism in the post-war period. This was introduced in 1995 and represented a further extension of the targeting of specific areas which have tourism potential but had fallen into varying forms of dereliction. Hotels and self-catering cottages are included as qualifying buildings in the designated resorts. The main fiscal measure is the tax expenditure represented in the accelerated capital allowances, the double rent reliefs and the tax-free rental incomes available on the construction or refurbishment costs of holiday homes.

While too early to evaluate, the scheme may simply divert tourists from non-resort to resort areas (since these depend heavily on domestic tourists) at a considerable cost in terms of tax foregone. Land values may also be driven up in the selected areas thus providing windfall gains for the local landowners. Nevertheless, there may be unexpected benefits should the resorts recover some of their former glories and also become attractive to overseas tourists through the variety of restaurants and cultural attractions which emerge.[37]

Business Expansion Scheme (BES)

The BES was introduced in 1984 as a means of stimulating a flow of equity capital to risky ventures initially in manufacturing only but extended to include tourism enterprises in 1987. Modelled on a similar UK scheme to overcome the equity or finance gap for small firms, the BES enables individuals to invest either directly or indirectly, through a designated investment fund, in qualifying companies which are engaged in qualifying trades.[38] Individuals who invest in BES ventures can reduce their taxable income by the amount invested thus securing tax relief at the top marginal rate (of 48 per cent in recent years). Investments must be held in the companies for at least five years. Over the period 1984/5–1994/5 tax years the total invested in tourism through the BES was IR£113.4 million or 32.5 per cent of the total of IR£349 million raised (Dublin BIC, 1995). Over 90 per cent of the tourism funds were invested in property asset-backed ventures and were thus regarded as low-risk investments, which led to their exclusion from the tax year, 1992 onwards. The tourism sector benefited most from the BES in the period 1988–1991 when its proportionate share of the total invested through the scheme was almost 42 per cent. Table 9.2 summarizes the relative importance of BES investments in Irish tourism.

The BES had a significant impact on the improvement and expansion of the tourism accommodation stock at the time when the first OP for Tourism was targeted at other product developments in the sector.[39] The costs in terms of tax foregone were not insignificant in comparison with the Government's contribution to the OP programme, 1989–1993. In the overlapping period with this first OP, the total tax expenditures for BES-funded tourism projects was IR£38.7 million (current prices) compared with IR£65 million (constant 1989 prices) expenditure on the OP. The proportionate contribution subsequently fell below 10 per cent of OP funding. In the absence of objective or official estimates of the impact and spread of the BES-led investments in tourism, one is left to speculate on the effectiveness of the scheme in terms of the alternative use of

Table 9.2 Business Expansion Scheme (BES) investments in Irish tourism, 1987/8–1994/5

Tax year	Total BES investment IR£ million	Tourism BES investment IR£ million	Tourism/total (%)	Estimated tax foregone* IR£ million
1987/8	10.3	0.5	4.9	0.2
1988/9	25.6	6.5	25.4	3.1
1989/90	79.0	24.0	30.4	11.5
1990/91	61.0	27.1	44.4	13.0
1991/2	61.5	27.0	43.9	13.0
1992/3	21.6	2.6	12.0	1.2
1993/4	25.3	3.1	12.3	1.5
1994/5	52.3	5.8	11.1	2.8

*On tourism investments at 48% marginal rate.
Source: Derived from Dublin BIC (1995), Quigley (1992) and other sources.

the funds, how closely the location and nature of the investments were consistent with the tourism development plan as outlined in the OP and to what extent they assisted in meeting the targets set out in this programme? The suspicion that the BES was largely used as a tax avoidance measure is strong and it was this which led to the exclusion of property-based investments as 'qualifying trades' in 1992, which led to a substantial drop in the flow of funds to the tourism sector thereafter. Some commentators (quoted in Naughton, 1995) have suggested that the BES led to considerable windfall gains for tourism investors. Given the tourism demand expansion in Ireland from 1987 to 1991, it is likely that much of the investment in additional accommodation would have occurred in any case, suggesting considerable 'deadweight loss' arising from the implementation of the BES in tourism. This 'loss' was, of course, at the expense of the Irish tax-payer.

Seed Capital Scheme

The Seed Capital Scheme (SCS) was introduced in 1993 as an adjunct to the BES and was aimed primarily at employees, unemployed persons or those recently made redundant to provide start-up capital to set up in manufacturing or tourism businesses. The individuals participating could qualify for a claw-back of income tax paid in the previous three years (later extended to five years) and invest in a qualifying business. Bord Failte have a role in 'certifying' that the business was new, with the potential to create sustainable employment without displacing existing employment. The take-up in the overall scheme has been very poor, with only IR£1.7 million raised in 1994–1995 (Dublin BIC, 1995), and its impact has been minuscule.

Policy instruments in future

The preference for direct cash transfers has been very evident in the manner in which Irish tourism has been subvented in the past 10 years. This has been heavily influenced by the availability of EU funding and the need for matching funding by the host country government. The 'dependency' culture has been continued and fostered in this scenario. The fiscal incentives were largely the by-product of schemes brought in to stimulate investment in the manufacturing sector and later extended to tourism. The advice of the Commission on Taxation has been largely ignored in this context, although the concept and application of area-based incentive programmes (Urban Renewal Scheme and Seaside Resort Scheme) have enabled some targeting to take place, which the BES reliefs failed to do.

The critical issue which needs to be addressed now in the preparation for the post-1999 period, when EU Structural Funds may have dried up, is how best to prepare the tourism sector for a situation where subventions return to a level akin to the mid-1980s. Supplementary to this is the issue of evaluating which are the best instruments to use in a context where the tourism industry should be both more mature and more self-reliant.

SUMMARY AND CONCLUSIONS

This chapter set out the broad policy context in which Irish tourism developed in the past 10–15 years. Certain parallels were drawn with the approach taken to industrial promotion and development. The organizational arrangements for the industry were outlined and the changing role of the national tourism organization (Bord Failte) was examined against a background of institutional initiatives (i.e. the Tourism Task force and the Tourism Council) and the implementation of the Operational Programmes for Tourism. In addition to its primary role in promoting Ireland overseas, Bord Failte had moved from being centrally involved in tourism policy design and delivery in the mid-1980s, through a development and promotional role in the early 1990s during the implementation of the first OP, to a reversion again to its core function of promoting Ireland as a holiday destination. These changes were driven by a re-appraisal of the organization and a repositioning of it in the context of a more mature tourism industry which requires less 'hand-holding' and can assume more responsibility for its future development. It remains to be seen if the industry is sufficiently mature to move on from the 'dependency' culture which characterized it for the past 40 years.

The policy process involved in the unprecedented nature and scale of investment in Irish tourism under the two OPs was analysed, and the central role of government in shaping and monitoring the programmes noted. The monitoring function is undertaken in partnership with the agencies, the tourism industry and an EU representative. This process is a new departure, particularly the inclusion of the private sector. While some evaluative work was undertaken towards the end of the first OP it seemed there was an undue emphasis on ensuring the funds were drawn down fully rather than determining that they were spent most effectively and efficiently. Such is the nature of public sector budgetary procedures. The second OP has a greater emphasis on evaluation with detailed measures on the supply and demand side of the industry built into the programme. While the financial subsidies arising from the two OPs were the dominant form of policy instrument used to achieve the targets set for Irish tourism, extensive use was made also of tax incentives, particularly to support an increase in tourist accommodation from 1988 to 1991, to facilitate the achievement of these targets. Some of these issues are revisited in the final chapter which examines the prospects for the future development of Irish tourism.

NOTES

1. Tansey Webster and Associates (1991) refer to the Irish tourist sector as essentially factor-driven with limited product development and over-reliance on beautiful scenery and friendly people to promote Ireland as a tourism destination; they liken it to the commodity trading stage of agriculture which features in less-developed economies whereas at a more developed stage more value added is created at home through processing these commodities and exporting the finished products. Product

development is deemed to be essential to convert a comparative into a competitive advantage.

2. Initially established under the Tourist Traffic Act, 1939, the Irish Tourist Board was reconstituted by statute in 1952 as Bord Failte and both it and Fogra Failte were integrated in the new tourism promotion body, Bord Failte Eireann, in 1955 (see page 21).

3. Neither has there been such a development plan for the industry sector but over the years there has been far greater emphasis and Government resources allocated to the development of manufacturing industry than there has been to develop tourism.

4. While one can argue the logic of placing tourism in any of these departments of state it appears to the authors that the importance of the transport sector to tourism is paramount and therefore, policies for both should be developed in tandem; a strategy of maximizing traffic through Irish airports may not be consistent with developing the international tourism sector in Ireland as increasing the flow of outbound Irish tourists may be one approach taken. The recent decision (effective from 1 January 1996) of the Minister for Transport, Energy and Communications to transfer responsibility for promoting traffic through Shannon Airport from a joint venture between the regional industrial and tourism development agency (Shannon Development) and the regional airport authority (Aer Rianta Shannon) to the latter indicates a potential conflict between the viability requirements of the airport and the tourism needs of the West of Ireland.

5. Shannonside was the RTO for the Mid-west region until 1987 when its functions were subsumed within Shannon Development.

6. The Mid-west region consists of the three counties of Clare, Limerick and Tipperary NR together with Limerick Co. Borough as defined in the original Regional Development Organization's geographical sphere of influence. South-west Offaly was added to the region in 1977, thus extending the geographical area of responsibility for Shannon Development in its industrial development support activities while North Kerry was added to define the broader Shannon Region for purposes of drawing up sub-regional plans in 1989 in connection with the first OP for Tourism.

7. For further discussion on regional structures, see Chapter 5.

8. These reports included: Improving the Performance of Irish Tourism (Price Waterhouse, 1987); Tourism Working for Ireland: A Plan for Growth (SKC, Peat Marwick and DKM, 1987); The EUROPEN Report – 1992 and the Tourism Sector (Stationery Office, 1990); The Operational Programme for Tourism (Department of Tourism and Transport, 1990); and Strategic Framework for the Development of Irish Tourism Enterprises (Tansey Webster and Associates, 1992).

9. By and large the evaluative measures used to gauge the effectiveness of marketing expenditures for tourism promotion are few and far between, though there has been a strong 'bandwagon' effect at work in recent years (largely industry-led) in convincing both the Irish Government and the EU Commission that substantial additional sums ought to be allocated to marketing Ireland as a tourist destination internationally.

10. The Community Support Framework (CSF) was one of the principal innovations introduced as part of the reform of the EU's Structural Funds in 1989, as part of the measures taken to promote economic and social cohesion in the European Union on foot of the lead up to the passing of the Single European Act (and completion of the Internal Market by 1992). Objective 1 regions, or those whose development was

lagging behind, received particular attention for co-ordinated application of the three Structural Funds – ERDF, ESF and AGGF – and the Community's loan instruments. The CSF was negotiated between the Member State concerned (all ROI was classified as an Objective 1 region) and the EU Commission, and it established the agreed development priorities which are to be the focus of Community support for the four-year duration of the development plan. For a fuller outline see CEC (1990a).

11. This was indeed a disappointment for the promoters of the OP though probably reflected the harsh reality of the low returns on investment in the sector and the consequent reluctance of rational investors to invest therein; it also reflected a misjudgement by the authorities of the readiness of the private sector to take the necessary financial risks and the tourism industry's still heavy reliance on the public sector to take the lead in developing it.

12. The provision of well-equipped indoor leisure facilities at Irish hotels was one of the few concessions in the first OP granted to the accommodation sub-sector; though the lack of such facilities was argued as a negative factor in attempting to attract overseas tourists, the utilization rates among these tourists appear (from anecdotal evidence) to have been much less than among domestic users, tourists or residents.

13. ESRI (1993) and SIS (1992), respectively. In the introduction to the second OP for tourism (Stationery Office, 1994) reasons for the fine performance of Irish tourism from 1989 to 1993 were attributed to the success of the first OP. The difficulties of attributing causality to specific measures was noted by Bachtler and Michie (1995) in a useful article which raises many of the relevant issues in evaluative studies of Structural Funds, e.g. time-lags, regional scales, additionality and displacement.

14. The proposal to build a National Conference Centre under the Second OP for Tourism is a case in point where the economics of the conference business is unlikely to justify the investment required but the secondary spinoffs in purchases of hotel accommodation, transport services and general shopping items may give a positive benefit to cost ratio in an overall sense.

15. The Culliton report represented the culmination of an extensive reappraisal of the Irish Government's strategy towards the development of the industrial sector in the early 1990s; it was published as a summary report with several background studies commissioned to consider various aspects of the wider economic environment which impacted on the development of the sector. This marked it apart from previous approaches, e.g. the Telesis report (NESC, 1982) which concentrated more specific-ally on the industrial sector itself.

16. Funds from Brussels have often been viewed as 'free goods' and thus there has been a tendency to be less concerned about the effectiveness with which the funds are used. This is not unrelated to a problem for which the EU Commission itself is partly responsible. This refers to the preoccupation with ensuring the funds are spent by particular deadlines, under threat of having the funds withdrawn. It is inevitable in such circumstances that certain marginal projects will attract funding which might not otherwise go ahead with an inevitable outcome being a poor return on investment or failure to survive. Many interpretative centres supported under the first OP are deemed to have serious viability problems primarily because insufficient attention was paid to the demand side of the market at the planning stage.

17. The Tourism Task Force (discussed later in this chapter) was strongly in favour of increased public sector-led marketing expenditures, using the EU Structural Funds available to support the Irish Exchequer contributions.

18. Hurley *et al.* (1994) estimated the income and employment effects of the planned increased investment in Irish tourism under the first OP. Using input–output techniques, they estimated multiplier values for both the planned investment and the expected increase in international tourism receipts (not actual amounts). Though the resulting income multiplier values were somewhat high (1.25 for international receipts, which excluded carrier receipts) they concluded that the employment targets would not be met without taking account of indirect and induced effects of the additional expenditures – a strange 'finding' given that the OP targets explicitly measured tourism employment and employment gains in this manner.

19. See Note 2 in Chapter 5.

20. While espousing private sector principles throughout its report and a more central role for the sector in future policy formation, the Task Force was not slow to suggest a major transfer of public funds (rather than funds from the industry itself) to spearhead a marketing drive for the sector!

21. Government press release announcing the establishment of the Council (30 September 1993).

22. Mr Charlie McCreevy, TD, Minister for Tourism and Trade. The quotation was contained in the press release for the launch.

23. Reports on issues such as seasonality, domestic tourism and the fiscal environment for tourism development have been commissioned but not made available to a wider public. Ironically the commissioning of such work belies the opening thrust of the press release referred to in the text above.

24. Arthur D. Little Ltd (London) were the consultants appointed.

25. It should be noted also that the state subvention for current spending on tourism administration and marketing to both Bord Failte and Shannon Development declined steadily in real terms from 1983 to 1992, during a period when the proportion of the total budget raised from own resources increased from 7 to 23 per cent. See Stationery Office (1994) for further details.

26. Decisions on funding, with a private sector involvement, have been delegated to two independent management boards, one each for Shannon Development and Bord Failte 'regions' with one representative from the Department of Tourism and Trade, two from the agencies and three independent business people on each of the two boards. These boards effectively replaced the two state tourism agencies in this final decision-making role on which projects to support.

27. These are the native Irish speaking parts of Ireland, principally confined to small pockets of development on the west coast.

28. The causal link between tourism marketing expenditures by national tourist organizations (NTOs) and eventual tourist numbers to these country destinations is very difficult to establish because of the many other influences on destination choice. Faulkner (1995) carried out some interesting work on this topic and suggested a range of approaches to be used in evaluating the marketing spend of NTOs. He noted from his review of research carried out hitherto that what had been done was 'both inconclusive and unconvincing' in establishing causal linkages.

29. Gray (1982) refers to the 'asset theory of tourism' which largely embraces the preservation of the natural and 'built' tourism products but he extends it also to the 'quality of service' which the human capital investment should be designed ultimately to support.

30. For example, the rhetoric on foreign language training for the tourism sector has not

transferred into any extensive use of French or German in Irish tourism delivery, according to an autumn 1995 telephone survey of leading hotels conducted by an Irish Sunday newspaper.

31. The Tourism OPs were supplemented by other smaller direct transfers of EU funds through the INTERREG and LEADER programmes and the OP for Rural Development (agri-tourism scheme); the IFI was a further source of external funding while Irish Government supports were channelled through the annual grant-in-aid to Bord Failte supplemented periodically with special project funding (e.g. overseas marketing initiatives, capital development fund).

32. For example, Shannon Development through its subsidiary company, Shannon Heritage Limited, operated no less than eight day-visitor attractions in the Mid-west region which attracted an aggregate of 491,000 visitors in 1992.

33. Two examples of accommodation support measures were the 'Grant Scheme for Hotels and Guesthouses' in 1978 and the 'Hotel and Guesthouse Re-construction and Development Scheme' in 1985. Grant rates were low and total allocations minuscule in relation to the objectives sought to secure meaningful improvements in the tourist accommodation stock at the time.

34. This Commission was established by the Government in the early 1980s to undertake a comprehensive review of the taxation system in Ireland and make recommendations on how it could be improved to enhance growth, productivity and equity in the economy. The Commission noted several distortions in the tax code through incremental adjustments over the years and argued for a holistic approach to reform which would greatly simplify the system. This proved much more difficult to implement than to propose.

35. Naughton (1995) noted that the removal of the 'accelerated' version of the capital allowance measure in 1992 had little appreciable impact on the subsequent tourism accommodation supply. This suggests that the measure was either unnecessary (no market failure evident) or that other incentives had replaced it.

36. Hotels did qualify for double rent reliefs in the designated urban areas.

37. A number of other incentives of benefit to tourism are available also including incentives to maintain and promote Ireland's culture and heritage. Examples include capital acquisitions tax exemptions for objects of national interest and for stately homes and gardens, tax relief for donation of heritage items to national collections and for repairs and maintenance of 'significant' buildings. The tax expenditures involved are generally very small.

38. Tourism enterprises, including hotels, guesthouses and self-catering accommodation, were classified as 'qualifying trades' in 1987 although these primarily asset/property-backed tourism enterprises were declassified in 1992.

39. While no systematic evaluation has been published of the BES investments in tourism, some measures of the 'outputs' have been made, e.g. 2418 additional bedrooms provided and over 2700 full-time and 1200 part-time jobs provided up to the end of 1990 (report by Simpson, Xavier Horwath, quoted in Naughton, 1995).

10 Prospects for Irish tourism

INTRODUCTION

Against a background of a rather poor performance in the 1970s and early 1980s the subsequent performance of Irish tourism has been very impressive. While views differ as to the reasons for the improved performance it would be generally correct to say that the liberalization of air traffic between Great Britain and Ireland from 1986 and the surge in demand for cultural/environmentally friendly holidays by European holiday-makers since the late 1980s have been major contributory factors. Undoubtedly, the increased emphasis placed by the government on tourism development in recent years has certainly helped to increase confidence in the sector and the attendant allocation of significant EU Structural Fund monies to tourism projects has greatly improved the physical plant. Despite these favourable developments it is vital to recognize that tourism, like any other business, is constantly subject to change. This change manifests itself through the customer, i.e. the tourist. Those involved in tourism development, either in the public or the private sector, must constantly appraise themselves of such market changes and be in a position to react. Rather than be complacent with a good performance it is necessary to fully understand what factors bring a certain performance and also what actions are necessary to sustain a situation where tourism makes a sustainable and significant contribution to the national economy and society. Previous chapters in this book have highlighted many instances where improvements can be made and this final chapter explores issues that will be crucial for the long-term development of Irish tourism.

KEY ISSUES IN IRISH TOURISM

In recent years the Irish government has been successful in controlling inflation and other fiscal measures implemented in the late 1980s, such as the reduction of VAT, have helped to make Ireland a more competitive tourism destination. This improvement in the macroeconomic environment must be sustained for long-term competitiveness. Twelve key policy issues directly affecting the tourism sector are explored below and potential improvements suggested.

Seasonality[1]

Seasonality in tourism is a problem confronted by most tourism destinations. The problems created by seasonality of arrivals include seasonal employment, low profitability, poor investment and under-utilization of capacity at one end, and congestion, environmental damage, saturation of transport infrastructure, increased risk of road accidents, higher prices and a negative impact on the tourism product at the other. Traditionally the problem has been associated with demand-side considerations whereby tourists were constrained to travel by work, school holidays and other commitments at certain times of the year, and on the supply side by the dearth of demand that made it unprofitable to open many tourist attractions. While this general scenario exists to some degree today it does appear as though the tourism industry in general has been slow to react to certain demand-side changes that could contribute to an alleviation of the seasonality problem. In particular, the ageing of many European country populations and the preference for environmentally green holidays indicate that significant cohorts of the tourism market are prepared to travel out of peak season. The poor response to such market changes reflects the generalized lack of innovation on behalf of small- and medium-sized enterprises in tourism and also certain supply-side problems which hitherto have been given scant attention in the tourism literature and also in planning documents for tourism development. Too often it has been assumed that all the problems of seasonality were due to demand-side constraints with little attention being placed on supply-side considerations.

It does appear as though certain constraints such as 'satisficing' by suppliers is a major element in the seasonality problem. By 'satisficing' we mean an approach whereby suppliers are happy with a certain level of business and generally view an extension of the season as burdensome. Despite this problem it should be recognized that certain institutional constraints can also play an important disincentive in the attempt to extend the season. For example, in certain cases the role of the social welfare system allows workers in tourism (and other industries) to work for a certain period and then to claim social welfare benefits or payments for the months when the tourism business is slack. This process in itself actually suits a certain cohort of the tourism workforce yet does contribute to the general sense of unprofessionalism in the industry. Any attempt to tackle seasonality must place due emphasis on institutional and other factors on the supply side that mitigate against extending the tourism season in addition to reacting positively to demand-side signals.

Seasonality has been a long-standing issue in Irish tourism with a very concentrated peaking of demand in July and August. Traditionally, the policy focus in Ireland on seasonality has had more to do with getting additional tourists to Ireland rather than any strategic approach to spreading the timing of arrivals for environmental reasons. Virtually every Government planning document concerned with tourism since the 1950s has made some reference to seasonality yet virtually no concrete action has been taken. While the launch of the 'An Tostal' campaign in the 1950s to tackle seasonality can be seen as a visionary approach the subsequent attempts made in the 1960s and 1970s were haphazard and lacked any real concerted effort.[2] In a major review of tourism policy conducted for the National Economic and Social Council in 1980 Deane stressed the problem of seasonality in Irish tourism and while recognizing that certain initiatives had been undertaken concluded that 'there has been no major and sustained commitment of marketing resources aimed at improving the seasonal pattern of demand' (NESC, 1980b). Deane, however, suggested that a strategy of staggering Irish school holidays should be considered in an attempt to alleviate seasonality associated with domestic tourism but unfortunately little work was undertaken to bring the idea to fruition.

Although seasonality was identified in subsequent tourism documents in the 1980s little if any progress was made in distinct policy terms until the Operational Programme for Tourism, 1989–1993.[3] The OP stressed that seasonality was a major issue constraining the development of the tourism sector and identified the alleviation of same as a strategic objective. Unfortunately, progress on seasonality during the growth period 1989–1993 was minuscule and not surprisingly the OP for 1994–1999 identified an attempt to tackle seasonality as a major objective. Specifically, the programme objective for seasonality aims to 'concentrate a significant proportion of growth in the shoulder and off-peak periods, e.g. outside the peak July/August period'. The aim is that by 1999, 75 per cent of visitors will arrive in Ireland outside this period, compared with about 70 per cent at present (Stationery Office, 1994). In order to achieve this target certain preferential marketing monies are to be allocated to private sector companies that market the shoulder and off-peak periods. The latest data available for 1995 show that no inroads have been made in achieving the target with 30 per cent of visitors arriving in the peak months of July and August.[4]

At a time when Irish tourism is showing growth rates above international norms the lack of progress will at some time in the near future cause serious difficulties for the industry. Already, certain sections of the industry in Dublin are suggesting that the city is facing overcrowding and supply-side problems during the peak season. At the same time, various scenic beauty spots across the country are overcrowded and the quality of the product is seriously under pressure. In this circumstance it is necessary that a far more proactive policy than heretofore be implemented to deal with the seasonality issue. Between 1989 and 1999 total investment in the tourism industry in Ireland will total somewhere in the region of IR£1 billion yet much of this plant will lie idle for considerable periods if a strategic response is not implemented immediately.

One important first step in this approach must be a significant re-appraisal of how marketing monies are allocated. Perhaps it is now appropriate to move the bulk of the marketing effort to the shoulder and off-peak periods. Certainly, an evaluation of such an approach is worth considering. In addition it is imperative that quality products and packages which make the off-season attractive to responsive markets be developed as a matter of priority. The problems associated with the peaking of domestic demand are also worthy of serious attention. For far too long the generalized acceptance that all schools should have holidays simultaneously is in need of serious attention. While it is important to recognize that such an approach will meet with resistance from certain vested interests it should not deter the authorities from tackling the issue. It should be recognized that other countries have staggered school and factory holidays to great effect. In the absence of these changes and a fundamental shift in policy to seriously tackle seasonality it seems inevitable that current problems will be compounded.

Access transport

Frequent and competitively priced access transport networks is generally regarded as a fundamental element in the development of any successful tourism destination. Ireland's peripheral location makes the development of such networks a vital priority, especially since the opening of the Channel Tunnel which leaves Ireland as the only EU member without a landbridge to the rest of Europe. For many years the lack of suitable and appropriately priced air and sea access acted as a serious constraint to the development of tourism traffic. In addition, the virtual monopoly position of Aer Lingus (the Irish national carrier), until 1988, on the Dublin–London route with exorbitant fares and infrequent departures compounded what was a very difficult situation.

In recent years there has been significant improvement on both air and sea access to Ireland. The liberalization of the Ireland–UK bilateral air agreement in 1986 and the arrival of Ryan Air on the route had brought significant change. From a position whereby air traffic between Dublin and London fell by 6 per cent between 1978 and 1985 the liberalization ushered in an explosion of air traffic. Between 1986 and 1989 passenger numbers on the route increased from 1 million to 2.3 million (Barrett, 1991). Passenger levels on the route in 1994 were in the region of 3 million. Most of this new growth is the result of increased competition on the route and the resultant price decreases that have followed. The liberalization has led to a situation whereby the Dublin–London route has become the second busiest intra-EU route, after London–Paris, and the seventh busiest international route in the world. Undoubtedly, the initial growth in Irish tourism from 1986 to 1990 can certainly be traced to the availability of cheaper and more frequent flights on the route.[5]

While the growth on the London–Dublin route has been spectacular the majority of intra-EU routes are too thin to sustain Dublin–London competition. In 1993 the Civil Aviation Authority claimed that all but 26 scheduled routes between airports within the EU were either monopolies or duopolies. Nonetheless, Ireland has enjoyed a significant increase in scheduled traffic from mainland Europe since 1993. Capacity on European scheduled routes grew by 26 per cent from 1993 to 1995, although from a relatively small base. Of the total capacity of 2.14 million seats in 1995, Dublin had 2.04 million, Cork had 96,000 and Shannon

50,000 seats. Interestingly, charter traffic which began from an extremely low base in the mid-1980s and which in 1995 accounts for roughly 177,000 seats has mainly been to Shannon (46 per cent), Dublin (35 per cent) and Cork (16 percent) (ITIC, 1996). Given the obvious advantage that Dublin has for the growth of scheduled traffic and the declining proportion of tourism growth accounted for by the regions outside of Dublin, the increase in tourism traffic through regional airports in future years should be a major priority of tourism policy. While the growth of charter traffic to Farranfore airport in Kerry and the airports in the west of Ireland in 1995 is to be welcomed, a significant increase in charter traffic is required, particularly in the off-peak months. This will require a co-ordinated effort from all players in the tourism industry and will necessitate a clear focus on elements of the tourism market that are demonstrably growth sectors. A legitimate focus in the forthcoming years could be senior citizens across Europe.

In recent years the issue of air access to Ireland has caused considerable debate and controversy. In essence, the Shannon stopover, whereby all arriving and departing planes from and to the USA had to touch down at Shannon, was seen as a major constraint to the development of North American tourism traffic. In particular, this arrangement was seen to lower the overall traffic to Ireland and secondly it was argued that the arrangement induced significant numbers of tourists to arrive in Ireland via the UK. This was believed to be particularly unfortunate as it led to lower revenues for Aer Lingus, lower expenditure by tourists as length of stay in Ireland was curtailed and thirdly because it curtailed traffic growth to Ireland from North American airlines. While it is undoubtedly correct that the 'stopover' proved a disincentive for a certain cohort of tourists the evidence that the removal of the stopover would lead to increased interest from American carriers was certainly far more uncertain than was often claimed. Most importantly, it should be recognized that the size of the Irish market is far too small to be of interest to American airlines who generally are seeking airports and destinations that can act as hub airports for onward traffic. In addition, it should be recognized that the level of 'backtracking' to Ireland from the UK and other parts of Europe is a reflection of changing consumer composition and demand to visit more than one destination on a visit to Europe.

Irrespective of the merits of the argument the Government (with a certain backlash in the Shannon region) decided to allow a direct transatlantic service to/from Dublin in 1994. The most recent figures available for 1995 shows that scheduled capacity between Ireland and the USA grew roughly 30 per cent from 1993. While this growth is to be welcomed, the anticipated increase of interest from American carriers has not materialized with only Delta Airlines showing any interest in increasing capacity to Ireland. This development together with the possibility that Delta and Aer Lingus may enter a codesharing[6] arrangement on the North Atlantic route suggests some interesting developments that will require monitoring by the Irish Government. While the agreement may bring increased capacity to the route it is also possible that competition could be stifled by a duopoly practice which could ultimately curtail growth. Whatever the decision on the Aer Lingus–Delta codeshare an immediate priority for tourism interests should be the identification of a mechanism to attract traffic from the west coast of the United States where outbound tourism growth is extremely buoyant. To date, direct services between Ireland and the US west coast have proved very difficult to maintain because of the competition provided by indirect routings via the UK. The level of backtracking is so great and the number of factors behind it so varied that the scope for reversing the trend seem limited. Even so, connecting services between the US west coast and Ireland, marketed under the code of a large US airline could both stimulate growth and attract a higher proportion of direct entrants. With due regard to maintaining competitive conditions an approach on codesharing may yet offer the best opportunity to increase traffic to Ireland from both the east and west coasts of the United States.[7]

Since 1989 there has been a marked increase in capacity on sea routes to Ireland, mainly due to the introduction of larger ships, high-speed ferries and increased frequencies on sea routes between Ireland and Britain. While the increased capacity in recent years has been important it is noticeable that in 1995, 59 per cent of holiday visitors arrived to Ireland by air and 42 per cent by sea compared with a roughly even split in 1993. The market share swing to air is evidenced in all source markets. Importantly, the number of mainland European residents arriving on holiday in Ireland by sea has declined on both direct and indirect routes over the period. The major elements of growth on sea access from 1993 to 1995 (+10 per cent) has been due to growth from the British market (ITIC, 1996). In view of the regional imbalances now prevalent in Irish tourism it is imperative that increased efforts should be made to encourage increased access to Ireland on direct ferry services from mainland Europe in the years ahead. It is also important that current constraints on car hire availability and price should be tackled in tandem with this initiative.

Human resource issues

A fundamental element in the sustainability of the current tourism boom will inevitably be the recruitment, training and education of new entrants to the tourism industry. The increased quality demanded by the ever more mobile international tourist requires that entrants to the tourism sector be imbued with a service ethic that has hitherto been absent from many sections of the industry in Ireland. No longer can an unprofessional and piecemeal approach be taken to the human resource function if tourists are to receive an overall quality of product that will generate repeat business. In recognition of this fact, the first OP for Tourism, 1989–1993, increased the budget allocated to CERT, the national training agency for tourism, by 50 per cent. The programme initiated for training placed emphasis on increasing the numbers on existing training programmes and on new programmes which included courses with a foreign language component. A review of the training initiatives undertaken for the EU Commission in 1993 concluded that placement rates on many of these programmes were close to 100 per cent (SIS, 1992). The review did, however, express some concern that the training outputs tended to be measured on a quantitative rather than a qualitative basis and that the indicators used revealed little about the quality of the trainees and subsequent performance in the industry. Little progress has been made since then to develop appropriate monitoring instruments for quality assessment.

The OP for Tourism 1994–1999 has allocated IR£110 million for all tourism training initiatives.[8] In tandem with the new focus on tourism, responsibility for CERT was transferred from the Department of Labour to the newly created Department of Tourism and Trade. The training strategy identified for the new programme is consistent with that identified in the Community Support Framework 1994–1999, namely:

- to boost human capital in Ireland by enhancing education and skill levels;
- to enhance the employment prospects of unemployed people and persons excluded from the labour market and to develop appropriate support and counselling measures (Stationery Office, 1994).

In executing its tourism training role, CERT is expected to co-operate closely with the Department of Education in pursuit of higher education and training standards on behalf of the hotel, catering and tourism industry.

While CERT and individual universities, regional technical colleges and other private institutions continue to concentrate efforts to produce quality personnel for the industry, a number of serious problems appear to be emerging. First and foremost, the expansion of the industry is so swift that certain categories of personnel are apparently in short supply. Regularly, articles appear in the daily newspapers suggesting a shortage of key staff and the need to recruit from the UK or further afield. While it could be expected that an expanding industry may encounter problems of this nature it does appear as though there are some fundamental structural problems that must be overcome if the required human resource contribution is to be achieved.

The structural problems encountered in the Irish tourism industry are similar to those found in many other countries. Primarily, there appears to be a certain mismatch between the aspirations of young school leavers and graduates and the conditions offered by both the hospitality and tourism sector at large. The tourism industry today and increasingly in the years ahead requires well-trained, educated and linguistically capable personnel, yet the industry at a broader level offers a poor career structure, poor wages and extremely long and unsocial hours. Recent work conducted on behalf of CERT found that three-quarters of those in the industry were earning less than IR£10,000 per annum compared to the average industrial wage of IR£14,000. The hours worked for such pay were particularly long, especially for professional cookery, bar service and supervisory staff in hotels. Just 37 per cent of graduates worked between 41 and 50 hours per week, while a further 20 per cent worked between 51 and 80 hours compared to a national average of 40.8 hours a week for industrial workers (CERT, 1996a).

At a time when the number of school leavers in Ireland is declining the tourism industry desperately needs to recruit additional staff to both craft and supervisory management positions. In this endeavour the industry must be more focused on the competition for this emerging labour force and also be appraised of the factors that influence the choice of career of young school leavers. A recent report commissioned by CERT on the attitudes of secondary school leavers towards the tourism industry found that a 'poor image' of the industry, especially for catering jobs must be tackled as a matter of priority if quality personnel are to be attracted in to the industry. Notable research findings were as follows (CERT, 1996b):

- careers advice for tourism appeared to work on a 'need to know basis' whereby pupils would only be given information on tourism if they specifically requested it. Even more alarmingly, teachers in general did not perceive that tourism would be a suitable career path for most of the brighter students and as a result tourism career information was distributed after university applications had been completed;
- only 7 per cent of a total sample of 1260 pupils expressed interest in a tourism career path;
- pupils attach significant importance to career progression in deciding on career choice.

Given these research findings, the declining number of school leavers and the projected expansion of the tourism industry it is apparent that the industry will need to address some fundamental issues as a matter of priority. Importantly, the industry must endeavour to improve working conditions, provide promotional opportunities and generally enhance the attractiveness of tourism as a sustainable and fulfilling career opportunity. In tandem, both CERT and the industry must be far more proactive in getting its message across to those still in the school system. It would be extremely unfortunate if the massive expenditure on tourism hardware, such as buildings and facilities, was not accompanied by the human resource element that ultimately defines a tourism experience as being memorable.

Role of the private sector

There has been a strong public sector involvement in the development of Irish tourism (as in other sectors of the economy) since the 1950s. This is not unusual in countries in the early stages of development – and Ireland was classified as underdeveloped by World Bank criteria up until the early 1970s. Successful arguments by the Irish Government to secure significant tranches of EU Structural Funds over the period 1989–1999 have prolonged and extended in scale the public sector subventions which the industry has attracted. Combined with fiscal-induced transfers, especially through the BES schemes, and other funding through the IFI and the EU's INTERREG and LEADER programmes, it is questionable how the Irish tourism industry can ever move to a more self-reliant basis and survive in a less subsidized and more openly competitive environment. The anticipated loss of EU Structural Funds post-1999 will undoubtedly cause greater exposure to the marketplace. The anticipated expenditure by the private sector during the period of the first Operational Programme for Tourism, 1989–1993, only partially materialized, even where significant co-funding was available.

The Northern Ireland tourism sector is not dissimilar to that in the Republic of Ireland in terms of its reliance on the public sector, though NI tourism differs in that it has operated in more of an insular fashion with a stronger reliance on the domestic market and on those visiting friends and relatives. Government policy documents in the late 1980s have stressed the need for greater self-reliance in NI tourism, citing the existence of market failure as the only rational basis for public intervention. The commencement of the 'peace process' in 1994 did generate substantially increased investment activity based on a new optimism for the future of the industry. This serves to highlight the weaknesses on the demand side of the industry prior to 1994 which in turn limited its growth.

The Arthur D. Little (1994) report on the re-organization of Bord Failte expressed this need to shift to a more market oriented approach in terms of the way in which mature tourism industries operate. There is less support from the state and, where this is deemed necessary as through a properly functioning national tourism organization (NTO), the latter should concentrate on its core functions of international destination marketing and provision of information and research services. All other non-core activities should be transferred or privatized according to the consultants.

There has been a dominant supply-side approach to Irish tourism development for the past 30 years, driven by the grants and subsidies available through the Exchequer, and augmented since the late 1980s by other funding sources. Unless and until the private sector sharply refocuses on the demand side of the business and develops a customer-oriented approach at all levels, the future looks uncertain. The lead advocated for the NTO (Bord Failte) is not just symbolic but represents an approach to business development which the private sector needs to follow, rather than direct energies in lobbying for further Government subventions for marketing spend on their behalf. International tourists will not continue to come to Ireland and generate the expected expenditure volumes unless they get value for money, receive quality services and have a sufficient variety and quality of product (and experience) to encourage repeat visits and open up new markets. It is not clear that many of the non-accommodation based ventures established in recent years are sufficiently attuned to international tourist trends to sustain them in the long term.

The scale and development of tourism in the Dublin region in recent years is such that the market has responded significantly to the opportunities presented with several new hotel investments and greater capacity utilization of other tourist facilities, e.g. restaurants, shops. Market failure is more likely to continue to be found in western regions where tourism buoyancy has masked the decline in relative regional market share. Where accommodation investments have been undertaken (e.g. in the Mid-west) on the basis of assumptions about national market growth, the excess capacity generated will put further pressure on margins. Public sector intervention which is focused to enhance the marketing efforts of private operators in western regions will be required to prevent potential disinvestment decisions by private operators there in the years ahead. The same argument (i.e. 'market failure') applies to continued product development interventions on a selective regional basis. Tourism innovation in both the private and public sectors is a key dimension for the future of Irish tourism.

Innovation in the tourism sector

The level of innovation in a firm is a critical determinant of its long-term capacity to grow and develop; it is no different at the industry level although the degree of fragmentation of the particular sector can influence the rate at which innovations occur.[9] Innovation has been defined in an MCSB (1989) study as 'exploiting or managing change as an opportunity to develop a different business; or provide a different service; or attract a different market or market segment'. Tourism is a fragmented industry though individual sub-sectors (e.g. transport operators) can develop appropriate scale economies to benefit from research and development expenditures leading to innovations, especially of a technical nature. The travel trade has adopted technological advances, especially in the information technology field, to improve operational efficiencies and deliver a better quality service to travellers. They have embraced these technological advances also to stay ahead of, or match, the competition. But innovation in tourism goes much beyond technological improvements and includes numerous new product combinations, alternative package tours, integrated holiday packages, new niche markets, new holiday experiences or new ways of delivering traditional products. Innovations can extend also to organizational changes which improve the delivery of tourism services in often imperceptible but effective ways. The objective is to ensure that the tourist (consumer) experiences a more enjoyable holiday, the viability of specific businesses are enhanced and the tourism destination is continually renewed and retains its attractiveness to visitors.

Innovative firms are characterized by one dominant consideration – focus on the customer. Given the largely supply-side approach (and public-sector dependence) to tourism development in Ireland, one would not expect to find an industry noted for its innovative approach to development. For much of the post-war period the comparative advantage which Ireland enjoyed as a tourist destination was predicated on the natural beauty of the scenery and the friendliness of the people, buttressed by the favourable price variables (pre-1970s and early 1990s). But there were a number of notable innovations also. The world's first duty-free shop was opened in Shannon Airport in 1947, medieval banquets were pioneered in the Mid-west region during the 1960s, the 'Rent-an-Irish-Cottage' scheme was initiated as a joint public–private sector initiative and Ireland's first regional tourism organization was established there in 1964. The Bunratty Folk Park, the first of several heritage centres subsequently developed on the island, was also initially developed in the 1960s.[10] More recently, rural communities have effectively used EU LEADER funds to develop innovative alternative tourism products in their areas with a focus on a combination of active holidays, walking routes, integrated packages and co-operative marketing. However, the record of innovation in Irish tourism since the 1960s has been remarkably weak as the MCSB (1989) study attested.[11] This was attributed to the small and fragmented nature of existing tourism operators, their tendency to confuse investment with innovation, shortage of finance, poor strategic planning and marketing in tourism and the lack of focus or support for an entrepreneurial approach to tourism development.

The lessening of the finance constraint in Irish tourism during the first and second Operational Programmes (since 1989) did lead to unprecedented investment in the industry, much of which was led by the public sector. It is not evident whether this was accompanied by a greater degree of innovation in the industry. However, it is clear that the long-term strategic development of Irish tourism will require a much greater emphasis on this dimension of change. Achieving this requires much closer analysis of competitors, much closer attention to changing customer needs and the flexibility to respond and the creation of a facilitative context at senior executive levels to enable innovations to emerge.[12] Organizational structures in tourism enterprises will need to become less rigid to encourage more innovation which requires 'flexibility, teamwork and creativity', and professional management with strong market orientation.[13]

Quality of tourism services

The strategic development of Irish tourism and the move towards attracting higher spending tourists will be constrained without concerted action to raise the quality of service within the industry. While there is limited scope to improve the attractiveness of a holiday destination with regard to natural resources, such as scenery, a great deal can be done to improve the quality of the provision and delivery of tourism services. Quality is also emerging as a key competitive component within the marketing strategies of the tourism industry. It is important to note that the perception which tourists have of quality is not based solely on the outcome of a service (its technical quality) but also on an evaluation of the process of service delivery (its functional quality). Furthermore, it is essential that any evaluation should look beyond the view of quality in its negative sense (concerned with avoiding service failures and customer complaints) to the adoption of a positive approach which focuses on setting and exceeding quality standards.

Difficulties involved in the measurement of quality arise from the nature of services – their intangibility (compared with tangible manufactured goods), simultaneity (of production and consumption) and perishability (inability to store unsold services). These features are compounded in tourism by the heterogeneity of tourism services which causes difficulty in applying uniform quality standards and the costs of monitoring improvements which rely heavily on surveys of tourists.

The quality of service provided by those employed in the industry and in the range of associated activities which constitute the total tourism 'experience' is dependent on a whole host of factors, many of which are ingrained in the pysche of the population. Attitudes to foreign visitors is generally very positive in Ireland and the traditional Irish reputation for hospitality – friendly and welcoming – provides a healthy basis for a thriving industry. However, tourism involves a certain degree of servility which can often run 'against the grain' of those in countries with a colonial past in which relationships with those being served were extremely unequal. Combine this with parts of an industry in which income levels are relatively low, employment forms are precarious and career progression prospects poor and one can begin to understand the problems of raising service quality to appropriate levels. Attempts to do so are linked particularly to the human resource development strategies used in the industry. The national training agency, CERT, has a key role in this process as noted above. It is responsible for the vast majority of those trained to enter the industry though its main evaluative focus tends to be on the immediate employability of its trainees rather than on their ultimate interface with customers (many of them tourists).

The industry itself also has responsibility for maintaining and improving quality standards, and it is generally recognized that these have improved in recent years (judged by the declining proportion of visitors indicating their low value for money (satisfaction) ratings of their Irish tourism visit). While there are some examples of outstanding service quality in, for example, the five-star hotels in Ireland, there is limited evidence to suggest that expenditure on and effectiveness of training for improved interface with customers is adequate. There is a dearth of information and research work in this field as most survey work tends to focus on the quantitative rather than the qualitative outputs in Irish tourism. Indeed, it is likely that very little is known about the expectations of tourists in regard to service quality; whether reliability (expectations fulfilled) is more important than responsiveness (to requests/complaints) or whether empathy (understanding of problems) ranks ahead of assurance (courteous and knowledgeable tourism personnel).

The service dimension of Irish tourism needs to be addressed in line with the strategic direction the industry is taking. This will require appropriate resourcing, direction from top managerial levels and effective incentives for all those delivering at the interface with the tourists themselves. Monitoring of outcomes is a critical component of any concerted effort at quality improvement.

Overseas tourism promotion

The primary purpose of all tourism organizations is to promote a particular country, region or area as a tourist destination amongst consumers and the travel trade. The activities undertaken by tourism organizations are very similar and include marketing campaigns, operation of tourist centres, consumer and travel trade shows, and provision of information in the form of guidebooks, brochures and travel manuals. In addition to the promotional spend of public sector agencies, there is also considerable (though often difficult to quantify) expenditure by private sector interests such as airlines and hotel groups. In Ireland, particularly in recent years, a great deal of emphasis has been placed on the need to increase and also to target promotional spending. A view, shared by many, appears to be that substantial monies have been expended on facilities and now the major job at hand is to promote same to the tourism consumer and trade.

In the attempt to improve the marketing of Ireland a major restructuring has taken place at Bord Failte and an additional layer of marketing has been introduced, now known as the overseas tourism marketing initiative (OTMI). The OTMI, originally established in 1993 brought together a voluntary group of marketing professionals in the tourism industry as a means of rejuvenating business, particularly from the USA which had declined since the Gulf War. In 1996, the OTMI budget totals IR£6.5 million, of which IR£4 million is from the EU, IR£1 million is from industry, IR£1 million from government and the balance comes from the Northern Ireland Tourist Board. Of this amount one-third of each expenditure will be spent in the US and British markets, respectively, and most of the remainder will be allocated to Germany and France.

The operation of the OTMI has been heralded by its supporters as a major success. Increases in market performance from the US and other markets in recent years have been attributed to the excellent work of the OTMI. While such a response is understandable, it does appear as being rather simplistic. For example, such claims can only be substantiated if it can be demonstrably proven that such growth would not have occurred without the intervention. While recognizing that such a task is fraught with many difficulties it is palpably clear that the tracking exercises required to substantiate the OTMI claims have not been undertaken to date. In essence, the performance could have more to do with general macroeconomic criteria in the source markets than any initiative undertaken. While such a view of the OTMI might appear very jaundiced it should be recognized that tourism growth to Ireland was increasing some years before the increased availability of marketing funds. More importantly, the growth in the late 1980s coincided with a period when the promotional budget of Bord Failte had been seriously reduced. The aforementioned is merely a plea that promotional expenditure be subject to more rigorous examination than heretofore.[14] On a more general level, more detailed work needs to be undertaken to ascertain whether promotional spending should be pro- or counter-cyclical, i.e. should promotion be increased in markets where disposable incomes are growing or alternatively in markets where disposable income is declining?

In line with the general reorganization of Bord Failte it appears as though some fundamental and welcome change is being introduced. The appointment of a new marketing director, appears to be a move that will usher in a very exciting and innovative period for Irish tourism. The new approach focuses on the need to fundamentally alter how Ireland is marketed abroad and currently a brand image for Ireland is being developed. The aim is to develop a marketing strategy along the lines of the Olympic games, where large branded corporations pay to be associated in some recognized way with the games. Obviously, this will raise a number of significant issues on property rights related to promotion of the country but is in principle a commendable idea.

The move to a brand image[15] and the approach being undertaken is particularly timely. Currently, the total public and private promotional spend for Ireland is estimated to be in the region of £IR60 million. While a considerable sum it is minuscule relative to the marketing budgets available to many private sector companies outside of Ireland. For example, British Airways recently spent £22 million on an advertising campaign in the USA. If a branding approach can be agreed it can certainly give economies of scale, avoid duplication of effort and also avoid conflicting marketing images of Ireland. It is currently estimated that once developed a branding scheme would still require an annual outlay of IR£30 million and plans are currently being developed to ascertain how such funding can be raised.

While generally embracing the idea of a branding image it should be recognized that certain factors be given due regard in the process. First, how does the current investment programme fit with the branding image that is emerging? Second, investors in the private sector who are considering investing in tourism ventures must be appraised of the vision of the future that is emerging. Third, whatever brand emerges it is vital that due regard be given to the two main factors that tourists to Ireland find attractive, namely the environment and the friendliness of the Irish people. In the effort to develop a slick brand image it should not be forgotten that the recent growth of Irish tourism and the future possibilities depend on protecting and nurturing these important assets.

Investment appraisal

The question of investment appraisal has become quite critical in the tourism sector in recent years in Ireland because of the substantial EU and public sector funds allocated to individual projects and the desire to ensure that the returns reflect sound investment decisions, given the alternative use of the funds sacrificed in the process. A number of well publicized 'failures' have given a new urgency also to the search for a more effective appraisal mechanism.[16] A major problem is the tendency to overestimate the demand for new tourist facilities and particularly the additionality generated by the investment, especially the increased overseas demand. Cost over-runs can occur also though these happen less frequently and are more predictable. The dominant supply-side approach to developing Irish tourism, encouraged by the EU structural fund transfers, is only slowly changing to take greater cognisance of international tourism trends and the changing needs of the overseas tourists.

The appraisal mechanisms used rarely take account of the wider cost–benefit framework which embrace impacts well beyond the immediate effects of the tourism projects themselves. These latter 'externalities' can seriously limit or enhance the cost–benefit ratios of individual projects, for example projects which attract 10,000 more visitors per day may cause excessive traffic congestion and physical disturbance of access routes to amenities such that positive commercial returns may be turned into negative net benefits. Positive externalities arise from the expenditures by tourists in areas where visitor attractions may be the prime reasons to visit; the local economy can benefit from expenditure on local accommodation, shopping, pubs and restaurants.

There is also a need to measure the extent of 'displacement' which occurs when, for example, an additional heritage centre in an area diverts demand from other heritage centres thereby reducing the net benefit to the economy of the proposed investment. This need to take account of competitive attractions is frequently overlooked though it should be a central element of the project appraisal mechanism. Displacement is not always a negative aspect of tourism policy, however. If visitors are diverted from low- to high-grade accommodation in an area or from small- to large-scale attractions with more facilities there may be additional expenditure (both on and off site) associated with the displacement and this would be regarded as a positive outcome. Furthermore, it may be an objective of tourism policy to encourage spatial displacement between sub-regions, from more to less congested areas or from areas of lower to higher unemployment both of which might be achieved through active displacement measures. Domestic tourists might be targeted for such strategies as their geographical redistribution could yield positive net benefits.

Gray (1995) provides a useful analysis of the core issues involved in public sector project appraisal methodologies. He stresses the need for individual projects to make a net economic return,[17] to ensure that more attractive alternatives are not overlooked and that the wider impact of investment decisions on the returns from other projects is also evaluated. 'Deadweight' effects should also be monitored to avoid the danger of allocating resources to projects which would have gone ahead even without the public sector funding, thus ensuring these resources are released for other purposes. The SIS (1992) report to the EU Commission on the Operational Programme for Tourism, 1989–1993, also cautioned on the failure to allow for displacement effects in project appraisal mechanisms used for tourism investments in Ireland. It was also critical of the absence of any qualitative assessment of tourism project promoters as part of the overall appraisal and the lack of any follow-up process to compare demand forecasts with outcomes in the implementation phase of the funded investments. The pressure (from the EU and the Irish Government) to use the funds available within the specified time-frame did not help in ensuring the best investment decisions were made in the first OP though there have been improvements in the latest OP.[18]

In spite of the measurement difficulties surrounding the effective use of cost–benefit analysis, it is a powerful basis for determining whether particular publicly funded tourism investments should go ahead. This technique is used to ensure a better return on taxpayers' funds and takes account of broader issues pertaining to the overall welfare of society.

Regional issues

The changing regional distribution of tourism expenditures critically impacts on the contribution of tourism to regional GDP and employment levels in Ireland. The Irish tourism industry made a disproportionate economic contribution to the less developed western regions of Ireland up to the early 1980s but since then there has been a redirection of relative expenditures towards the eastern regions, especially Dublin. This latter trend has become more pronounced since 1989 with British and mainland European visitors being primarily responsible for the 'diversion' from western regions.[19] While various factors are advanced for these changing trends such as the growth of city tourism, greater tourist flows through east-coast access ports, the lower incidence of motoring tourists and the growth of the 'short-break' market from Britain, the supply-side responses have not been tailored to these changed market preferences. This will be a major challenge in future years for tourism promoters in the least developed parts of Ireland to ensure the industry can recover lost ground. Those concerned with regional development in the western regions will need to design an appropriate long-term strategy, firmly based on changing market trends, to develop the tourism sector and ensure it makes an appropriate contribution to the regional economy.

Niche tourism markets, such as rural tourism, can make important though modest contributions to the revitalization of the industry. The over-reliance on existing natural attractions and on the development of interpretative-style centres are often based on a limited understanding of market trends and an exaggeration of the likely demand. Problems of displacement are rarely included in the assessment of EU-funded projects though these can substantially reduce the net impact of the investments made in employment terms. Tourist preferences for active rather than passive holidays, for short- rather than long-stay vacations, and for cultural experiences through interaction with the resident population need to be understood and matched by tourism providers in all tourism regions but particularly in those attempting to regain market share, i.e. western regions. The focus at national level on marketing 'Ireland Inc.' as a tourist destination makes no differentiation between regions. It would be unfortunate if the new opportunities likely to follow a successful brand image marketing strategy were to lead to a further widening of regional disparities. It is left to individual RTOs to promote their regions on the basis of the throughput of numbers generated nationally and the product mix, innovative ideas and tourist resources at their disposal. Event tourism, which may attract an international audience, can be an effective regional promotional tool though one which can put pressure on available capacity at specific times. The problems of scale in Irish tourism can lead also to limitations on developing the industry in the more remote regions while sustainability arguments serve to limit the expansion of some attractions there and access to them.

Much, perhaps too much, is expected in terms of the economic contribution of tourism to regional development and the RTOs are seen as key organizations to deliver on these expectations. The RTOs lack true autonomy though have become less dependent on Bord Failte subventions in recent years, particularly in the better performing tourism regions. More specifically, the RTOs have only partial control over the public sector subventions to tourism with the LEADER programmes I and II, the INTERREG and the IFI funds being outside its remit. This makes it difficult to introduce coherence into the implementation of tourism policy at regional level and impossible to develop strategic plans. The move to develop organizational structures at the sub-regional, i.e. county, levels is a further undermining of the regional structures. The accumulated knowledge and expertise of the RTOs need to be effectively mobilized, within a rationalized framework, to ensure a better regional distribution of the benefits of tourism in Ireland.

Environmental issues

In recent years the protection of both the natural and physical environment is evidenced across the world by numerous international conferences and the introduction of legislation. Ireland, more by accident than design, is deemed to possess a relatively clean and unspoilt environment and as a result has been an attractive tourism destination, particularly for Europeans in recent years. While the perception that Ireland is 'clean and unspoilt' is generally accurate, there is evidence that a certain degree of complacency surrounds the area of environmental protectionism. Tourism is legitimately targeted by Government as a growth sector of the economy yet the environmental asset is given scant or very vague attention in planning documents, e.g. the OP for Tourism, 1994–1999, allocates just 14 lines of a 130-page document to the environment.

In the current market conditions where the tourism sector is booming such scant attention to the environment is deemed a serious flaw. Already there have been a number of controversies surrounding the development of interpretative centres in sensitive areas of natural beauty and environmental bodies have expressed concern over the development of golf courses and other tourism amenities. The reasons for such controversies can often be multifaceted yet the major factor behind many of the disputes is the absence of a firm policy statement and guidelines that govern the fragile relationship between tourism and the environment. The growth of tourism numbers to many regions of the country, particularly in the peak months of July and August, is cause for concern yet a clear policy response has been slow to emerge. To date there has been little debate in Ireland about the use of market-based solutions to environmental problems which could offer some part of a solution to the problems encountered by tourism development. Too often policy decisions have been guided not by a vision of the future based on the common good but, rather by reactions to pressure from powerful groups to serve their own interests. Problems of congestion, whether they be at a scenic beauty spot or alternatively in the increasingly overcrowded Dublin, are deleterious to the long-term development of a sustainable tourism industry and require immediate attention.

An important factor in the environmental problem has been the emphasis on tourism numbers rather than revenues. For an important period in the late 1980s and the early 1990s the government adopted a numbers target for tourism as the barometer of success. While the current Operational Programme has correctly moved to an approach of emphasizing revenue as the objective target, a more coherent strategy is required. Such an approach would target the more affluent tourist, tourists who tend to travel out of peak season and also those who travel geographically across countries thus alleviating congestion problems in certain locations and contributing to regional development. Failure to adopt such a strategic approach will lead to the deterioration of the environment, negative consumer reaction and the loss of sustainable jobs which the economy so badly requires.

North–South dimensions

The similarities in product and touristic experiences in Northern Ireland and the Republic of Ireland for the past 30 years have been noted earlier, especially in Chapter 8. The 'peace process', which commenced with the announcement of the IRA ceasefire on 31 August 1994, has been a particularly significant catalyst in stimulating the key players (tourism operators, policy-makers, tourism agency representatives) to focus on the potential for joint activities and initiatives, North and South, to enhance the benefits to be derived from the tourism sectors on the island. This 'peace process' has undoubtedly been instrumental in attracting more visitors to both parts of the island (e.g. in 1994–1995) and encouraging a higher proportion of visitors to the ROI to include NI as part of their trip. While the latter may reduce the revenue yield from a given volume of overseas visitors to the ROI, this can be compensated for though an overall expansion of the market.

The supply-side deficiencies in the NI tourism product, because of low investment levels over several years and the limited proportion of 'pure' tourists visiting there, are being remedied in recent years. In this regard, the experience of the ROI in tourism development since 1987 is a convenient learning context for those charged with development in NI tourism, both to learn from mistakes as well as from the more positive outcomes. A number of joint projects have been initiated under the EU's INTERREG programme and others funded in border counties through the International Fund for Ireland (IFI). The IFI has been quite supportive in promoting Ireland (NI and ROI) as a single destination through funding exhibition stands and overseas tourism offices while the joint computer-based reservations system – GULLIVER – was also financed from this source.[20] EU Structural Funds have also supported product developments with North–South dimensions, for example the Ballinamore–Ballyconnell canal.

Teague (1993) refers to a 'co-ordination deficit' which has limited the degree of North–South co-operation in economic matters, and points out how 'this deficit is reflected in the remarkably thin economic relations between North and South'. Tourism is a sector which lends itself very much to co-operative initiatives, and while the onset of the 'troubles' in 1970 limited the extent of this co-operation for a number of years, this has gradually improved since the early 1980s as the actors on both sides perceived the benefits to be gained. The concept of 'co-operative competition' is relevant here, borrowed from the experience of the industrial districts in northern Italy. The theory of co-operative competition suggests that it is best to co-operate to expand the market, and once consolidated then competition can develop to share the enlarged market revenues. Both parties co-operate in terms of market research, product development and promoting all of Ireland as a tourism destination but compete in terms of products available in each part of the island. The promotional efforts can emphasize the benefits of visiting 'two destinations for the price of one' while attractive all-Ireland tourism packages should be developed which stress the complementary nature of the product offerings. Product promotion could benefit also from the use of the World Wide Web (Internet) facility to market Ireland as a holiday destination to over 40 million users, using this modern technological means of communication.

Further co-operative possibilities

There are opportunities for further enhancement of all-Ireland tourism through initiatives in product development, access transport, and human resource development. There is significant scope for cross-border co-operation in the area of market research, especially to identify prospective tourist patterns and tastes and to determine motivational reasons for visiting Ireland, of which very little is known. There is considerable scope for improving the quality and accuracy of tourism data, especially in regard to expenditure patterns.[21] There is also a need to develop mechanisms to evaluate tourism quality factors which would provide useful insights into future product developments. Similarly, tourism innovation could benefit from developments on both sides of the border helping to overcome the diseconomies of small-scale operations.

Turning to access transport, an island destination is continuously constrained by the frequency and cost of access transport services. There are no direct transatlantic flights from North America to Belfast and only two scheduled air services from mainland Europe. Thus, NI is heavily dependent on traffic channelled through UK airports either from mainland Europe or backtracking from flights originating in North America. North–South air services are also limited and could benefit from initiatives such as the Belfast–Shannon–Boston service originated in 1995. Irish regional airports could play a strategically important role in the development of tourism within the island given their location in key tourism regions. One positive example is the recently introduced charter service from Belfast to Farranfore airport in the south-west (Kerry). Poor internal transport linkages between North and South also need attention. There are only four cross-border public bus services and the rail service between the two 'capitals' needs upgrading. The intention to develop the 'economic corridor' between Dublin and Belfast includes extensive infrastructural developments along the route which should benefit cross-border flows considerably.

Human resources issues in international tourism will be critical in the years ahead and this will be particularly concerned with the quality of employees, their training and qualifications, and their ability to manage in high quality, sustainable tourism destinations. Ireland is positioning its tourism in this framework and will be unable to maintain its competitive edge without due attention to the training and human resource requirements of the sector. The sophisticated tourism industry of the future will require well-educated, fluent and professional employees with a thorough knowledge of the industry, an appreciation of the main market trends and the capacity to service customers' requirements. Northern Ireland tourism has developed in a framework of a quasi-domestic industry while the primary training focus in the ROI has been developed from the craft side with a bias towards the hotel and catering end of the business. This means there are mutual benefits to supporting initiatives which can jointly address the human resource deficiencies in the industry.

There are mutually beneficial reasons for North–South co-operation in tourism development. Both parts of the island need to ensure an appropriate balance between tourism development and the environment, the raising of quality standards and a better understanding of changing markets through proper research work. Progress along these lines should ensure a vibrant and sustainable tourism industry. Co-operation between tourism agencies on both sides of the border does not mean that the respective industries will not compete for the available business. This would be an unrealistic and undesirable outcome as tourism by its nature is competitive. What is important is that there should be significant co-operation in product development, research and in areas where significant economies of scale exist.

Beyond this competitive forces will operate as they do between east and west. This model of co-operative competition offers significant benefits to Irish tourism, especially in the context of the somewhat fragile 'peace process' in place at the time of writing.

Research and information issues

In the enthusiasm to develop the tourism sector in Ireland it has been apparent that a great deal of investment and strategy have taken place in the absence of good detailed information. In some respects it appears as though policy-makers are of the misguided opinion that tourism investment does not require the same degree of research underpinning as other sectors of the economy. A critical issue in this regard are the tourism data. The Central Statistics Office (CSO) in Ireland is responsible for collating tourism data yet the information provided is inadequate for a sector of the economy that exhibits such massive growth as in recent years and one which is so important to the Irish economy. Essentially the CSO considers its function is be the delivery of data for a balance of payments input which is unfortunately inappropriate for policy-making purposes. While the data provided by the CSO are provided in a more user-friendly format by the research staff at Bord Failte, serious gaps still remain in our knowledge of expenditure patterns, preferences of tourists and perceptions of the quality of the tourism product.

The lack of attention to the tourism data permeates other issues on the research function related to Irish tourism. While there has been significant investment in tourism hardware issues such as buildings and facilities, the commensurate research on investment appraisal mechanisms has been sadly lacking. A vibrant tourism industry of the future requires that funding be made available to appropriate bodies such that both private and public investment decision-makers can avail of detailed and informed research findings. Of vital importance is the need to have accurate, reliable and informed information on market trends, preferences and expenditure patterns of tourists. To date, this information has not been available or alternatively is in such a format that is broadly inaccessible to the small- and medium-sized enterprises in Ireland that are considering investing in tourism ventures. Mechanisms must be developed whereby these enterprises can avail of quality research information and also receive advice from experienced tourism professionals. Finally it is imperative that short-term expediency should not deflect policy-makers from the pursuit of strategic research that focuses on long-term issues crucial to the development of the tourism sector.

CONCLUDING REMARKS

The recent performance of Irish tourism has led many prominent public and private interests to herald the sector as the boom industry for Ireland in the latter part of this century and into the next. Such a response is understandable for an economy with an endemic unemployment problem but is also rather strange in an historical context. In many ways Irish tourism is very much a Cinderella industry. For many years, the Irish Government and resultant public policy paid scant attention to tourism, whereby a rather laissez-faire approach was taken to the contribution tourism could make to economic development. In fact, it could be argued that the impetus to tourism development that occurred in the 1950s came at the behest of the government of the United States and significant investment in the late 1980s and early 1990s also arose due to the availability of similar external funding, this time from European Union sources. While government sources and the private sector in Ireland have been quick to claim credit for the recent tourism boom it is wise to be cautionary as a good deal of Irish tourism growth occurred before a policy for tourism was implemented and certainly before much of the recent investment occurred.

It has been argued in this book that Ireland does possess many of the attributes currently in demand by the increasingly mobile international tourist of the 1990s. A clean environment, beautiful scenery and friendly people, often taken for granted by natives, is deemed particularly attractive by many Europeans and visitors from further afield. The issues addressed in this final chapter of this book suggest that the future of Irish tourism is dependent on the necessity to respond very promptly to some serious policy failures of the past. In essence, it is important that we fully understand the factors that have contributed to recent growth and implement policies that will sustain recent developments.

NOTES

1. The authors will like to acknowledge the advice and documentation provided by Liz Kennedy, graduate student of the NCTPS in the completion of this section.
2. The June Holiday Plan was launched by Bord Failte in 1961 and was aimed primarily at the domestic tourism market with the stated aim of attracting tourists outside the peak months of July and August. The Second and Third Programmes for Economic Expansion (Stationery Office, 1964, 1969) also expressed a desire to extend the tourism season outside the peak months of July and August yet little concrete action was taken or progress made. Throughout the 1970s planning documents continued to mention seasonality yet the same laissez-faire approach prevailed.
3. The White Paper on 'Tourism Policy' of 1985 suggested that 'our climate and the general pattern of holiday taking in our major markets would seem to militate against any significant increase in holiday business in the period October to April for the foreseeable future' (Stationery Office, 1985).
4. While there has been little progress made in achieving the Government target it should be recognized that the overall increase in the volume of tourists has led to an improved position in the shoulder months for many establishments.
5. It should be recognized that a major element in the traffic growth during the period would have been Irish emigrants returning to Ireland for short breaks. The exodus of significant numbers of well-educated university graduates to well paid jobs in the buoyant UK economy at the time was extremely important in this growth. It is noticeable that the numbers dipped slightly in the early 1990s as the UK economy went in to recession.
6. Codesharing is the marketing practice whereby connecting flights of different airlines are offered to the consumer under the same airline designator code.

7. For a more detailed discussion of codesharing and the implications for Ireland see Crosbie (1996).
8. Of the total outlay of IR£110 million CERT will receive IR£73 million and the Department of Education the remainder.
9. Agriculture is a case in point where the large number of small farmers cannot justify the necessary investment in research and development in terms of the likely return expected. Government steps in to correct this implied 'market failure' with funding of agricultural research organizations from which all producers can benefit. By contrast, the large food firms (many originating as farmer co-operatives) have introduced several innovations in food products as they have been able to benefit from the economies of scale possible. In turn, the farmer-producers have benefited from the continuing demand for their output.
10. It is interesting to note the concentration of tourism innovations in the Mid-west region during this early period and to examine the factors responsible. The region was fighting for survival as the overfly of the transatlantic jets posed a significant threat to Shannon airport's future. Tourism was poorly developed in the region which largely served as a 'gateway' to other more attractive parts of Ireland. The tourist innovations were specifically developed to encourage the transiting tourists to spend one or two extra nights in the region. Thus, an innovative approach was fostered by crisis conditions and an imaginative response which was executed by focusing on the tourist's needs and developing proximate products to suit.
11. This was the first national study of innovation in Irish tourism and was commissioned by Shannon Development's Tourism Innovation Centre.
12. There is a role here for partnerships between the public and private sectors, the educational and training institutions, research bodies and the tourism agencies with some unifying vision or long-term strategic planning for the industry as a key component. Recommendations to establish a strategic planning unit in the relevant Government department were made in SIS (1992) but never acted upon, partly due to re-structuring of departments and turnover of civil servants but largely due to lack of commitment to the concept.
13. Noted in MCSB (1989) summary report.
14. This point is also made by Gray (1995).
15. For a more detailed discussion of the Brand Image concept, see *Business and Finance*, 4 April 1996.
16. Celtworld in Tramore, Co. Waterford, is one example of such a failure where the investment of IR£6 million was reduced to IR£600,000 following closure and re-sale attempts in 1995–1996.
17. At least equivalent to the real rate of interest on Government borrowing.
18. A more sanguine approach is being taken in the current OP (1994–1999) with independent Management Boards given the task of adjudicating on the merits of specific cases. (See Chapter 9).
19. Two recent reports from the Irish Tourism Industry Confederation (ITIC, 1995, 1996) focus on the changing regional disparities in tourism expenditures within Ireland and possible determinants of these variations, respectively.
20. Although the GULLIVER project has come in for significant criticism from the industry for a variety of reasons largely concerned with efficiency and effectiveness.
21. The 'diary method' of tracking holiday expenditure provides a rich source of such data. The methodology relating to a 1994 survey is outlined in Deegan and Deegan (1995).

Appendix

Table A1 Tourism flows to Ireland from principal origin zones, 1970–1980

	Britain	North America	Mainland Europe	(000s) Other overseas	Total overseas	Northern Ireland	Total out-of-state
1970	1061	258	110	30	1459	299	1758
1971	947	279	135	36	1397	295	1692
1972	750	259	127	28	1164	294	1458
1973	845	261	148	30	1284	330	1614
1974	820	252	165	28	1265	363	1628
1975	817	256	188	28	1289	399	1688
1976	797	266	207	27	1297	423	1720
1977	864	297	252	55	1468	495	1963
1978	1055	309	320	71	1755	544	2299
1979	1077	293	358	66	1794	566	2360
1980	1068	260	336	67	1731	527	2258

Source: As for Figure 3.3 (Chapter 3).

Table A2 Expenditure by tourists to Ireland by origin zones, 1970–1980

	UK	North America	Europe overseas	(IR£ million)* Other	Total overseas	NI	Total
1970	268.2	159.8	44.8	15.5	488.4	50.5	538.9
1971	234.2	182.6	59.9	20.2	496.8	50.9	547.7
1972	173.0	161.9	55.1	15.2	405.2	46.2	451.3
1973	215.8	158.3	52.6	9.9	436.5	50.7	487.2
1974	209.9	166.0	66.6	8.5	451.0	52.3	503.3
1975	199.0	150.5	70.0	9.6	429.1	47.2	476.3
1976	176.1	154.6	79.7	11.9	422.2	47.1	469.3
1977	191.8	168.3	100.8	23.5	484.5	79.3	563.7
1978	239.4	159.7	115.2	24.2	538.6	78.8	617.4
1979	255.3	154.7	140.0	31.9	581.9	70.1	652.0
1980	257.6	115.2	125.6	30.6	529.1	71.1	600.2

*1993 prices.
Source: As for Figure 3.4 (Chapter 3).

Table A3 Regional tourism employment as a percentage of total regional employment, 1981–1994*

					Per cent			
	Dublin–East	South-east	South-west	Mid-west	West	North-west	Midlands	Ireland
1981	3.8	4.3	6.0	5.2	6.5	7.4	2.4	4.6
1982	3.8	4.6	5.9	4.3	6.5	6.6	2.7	4.5
1983	3.6	4.2	6.5	5.1	6.0	6.8	2.5	4.5
1984	3.7	4.4	5.7	4.6	6.6	6.7	2.4	4.4
1985	4.2	4.4	6.3	5.4	7.0	7.2	2.6	4.9
1986	3.6	4.2	5.8	3.9	5.8	6.0	2.4	4.2
1987	4.1	4.4	6.3	5.3	7.1	7.4	2.7	4.9
1988	4.6	4.5	7.4	5.5	7.2	7.4	3.4	5.3
1989	4.8	4.6	6.7	7.7	10.4	8.3	3.5	5.8
1990	5.4	4.8	7.3	8.1	11.1	8.8	4.2	6.4
1991	6.2	6.9	9.4	8.6	12.7	9.9	4.0	7.5
1992	5.8	6.9	9.4	7.5	11.3	8.7	3.7	7.0
1993	5.9	7.1	9.7	8.0	12.0	9.2	3.9	7.3
1994	6.0	7.1	10.2	8.6	12.3	10.0	4.5	7.5

*Using the 'old' regions with Dublin and the East combined as one region.
Source: As for Figure 5.7 (Chapter 5).

References

Arthur D. Little Ltd (1994) Review of Bord Failte Eireann. Report to Minister for Tourism and Trade, Dublin.

Akehurst, G. (1992) European Community Tourism Policy, in *Perspectives on Tourism Policy* (eds P. Johnson and B. Thomas), Mansell Publishing, London, pp. 215–32.

Aldridge, D. (1974) Upgrading park interpretation and communication with the public, in *Second World Conference on National Parks*, IUCN, Switzerland.

An Foras Forbartha (1966) Planning for Amenity and Tourism. An Foras Forbartha, Dublin.

An Foras Forbartha (1968) Planning for Amemity, Recreation and Tourism. An Foras Forbartha, Dublin.

An Foras Forbartha (1985) The State of the Environment. Report for An Foras Forbartha, Dublin.

An Taisce (1992) Structural Funds and the Environment. Report prepared by J. Meldon. An Taisce, Dublin.

Archer, B.H. (1977) Tourism multipliers: the state of the art, in *Bangor Occasional Papers in Economics, No. 11,* University of Wales Press, Cardiff.

Bachtler, J. and Michie, R. (1995) A new era in EU Regional Policy evaluation? The appraisal of the Structural Funds. *Regional Studies*, **29**(8), 745–51.

Barrett, S.D. (1991) *Transport Policy in Ireland*, Gill and Macmillan, Dublin.

Barry, K. and O'Hagan, J. (1972) An econometric study of British tourist expenditure in Ireland. *Economic and Social Review*, **3**(2), 143–61.

Bord Failte (1973) An Outline Product Policy for Irish Tourism. Bord Failte Eireann, Dublin.

Bord Failte (1987) Trends in Irish Tourism, Tourism Numbers and Revenue 1960–91. Bord Failte Eireann, Dublin.

Bord Failte (1988a) Strategy for Growth. Bord Failte Eireann, Dublin.

Bord Failte (1988b) Trends in Irish Tourism, 1979 to Sept. 1987. Bord Failte Eireann, Dublin.

Bord Failte (1988c) The Regional Tourism Organisations. Bord Failte Eireann, Dublin.

Bord Failte (1992) Heritage Attractions Development. Bord Failte Eireann, Dublin.

Bord Failte (1994a) Perspectives on Irish Tourism – Regions, 1989–93. Bord Failte Eireann, Dublin.

Bord Failte (1994b) Perspectives on Irish Tourism – Visits to Tourist Attractions, 1989–93. Bord Failte Eireann, Dublin.

Bord Failte and An Foras Forbartha (1972, 1973) National Coastline Study, Vols 1–3. Bord Failte Eireann, Dublin.

Bord Failte and Office of Public Works (1975) The Shannon Study. Bord Failte Eireann, Dublin.

Bradley, J., Digby, C., Fitzgerald, J.D., Keegan, O. and Kirwan, M. (1981) Description, Simulation and Multiplier Analysis of the MODEL-80 Econometric Model of Ireland. Research Paper 2/81, Department of Finance, Dublin.

Brady Shipman Martin (1983) West Region Study: Development Strategy to 2004, Vol. 2. Report prepared for the West Regional Development Organisation and the Commission of the European Communities.

Breathnach, P. (1992) Employment in Irish tourism: a gender analysis. *Labour Market Review*, **3**(2), Winter, 15–26.

Brunt, B. (1988) *The Republic of Ireland* (Series: *Western Europe – Economic and Social Studies*), Paul Chapman Publishing, London.

Buckley, P.J. and Klemm, M. (1993) The decline of tourism in Northern Ireland. *Tourism Management*, **14**(3), June, 184–94.

Butler, R.W. (1980) The concept of a tourist area, cycle of evolution and implications for management. *The Canadian Geographer*, **24**, 5–12.

Byrne, A., Edmondson, R. and Fahy, K. (1993) Rural tourism and cultural identity in the west of Ireland, in *Tourism in Ireland: A Critical Analysis* (eds B. O'Connor and M. Cronin), Cork University Press, Cork.

Byrne, J.P. and Palmer, N.T. (1981) Some economic aspects of Irish tourism. *Irish Journal of Business and Administrative Research*, **3**(1), April, 87–93.

Cardosa e Cunha (1990) Inanguration of the European Year of Tourism, 1990, Speech made in Dublin, 30 January.

CERT (1996a) Where are they now? Employment and Career Prospects of CERT–NTCB graduates, 1982–1994, CERT – The State Tourism Training Agency, Dublin.

CERT (1996b) Images of Employment in the Tourism Industry. Report prepared by the National Centre for Tourism Policy Studies, University of Limerick. CERT – The State Tourism Training Agency, Dublin.

Clark, W. and O'Cinneide, B. (1981) Tourism in the Republic of Ireland and Northern Ireland. Paper V in the series *Understanding and Cooperation in Ireland*, Cooperation North, Dublin and Belfast.

Clark, W. and O'Cinneide, B. (1991) Tourism Operational Programme Northern Ireland, 1990–1993. Technical Assistance Final Report to the Commission of the European Communities, DGXVI – Regional Policy. LRDP, London.

Colleran, E. (1992) Interpretative centres, tourism and environment in Ireland, in *Environment and Development in Ireland*, Environmental Institute, Dublin.

CEC (1984a) Council Resolution of 10 April 1984 on a Community Policy for Tourism. *Official Journal of the European Communities*, April 30.

CEC (1984b) Council Regulation (EEC) No. 1787/84 of 19 June on The European Regional Development Fund. *Official Journal of the European Communities*, June 28.

CEC (1985) The European Community and its Regions: 10 years of Community Regional Policy and of European Reional Development Fund (ERDF), Office for Official Publications of The European Communities, Luxembourg.

CEC (1986) Community Action in the Field of Tourism. *Bulletin of the European Communities, Supplement 4/86*. Commission of the European Communities, Brussels.

CEC (1988a) Amended Proposal for a Council Decision on An Action Programme for the European Tourism Year (1990). Com (88) 803 Final. Commission of the European Communities, Brussels.

CEC (1988b) The Future of Rural Society. *Bulletin of the European Communities, Supplement 4/88*. Commission of the European Communities, Brussels.

CEC (1988c) Council Regulation (EEC) No. 2052/88 of 24 June, 1988 on the tasks of the Structural Funds and their effectiveness and on coordination of their activities between themselves and with the operations of the European Investment Bank and the other existing financial instruments, OJL 185 15/07/1988, p. 9.

CEC (1988d) Council Regulations (EEC) Nos 4253/88, 4254/88 and 4255/88 of 19 December 1988 laying down provisions for implementing Regulation (EEC) No. 2052/88, OJL 734, 31/12/1988, pp. 1, 15 and 21.

CEC (1989) Council Decision of 21 December 1988 on an Action Programme for European Tourism Year (1990) (89/46/EEC) OJL 17, 21/01/89, p. 53.

CEC (1990a) Community Support Framework – 1989–93: Ireland. Commission of the European Communities, Luxembourg.

CEC (1990b) Community Action to Promote Rural Tourism. Communication from the Commission. COM (90) 438 Final. Commission of the European Communities, Brussels.

CEC (1991a) *Guide to Community Initiatives*. Office for Official Publications of the European Communities, Luxembourg.

CEC (1991b) Community Action Plan to Assist Tourism. Com (91) 97. Commission of the European Communities, Brussels.

CEC (1991c) Report from the Commission to the Council, the European Parliament and the Economic and Social Committee on Community Measures Affecting Tourism. Office for Official Publications of the European Communities, Luxembourg.

CEC (1991d) Report by the Commission to the Council and the European Parliament on the European Year of Tourism. Com (91) 95. Office for Official Publications of the European Communities, Luxembourg.

CEC (1992a) Treaty on European Union. Office for Official Publications of the European Communities, Luxembourg.

CEC (1992b) Towards Sustainability, A European Community Programme of Policy and Action in relation to the Environment and Sustainable Development. Commission of the European Communities, Brussels.

CEC (1992c) Council Decision 92/421 on a Community Action Plan to Assist Tourism, OJL 231, 13 August.

CEC (1993) Eurostat DGXXIII – Tourism in Europe Key Figures, Office for Official Publications of the European Communities, Luxembourg.

CEC (1994) Report from the Commission to the Council, the European Parliament and the Economic and Social Committee on Community measures affecting tourism (Council Decision 92/421/EEC Com (94)) 74, Final, Brussels.

CEC (1995a) Eurostat DGXXII – Tourism in Europe. Office for Official Publications of the European Communities, Luxembourg.

CEC (1995b) The Role of the Union in the Field of Tourism. Commission Green Paper, Com (95) 97 Final. Commission of the European Communities, Brussels.

Convery, F. (1982) The physical environment. *Administration*, **30**(2/3), 243–65.

Convery, F. (1994) Theory and practice: achieving the aims of the Fifth Environmental Action Programme. *Living Heritage*, **11**(2), 27–39.

Coughlan, A. (1986) *EEC Political Union: Menace to Irish Neutrality and Independence*, Irish Sovereignty Movement Publications, Dublin.

Crick, M. (1989) Representations of international tourism in the social sciences: sun, sex, sights, savings and servility. *Annual Review of Anthropology,* **18**, 307–44.

Crosbie, N. (1996) Airline Deregulation and the North Atlantic Air Travel Market: Implications for Ireland. Unpublished Master's in Business Studies Thesis, College of Business, University of Limerick, Limerick.

Crotty, R. (1988) *A Radical's Response*, Poolbeg Press, Dublin.

CSO (1960) *Irish Statistical Bulletin, 1959.* Central Statistics Office, Dublin.

CSO (1988) *Trend of Employment and Unemployment 1979–1985.* Central Statistics Office, Dublin.

CSO (1991) *Census of Distribution, 1988.* Central Statistics Office, Dublin.

CSO (1992) *Census of Industrial Production, 1989.* Central Statistics Office, Dublin.

CSO (1993) *National Income and Expenditure.* Central Statistics Office, Dublin.

Culliton, J. (1992) A Time for Change: Industrial Policy in the 1990s. Report of the Industrial Policy Review Group (Chairman – J. Culliton). Stationery Office, Dublin.

Curran, C.P. (1926) Tourist development at home and abroad. *Studies*, **XV**(58), 299–309.

De Kadt, E. (1990) Making the alternative sustainable: lessons from development for tourism. Paper to the Centre for Environmental Management and Planning Conference, Valetta.

Deane, B. (1987) Tourism in Ireland: an employment growth area. *Administration*, **35**(3), 337–49.

Deane, B.M. and Henry, E.W. (1993) The economic impact of tourism. *The Irish Banking Review*, Winter, 35–47.

DED (1984) Discussion Paper on Tourism Development in Northern Ireland. Department of Economic Development, Belfast.

DED (1986) Northern Ireland Tourism – Policy Guidelines Statement. Department of Economic Development, Belfast.

DED (1989a) A Review of Government Policy Towards the Tourism Industry in Northern Ireland. Report by the Tourism Review Group, Belfast.

DED (1989b) Tourism in Northern Ireland, A View to the Future. Department of Economic Development, Belfast.

DED (1989c) Tourism Operational Programme, Northern Ireland, 1990–1993. Department of Economic Development, Belfast.

DED (1995) Growing Competitively – A Review of Economic Development Policy in Northern Ireland. Department of Economic Development, Belfast.

Deegan, J. (1991) Environmental problems associated with tourism: is alternative tourism the answer? *Irish Business and Administrative Research*, **12**, 104–14.

Deegan, J. (1994) Hospitality delivers jobs: the tourism dimension. Paper given at the Irish Hotel and Catering Institute Annual Conference, Cork.

Deegan, J. and Dineen, D.A. (1992) The employment effects of Irish tourism projects – a microeconomic approach, in *Perspectives on Tourism Policy* (eds P. Johnson and B. Thomas), Mansell Publishing, London, pp. 137–56.

Deegan, J. and Dineen, D.A. (1993) Irish Tourism Policy: targets, outcomes and environmental considerations, in *Tourism in Ireland: A Critical Analysis* (eds B. O'Connor and M. Cronin), Cork University Press, Cork, pp. 115–37.

Deegan, J. and Dineen, D.A. (1995) The use of a diary method to measure tourism expenditure: some preliminary results and policy implications. Paper to the International Conference on the Economics of Tourism, Rethymno, Crete. Organized by University of Crete and Fondazione ENI Enrico Mattei, Milan.

Department of Finance and Personnel (1994) The Northern Ireland Single Programming Document. Department of Finance and Personnel, Belfast.

Department of Finance and Personnel (1995) Northern Ireland Annual Abstract of Statistics, Policy Planning and Research Unit, Belfast.

Department of Tourism and Transport (1989) Operational Programme for Tourism, 1989–93. Department of Tourism and Transport, Dublin.

DKM Economic Consultants (1994) The Economic Impact of the Northern Ireland Conflict. Report. DKM Economic Consultants, Dublin.

Dowling, B. and Keegan, O. (1992) Fiscal policies and the built environment, in *Environment and Development in Ireland*, Environmental Institute, Dublin.

Dublin BIC (1995) *Business Expansion Scheme: 11th Year and 11th Hour*, Dublin Business Innovation Centre, Dublin.

Edwards, A. (1992) International Tourism Forecasts to 2005. Special Report No. 2454. The Economist Intelligence Unit, London.

EIU (1991) The Republic of Ireland, EIU International Tourism Report No. 4. The Economist Intelligence Unit, London.

ESRI (1993) EC Structural Funds, the Community Support Framework, Evaluation and Recommendations. Economic and Social Research Institute, Dublin (in association with DKM Economic Consultants, G. Boyle and B. Kearney and Associates).

Euradvice Ltd (1994) A Crusade for Survival. Final Report of Study of the West of Ireland, Developing the West Together, Galway.

European Parliament (1993) Directorate General for Research: Working Paper on The Role of the EC in Regard to Tourism and Regional Development (Regional Policy Services) by Fitzpatrick and Associates, Dublin.

Faulkner, B. (1995) The Evaluation of National Tourism Promotional Programs. Centre for Tourism and Hotel Management Research, Griffith University, Gold Coast, Australia.

Feehan, J. (ed.) (1992) *Tourism on the Farm,* Environmental Institute, University College, Dublin.

Fitzpatrick and Associates (1994) Irish Operational Programme for Tourism, 1994–1999 – Prior Appraisal. Fitzpatrick and Associates, Dublin.

Fitzpatrick, J. (1961) The role of the ITA in tourist development. *Administration*, **9**(3), 236–7.

Gillmor, D.A. (1985) *Economic Activities in the Republic of Ireland: A Geographical Perspective*, Gill and Macmillan, Dublin.

Gray, A.W. (1995) *EU Structural Funds and Other Public Sector Investments: A Guide to Evaluation Methods*, Gill and Macmillan, Dublin.

Gray, H.P. (1982) The contribution of economics to tourism. *Annals of Tourism Research*, **9**, 105–25.

Halpern, S.L. (1993) The United Nations Conference on Environment and Development – Process and Documentation. Academic Council on the UN System, Providence, Rhode Island.

Hannigan, K. (1994) A regional analysis of tourism growth in Ireland. *Regional Studies*, **28**(2), 208–14.

Heneghan, P. (1976) The changing role of Bord Failte, 1960–1975. *Administration*, **24**(3), 394–406.

Henry, E.W. (1990–1) Estimated employment and Gross National Product impacts of 1989 tourism in Ireland. *Journal of the Statistical and Social Inquiry Society of Ireland*, **XXVI**, Part III, 339–85.

Henry, E.W. (1991) Estimated employment and Gross National Product impacts of 1989 tourism in Ireland. Paper read before the Statistical and Social Inquiry Society of Ireland.

Henry, E.W. (1993a) *Irish 1990 Input–Output 13 – Sector Approximate Structures, with Derived Multipliers for Employment, GNP, and Imports. ESRI Technical Series 9*, Economic and Social Research Institute, Dublin.

Henry, E.W. (1993b) Estimated GNP and Employment Impact of the Irish 1991 and 1992 Tourist Trade. Unpublished Report to Bord Failte, Dublin.

HMSO (1995) Expenditure Plans and Priorities, Northern Ireland, The Government's Expenditure Plans 1995–96 to 1997–98. Com 2816. HMSO, London.

Hong, E. (1985) *See the Third World While it Lasts:the Social and Environmental Impact of Tourism with Special Reference to Malaysia*, Consumer Association of Penang, Penang.

Horwath and Horwath (UK) Ltd (1980) Northern Ireland Tourism Study, Horwath and Horwath (UK) Ltd, London.

Horwath and Horwath (UK) Ltd (1984) Tourism in the Northern Ireland Econnomy, Horwath and Horwath (UK) Ltd, London.

Hurley, A., Archer, B. and Fletcher, J. (1994) The economic impact of European Community grants for tourism in the Republic of Ireland. *Tourism Management*, **15**(3), 203–11.

Institut du Transport Aerien (1970) The effects of currency restrictions on British travel abroad. *Institut du Transport Aerien Magazine*, **15**, 261–6.

Industry Department for Scotland (c. 1989) *Tourism in Scotland: Visitor Externalities and Displacement*, Report prepared by PA Cambridge Economic Consultants, ESU Research Papers No. 19, Industry Department for Scotland.

IFI (1993) Annual Report , 1993, IFI – International Fund for Ireland, Belfast and Dublin.

Irish Independent (1946) Tourist board and tourists. (1 May.)

ITIC (1986) *Tourism and the Environment*, Irish Tourist Industry Confederation, Dublin.

ITIC (1995) Analysis of Regional Distribution of Overseas Tourism, 1989–94. Report prepared by Tourism Development International for ITIC, Dublin.

ITIC (1996) Regional Distribution of Tourism in Ireland: Responding to Changing Market Trends. Report prepared by Tourism and Leisure Partners for ITIC, Dublin.

Johnson, P. and Thomas, B. (1992) *Tourism, Museums and the Local Economy*, Edward Elgar, Aldershot.

Johnson, P. and Thomas, B. (1994) The notion of 'capacity' in tourism: a review of the issues, in *Progress in Tourism Recreation and Hospitality Management* (eds C. Cooper and A. Lockwood), John Wiley, Chichester.

Keane, M.J., Brophy, P. and Cuddy, M.P. (1992) Strategic management of island tourism – the Aran islands. *Tourism Management*, **13**(4), Dec., 406–14.

Keane, M.J. and Quinn, J. (1990) *Rural Development and Rural Tourism*, SSRC, University College, Galway.

Kearney, B., Boyle, G.E. and Walsh, J.A. (1994) EU LEADER I Initiative in Ireland: Evaluation and Recommendations. Department of Agriculture, Food and Forestry/Commission of the European Communities, Dublin.

Kennedy, K.A. (1988) Ireland and European integration – an economic perspective. Paper delivered to the Conference on Britain, Ireland and European Integration, University College, Cork.

Kennedy, K.A. and Dowling, B.R. (1975) *Economic Growth in Ireland: The Experience Since 1947*, Gill and Macmillan, Dublin, in association with the Economic and Social Research Institute, Dublin.

Kennedy, K.A. and Foley, A. (1977) Tourists trends in Ireland. *Business & Finance*, 7 April, 16–17.

Lavery, P. and van Doren, C. (1990) *Travel and Tourism: A North American – European Perspective*, Elm Publications, Cambridge.

Leslie, D., (1991) Tourism and Northern Ireland – a troubled time. M.Phil. thesis, University of Ulster. (2 Vols.)

Lipman, G. (1994) Foreword to WTTERC Third Annual Review, World Tourism and Environmental Research Centre, London.

Local Government Act 1925.

Lynch, P. (1969) The Irish economy since the war, 1946–51, in *Ireland in the War Years and After 1939–51* (eds K. Nowlan and T. Williams), Gill and Macmillan, Dublin.

Lyons, F.S.L. (1985) *Ireland Since the Famine*, Fontana Press, London.

MCSB (1989) The Practice of Innovation in Irish Tourism. Study by the Marketing Centre for Small Business,University of Limerick, commissioned by the Tourism Innovation Centre of Shannon Development, Shannon.

Mathieson, A. and Wall, G. (1982) *Tourism: Economic, Physical and Social Impacts*, Longman, New York.

Mawhinney, K. and Bagnall, B. (1976) The integrated social, economic and environmental planning of tourism. *Administration*, **24**(3), 383–93.

McDonald, M. (1990) Can Europe really help? Paper to the Environmental Protection and the Impact Of European Community Law Conference, Irish Centre for European Law, Dublin.

McNutt, P. and Rodriguez, J. (1993) Economic strategies for sustainable tourism in islands: the case of Tenerife. Paper presented at the International Conference on Sustainable Tourism in Islands and Small States, University of Malta, Valetta.

Minister of Tourism and Transport (1988) Report of Working Group on Tourism and Employment, Department of Tourism and Transport, Dublin.

Mitchell, F.M. (1992) Golf course on Valentia Island would erase our archaeological history. *Living Heritage,* **9**(2), 13–15.

Moles, R. (1993) Should the Burren Interpretative Centre be completed? An exploration of some of the issues. *Newsletter of the Geographical Society of Ireland*, No. 34, 14–23.

Moorhead, P. (1991) An examination of the relationship between terrorism, the media and tourism, with reference to the Northern Ireland tourism product. M.Sc. in Tourism Studies dissertation, University of Surrey.

Murray, J.A. (1977) Perspectives on Irish tourism. *Irish Banking Review*, 13–18 Sept.

National Archives of Ireland – D/T S13087A.

National Archives of Ireland – D/T S13087B.

National Archives of Ireland – D/T S13087C.

National Archives of Ireland – D/T S13087D.

Naughton, D.A. (1995) An analysis of the impact of the tax incentives to the Irish hotel and tourism industries. Masters in Accounting thesis, Graduate School of Business, University College, Dublin.

NESC (1980a) Personal Incomes by County in 1977. Report No. 51. National Economic and Social Council, Dublin.

NESC (1980b) Tourism Policy. Report No. 52. Stationery Office, Dublin.

NESC (1982) A Review of Industrial Policy. Report No. 64 ('Telesis Report'). Stationery Office, Dublin.

NIEC (1995) The Economic Implications of Peace and Political Stability for Northern Ireland. Occasional Paper 4. Northern Ireland Economic Council, Belfast.

NITB (1981) Tourism in Northern Ireland, 1981. Research Department, Northern Ireland Tourist Board, Belfast.

NITB (1982) Tourism in Northern Ireland, 1982. Research Department, Northern Ireland Tourist Board, Belfast.

NITB (1990) Tourism in Northern Ireland – An Indicative Plan. Northern Ireland Tourist Board, Belfast.

NITB (1992) Corporate Plan, 1992–5. Northern Ireland Tourist Board, Belfast.

NITB (1993a) Visitor and Domestic Tourism in Northern Ireland, 1993 Report. Research Department, Northern Ireland Tourist Board, Belfast.

NITB (1993b) Tourism in Northern Ireland – A Sustainable Approach. Northern Ireland Tourist Board, Belfast.

NITB (1993c) Annual Report, 1993, Northern Ireland Tourism Board, Belfast.

NITB (1994) Survey of Hotel Occupancy, 1993, Annual Report. Research Department, Northern Ireland Tourist Board, Belfast.

NITB (1995a) Corporate Plan, 1995–8. Northern Ireland Tourist Board, Belfast.

NITB (1995b) Tourism in Northern Ireland – A Development Strategy, 1995–2000. Northern Ireland Tourist Board, Belfast.

Norton, D.A.G. (1982) Export tourism input–output multipliers for Ireland. *Quarterly Economic Commentary*, May, 34–50.

O'Cinneide, M. (1992) Approaches to the development of peripheral rural areas: some lessons from the Irish experience, in *Development Issues and Strategies in the New Europe: Local, Regional and Interregional Perspectives* (ed. M. Tykkylainen), Avebury, Aldershot, pp. 77–88.

O'Cinneide, M. and Walsh, J.A. (1990–1) Tourism and regional development in Ireland. *Geographical Viewpoint*, **19**, 47–68.

O'Cinneide, M.S. and Keane, M.J. (1988) Local Socio-economic Impacts Associated with the Galway Gaeltacht. Research Report No. 3. Social Sciences Research Centre, University College, Galway.

O'Connor, P. (1995) Tourism and development in Ballyhoura: women's business? *Economic and Social Review*, **26**(4), 369–401.

O'Connor, P. (1996) *Invisible Players? Women, Tourism and Development in Ballyhoura*. Women's Studies, Department of Government and Society, University of Limerick, Limerick.

O'Hagan, J. (1972) Export and import visitor trends and determinants in Ireland. *Journal of the Statistical and Social Inquiry Society of Ireland*, **XXII**(V), 17–18.

O'Hagan, J. and Duffy, C. (1994) Access and admission charges to museums: a case study of the National Museum. Paper to the Statistical and Social Inquiry Society of Ireland.

O'Hagan, J. and Mooney, D. (1983) Input–output multipliers in a small open economy: an application to tourism. *The Economic and Social Review*, **14**(4), 273–80.

O'Hagan, J. and Waldron, P. (1987) Estimating the magnitude of tourism in the European Community: data deficiencies and some results. *Journal of the Statistical and Social Inquiry Society of Ireland*, **XXV**, Part IV, 89–126.

O'Malley, E. (1987) *Industry and Economic Development – The Challenge for the Latecomer*, Gill and Macmillan, Dublin.

O'Riain, M. (1986) *Aer Lingus 1936–1986 – A Business Monograph*, Gill and Macmillan, Dublin.

O'Riain, M. (1992) Modal competition on the Irish Sea. Paper read to the Chartered Institute of Transport in Ireland (Eastern Section), Dublin.

O'Toole, F. (1994) *Black Hole, The Disappearance of Ireland – Green Card,* New Island Books, Dublin.

OECD (1990) State of the Environment. Organization for Economic Cooperation and Development, Paris.

OECD (1992) Tourism Policy and International Tourism in OECD Member Countries. Organization for Economic Cooperation and Development, Paris.

Oliver, F.R. (1971) The effectiveness of the UK travel allowance. *Applied Economics*, **3**(3), 219–26.

Palma, G. (1978) Dependency: a formal theory of underdevelopment or a methodology for the analysis of concrete situations of underdevelopment. *World Development*, **6**, 881–924.

Pearce, D. (1992) Tourism and the European Regional Development Fund: the first fourteen years, *Journal of Travel Research*, **30**(3), Winter, 44–51.

Pearce, D., Markandya, A. and Barbier, E. (1989) *Blueprint for a Green Economy*, Earthscan Publications, London.

Pearce, D.G. (1990) Tourism in Ireland: questions of scale and organisation. *Tourism Management*, **11**(2), June, 133–51.

Plimmer, N. (1994) Everyone benefits? The case of New Zealand, in *Environment and Development Bulletin, No. 4,* World Travel and Tourism Research Centre, London, pp. 2–3.

Price Waterhouse (1987) Improving the Performance of Irish Tourism. Report by Price Waterhouse, Dublin.

Quigley, M. (1992) Fiscal Incentives for Tourism Infrastructure Investment. Mimeo, College of Business, University of Limerick.

Quinlan, A. (1988) Ireland and the Atlantic-Shannon, in *World Aviation – The Complete Story* (eds L. Skinner and T. Cranitch), Director Publications, Dublin, pp. 39–52.

Quinn, G. (1961) Tourism in the Irish economy. *Administration*, **9**(3), 155–63.

Quinn, J. and Keane, M.J. (1991) Community tourism in rural Ireland, in *Rural Crisis: Perspectives on Irish Rural Development* (eds T. Varley, T.A. Boylan and M.P. Cuddy), Centre for Development Studies, University College, Galway.

Richards, G. (1975) The role of tourism in the Northern Ireland economy. M.A. thesis, University of Surrey.

Samuelson, P.A. (1954) The pure theory of public expenditure. *Review of Economics and Statistics*, **36**(2), 387–9.

Scott, R. and Guy, N. (1992) The Economic Impact of Tourism in Northern Ireland, Working Paper No. 2, Northern Ireland Economic Research Centre, Belfast.

Shannon Development (1990) A Critical Assessment of the Tourism Consultative forum and the Company's Interface with the Regional Tourist Industry. Internal Briefing Document.

Share, B. (1992) *Shannon Departures: A Study in Regional Initiatives*, Gill and Macmillan, Dublin.

SIS (1992) Tourism and Regional Development in Ireland. Report for the Commission of the European Communities (DGXVI). Structure Intermediare de Support, Brussels.

SKC, Peat Marwick and DKM (1987) Tourism Working for Ireland: A Plan for Growth. Report for the Tourism Policy Committee of the Irish Hotels Federation, Dublin.

Smyth, R. (1986) Public policy for tourism in Northern Ireland. *Tourism Management*, June, **7**(2), 120–6.

Solow, R.M. (1993) Sustainability: an economist's perspective, in *Economics of the Environment* (eds R. Dorfman and S. Dorfman), Norton, London, pp. 179–87.

Stationery Office (1946) Tourist Development Programme. Stationery Office, Dublin.

Stationery Office (1951) Synthesis of Reports on Tourism, 1950–51. Stationery Office, Dublin.

Stationery Office (1952) Dail Debates. Dail Eireann, Dublin.

Stationery Office (1955) Dail Debates. Dail Eireann, Dublin.

Stationery Office (1958a) First Programme for Economic Expansion. Stationery Office, Dublin.

Stationery Office (1958b) Tourist Development Programme, Stationery Office, Dublin.

Stationery Office (1963) Dail Debates. Dail Eireann, Dublin.

Stationery Office (1964) Second Programme for Economic Expansion. Stationery Office, Dublin.

Stationery Office (1969) Third Programme: Economic and Social Development 1969–72. Stationery Office, Dublin.

Stationery Office (1970) Dail Debates. Dail Eireann, Dublin.

Stationery Office (1975) Dail Debates. Dail Eireann, Dublin.

Stationery Office (1984) Direct Taxation, the Role of Incentives. Second Report of the Commission on Taxation, Dublin.

Stationery Office (1985) White Paper on Tourism Policy. Stationery Office Dublin.

Stationery Office (1987) Programme for National Recovery. Government Publications, Dublin.

Stationery Office (1989) National Development Plan, 1989–1993. Stationery Office, Dublin.

Stationery Office (1990) The EUROPEN Report – 1992 and the Tourism Sector. Stationery Office, Dublin.

Stationery Office (1991) Programme for Economic and Social Progress. Stationery Office, Dublin.

Stationery Office (1992) Report of the Tourism Task Force to the Minister for Tourism, Transport and Communications, Dublin.

Stationery Office (1993) Ireland: National Development Plan, 1994–1999. Stationery Office, Dublin.

Stationery Office (1994) Operational Programme for Tourism, 1994–9. Government Publications, Dublin.

Steinecke, A. (1979) An analysis of differences between the travel attitudes and demand patterns of diverse visitor groups and their reaction to political–military conflicts: the Republic of Ireland as a case study. *Weiner Geographische Schriften*, **53/54**, part 2, 115–31.

Tansey, P. (1995) Tourism: a product with big potential, in *Border Crossings – Developing Ireland's Island Economy* (eds M. D'Arcy and T. Dickson), Gill and Macmillan, Dublin, pp. 197–207.

Tansey Webster and Associates (1991) Tourism and the Economy, A Study of the Economic Impact of Tourism in Ireland (1985–90). Report prepared for the Irish Tourist Industry Confederation, Dublin.

Tansey Webster and Associates (1992) Strategic Framework for the Development of Irish Tourism Enterprises. Report for the Irish Tourist Industry Confederation, Dublin.

Tanzi, V. (1986) Public expenditure and public debt, in *Public Expenditure, The Key Issues*, I.P.A., Dublin.

Teague, P. (ed.) (1993) *The Economy of Northern Ireland – Perspectives For Structural Change*, Lawrence and Wishart, London.

Thomas, B. (1995) Tourism; is it underdeveloped?, in *The Northern Region Economy: Progress and Prospects in the North of England* (eds L. Evans, P. Johnson and B. Thomas), Mansell Publishing, London, pp. 59–77.

Tourist Traffic Act 1939, Stationery Office, Dublin.

Tourist Traffic Act 1952, Stationery Office, Dublin.

Tourist Traffic Act 1955, Stationery Office, Dublin.

Tourist Traffic Act 1957, Stationery Office, Dublin.

Tourist Traffic Act 1959, Stationery Office, Dublin.

Tourist Traffic Act 1961, Stationery Office, Dublin.

Tourist Traffic Act 1963, Stationery Office, Dublin.

Tourist Traffic Act 1966, Stationery Office, Dublin.

Tourist Traffic Act 1970, Stationery Office, Dublin.

Tourist Traffic Act 1972, Stationery Office, Dublin.

Tourist Traffic Act 1975, Stationery Office, Dublin.

Tourist Traffic Act 1979, Stationery Office, Dublin.

Tourist Traffic (Development) Act 1931.

US Department of Commerce (1960) Survey of Current Business. US Department of Commerce, Washington, DC.

Walsh, M.C. (1994) Irish tourism demand analysis. Unpublished Masters in Business Studies thesis, College of Business, University of Limerick.

Wilson, D. (1993) Tourism, public policy and the image of Northern Ireland since the troubles, in *Tourism in Ireland: Critical Analysis* (eds B. O'Connor and M. Cronin), Cork University Press, Cork, pp.138–61.

World Commission on Environment and Development (1987) (Brundtland Report), in *Our Common Future,* Oxford University Press, Oxford.

WTO (1991) Tourism to the Year 2000; Qualitative Aspects Affecting Global Growth. (Executive Summary.) World Tourism Organization, Madrid.

WTTERC (1994) *Third Annual Review,* World Tourism and Environmental Research Centre, London.

Index